I0888698

# Green Finance Innovations and the Future of Sustainable Investing

Revenio Jalagat
https://orcid.org/0000-0002-8878-3825
*Al Zahra College for Women, Oman*

Karima Toumi Sayari
*Al Zahra College for Women, Oman*

Rafat Al Batayneh
*Al Zahra College for Women, Oman*

IGI Global
Scientific Publishing
Publishing Tomorrow's Research Today

| | |
|---|---|
| Vice President of Editorial | Melissa Wagner |
| Director of Acquisitions | Mikaela Felty |
| Director of Book Development | Jocelynn Hessler |
| Production Manager | Mike Brehm |
| Cover Design | Jose Rosado |

Published in the United States of America by
IGI Global Scientific Publishing
701 East Chocolate Avenue
Hershey, PA, 17033, USA
Tel: 717-533-8845 | Fax: 717-533-7115
Website: https://www.igi-global.com E-mail: cust@igi-global.com



Copyright © 2026 by IGI Global Scientific Publishing. All rights reserved. No part of this publication may be reproduced, stored or distributed in any form or by any means, electronic or mechanical, including photocopying, without written permission from the publisher. Use of this publication to train generative artificial intelligence (AI) technologies is expressly prohibited. The publisher reserves all rights to license its use for generative AI training and machine learning model development.

Product or company names used in this set are for identification purposes only. Inclusion of the names of the products or companies does not indicate a claim of ownership by IGI Global Scientific Publishing of the trademark or registered trademark.



Library of Congress Cataloging-in-Publication Data

Names: Jalagat, Revenio Cabanilla, Jr., 1978- editor | Sayari, Karima, 1978- editor | Al-Batayneh, Rafat, 1982- editor

Title: Green finance innovations and the future of sustainable investing / [edited by] Revenio C. Jalagat, Jr., Karima Sayari, Rafat Al Batayneh.

Description: Hershey, PA : IGI Global Scientific Publishing, [2026] | Includes bibliographical references and index. | Summary: "This book explores emerging innovations in green finance and sustainable investing, highlighting technologies, policies, and financial instruments driving low-carbon development. Through global case studies and forward-looking strategies, it examines how green bonds, carbon markets, and sustainable investment tools support climate resilience and the transition to a greener economy"-- Provided by publisher.

Identifiers: LCCN 2026002292 (print) | LCCN 2026002293 (ebook) | ISBN 9798337382876 hardcover | ISBN 9798337382883 paperback | ISBN 9798337382890 ebook

Subjects: LCSH: Finance--Environmental aspects | Investments--Environmental aspects | Finance--Technological innovations

Classification: LCC HG101 .G745 2026 (print) | LCC HG101 (ebook) | DDC 332--dc23/eng/20260219

LC record available at https://lccn.loc.gov/2026002292

LC ebook record available at https://lccn.loc.gov/2026002293

British Cataloguing in Publication Data
A Cataloguing in Publication record for this book is available from the British Library.



All work contributed to this book is new, previously-unpublished material.
The views expressed in this book are those of the authors, but not necessarily of the publisher.
This book contains information sourced from authentic and highly regarded references, with reasonable efforts made to ensure the reliability of the data and information presented. The authors, editors, and publisher believe the information in this book to be accurate and true as of the date of publication. Every effort has been made to trace and credit the copyright holders of all materials included. However, the authors, editors, and publisher cannot assume responsibility for the validity of all materials or the consequences of their use. Should any copyright material be found unacknowledged, please inform the publisher so that corrections may be made in future reprints.

# Table of Contents

# Detailed Table of Contents



Recently, the concept of sustainability has received significant attention from governments, technologists, and practitioners due to increased industrialization. Sustainable development indicates the outcome of the environmental, economic, and social conditions of a nation, region, and global area, where life can develop, prosper, and reach an enhanced level. There is an increased expectation for global economic development to be compatible with environmental protection and sustainability. While green foreign direct investment (GFDI) fosters cross-border capacity building, knowledge spillovers, and technology transfer, green financing instruments enable the mobilization of necessary resources. Both strategies have different but complementary benefits. The chapter introduces a novel conceptual framework demonstrating how green finance and green foreign direct investment work together to drive sustainable economic development. Furthermore, it provides useful information for policymakers seeking to develop integrated policies that leverage GFDI to build strong green economies.



The imperatives of climate change coupled with a global momentum towards sustainable development are changing the face of personal finance and investment. This chapter, explores the way financial markets, institutions, and instruments are growing to enable individual investors to fund environmental sustainability and

more difficult to quantify and less standardized. The analysis reveals synergies in projects that combine carbon sequestration and biodiversity but also conflicting goals. The findings underscore the importance of local participation, transparency, and regulatory clarity, and inform recommendations for improving the governance of both instruments and their integrated use to advance climate goals and biodiversity protection.



Green and Sustainability Sukuk issuance has maintained a strong growth momentum and marked a consecutive record of annual issuance since the market's inception in 2017. Saudi Arabia, the United Arab Emirates (UAE), Malaysia, and Indonesia are the top four Green and Sustainability Sukuk-issuing countries in the world. Saudi Arabia is the leading issuer within the Gulf region, followed by the UAE. If Malaysia is known as the world's first Green Sukuk issuer, Indonesia is known as the world's first sovereign Green Sukuk as well as the world's first retail Green Sukuk. Therefore, through a literature review by gathering data mainly sourced from the official publications of the related ministry and institutions, this chapter focuses on discussing: (1) Green and Sustainability Sukuk framework in Saudi Arabia, UAE, Malaysia, and Indonesia; (2) Green and Sustainability Sukuk performance for the four countries; (3) the impacts of their Green and Sustainability Sukuk for SDGs targets.



Green bonds play a key role in financing climate resilience and sustainable development by directing investments toward projects with measurable environmental benefits, such as renewable energy and climate-resilient infrastructure. These bonds align capital flows with global sustainability goals, leveraging transparency and adherence to frameworks like the Green Bond Principles to attract investors. However, challenges like high issuance costs, inconsistent standards, and greenwashing risks limit their adoption. This study explores green bonds' opportunities, challenges, and policy implications, analyzing market trends, innovative practices, and regulatory frameworks. The findings highlight the need for harmonized standards, capacity-building initiatives, and technological tools to enhance green bonds' impact in driving sustainability.

Green finance is fast becoming a key tool for solving global issues such as climate change, natural resource scarcity, and social inequality. Green finance mobilizes financial resources as investments with environmental benefits that contribute and activate investments based on sustainable development goals (SDGs) to help steer the economy into one focusing on long-term ecological, social wellbeing. This chapter investigates the role of green finance for sustainable development, more specifically which financial instruments help shaping a more sustainable economic model. Globally, the use of green bonds and sustainability linked instruments have picked up in both developed and emerging economy jurisdictions indicating a universal commitment to deliver the sustainability objectives. This chapter indicates that firms which issue green bonds tend to see a financial benefit as investors realign themselves to meet the needs of portfolio responsibilities.



This chapter explores the synergistic relationship between green finance and green technology in accelerating the transition to a low-carbon, sustainable economy. Green finance through instruments such as green bonds, sustainable loans, and climate funds mobilizes capital for the development and adoption of clean technologies, including renewable energy, energy-efficient systems, and sustainable agriculture. Case studies from China and Brazil highlight successful models of policy and financial integration. However, the chapter identifies persistent barriers financial, technological, institutional, and policy-related particularly in low-income countries. It offers strategic recommendations for scaling green finance, enhancing institutional capacity, and aligning national policies with global climate goals. The chapter concludes with future research directions and emphasizes the need for global collaboration to ensure equitable access to green technologies and to integrate climate action with broader sustainable development objectives.

# Preface

The twenty-first century has seen the emergence of an urgent global consensus: achieving sustainable development requires the alignment of financial systems with environmental and social objectives. *Green Finance Innovations and the Future of Sustainable Investing* brings together a collection of scholarly works that explore the dynamic and evolving relationship between finance, technology, and sustainability. This edited volume gathers diverse perspectives from global scholars and practitioners, highlighting how green financial instruments, innovative technologies, and policy mechanisms are shaping the transition toward low-carbon, inclusive, and resilient economies.

At the heart of this book lies a shared belief that sustainable investing is no longer a niche concept but a central pillar of global economic transformation. Each chapter delves into the ways in which green finance channels capital toward environmentally sound projects, from renewable energy investments to biodiversity conservation and the development of green financial instruments such as bonds, sukuk, and credits. The volume further examines the vital role of emerging technologies, governance frameworks, and individual investor participation in driving sustainable change.

This book aims to inform policymakers, investors, academics, and students about the practical, theoretical, and institutional innovations reshaping the financial landscape. By bridging research and practice, the volume offers critical insights into how green finance can foster a balanced integration of the core tenets of sustainable development.

# OVERVIEW OF CHAPTERS

## Chapter 1: Examining the Synergistic Relationship Between Green Finance and Green FDI in Building a Sustainable Green Economy

This chapter develops a conceptual framework linking green finance and green foreign direct investment (GFDI) as complementary strategies for achieving sustainable economic development. It emphasizes how the interaction between these two forces mobilizes resources, facilitates technology transfer, and strengthens policy integration for building resilient green economies.

## Chapter 2: Future Directions in Sustainable Investing: Empowering Individual Investors for Green Development

Exploring the intersection of personal finance and sustainability, this chapter examines how individual investors are influencing the evolution of green financial markets. It identifies key trends such as technological innovation, regulatory reform, and financial inclusion that empower retail investors to actively contribute to environmental sustainability through green bonds, ESG funds, and impact investing.

## Chapter 3: Green Finance: Trailblazing Towards Sustainable Growth in Renewable Energy Investments

Focusing on renewable energy, this chapter demonstrates the crucial role of green finance in facilitating the global energy transition. It reviews various financial instruments—green bonds, green loans, and blended finance models—while discussing investment trends, risk-return dynamics, and policy interventions needed to accelerate renewable energy adoption.

## Chapter 4: Carbon Credits and Biodiversity Credits: Opportunities, Risks, and Global Perspectives of a Market-Based Environmental Policy

This chapter offers an analytical comparison of carbon and biodiversity credit systems, drawing on international case studies. It discusses their potential for environmental conservation, the governance challenges they face, and the need for transparent, locally inclusive frameworks that align market mechanisms with ecological goals.

## Chapter 5: Green and Sustainability Sukuk for SDGs: Lessons From Saudi Arabia, UAE, Malaysia, and Indonesia

Highlighting Islamic finance innovations, this chapter examines the rapid growth of Green and Sustainability Sukuk across leading issuing nations. Through comparative analysis, it explores how these instruments contribute to achieving the Sustainable Development Goals (SDGs), emphasizing regulatory frameworks, performance outcomes, and cross-country lessons.

## Chapter 6: The Role of Green Bonds in Financing Climate Resilience Projects

Dedicated to the rise of green bonds, this chapter investigates their role in financing climate-resilient infrastructure and renewable energy. It addresses the barriers of standardization and greenwashing while proposing harmonized regulatory approaches and capacity-building initiatives to enhance transparency and investor confidence.

## Chapter 7: Green Finance: Unlocking Sustainable Development and Navigating the Greenwashing Challenges

This chapter explores how green finance mobilizes capital toward achieving the SDGs, while confronting the pressing issue of greenwashing. It provides evidence that sustainable financial instruments not only drive environmental benefits but also improve corporate profitability and investor alignment with sustainability goals.

## Chapter 8: Green Finance, Green Technology Adoption, and Low-Carbon Emissions: Pathways to Achieving the Sustainable Development Goals

Investigating the symbiosis between green finance and green technology, this chapter offers empirical insights into how financial innovation accelerates low-carbon transitions. Drawing from global case studies, it presents actionable strategies for overcoming barriers in financing, governance, and technology adoption in developing economies.

## Chapter 9: The Triple Bottom Line of Green Finance: Profitability, Planet, and People in the Context of SDGs

Concluding the volume, this chapter revisits the *Triple Bottom Line* framework, examining how green finance integrates economic viability with environmental and social imperatives. It underscores the importance of standardization, transparency, and policy innovation to ensure that green finance truly serves as a foundation for inclusive and sustainable growth.

Together, these ten chapters weave a comprehensive narrative on how financial innovation can be harnessed to secure a sustainable global future where economic prosperity coexists with ecological stewardship and social equity.

Chapter 1

# Examining the Synergistic Relationship Between Green Finance and Green FDI in Building a Sustainable Green Economy

**Karima T. Sayari**
https://orcid.org/0000-0001-7564-022X
*Al Zahra College for Women, Oman*

**Rafat C. Al Batayneh**
*Al Zahra College for Women, Oman*

**Revenio C. Jalagat**
https://orcid.org/0009-0007-5535-6919
*Al Zahra College for Women, Oman*

## ABSTRACT

*Recently, the concept of sustainability has received significant attention from governments, technologists, and practitioners due to increased industrialization. Sustainable development indicates the outcome of the environmental, economic, and social conditions of a nation, region, and global area, where life can develop, prosper, and reach an enhanced level. There is an increased expectation for global economic development to be compatible with environmental protection and sustainability. While green foreign direct investment (GFDI) fosters cross-border*

DOI: 10.4018/979-8-3373-8287-6.ch001

© 2026, IGI Global Scientific Publishing. Copying or distributing in print or electronic forms without written permission of IGI Global Scientific Publishing is prohibited. Use of this chapter to
nerative artificial intelligence (AI) technologies is expressly prohibited. The publisher reserves all rights to license its use for generative AI training and machine learning model development.

*capacity building, knowledge spillovers, and technology transfer, green financing instruments enable the mobilization of necessary resources. Both strategies have different but complementary benefits. The chapter introduces a novel conceptual framework demonstrating how green finance and green foreign direct investment work together to drive sustainable economic development. Furthermore, it provides useful information for policymakers seeking to develop integrated policies that leverage GFDI to build strong green economies.*

## 1. INTRODUCTION

Green finance is increasingly playing a significant role in developing sustainable economic advancement in both developed and developing countries to protect the environment. It is a financial thought in which the green issue is included in financial policies with the goal of eliminating environmental problems brought on by human activity. The issue of green securities, green credits, and green investment by financial services companies to the business units drives them to invest in environmentally friendly practices while carrying out the economic operations (Zhang, 2022). GFDI aims to protect environmental commitments concerning investments, technologies, and practices that help protect the natural environment. Sound financial systems are the most fundamental prerequisites of economic development and have an influential role in the growth of green investment. Environmentally, green technology and knowledge transfer from environmentally innovative developed countries operate as the most sustainable and long-lasting factors in driving FDI to poor countries.

To address environmental and pollution issues, green investment needs green technology, as well as green finance, to resolve environmentally sound technology FDI and leverage sustainable investment elements. Each year, the global economic growth rate shows remarkable acceleration, increasing environmental degradation, reduction of natural resources, and rise in emission gas levels, such as carbon dioxide (CO2) emissions. Investment in green projects like natural services, reforestation, air quality mitigation, artificial intelligence carbon capture is recognized as a positive role building a sustainable green economy by focusing on cultivating the green finance investment point of view (Muganyi et al., 2021). Besides that, the potential of task fall on fostering economic growth, generating financial prosperity, eradicating poverty, and assisting with interconnected green projects, which could sustainably secure the trade, investment, and environmental policy benefits by understanding and jointly implementing stakeholders in developing a sustainable green economy.

## Research Gaps

A mounting consensus on the urgency to fight climate change as well as depletion of resources has expanded into an array of international engagement and domestic actions. Previous works have demonstrated how GFDI, and green economic reforms can interact in improving the environment while sustaining economic growth.

There is a lack of research explaining the synergistic relationship between green finance and GFDI. In the existing literature on green finance, the focus is mainly on green banking, green bonds, green insurance, and carbon finance. Additionally, the literature on GFDI largely targets environmental regulations. The research question addressed is: How does green finance influence GFDI? Specifically, how does the supply of green investment funds and de-risking green projects financially affect MNEs' GFDI decisions?

This financial support, on the one hand, encourages MNEs' establishment of green operations in these countries; and, on the other hand, demands that MNEs' GFDI projects comply with strict green financing requirements. Thus, firms may utilize a wide variety of green investment vehicles, such as greenfield investment, M&As of pre-existing green entities, merger-of-equals with green firms, and partner with reputable green companies. Hence, the host governments will be more amicable to approve GFDI projects that can simultaneously bring new green operations and positive environmental externalities.

## Research Aim and Objectives

The aim of the chapter is to explore the synergistic relationship between green finance and green FDI in building a sustainable green economy. The ultimate purpose of the research is to provide comprehensive evidence and policy recommendations. The focus will be on research questions: (1) How to understand green finance and GFDI ?; (2) What is the development of GFDI in both the global and the national level?; (3) What are the patterns and determinants of GFDI based on different financial instruments?; (4) Is there a synergistic relationship between green finance and GFDI?; (5) How to promote the sustainable green economy by improving policy-based evidence?

To leverage and support the synergy-effect between green finance and GFDI in building a sustainable green economy, this research applies linkage analysis from a conceptual framework. The design of the research is organized as follows: Section 2 explains the concept of green finance, its development and origin. Section 3 describes GFDI and different drivers that influence FDI's greening impact by focusing on political and regulatory framework and analyzing the role of green taxonomies. Section 4 discusses the synergies between Green Finance and Green FDI, by analyzing the effects of green finance financial instruments on financing GFDI. The discussion ends with the development of a conceptual framework on this synergistic relationship. Finally, the conclusion will be provided in the summary section.

## 2. GREEN FINANCE: DEFINITION AND COMPONENTS

The defining green finance is a relatively young field. It has emerged as a brand-new topic discussed in the past 5 years along with the popularity of sustainable economic development and especially the realization of Paris Agreement. Green finance is any financial instrument or investment flowing into the sectors such as sustainable agriculture, clean and renewable energy, biodiversity conservation, pollution prevention, fallow land reclamation, clean transportation, and sustainable production to protect and improve the environment casting the premise of stability and green economic growth or receiving a lower punishment

There is growing consensus that the world economy is only beginning its transition to a green economy. An economy that fosters economic development and sustainability is known as a "green economy." It is a good substitute for the prevailing economic model of today, which increases inequality, encourages waste, depletes resources, and presents several risks to the environment and public health (El Madnaoui et al., 2021). Agarwal (2020) defined the green economy as the one that attempts for sustainable growth without damaging the environment and that attempts to lower ecological scarcities and environmental dangers.

The over-dependence on traditional economic growth models has led to the problem of scarcity of natural resources, the low efficiency of resource utilization and environmental pollution, and so forth. Transforming traditional economic growth model and striving to achieve the green and sustainable economic development are core requirements for global countries. In this regard, green finance, low-carbon technology, green products and other green resources have emerged in an endless stream in the global economic development. Green finance and GFDI can support each other in green development.

According to Fu et al. (2024), many aspects of green finance have been studied, including the role of greenhouse gas emissions, environmental disclosures, the risk of climatic disasters, the economic effects of global warming, temperature shifts, the relationship between temperature and aggregate risk, the impact of climate policy risk on the financial system, how to manage investment risk in the shift to a lower-carbon economy, how to quantify investment risks and policy uncertainty, and the macroeconomic effects of climate change and private debt dynamics.

Green financing is now essential in the worldwide effort against environmental harm and climate change. Given the dire consequences of climate change for the world and its people, immediate action is necessary. The rate of loss of biodiversity is accelerating so dramatically that a million or more species might become extinct. Rising sea levels also threaten the lives of countless families (Fu et al., 2024).

Fu et al. (2023) conducted an empirical analysis that focuses on evaluating the effects of fossil fuel efficiency and green financing on sustainability in 15 OECD nations between 2005 and 2021. Their findings revealed that, by funding environmentally friendly initiatives and facilitating the shift away from fossil fuels, the green finance method facilitates the transition to a more ecologically sustainable future. This approach includes climate-smart blue economies, funding sustainable natural resource-based economies, and investing in clean and renewable technology. In order to achieve carbon neutrality and foster sustainable economic development, green money may be essential.

Chandrashekara (2022) identified the trends of green finance and sustainable investment which are incorporating environmental, social, and governance (ESG). The assessment of a company's sustainability performance included (ESG) considerations into investment strategies. Additionally, green Bonds, which provide money for eco-friendly initiatives, have become more popular. By issuing these bonds, issuers may lessen their dependence on certain markets and diversify their sources of funding. Investors interested in sustainable and responsible investing and those that satisfy ESG (Environmental, Social, and Governance) standards have shown a particular interest in green bonds.

In recent years, attitudes about investment have altered as a result of a growing understanding of the dangers and difficulties presented by climate change. Due to investors' growing interest in creating a more sustainable portfolio, new investment standards like ESG investing have fueled the expansion of various financial products and transparency measures in the financial industry. Green bonds are fixed-income financial instruments that are issued to finance and develop environmentally friendly initiatives in a variety of sectors. The market for green bonds, which have reached a value of over 600 billion US dollars globally and are a crucial tool for mitigating climate change, has grown rapidly between 2014 and 2020.

## Green Finance Development and its Origin

Green finance has been a focus area as world knowledge of environmental relevance grows. This section explores the development of green finance in response to this trend; this review will provide a clear picture on its development at national and international level will provide interesting insights. Moreover, we review the historical development of green finance, looking at its basic ideas, considering the driving forces and challenges.

The report on the State of Green Banks (2025) provide a snapshot on the state of green finance and how green banks help to create a robust economy. These banks play an important role in overcoming certain obstacles to mobilizing sustainable investing. In emerging markets and developing economies, the adoption of green banks has been slower compared to developed ones. They use concessional worldwide funding by reducing and spreading risks related to developing clean technology. However, they confront several challenges, including insufficient funding, regulations, inconsistent policies, a lack of technical expertise, and ineffective risk-sharing arrangements. They may avoid poor policy settings, enable extended investment horizons, and overcome asymmetries in fundamental knowledge to provide more low-cost, fit-for-purpose capital.

In a bibliometric analysis study, Tung et al. (2025) examined the research development trajectory from 3712 publications linked to green finance of main path analysis (MPA) in order to promote the growth of green finance. This research classifies the green knowledge trajectory in the following phases:

*Figure 1. The timeline illustrates how climate adaptation finance has transformed over 15 years, moving through distinct developmental stages*

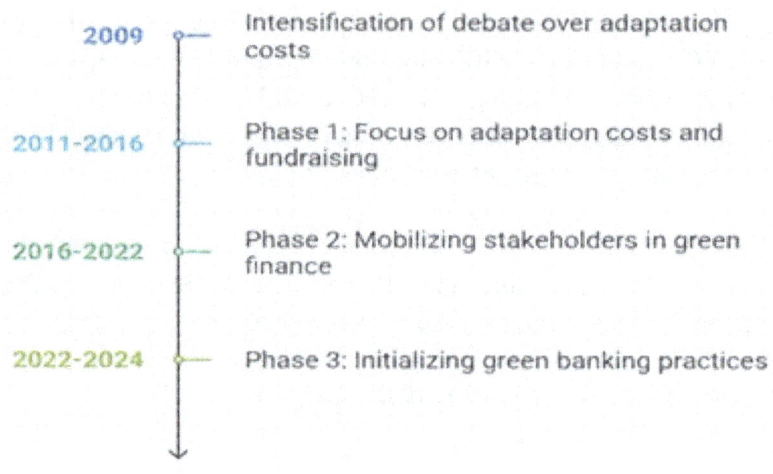


The first step requires early considerations aimed at serious financial deficits for adaptation, especially for the vulnerable poor countries most affected by climate change impacts. The start of the adoption process involves the establishment of funding channels and approximating the cost of adaptation. In major breakthroughs, there was establishment of the Green Climate Fund (GCF), unlocking of the Adaptation Fund, and incorporation of some of the adaptation financing commitments into the 2015 Paris Agreement. This came after the setting up of the era of a large-scale adaptation of green finance which branched out into non-government driven initiatives to involve different actors. Financial institutions, private sector operators, and multilateral development institutions became part and parcel of the adaptation finance. Throughout this period, the financial architecture witnessed the emergence of new models like blended finance models, public-private partnerships, and customized financial instruments specific to adaptation projects. Finally, the most recent phase, a mature phase, is characterized by an adaptation of green finance becomes as it became embedded in mainstream financial systems.

## 3. GREEN FDI: DEFINITION AND SIGNIFICANCE

According to the OECD, "green investment" encompasses funding for green infrastructure and greening of existing infrastructure, sustainable management of natural resources and activities within the environmental goods and services sector, as well as across entire segments of green value chains and greening of existing ones (Green FDI in Developing countries, 2017).

Theoretically, under the neoclassical growth model, FDI boosts economic development by improving investment efficiency (Li and Liu, 2005). According to the endogenous growth model, FDI stimulates economic development by facilitating technology diffusion from the developed world to the host nation. FDI is a composite bundle of capital assets, know-how, and technology. Through skill acquisition and dissemination, labor training, and the introduction of alternative organizational structures and management techniques, it may enhance the recipient economy's current knowledge base.

Most people think that the world economy is only beginning its green revolution. As a result, many multinational corporations (MNEs) have started to globalize their green initiatives and are looking to improve their capacity for sustainable innovation. Through their study, Amendolagine et al. (2021) revealed that green foreign direct investments strengthen multinational corporations' broader focus on sustainability. They boost MNEs' specialization in certain green technologies in addition to having a greening influence on the technological base. Moreover, the level and caliber of MNEs' inventive capabilities in sustainability-oriented technologies are greatly enhanced by GFDI. This indicates that multi-technology companies tend to deepen innovation in certain green technologies while simultaneously pushing their overall inventive skills in a more sustainability-oriented direction.

GFDI is essential for all countries, not only as an alternative source of capital, but also as a means of technological and managerial improvement in the EGS sectors. This type of FDI has been overlooked so far and there's no agreed definition (Golub et al., 2011). Building a set of suitable policies to attract green FDI is identified as a complex challenge, and firms as the main generators of GFDI are influenced by a broad set of factors thanks to the growing interest in environmental issues in the last decades. Understanding the influence of environmental regulation and awareness on investing abroad in EGS sectors is deemed relevant for policymakers to design a set of efficient policies.

To increase economic growth, both developed and developing nations seek to attract FDI. However, the literature has revealed the negative effects of FDI on the environment, so nations must take climate change into account by changing their focus from purely economic growth to Green Growth, which is economic growth that also takes environmental depletion into account (Caetano et al., 2022). These authors found that attracting investment in renewable energy infrastructure and electrifying the economy, particularly in poorer nations, may be crucial to mitigating the negative effects of the energy transition. FDI is one of the pillars to achieve green development. Through its crucial role to increase economic output, support sustainable renewable sources, and speed up the development of renewable energy, FDI seems to have the potential to aid nations in achieving Green Growth more easily through the energy transition.

Ofori et al. (2023) identified a substantial research gap, that FDI and economic freedom promote growth and environmental sustainability, yet insufficient empirical study on whether these factors condition one another's effects on inclusive green growth (IGG).

## What are the Factors That Influence FDI's Greening Impact?

Apart from domestic climate policy, nations can increase certain forms of GFDI by using strong domestic fundamentals and external factors to their advantage. GFDI volumes were greater where there existed higher institutional quality, higher trade and capital account openness, and openness levels. With green hydrogen, favorable terms for renewable energy production and overall national hydrogen policy using worldwide efforts to promote increased production seem to be a prime driver of FDI inflows (Jaumotte et al., 2024) .

Strong environmental laws and their enforcement have generally been shown to be important motivators for businesses looking to green their operations and purchase environmentally friendly technology. Johnstone et al. (2007) found that the greatest important effect on enterprises' environmental performance is the perceived stringency of the legislative regime. The strictness of environmental regulations in the home country has also been shown to have a major impact on foreign investment's ability to go green.

Certain governments have made the decision to actively promote GFDI by offering particular investment incentives, such as subsidies. For instance, the German government mandates the development of renewable energy facilities and offers direct incentives for their construction.

Comprehensive climate policies are linked to an increase in FDI in renewable energy, especially in nations with solar potential and a low reliance on fossil fuels, according to research that combines economic analysis with national case studies. By implementing climate policies like those of industrialized nations, emerging markets and developing economies may close 40% of their private renewable investment gap and quadruple their GFDI-to-GDP ratio. With strong climate policy support, renewable investment may be able to overcome the high financing costs that often restrict developing and emerging market economies.

GFDI is more likely to be attracted to nations with strong institutions and free trade policies in addition to climate restrictions. Geopolitical fragmentation jeopardizes this potential since studies indicate that green investments are less common in countries with political divisions. Comprehensive national policies that are in line with international initiatives and favorable renewable energy conditions are the best ways to attract FDI.

Jaumotte et al. (2024) had an in-depth IMF staff climate note examining evidence-based strategies for emerging markets and developing economies to participate and optimize GFDI, highlighting policy frameworks that allow environmental objectives to balance with economic development goals.

Their study reveals the following findings: *For climate policies & Green FDI Relationship*, additional climate policies are linked to higher renewable energy FDI flows, and low-fossil-fuel-intensity and high-solar-resource countries are most advantaged. Closing the climate policy gap between emerging markets and developing countries and developed economies can potentially triple the green FDI-to-GDP ratio in representative EMDEs and close 40% of their private renewable investment gap (excluding China). Strong climate policies, especially, allow EMDEs to overcome high financing costs that would otherwise deter investment.

*Regarding sector-specific FDI Trends*, GFDI in electric and hydrogen shows no heightened responsiveness to home country climate policy, compared to investments in renewable energy. This absence of responsiveness is probably due to the early development stages of these industries, which have not yet formed mature market structures nor discernible patterns of investment.

The novelty of these sectors suggests that investors remain primarily driven by factors such as strategic positioning in new value chains, access to dominant raw materials, and positioning relative to global automotive industry change rather than responding to national-level climate policy architecture. As these industries mature and regulatory systems become more uniform around the world, the connection between domestic climate policy and investment flows may become more direct, as it has with the more developed renewable energy industry.

According to Statista, in 2023, there were over 619 billion US dollars invested globally in renewable energy technologies. Compared to the prior year, this represented a rise of 8%. Over the last ten years, global financing for renewable energy has been increasing significantly. Which confirm the global priority for sustainable development . Investments in clean energy amounted to 263 billion dollars in 2014 and reached a high of 619.1 billion dollars in 2023. The sector has significantly developed, as seen by the notable growth in investment financing. Clean energy investment has been steadily increasing because of policy backing for renewable sources, an expanding sector, and the advent of publicly traded corporations that control renewable energy assets. With 273 billion dollars invested in renewable energy in 2023, China leads in this investment . Nonetheless, the largest investments are in wind and solar power. The amount of money invested worldwide in solar photovoltaic energy has increased dramatically in recent years, from 126 billion dollars in 2019 to around 300 billion dollars in 2022.

Governments must, however, not only put laws into place to foster investment-attracting environments but also protect against exploitation by making sure social and environmental standards are fulfilled, offering local possibilities, and transferring technology.

## Green FDI and Environmental Taxation

FDI patterns and environmental taxation are a relevant policy nexus for advanced countries like the UK and EU. The significance of sector-specific FDI patterns in addressing environmental challenges and minimizing the tax burden of environmental taxes through incentive green investment is emphasized in this part of the chapter.

The UK and EU have witnessed incredible transformations in FDI patterns with increased emphasis on green sectors (UNCTAD, 2023). Traditional carbon-intensive industries are losing investment appeal due to charges under policies and carbon pricing schemes (Dechezleprêtre & Sato, 2017). The UK Net Zero Strategy and European Green Deal have transformed the investment arithmetic of multinational firms (European Commission, 2019). Among key sectors witnessing transformation are:

*Energy:* Green energy FDI has been on the rise, with offshore wind registering substantial investment in UK and EU economies (OECD, 2023). This reduces the reliance on fossil fuel imports and allied carbon charges (Balsalobre-Lorente et al., 2020).

*Manufacturing:* Green manufacturing technologies and circular economic initiatives progressively become drivers of FDI, particularly for automobiles (electric cars) and chemicals (biobased chemical products).

*Technology:* Digitalization investment and clean tech advance the environment in addition to economic competitiveness.

## Environmental Taxation as FDI Determinant: Tax Policy Framework

Environmental tax has two direct functions: internalizing the environmental expenditure and generating revenue to finance green transformation (European Environment Agency, 2022). Nevertheless, excessive use of environmental tax can deter FDI and induce carbon leakage. The issue is, therefore, how to formulate tax systems conducive to green investment without sacrificing economic competitiveness (Garsous et al., 2017).

## Strategic Tax Incentives for Green FDI

Governments of the UK and EU have implemented targeted tax incentives to attract environmentally friendly FDI (UK Department for Business, Energy & Industrial Strategy, 2021):

*Green Investment Tax Credits*: tax depreciation of renewable energy and green machinery and green infrastructure

*R&D Tax Incentives*: Overstated tax relief on environmental technology development (Calel & Dechezleprêtre, 2016).

*Carbon Tax Exemption*: Temporary or permanent exemption of certified low-carbon activities

GFDI and environmental taxation complement each other when appropriately designed. Environmental taxation brings green technologies within economic reach by providing market signals, whereas green FDI provides the technology and finance necessary for environmental change.

The interaction is in several ways: 1-Technology Transfer: Green FDI brings in innovative green technologies reducing the tax burden on local firms (Dechezleprêtre & Sato, 2017). Capacity Building, as green sector foreign investment builds indigenous capacity, reducing long-term reliance on environmental tax revenues. Market Development can also be achieved because FDI facilitates market development for green products and services, going green becoming less expensive. For that, effective policy coordination between FDI attraction and environmental taxation can be accomplished and industries where GFDI can play the greatest role in the environment and, at the same time, address economic objectives. Also, the temporal sequencing of the GFDI-driven transition to leave space for environmental taxes.

In the United Kingdom Context, there is greater flexibility in the UK post-Brexit on the extent of coordinated FDI-environmental tax policy. The UK approach includes green financing structures for promoting green investment, offshore wind and nuclear sectoral FDI approaches and carbon pricing structures for the purpose of supplementing, not substituting for, green investment.

For the European Union Framework, EU coordinated approach is challenging and promising. The European Green Deal envisages a soundly conceived framework integrating FDI and climate policy. It must be implemented with thoughtful consideration of the principles of state aid in framing green FDI incentives. Cross-border coordination is essential to successful carbon leakage prevention.

Attaining economic competitiveness and environmental policy objectives balance forms the central policy dilemma in balancing FDI attraction and environmental taxation. This delicate balance requires policy flexibility in adjustment through ongoing monitoring and consequent readjustment of tax prices and FDI incentives based on evolving market conditions, as well as encouraging international cooperation among jurisdictions to prevent regulatory arbitrage that undermines policy effectiveness. Success is dependent on implementing industry-specific techniques that recognize the varying investment trends and environmental impacts in specific industries. To achieve these objectives, the policymakers should focus on harmonized policy design that generates harmonious structures for managing both FDI attraction and environmental taxation simultaneously, establish robust monitoring mechanisms with clear benchmarks for tracking GFDI performance in reducing environmental tax challenges, and employ ongoing stakeholder engagement that triggers the incorporation of industry stakeholders, environmental stakeholders, and foreign partners into the policymaking. This integrated approach would allow economic competitiveness and environmental objectives to be followed in conjunction, and not as competitive alternatives.

The linking of sectoral FDI flows with environmental taxation is a core policy frontier for the UK and EU. It requires top-level policy formulation that employs green FDI to drive environmental objectives without diminishing economic competitiveness. The reality is that astutely crafted GFDI measures really reduce onerous environmental taxation and drive environmental changes.

## 4. SYNERGIES BETWEEN GREEN FINANCE AND GREEN FDI

To mitigate the ecological negative impact of economic activities, the concept of green finance defines the exploitation of all forms of assets and financial services investing in green projects in food, economy, and housing sector, and binds the era of sustainable green economic development.

Given the significance of utilizing green finance to develop green economic activities, research regarding GFDI as a main policy in green sector and the financial industry supporting it have also been extensively carried out. There are many national policies and provisions to publicly safeguard the nicety of GFDIs. The mention indicates that the rise of GFDI should not be spurred by itself noticeably. However, with the enforcement of GFDI policy, there must be a variety of policies designed to sustain and motivate it, of which the most outstanding is green finance support. Financing is irreplaceable in green project development, such as recycling waste, emissions, atmosphere and water purification, ecosystem construction, and low carbon & energy efficiency improvement. Incorporating GFDI policies, the financial system is isolated, and the exclusive financial policy enables us to cope with great measures of financial assistances to green project over the relative years. In this sense, expansion of green finance can be expected in two ways reduction: 1) qualified/incentive financial policy obligations enacted to enhance the work of administrative department of finance that promotes the quantities of credit/investment granted to green areas and 2) development of financial mechanism extending to reuse and leverage the green FDI's societal connections and market perceptions to fetch more financial establishments (Li et al., 2021).

This section investigates the synergetic relationship between green finance and GFDI, attempting to further develop this field in theoretical and methodological terms. Aiming at garnering the green economy, a green finance system has been developed in many countries providing loans and fiscal subsidies for green construction projects in energy, transportation, and other sectors (Tufail et al., 2024). At the same time, more investments are being attracted to these sectors through green FDI because these sectors are central to environmental quality and sustainable growth. On the one hand, financial facilities are employed to aid the operation and the establishment of green industries. For the operation of these facilities, green finance is developed. On the other hand, foreign investments also aim for this goal are attracted, i.e., GFDI. Efforts are made by the government to lift green finance and FDI in green industry, leading to the creation of a virtuous cycle in a green economy.

Growing environmental consciousness and the need to address climate change have made green finance and sustainable investing subjects in the financial sector more and more relevant.

Today, as climate change is regarded as a very serious issue, more countries are trying to build a green economy and to cope with climate change. Many scholars agree that both green technology and financial provision are essential for green economic development.

The financial sector may greatly impact Green Economies and attempts to adapt to climate change by promoting Green Finance as a strategic approach to address present shortcomings in terms of funding and risk mitigation. Green finance is a tactic used to include the financial industry into efforts to transition to resource-efficient and low-carbon economies to prepare for climate change (Almazrouei and Nobanee, 2021). Two of the most notable instruments within the green finance framework is green bonds and green loans.

## Green Bonds

Issuing green bonds whose earnings are designated for financing climate and environmental-friendly projects—is a successful and growingly popular strategy. The entire amount of yearly green bond issuance increased more than 100 times in less than ten years, from USD 1.5 billion in 2007 to USD 167 billion in 2018. While China has yet to issue a single green bond in 2015, it already accounted for 40.9% of worldwide green bond issuance in 2016 (followed by 24.6% in 2017 and 23.0% in 2018), indicating that bond issuers in Asia are increasingly adopting the technique (Larsen, 2019).

Recognition of the serious threats posed by global warming and environmental degradation has elevated the issue of how to promote green growth to the top of the policy agenda. A key issue is how to scale up the financing and foster the dissemination of environmentally-sound technology and practices in countries that host vital ecosystems and account for a rising share of global emissions of greenhouse gases and other pollutants (Golub et al., 2011). First literature has concerned how to identify the multiple drivers of green FDI, the cornerstone of virtually all cross-border private green capital flows, and an essential vehicle to disseminate green technology—and green finance; it has also dealt with how to define and measure these concepts.

Green bond markets may be exploited to create favorable investment climates and green foreign direct investment possibilities. The money raised from green bonds may be used to construct climate-resilient and environmentally friendly buildings and infrastructure, boost the supply of renewable energy, boost energy efficiency, finance green projects at a reasonable cost, and assist the development of important green growth sectors.

They make it possible for issuers and project developers to access the asset pools of institutional investors, such as insurance and pension funds, who often don't make direct investments in developing nations but are instead searching for long-term, sustainable prospects. The market can be expanded, more investment opportunities can be presented, and financing for GFDI projects can be made easier with the help of initiatives to promote and guarantee the "green" integrity of green bonds, increase securitization of green bonds, broaden the range of issuers, and increase the use of project bonds (Green FDI in developing countries, 2017).

Green financing has the financial strength to promote good environmental initiatives and steer clear of those that deplete natural resources, so creating positive externalities. This entails reorienting state policies and mobilizing financial resources to assist the private sector in its multifaceted transformation. Effective climate policies are essential to green finance's success (Mishra, 2021).

The figure below represent a strategic positioning of green finance (more precisely, green bonds) and FDI based on a quadrant model. Each of the quadrants illustrates different circumstances in the green finance environment.

*Figure 2.*

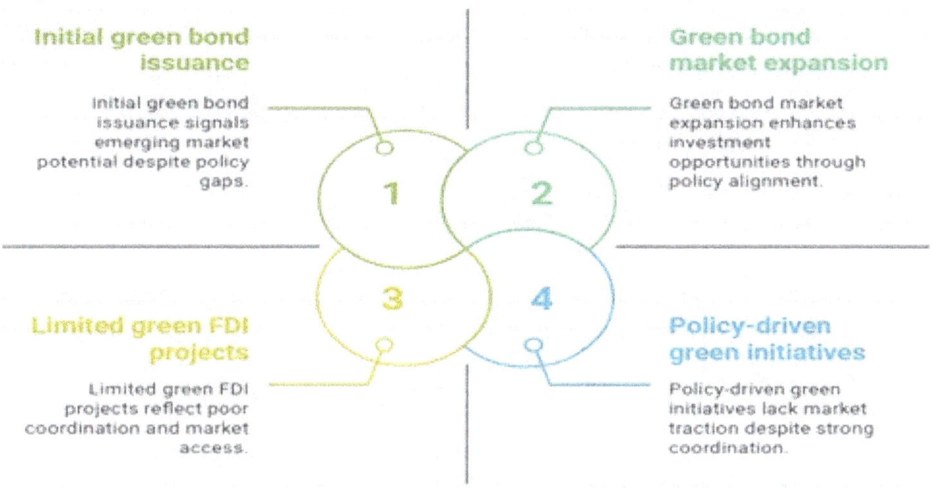


The process of changing national green growth models demonstrates how crucial it is to use the money generated by the green finance system to help green the economy. When nations successfully employ the mobilized green capital to create an economy that guarantees sustainable development and raises people's quality of life, they are said to have successfully transformed the green growth model (Nguyen et al., 2024).

GFDI, or FDI in low-carbon technology-related industries, has increased recently. As a percentage of global GDP, GFDI quadrupled between 2014 and 2022 after accelerating since 2016. Examining US$ FDI inflows, which rose from about \$40 billion in 2014 to \$80 billion in 2019 and over \$200 billion in 2022, further demonstrates the growing trend in GFDI.

## Green Loans

Green loans are seen as a particular kind of finance that promotes "green production." Businesses might accelerate the process of method innovation that can result in clean manufacturing, and it could allocate "the economic resources" via those economic activities that can assess environmental quality, address climate change, and save resources (Alnassar, 2022).

According to the world bank (2021), A loan cannot be considered a "green loan" unless it is created in compliance with the Green Loan Principles, which establish an international standard based on the following four crucial components:

1- The use of Proceeds: The borrower will assess, measure, and report on the obvious environmental advantages that approved green initiatives provide.
2- The process of evaluating and selecting which projects will get loan resources should be made explicit by the borrower of a green loan. Additionally, the borrower explains how it plans to manage the environmental and social risks related to eligible projects.
3- Profit management: The borrower should keep an eye on the earnings of a green loan or credit them to a designated account in order to ensure transparency and the product's integrity.
4- Reporting: The guidelines state that wherever feasible, both qualitative and quantitative performance indicators should be employed, including energy capacity, power output, and the prevention or reduction of greenhouse gas emissions.

## Political and Regulatory Framework for Green Finance

A number of particular commitments and international agreements have assisted in refocusing global emphasis, even if there are many motivators and motivations for accomplishing global climate and sustainable development goals. The most well-known of these are the UN Sustainable Development Goals (SDGs), the UNFCCC Paris Agreement on climate change, and the Convention on Biological Diversity (CBD) Aichi objectives for biodiversity. Even while these internationally planned commitments are admirable and almost universally accepted, there will still be ongoing difficulties in putting them into practice and eventually achieving their lofty objectives.

Since it offers a framework for figuring out what constitutes an ecologically sustainable investment, the idea of "green taxonomy" has attracted a lot of interest lately. Businesses and investors may support the green economy and make wise choices by being aware of its goals and constituent parts. sustainable finance taxonomies is crucial in scaling up sustainable financing and are at the heart of the synergistic relationship between Geen finance and green FDI mobilization.

This section deals with green and sustainable taxonomies. According to green taxonomy report (2023), a green taxonomy is a framework designed to identify the investments, goods, and activities that provide environmental, social, or green (ESG) benefits in order to assist direct funds toward priority sustainable initiatives for the shift to net zero and net positive. To create and organize green financial products (loans, bonds, credits, guarantees, securities, stocks, ETFs, etc.) and meet sustainability standards for impact investments, financial institutions might benefit from using a green taxonomy.

A green taxonomy, on the other hand, is a categorization system used by governments to identify investments or activities that would help a city or nation reach certain goals associated with important environmental objectives. Banks, investment funds, project developers, and institutional investors are the primary target consumers for green taxonomies. Since the target users compel all sectors to shift to a low carbon economy, setting national objectives (such Nationally Determined Contributions) is the absolute minimum to meet. A number of government organizations, stock exchanges, and regulators have released guidelines or green taxonomies that aim to provide more thorough definitions in an effort to stimulate sustainable finance. A number of ministries, organizations, and agencies have released guidelines or green taxonomies that aim to provide more thorough definitions in an effort to promote green investments.

There are two kinds of taxonomies: those that serve as rules for certain financial instruments (bonds, loans, checks, etc.) and those that provide a broad framework and classification of sustainable practices connected to particular social and/or environmental consequences.

Taxonomies are beginning to be recognized by policymakers and industry players as a potent instrument for mobilizing green capital for the shift to an ecologically sustainable economy.

Taxonomies are either currently in existence or actively being drafted into a large number of countries worldwide. However, some challenges needs an effort to be addressed.

*Table 1. Green Taxonomy Frameworks in Asia*

| Country/ Issuing Authority | Framework Name | Year Established | Key Features |
|---|---|---|---|
| ***ASEAN Region*** | ASEAN Taxonomy | Under development | • as the first regional taxonomy It is the first regional taxonomy in development. • Its purpose is to provide member nations a standard definition for financial instruments and economic activity. |
| ***China/*** People's Bank of China (PBOC) | Green Bond Endorsed Project Catalogue | 2015, updated 2021 | • Defines eligible green projects • Defines the criteria for project classification • 2021 revision has excluded coal and fossil fuels. |
| ***Bangladesh/*** Bangladesh Bank | List of Green Products Eligible for Financing | 2017, updated 2020 | • Bangladesh Bank specifies 8 categories of green products • lists 52 specific green products/projects |
| ***India /*** Securities and Exchange Board of India (SEBI) | Consultation Paper on Green and Blue Bonds | 2022 | • Extended green debt securities definition • Blue bonds concept introduction • Focus on eliminating 'greenwashing' |
| ***Indonesia/*** Financial Services Authority of Indonesia | Green Taxonomy | 2022 | • Sustainable Finance Roadmap feature • Policy development guidelines |
| ***Mongolia/*** Mongolian Financial Stability Council | Mongolian Green Taxonomy | 2019 | • Sustainable finance classification system |
| ***Russia/*** State Development Bank VEB. | Russian Green Taxonomy | 2021 | • Green taxonomy applies to multiple sectors like waste, energy, construction • Adaptation criteria to climate risk included |

Source: adapted from Green Taxonomy Report, 2023.

*Table 2. Green Taxonomy Frameworks in Latin America and the Caribbean*

| Country/ Issuing Authority | Framework Name | Year Established | Key Features |
|---|---|---|---|
| ***Brazil*** Brazilian Government | Brazilian Sustainable Taxonomy Framework | Developed under Bolsonaro (not yet validated) | • Consistent with the climate policies of the present administration • Need approval from four government bodies. It will probably take years. |
| ***Chile*** Ministry of Finance in collaboration with Climate Bonds Initiative | Chilean Green Taxonomy (in progress) | Roadmap published in 2021, still in development | •Priority sectors include energy, transportation, construction, and mining; it would be the first taxonomy in the world to include the mining sector |
| ***Colombia*** Financial Superintendence in collaboration with Ministry of Finance and Public Credit | Colombian Green Taxonomy | Published in April 2022 | • The first green taxonomy to be formally introduced in Latin America • It aims to stop greenwashing • It promotes the growth of green financial markets. |
| ***Dominican Republic*** | Dominican Republic Green Taxonomy | Project launched in 2022, under consultation as of June 2023 | • First in the Caribbean to introduce a green taxonomy initiative. • Aims to encourage sustainable capital market development. • Helps mitigate climate change. |
| ***Mexico*** Ministry of Finance and Public Credit | Mexican Sustainable Taxonomy | Published in March 2023 | • Addresses three major sustainability challenges: climate change, gender inequality, and access to basic services • Includes social objectives beyond environmental concerns |
| ***Peru*** | Peruvian Green Taxonomy (in progress) | Consultations began in January 2022, still in development | • Comparable structure to the EU and Colombian taxonomy • Separate from the Peru Sustainable Bond Framework; • Intended to serve as a pillar of the nation's sustainable finance roadmap |

Source: adapted from Green Taxonomy Report, 2023.

*Table 3. Green Taxonomy in OCEANIA and other countries*

| Country / Issuing Authority | Framework Name | Year Established | Key Features |
|---|---|---|---|
| ***Australia/*** Australian Sustainable Financial Institute (ASFI) | Australian Sustainable Finance Taxonomy | In development | • Led by 20-25 expert Technical Expert Group<br>• Coordinating with Asia-Pacific, Canada, EU, and UK taxonomies |
| New Zealand/ New Zealand Government | New Zealand Green Taxonomy | Expected by 2024 | •Establishing definitional instruments for green investments.<br>• working together with academia, industry, and science; and adhering to global best practices |
| **Green Taxonomy in Other Countries** | | | |
| ***South Africa*** | South Africa's Green Finance Taxonomy | Released April 2022 | • Listing of "green" assets, projects, and sectors<br>• Supports national policy and private sector initiatives<br>• Leverages EU taxonomy for global interoperability |
| ***United Kingdom/*** Green Technical Advisory Group (chaired by Green Finance Institute) | UK Green Taxonomy | In development (as of June 2023) | • Helps investors identify 'green' activities/products<br>• Independent advisory system |
| ***Canada/*** Sustainable Finance Action Council (SFAC) | Canadian Green Taxonomy | Roadmap approved September 2022 | • Defines green taxonomy<br>• Research and stakeholder engagement-based<br>• Expert-prepared Taxonomy Roadmap Report |

Source: adapted from Green Taxonomy Report, 2023.

Ambitious sustainability promises have been made by international accords such as the Paris Climate Agreement, the UN Sustainable Development Goals (SDGs). Significant increases in investments in renewable energy (RE) are necessary to meet the objectives of the Paris Agreement.

To fund Renewable energy projects, policymakers are increasingly turning to State investment Banks (SIB), as publicly funded financial institutions with autonomous operations.

Waidelich & Steffen (2024) revealed that according to existing research, either public financing in general has an impact on RE investments without examining the role of specific institutions or bank syndicates are affected by public financial institutions' involvement without taking energy technologies or SIB into account. However, policymakers that are thinking about creating a new, green SIB or incorporating renewables into the mandates of already-existing institutions might be guided by quantitative information about whether the RE financing operations of SIBs are consistent with theoretical justifications. The authors examines how SIBs' funding practices for RE technologies vary from those of commercial banks and if this aligns with their stated function.

The study used finance database to identify all SIBs in a sample of 4,999 debt financing transactions for RE projects in OECD member nations in order to evaluate these predictions. The findings demonstrates that SIBs play a crucial role in funding the clean energy transition, as seen by the fact that they are engaged in 11% of RE projects in our sample overall and roughly double the loan activity of all other public sector organizations put together.

For the same group of countries, Polzin et al., (2017) compared investments in electricity-generating capacity made by institutional investors (banks, insurance firms, and investment/pension funds), and they investigated the effects of various policy initiatives on the proliferation of renewable energy (RE) on a sample of OECD nations over a 12-year period (2000-2011). According to the findings, technology-specific rules that consider the current state of the market and the stage of the technology life cycle are necessary. Economic/fiscal incentives like feed-in tariffs (FIT) are recommended policy tools to enhance the climate for institutional investments; grants and subsidies are less successful in this regard.

Clark et al. (2018) review the Key Barriers to Private Investment as nothing is known about the present magnitude of private investment flows into environmental remediation, climate action, the forest industry, landscape methods, etc. The authors highlight the difficulty to entirely comprehend the current state of private financing and identify areas of potential opportunity because of a number of factors, such as the lack of systematic and coordinated efforts to gather information on investment flows, the absence of mandatory reporting requirements, and an overall lack of transparency.

## Economic and Financial Aspects

Climate change poses financial stability challenges to central banks, regulators and supervisors. Bolton et al., (2020) reveals that the risk of climate change amplifies catastrophic financial events with a potential to create a system crisis. Excessive levels of uncertainty and constraints of conventional models of risk render it difficult for central banks to introduce climate risk analysis into their financial stability oversight. Central banks are not capable of addressing climate change individually, though they must assist in scenario analysis in advance.

Moreover, the authors contend that central banks can enable more aggressive action by governments, business, civil society, and the international community through policies like carbon pricing, green financial policy, and innovative international financial architecture. Such collective efforts are necessary to ensure sustainable budgeting in the era of climate change, albeit redistributive and complex.

Geddes et al. (2018) stated that the role of finance has only been briefly examined, despite the fact that a large portion of transitions research has concentrated on energy transitions generally and technology-related elements specifically. However, every big socio-technical shift, especially the energy transition, necessitates a substantial and fundamental shift in financial resources from established solutions to new ones. As part of the current regime, the multi-level perspective (MLP) often encompasses financial markets and has a broader view of changes. Based on 56 interviews, the authors examined how State Investment Bank interventions in Germany, the UK, and Australia to learn more about how the banks fund energy projects. The researchers sought to determine whether the banks use more flexible, learning-based strategies or more traditional financial procedures (such as lending money and lowering investment risk).

The fundamental conclusion is that the methods in which funds are raised to promote sustainable technology cannot be explained by conventional economic theories alone. According to the report, state investment banks have two options when they step in: they may force the financial system to change to accommodate new clean technologies, or they can work to completely restore the system to better fund these advancements.

To accelerate sustainable transitions, policy measures need to become more nuanced and multifaceted in order to be able to steer funds away from carbon-intensive technologies and toward sustainable ones.

## 6. MONITORING AND EVALUATION

Impact measurement constitutes another concern. Regretfully, the effort does not devote enough attention to creating metrics for assessing the environmental effect of green finance-promoted GFDI.

The need for a more comprehensive and integrated conception of the shift to a sustainable low-carbon economy has been made even more urgent by the newly established sustainable development objectives and global climate agenda. In fact, although the idea of "green finance" is becoming more and more popular, there hasn't been as much actual data to support the success of initiatives that support sustainable development and climate change, both in terms of quantifiable performance and financial return.

Bhandary et al., (2021) conducted review of the literature and case studies to measure the effectiveness of climate finance. Their finding reveals that every climate financing policy has advantages and disadvantages. Moreover, targeted lending, transparency, and green bonds, feed-in tariffs, tax credits, loan guarantees, and national development banks are all successful in attracting private capital. Regarding the empirical effects of climate finance policies, particularly their effects on equality and the environment, there are substantial data and study gaps, as little to no data supporting the efficacy of national climate funds.

A balance between economic efficiency, environmental integrity, equality, and mobilization efficacy should be achieved when choosing climate financing strategies. The framework diagram illustrates the synergistic relationship between these key components by showing their directional interconnectedness and mutual reinforcement effects.

The "Synergistic Framework of Green Economics Development" Diagram illustrates the interrelationship of three fundamental components:

- The Financial Mechanism, often called Green Finance, encompasses "green bonds.", as financial tools destined particularly to assist environmentally good projects. ESG funds are investment vehicles that give environmental, social, and governance issues primary attention. Additionally, banking practices that include environmental impacts are referred to as "sustainable banking."
- The second component is the Green FDI (Investment Channels). The cross-border flow of environmentally friendly innovations is called technology transfer. Capital flows are money set aside for eco-friendly projects. Expertise sharing in the green industry is the exchange of knowledge and abilities.
- The synergy between green finance and green economy reinforces the green economy and sustainable growth through activities that conserve natural resources and ecosystem, which by consequent job opportunities development that meet present needs job Creation: Green Industry Employment Opportunities.

*Figure 3.*

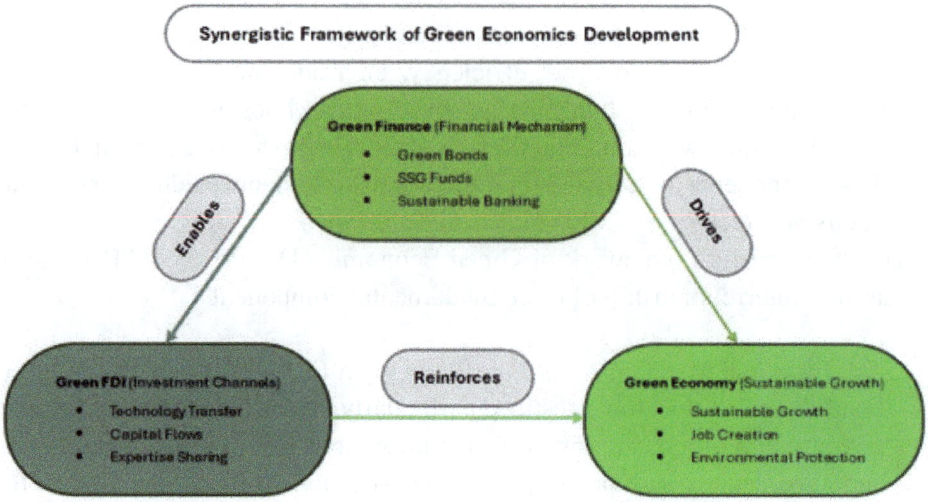


First and foremost, the framework values the fact that green finance and green FDI are not isolated forces but complementary and reinforcing forces reinforcing each other toward building sustainable economies. Green finance provides the channel of capital (e.g., green bonds, sustainability-linked loans, and ESG funds) capable of mobilizing and redirecting investments towards environmentally preferable projects, and green FDI is the cross-border flows of investments that introduce complementing resources, expertise, and technology to construct these projects.

## CONCLUSION

The maximization of social welfare has always been a slogan for human well-being. Under the context of building a sustainable green economy, countries have been trying to find the best solution to maximize the synergistic effects between resources.

Since the United Nations 2030 Agenda for Sustainable Development, more and more countries have incorporated green finance into policy-making and strategic development for building a sustainable green economy.

Innovative financing techniques are to mobilize investments in sustainable infrastructure. Among them, green financing is becoming more and more recognized as a potentially effective instrument for expanding and enabling investment in the infrastructure sector. Green finance promotes climate change mitigation and improves resource efficiency via impact investment and socially responsible investing techniques.

The ability of green finance to support Green FDI can be achieved through the development of sustainable financial instruments has facilitated this connection. Green FDI can not only significantly improve the ability to cope with environmental risks and social responsibility but also significantly increase the ecological efficiency and environmental productivity from the sustainable green economy recovery. Green FDI is also increasingly becoming an integral part of the national and multilateral framework and measures for promoting a green sustainable recovery green economy (Xu & Xu, 2022).

Despite their interdependence, the links between green FDI and green finance have yet to be addressed in the academic sphere. Three mechanisms are found to illustrate how green finance conditions the location and the intensity of green FDI, which, in turn, promotes the accessibility, the quantum and the terms of green finance. The essence of the work prompts further interest and exploration from researchers and policymakers regarding this two-way relationship between green FDI and green finance on the way to speeding the formation of a sustainable green economy.

Faced with a complex and changing global environment, the synergy between green economy recovery and green finance should be innovatively promoted. The United Nations 2030 Agenda for Sustainable Development also emphasizes that green finance should be integrated into national development strategies, green finance sub-goals, and goals should be planned, investments in green FDI and green trade should be significantly increased, and synergies should be systematically promoted.

## REFERENCES


Agarwal, M. (2020). Green economy research paper. *The International journal of analytical and experimental modal analysis, Volume XII, Issue* IV.

Almazrouei, H., & Nobanee, H. (2021). *Green Finance and Sustainable Growth.*

Alnassar, W. (2022). THE EFFECT OF GREEN LOAN AND ECOLOGICAL SUSTAINABILITY ON POLLUTION DEPLETION: PRACTICAL EVALUATION IN DEVELOPING AND OECD ECONOMIES. *Academy of Strategic Management Journal, 20*, 2021.

Amendolagine, V., Lema, R., & Rabellotti, R. (2021). Green foreign direct investments and the deepening of capabilities for sustainable innovation in multinationals: Insights from renewable energy. *Journal of Cleaner Production, 310*, 127381. DOI: 10.1016/j.jclepro.2021.127381

Balsalobre-Lorente, D., Shahbaz, M., Roubaud, D., & Farhani, S. (2020). How economic growth, renewable electricity and natural resources contribute to CO2 emissions? *Energy Policy, 113*, 356–367. DOI: 10.1016/j.enpol.2017.10.050

Bhandary, R. R., Gallagher, K. S., & Zhang, F. (2021). Climate finance policy in practice: A review of the evidence. *Climate Policy, 21*(4), 529–545. DOI: 10.1080/14693062.2020.1871313

Bolton, P., Després, M., da Silva, L. A. P., Samama, F., & Svartzman, R. (2020). *The green swan.* https://www.bis.org/publ/othp31.htm

Caetano, R. V., Marques, A. C., & Afonso, T. L. (2022). How Can Foreign Direct Investment Trigger Green Growth? The Mediating and Moderating Role of the Energy Transition. *Economies, 10*(8), 8. Advance online publication. DOI: 10.3390/economies10080199

Calel, R., & Dechezleprêtre, A. (2016). Environmental policy and directed technological change: Evidence from the European carbon market. *The Review of Economics and Statistics, 98*(1), 173–191. DOI: 10.1162/REST_a_00470

Chandrashekara, T. (2022). Green finance and sustainable investment: Trends, challenges, and opportunities. *International Journal of Research and Analytical Reviews, 9*(4), 282. https://www.ijrar.org

Clark, R., Reed, J., & Sunderland, T. (2018). Bridging funding gaps for climate and sustainable development: Pitfalls, progress and potential of private finance. *Land Use Policy, 71*, 335–346. DOI: 10.1016/j.landusepol.2017.12.013

Dechezleprêtre, A., & Sato, M. (2017). The impacts of environmental regulations on competitiveness. *Review of Environmental Economics and Policy, 11*(2), 183–206. DOI: 10.1093/reep/rex013

El Madnaoui, A., Cheedella, S. S., Okolo, K., Wang, K., Jatin, P., Agrawal, A., & Priya, S. (2021). *The Case for a Green Economy*. DOI: 10.5281/ZENODO.4740628

Fu, C., Lu, L., & Pirabi, M. (2024). Advancing green finance: A review of climate change and decarbonization. *Digital Economy and Sustainable Development, 2*(1), 1. DOI: 10.1007/s44265-023-00026-x

Garsous, G., & Kozluk, T. (2017). Foreign direct investment and the pollution haven hypothesis: Evidence from listed firms (OECD Economics Department Working Papers No. 1379). OECD Publishing. https://doi.org/DOI: 10.1787/5jlv2g5b3w9n-en

Geddes, A., Schmidt, T. S., & Steffen, B. (2018). The multiple roles of state investment banks in low-carbon energy finance: An analysis of Australia, the UK and Germany. *Energy Policy, 115*, 158–170. DOI: 10.1016/j.enpol.2018.01.009

Golub, S., Kauffmann, C., & Yeres, P. (2011). Defining And Measuring Green FDI: An Exploratory Review Of Existing Work And Evidence. *OECD Working Papers On International Investment*. DOI: 10.1787/18151957

Jaumotte, F., Kim, J., Pienknagura, S., & Schwerhoff, G. (2024). *Policies to foster green FDI: Best practices for emerging market and developing economies (IMF Staff Climate Notes 2024/004)*. International Monetary Fund., DOI: 10.5089/9798400289927.066

Johnstone, N., Serravalle, C., Scapecchi, P., & Labonne, J. (2007). *Public environmental policy and corporate behaviour: Project background, overview of the data and summary results* (OECD Working Paper). Organisation for Economic Co-operation and Development.

Larsen, M. L. (2019, November 22). *A growing toolbox of sustainable finance instruments – Green Finance & Development Center*. https://greenfdc.org/a-growing-toolbox-of-sustainable-finance-instruments/

Li, X., & Liu, X. (2005). Foreign direct investment and economic growth: An increasingly endogenous relationship. *World Development, 33*(3), 393–407. https://doi.org/ https://doi.org/10.1016/j.worlddev.2004.11.001. DOI: 10.1016/j.worlddev.2004.11.001

Mishra, M. S. N. (2021). *Future of Green Financing: Challenges and Opportunities. 1*(1).

Muganyi, T., Yan, L., & Sun, H. (2021). Green finance, fintech and environmental protection: Evidence from China. *International Journal of Environmental Research and Public Health, 18*(9), 4771. DOI: 10.3390/ijerph18094771 PMID: 33947122

Nguyen, D. T., Oanh, T. T. K., Bui, T. D., & Dao, L. K. O. (2024). The impact of green finance on green growth: The role of green energy and green production. *Heliyon, 10*(16), e36639. DOI: 10.1016/j.heliyon.2024.e36639 PMID: 39262964

Ofori, I. K., Figari, F., & Ojong, N. (2023). Towards sustainability: The relationship between foreign direct investment, economic freedom and inclusive green growth. *Journal of Cleaner Production, 406*, 137020. DOI: 10.1016/j.jclepro.2023.137020

Polzin, F., Sanders, M., & Tauebe, F. (2017). A diverse and resilient financial system for investments in the energy transition. *Current Opinion in Environmental Sustainability, 28*, 24–32. DOI: 10.1016/j.cosust.2017.07.004

Tufail, M., Song, L., & Khan, Z. (2024). Green finance and green growth nexus: Evaluating the role of globalization and human capital. *Journal of Applied Econometrics, 27*(1), 2309437. DOI: 10.1080/15140326.2024.2309437

Tung, P.-H., Chiu, Y.-H., & Huang, C.-H. (2025). Exploring the research development trajectory and trends of green finance. *Asia Pacific Management Review, 30*(3), 100329. https://doi.org/ https://doi.org/10.1016/j.apmrv.2024.10.001

UNCTAD. (2023). *World Investment Report 2023: Investing in sustainable energy for all.* United Nations Conference on Trade and Development. https://unctad.org/publication/world-investment-report-2023

Waidelich, P., & Steffen, B. (2024). Renewable energy financing by state investment banks: Evidence from OECD countries. *Energy Economics, 133*, 107455. https://doi.org/ https://doi.org/10.1016/j.eneco.2024.107455. DOI: 10.1016/j.eneco.2024.107455

Xu, L., & Xu, C. (2022). Does green finance and energy policy paradox demonstrate green economic recovery: Role of social capital and public health. *Frontiers in Public Health, 10*, 843314. DOI: 10.3389/fpubh.2022.951527 PMID: 36438284

Zhang, Y. (2022). How Economic Performance of OECD economies influences through Green Finance and Renewable Energy Investment Resources? *Resources Policy, 79*, 102925. DOI: 10.1016/j.resourpol.2022.102925

# Chapter 2
# Future Directions in Sustainable Investing:
## Empowering Individual Investors for Green Development

**Menaka Biswal**
*HLM Group of Institutions, India*

**Jyoti Tyagi**
https://orcid.org/0009-0006-1206-9437
*IAMR Group of Institutions, India*

**Mukesh Sehrawat**
https://orcid.org/0009-0008-7928-1568
*G.L. Bajaj Institute of Management and Research, Greater Noida, India*

**Vishal Jain**
https://orcid.org/0000-0003-1126-7424
*School of Engineering & Technology, Vivekananda Institute of Professional Studies - Technical Campus, New Delhi, India*

## ABSTRACT

*The imperatives of climate change coupled with a global momentum towards sustainable development are changing the face of personal finance and investment. This chapter, explores the way financial markets, institutions, and instruments are growing to enable individual investors to fund environmental sustainability and social responsibility efforts. It starts by discussing how green finance - focused on financing projects that help to mitigate climate change - is related to broader concepts of sustainable finance that involve other social and governance factors. Individual investors have contributed to demand for green bonds, ESG funds, and*

DOI: 10.4018/979-8-3373-8287-6.ch002

© 2026, IGI Global Scientific Publishing. Copying or distributing in print or electronic forms without written permission of IGI Global Scientific Publishing is prohibited. Use of this chapter to nerative artificial intelligence (AI) technologies is expressly prohibited. The publisher reserves all rights to license its use for generative AI training and machine learning model development.

*impact investing opportunities. The key emerging trends in sustainable investing include: technological innovation, regulatory developments, and affordable individual financial instruments. By considering the emerging trends and solutions, this chapter aims to inspire and motivate individual investors in taking active roles in making green development and a sustainable future.*

## 1. INTRODUCTION

The accelerating climate emergency and increasing inequality globally has led to the rapid transition to sustainable investing, which incorporates environmental, social and governance factors (ESG) into investment strategies. As economies transition toward low-carbon, inclusive and resilient economies, the pressure to innovate on financing green development and to facilitate inclusive participation in green development increases. Of the groups arguably most crucial, yet least engaged with, in this transition, are individual investors. The chapter examines the changing landscape of sustainable investing with a particular focus on financial and public empowerment of retail and individual investors. While governments and institutional investors have driven the initial enthusiasm in green finance, progress in the sustainable development space will require individuals who are not only interested in the financial return but also in contributing to the welfare of society and the health of the planet.

In the beginning by framing the importance of sustainable investing, this chapter highlighting the potential of green finance to deliver on the United Nations Sustainable Development Goals (SDGs). It will detail the urgent action needed to develop investor empowerment for individual investors through education, transparency, and inclusive policy design. By unpacking the psychological, social, and regulatory factors that drive investor empowerment, the chapter highlight how informed and motivated individuals can have an impact on corporate policy, market behaviour, and environmental outcomes. Additionally, the chapter discusses the core principles of green finance, upcoming market instruments, ESG investing developments, and the role of finance markets in enabling sustainability. In conclusion, this chapter discusses potential green finance challenges and opportunities along with highlighting not just the current development of sustainable investing, but also the potential-altering capacity of enabling individual investors as agents of green development.

### 1.1. Overview of Sustainable Investing and its Significance

In last two decades, we have witnessed a fast-growing trend transforming sustainable investing from niche ethical screening practices to mainstream financial strategies that consider aspects in the environment, social, and governance (ESG). Sustainable investing integrates long-term environmental, social, and governance (ESG) factors into the investment decision-making process in an attempt to realize improved risk-adjusted returns (Sikken, 2011).The practice of sustainable investing has evolved from basic screening methods to more sophisticated strategies, including "best-in-class" approaches and "impact investing" (Beisenbina et al., 2022). Sustainable investing initially promoted by institutional investors such as pension funds and sovereign wealth funds; sustainable investing has now entered the stock markets as its core component. This shift is caused by the increasing evidence that ESG investments can return equally or better risk-adjusted returns while contributing to social and environmental causes. Climate change, social inequality, corporate accountability, and other urgent issues have made sustainable finance an urgent catalyst to achieve long-term green development goals and the United Nations Sustainable Development Goals (SDGs).

The significance of sustainable investing comedown dual purposes:

- Providing competitive returns on the investment.
- Providing outcomes that are positive for society, the environment, climate action, human rights, corporate accountability, and inclusive development. Sustainable investments are starting to be seen as necessary mechanisms to help solve global issues like climate change, social inequality, and governance (Hachigian & McGill, 2012).

This shift involves moving away from traditional investment mechanisms, and instead, aligning the investment with world development goals and sustainable development goals/compacts (Johnson et al., 2019).

The key to this change is the inclusion of environmental, social, and governance (ESG) considerations in the investment decision-making process (Urwin, 2010). Recent research highlights the growing importance of integrating ESG considerations into investment strategies. In fact, ESG portfolios have demonstrated better financial performance than traditional ones, boasting average annual returns that are 4.3% higher (Pramitasari, 2024). Plus, these portfolios tend to be less volatile and more resilient during market downturns. Research indicates a positive relationship between corporate sustainability practices and financial performance. A comprehensive meta-study found that 88% of reviewed sources linked robust sustainability practices to better operational performance and cashflows (Clark et al., 2015). Similarly, a study on REITs demonstrated that investing in sustainability enhances operational performance while lowering risk exposure and volatility (Fuerst, 2015). In the materials industry, companies with higher environmental sustainability rankings showed lower growth rates in operational expenses, suggesting improved operational efficiency

(Brown, 2018). As sustainable finance starts to accelerate on a global scale, it is already changing the investment scene. Institutional investors, governments, and multilateral institutions are channelling capital towards ESG-categorized assets. However, to capitalize on the full potential of sustainable investment, access to markets will need to be democratized to allow individual investors to engage meaningfully in the transition to a greener and more equitable economy.

## 1.2. Overview of Sustainable Development Goals and Their Implementation

The Sustainable Development Goals (SDGs) are a comprehensive framework established in 2015 by the UN, consist of 17 sustainable development goals with 169 targets and 248 indicators, all aimed at challenging global issues by 2030 (Wadhwani &Malpani, 2023). The SDGs encompass a broad spectrum of issues that include poverty, inequality, climate change and environmental sustainability (Gigliotti et al., 2019). The SDGs build on the MDGs (Millennium Development Goals), but place greater emphasis on local action and stakeholder involvement to facilitate the achievement of the SDGs (Wadhwani &Malpani, 2023). The SDGs represent a comprehensive and ambitious global agenda and potentially one of the most far-reaching agendas since the 1945 UN Charter (Langford, 2016). The success of SDGs will be reliant on updated datasets, sound indicators, and awareness of the interdependence between goals and targets (Gigliotti et al., 2019). Achieving the SDGs will require substantial investment, innovation, and policy change at all levels (Wadhwani &Malpani, 2023).

- The SDGs have been adopted universally by all 193 UN member states and have been developed as a common vision for sustainable development. They are often referenced in government documentation and speeches and most countries have submitted Voluntary National Reviews on progress (Bai, 2024).
- Research on the SDGs has grown dramatically, with more than 9000 articles produced, and this is indicative of a growing awareness and acknowledgement and collaboratively in interdisciplinary ways to tackle global issues (Bai, 2024) (Yumnam et al., 2024).
- While the goals are meant to be universal, they need to be applied to a specific context with consideration of local conditions and priorities. Additionally, the pandemic made it clear we need strategies that are "resilient and adaptable" to achieve the SDGs, which will be achieved through sustainable development plans and support for health and economic recovery in the future (Markina, 2022) (Smith et al., 2018).

## 1.3. Definition and Key Principles of Green Finance

Green finance serves as an important aspect in reaching sustainable development by promoting activities and projects with a green purpose (Chala & Demidov, 2024). It encompasses a wide variety of financial instruments ranging from green banking, green debt markets, to green structured funds (Berensmann& Lindenberg, 2019). While green finance does not have a universal definition, common themes include funding for public and private green investments, goods and services for the environment, and policies to protect and enhance the environment and mitigate climate change (Lindenberg, 2014). It is anchored on key principles of an equitable interdependence of economic growth, environmental conservation, and social well-being (Chala & Demidov, 2024). Green finance currently faces many hurdles, including a lack of scale, wish-wash in market definitions and rules, and global cooperation (Chala & Demidov, 2024). An enabling environment that is transparent with definitions, voluntary principles, and guidelines will need to envelop all asset classes (Berensmann& Lindenberg, 2019) if these challenges are overcome. Green development finance will be collaboratively developed among international financial institutions, governments, and the business sector (Bhattacharyya, 2021). Green finance is a set of financial flows that aim to support sustainable development and adhere to the new norms of environmental, social, and governance (ESG). It includes different types of instruments or structures that incentivize investment into environmentally benign projects and/or technologies.

**Definition of Green Finance:** Green finance refers to a financial activity that can support the Sustainable Development Goals (SDGs) and corporate environmental responsibility. It consists of public subsidies, private investments, lending, and a host of other transactions according to ESG principles (Trukhachev&Dzhikiya, 2023). Following are the principles of governing green finance:

**Decarbonization:** Green finance constitutes, directly and indirectly, the socio-political strategies of economic transitions toward low-carbon economies, whereby energy consumption structures are decarbonized (Zhu et al., 2024). Together, these pillars create a financial system that links economic growth with environmental sustainability and climate objectives. Forming this system and establishing it as a prerequisite, we now need to explore how green finance facilitates environmental and social, as evidence of its meaningful application in inclusive, low-carbon, and resilient development in every sector.

## 1.4. Role of Green Finance in Achieving Sustainable Development Goals (SDGs)

Green finance plays a key role in achieving Sustainable Development Goals (SDGs) by promoting investment in sustainable infrastructure, green technology innovation, and corporate environmental responsibility as shown in figure 1. The three-pronged approach not only addresses environmental concerns but also initiates economic growth and social justice.

*Figure 1. Role of green finance in achieving sustainable development*

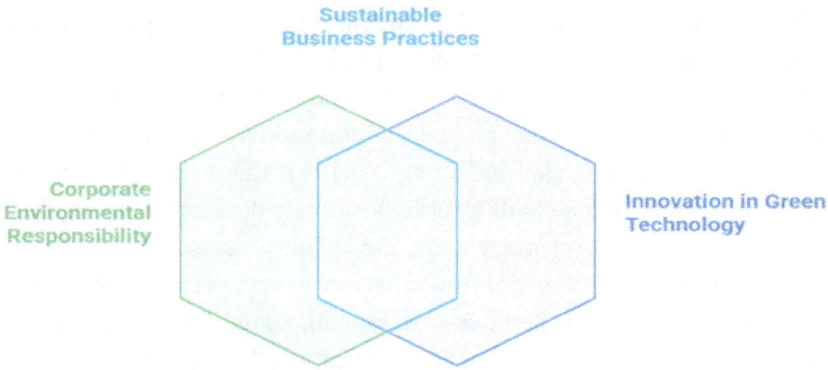


**Green Finance and Sustainable Infrastructure**: Green finance plays a significant role in the development of sustainable infrastructure, particularly in initiatives like the Belt and Road Initiative (BRI) (Mahmood et al., 2024). Green finance facilitates projects that are pollution-reducing and environmentally sustainable, essential in achieving SDGs on clean water, sustainable cities, and climate action.

**Innovation in Green Technology:** Green finance investment promotes green technology innovation, essential for a low-carbon economy (Mahmood et al., 2024) (Kholaif& Tang, 2024). The use of cutting-edge technologies, such as big data analytics, further enhances the effectiveness of green finance in promoting sustainable measures (Kholaif& Tang, 2024).

**Corporate Environmental Responsibility:** Green finance policies drive corporate responsibility by providing financial incentives for environmentally sustainable practices (Yuan et al., 2024). Evidence shows that such policies initiate improved corporate environmental performance, particularly in nations with strong regulatory regimes (Yuan et al., 2024.

While governments and institutions have been influential in driving such change, active contribution from all players, including retail investors, will be necessary on the road towards a genuine, sustainable future. For building a green and robust financial ecosystem which is inclusive as well as resistant to potential disruption, there must be inquiry as to how investors can be encouraged to invest toward sustainable development with informed, responsible investment decisions.

## 1.5. The Need to Empower Individual Investors in the Green Investment Landscape

Recent developments confirm that the empowerment of individual investors forms a basis to promote sustainability in finance. Researchers admit that investor empowerment is an essential driver toward sustainability in capital markets, and he speaks about the need for coordination of engagement activities by institutional investors and platforms. Individuals transform the paradigm of investing into greener capital sources, ensuring inclusive participation, sustainable behaviour, and faster movement towards the low-carbon sustainable future. Individual investors, for both monetary and non-monetary reasons, have shown an overwhelming rebel to achieve sustainability funds, which has been due to issues of financial literacy combined with personal and environmental values and the factor of warm glow perception (Gutsche et al., 2023). Gao et al. (2023) present evidence that individuals with stronger preferences for green investment tend to invest more in green mutual funds based on their aversion to climate change risks rather than for financial gains. Gonzalez-Arcos et al. (2023) highlight micro-investing platforms, which show that sustainability value and empowerment feelings are important motivators for sustainable investments that uniquely shape investors' willingness to forgo financial returns. Therefore, these studies put together give credence to the important role of individual investor participation as a favourable drive for sustainable finance and that investments in platforms, education, and options reflecting investors' values will be key to moving ahead in the green investment landscape (Ringe, 2023; Gao et al., 2023; Gonzalez-Arcos et al., 2023). Key reasons for empowering individual investors in the green investment landscape may be as follows:

**Unlocking Green Capital:** By choosing from an increasing menu of sustainable investments available through micro-investing platforms (Gonzalez-Arcos et al., 2023), individual investors have their potentials to substantially contribute to green finance. Individual investment decisions, when considered at large, could bridge the 'efficiency gap' in the adoption of green technology, thus rewarding both the environment and financial gain (Amram & Kulatilaka, 2009).

**Inclusive Participation:** By democratizing access to sustainable investments, micro-investing platforms attract a wider audience into the green finance movement (Gonzalez-Arcos et al., 2023). Financial literacy and awareness of environmental matters would be further enhanced by micro-investing platforms to make sustainable investment practices more inclusive (Gutsche et al., 2023).

**Promoting Sustainable Behavior:** Positive feelings and social preferences drive sustainable investment behavior and encourage individuals to align their financial decisions with environmental values (Gutsche et al., 2023). Such policies that act at the local level would become a catalyst in the field for private investors to discover profitable opportunities away from the sustainable path (Amram & Kulatilaka, 2009).

**Accelerating the Transition:** Individual investors, along with institutional actors, are vital participants in the transition out of fossil fuel reliance with their investments directing firms toward new strategic paths (Dordi et al., 2022). Reforms in the global financial architecture favouring ecological assets would further entice individual investors to back sustainable ventures (Triggs, 2023).

## 1.6. How Green Finance Supports Environmental and Social Sustainability

Green finance is an important tool for environmental sustainability and to resource green projects (Chua & Ho, 2023). It covers instruments like green bonds, renewables investment, and sustainable infrastructure (Ali et al., 2023). Green finance has shown increased environmental sustainability in countries where climate protective investment is a priority (Zakari & Khan, 2021). Though not all the effects of green bond financing have a positive effect on environmental and social sustainability. Some researchers have argued that they may have a slow detrimental transformational effect in environmental and social sustainability (Sinha et al, 2021). In any event, green finance has a key role to play toachieve the Sustainable Development Goals by financing all sorts of projects that achieve environmental preservation, social equity and economic development (Ali et al, 2023). Green finance and its effect on sustainability and alignment with ESG standards is still a key focus of investigation, the following sections present how green finance enables the above.

**Economic Contributions:** Green finance deploys capital to renewable energy, energy efficiency and green infrastructure projects that are important in economic development but with a lesser environmental footprint (Ali et al, 2023). Green finance helps managers improve the management of green in green supply chain management (GSCM) especially when aided with advanced technologies such as big data analytics, yielding improved economic performance and sustainability performance (Kholaif& Tang, 2024).

**Environmental Impact:** Green finance works to combat climate changes via the funding of green technologies and low-carbon initiatives (Chala & Demidov, 2024). A crucial part of funding projects with a goal of reducing carbon emissions is the issuance of green bonds and investments made by sustainable organizations (Ali et al., 2023).

**Social Sustainability:** Green finance helps to facilitate corporate social responsibility (CSR) activities and promotes social equity and community well-being through conscious investment practices (Cai & Song, 2022). It creates social inclusion by developing projects aimed at environmental sustainability and social welfare, allowing financial efforts to be aligned with social drivers (Ali et al., 2023). Overall contributions like this can strengthen the case that green finance is a contributing component to responsible economic, sustainable environmental and social equity projects. To improve understanding of the evolving role of green finance, it is essential to consider how green finance will fit into the great complexity of the sustainable finance lens at which a multitude of financial tools, rules, and global policies are aimed at improving the sustainability agenda on a broader long-term basis.

## 1.7. The Interconnection Between Green Finance and Broader Sustainable Finance Framework

Green finance and sustainable finance are generally interrelated in terms of their principles regarding environmental problems and economic growth. It is solely concerned with financing for projects with environmental positive effects, while the latter includes a wider range of financial activities against social and governance factors, besides environmental factors. They are connected together in many respects and more exploration will now ensure:

### Climate Risks Integration with Regulatory Frameworks

The initiatives inherent to green finance now enter the national regulatory framework, like, for example, Saudi Arabia Vision 2030 with its sustainability goals that marry economic diversification (Alhejaili, 2024). To improve market readiness, social acceptance for green finance is facilitated by regulatory frameworks, which would complement the increased transformation to sustainable business practice processes.

### Impact on Sustainable Development

Green finance has proved to have a positive effect on sustainable development, particularly up to sub-Saharan Africa, where it deals with the environmental, social, and economic dimensions-potentials. (Nile, Udo, Jack, Abner, 2024). Strong financial instruments such as green bonds are reported to propel the achievement of the UN Sustainable Development Goals (SDGs) because they mobilize funds for renewable and conservation projects (Raman et al., 2025) (Zhang & Umar, 2023).

### Interconnectivity of Financial Instruments

The relationship coming out of green bonds, renewable energy, and the carbon market illustrates the dynamic spillover effects across the green finance ecosystem in general, pointing towards complementary roles in promoting sustainability(Zhang & Umar, 2023).Financial instrument innovations, such as green fin-tech and social impact bonds, will create pathways for unlocking further progress of development in sustainability while mitigating some of the impacts on the environment(Raman et al., 2025).

## 2. THE ROLE OF FINANCIAL MARKETS IN SUSTAINABLE INVESTING

The role of financial markets in sustainable investing is multifaceted, encompassing capital allocation, corporate accountability, and innovation. Financial markets enable the mobilization of capital towards sustainable initiatives, hence enabling the transition towards a low-carbon economy. The market for sustainable finance was $5.8 trillion in 2022, a clear demonstration of strong demand for green investments amidst economic difficulties ("Capital markets and sustainable finance", 2023). Sustainable investing has the financial markets as capital mobilizers, price-setters, transparency enablers, innovation drivers, and policy implementers, thus making these markets key to channelings funds toward sustainable projects, setting prices that reflect ESG characteristics, and providing a transparent environment through the distribution of credible ESG data. Furthermore, financial markets support innovation by launching new financial products and technologies and implementing their policies in the service of sustainability. There is great need for reinforcing the above-mentioned roles to empower individual investors and to create a resilient sustainable finance system.

### 2.1. Advantages of Financial Markets

#### Capital Mobilization

Financial markets facilitate the application of capital into sustainable projects. An example are green bonds, the prime financing source for green initiatives (Zioło et al., 2024). The mainstreaming of integrating ESG criteria in investment decisions has triggered interest among socially responsible investors and those pursuing purely financial goals (Hunt, 2022).

### Price Setting and Transparency

More green opportunities have been considered by markets, with firms with significant green revenues experiencing positive financial returns post climate agreements (Kruse et al., 2023). A better transparency concerning ESG aspects of financial products is appreciated although the insufficiency of current regulatory frameworks remains to hamper the full mobilization of private capital into sustainable investments (Brühl, 2022).

### Innovation and Policy Implementation

Financial markets allow for an innovation route through the establishment of green financial products and technologies such as blockchain and fintech that provide innovative approaches to sustainability (Ziolo et al., 2024). The role of state regulation and the SRI movement is very important in creating an enabling environment for climate finance (Richardson, 2014).

## 2.2. Development of Financial Markets Towards Sustainability

Financial markets' development toward sustainability is reflected by the increased integration of environmental, social, and governance (ESG) considerations into investment plans, and the development of green finance. The shift is indicative of the increased recognition of the need for sustainable economic behaviors driven by both regulatory action and market forces.

Financial markets are evolving to become more sustainable by including environment, social and governance (ESG) factors in investment choices (Busch et al., 2015). The shift is an expression of the enhanced awareness of sustainable development and the corporate social responsibility in the global economy (Janicka, 2016). Socially responsible financial markets are intended to create leverage for economic, social, and environmental impacts, subsequently influencing market organization, legal systems, and financial products (JednakJednak, 2019). However, there are still issues like the need for a long-term investment strategy and better reliable ESG data (Busch et al., 2015). Climate change is an alarming threat, and the concept of "stranded assets" of fossil fuel industries comes into the picture (Caldecott, 2018). Financial activity is shifting towards a paradigm of green energy investment and the proper respect of natural capital and its role in generating wealth (Clarke, 2015). Despite progress, socially responsible practices in financial markets have much to give and there is still room to better meet full implementation (JednakJednak, 2019). The subsequent sections identify the main aspects of this evolution.

**Growth of Sustainable Finance:** The sustainable finance sector, once a niche, has seen rapid growth as ESG issues entered the mainstream investment process (Dimmelmeier, 2023). Green finance research is developing the trends toward energy efficiency and carbon reduction especially in emerging economies (Qadri et al., 2024).

**Role of FinTech:** Fin-Tech has become one of the major engines for sustainable development in resource-poor areas. The contributions provided by Fin-tech to sustainability show a U-shaped pattern: signifying that greater impact is exerted towards sustainability when Fin-Tech has moved onto a matured phase (Yu & Li, 2024). Fin-Tech creates an environment for sustainable development, dependent on market conditions and advancement in green technologies (Yu & Li, 2024).

**Market Interconnectedness:** The interconnectivity of ESG markets during geopolitical crisis situations indicates that sustainability-focused investments are capable of transmitting and absorbing market volatility (Ullah et al., 2024). This phenomenon, in turn, necessitates the watchfulness of these markets to avert systemic risks.

This evolution in green finance is also seen in the emergence of certain financial products, which demonstrate those principles at scale. Green bonds, ESG funds, and sustainable ETFs have emerged as important vehicles to align investment themes with long-term environmental and social objectives.

## 2.3. Green Bonds, ESG (Environmental, Social, and Governance) Funds, and Sustainable ETFs

Green bonds, ESG funds, and sustainable ETFs are increasingly a key component of the investment universe, highlighting environmental, social, and governance factors. They not only seek to deliver returns but also to promote sustainability. The following discuss their characteristics, performance, and implications for investors:

**Green Bonds:** Green bonds are specifically designed to finance projects with a beneficial impact on the environment, and they substantially improve corporate ESG performance through financing and signaling mechanisms (Ge et al., 2024). They have been known to improve the environmental and social dimensions of ESG, though their influence on governance elements remains limited (Ge et al., 2024). The green bond issuance can also assist in mitigating the adverse effects of policy uncertainty on the ESG performance of firms, underscoring their strategic position in sustainable finance (Ge et al., 2024).

**ESG Funds and Sustainable ETFs:** ESG ETFs have been revealed to offer competitive financial performance, frequently outperforming traditional benchmarks such as the Dow Jones and Russell 2000, particularly in times of market turmoil (Valadkhani& O'Mahony, 2024). These funds' performance is influenced by market conditions, with European ETFs registering reduced volatility and more resilience in the face of geopolitical tensions (Xu et al. 2024). Notably, ESG ETFs have exhibited safe-haven behavior, especially during crises, and have outperformed conventional assets like gold (Azad & Devi, 2024) (Bhattacherjee et al., 2024).

**Investment Implications:** Investors are increasingly aware of the dual advantages of sustainable investments, achieving financial returns while endorsing ethical practices (Valadkhani & O' Mahony, 2024). However, the risk of green washing is a concern, making it essential to carefully choose investment products to ensure they genuinely support sustainability efforts (Ge et al., 2024). As sustainable finance instruments such as green bonds, ESG funds and sustainable ETFs grow in popularity, their effects extend beyond short-term market performance. Now we will examine the ways in which these instruments build and reinforce long-term investment strategies so investors can have portfolios that align to long-lasting environmental, social and governance goals, avoid risks and generate future-oriented financial returns.

## 2.4. The Impact of Sustainable Financial Instruments on Long-Term Investment Strategies

The impact of sustainable financial instruments on long-term investment strategies becomes increasingly stronger over the years as investors look to have financial returns from the environmental and social governance (ESG) principles. Studies suggest that sustainable investments perform equally well as their traditional counterparts and can even lead to better results in the long run. Sustainable financial instruments, including green bonds and ESG funds, increasingly are becoming the accepted means of embedding environmental and social aspects in financial decision-making and, therefore creating long-term value. In addition to the benefits of being able to diversify the portfolio, these instruments can help to mitigate climate and regulatory risk, while also making capital allocation decisions more aligned with sustainability objectives. The shift towards sustainable finance is a key enabler of resilience-based approaches to investors' strategies for growth, as it provides a pathway towards investing for the future, rather than responding to current environmental and social governance (ESG) factors.

**Portfolio Diversification and Risk Mitigation:** Publicly and privately, there has been a growth in interest surrounding portfolio investments in green bonds, particularly as they provide some risk-diminishing characteristics that can appeal to institutional investors and socially responsible investors, increasing investor demand for green bonds even as their prices remain relatively high. This is being driven (and aided) by the growing size of the green bond market, along with better allocation of funds towards renewable energy, clean water and low-carbon transport projects (Marín-Rodríguez et al., 2023). ESG funds along with green bonds also reduce regulatory risks to varying degrees as they were created in response to evolving environmental policies and standards. Thus, at a minimum, they provide investors with a means of orienting to this evolving future and fulfilling their compliance obligations under international agreements (Zairis et al., 2024).

**Resilience and Long-term Value Creation:** Financial instruments that are sustainable contribute to the journey of a transition to a sustainable economy because they incorporate financial, social and environmental value into all investment decision-making. This incorporation contributes to long-term value creation through resilience and adaptability in the wake of environmental and social challenges (Schoenmaker &Schramade, 2019). The focus on environmental factors while developing green finance investment strategies highlights the necessity of governance and social factors that produce sustainable and ethical investment strategies (Meng & Shaikh, 2023).

**Performance Comparison:** According to the studies, funds screened under ESG criteria yield better retirement outcomes, which increase pension size by 10.4% compared to non-screened index funds (Owadally et al., 2021). Data over the years, from 1994 to 2020 with observations conducted over such a long time have shown that there is no significant performance difference between ESG funds and conventional funds, meaning that it is quite possible to invest in sustainable investments without impairing performance or returns (Owadally et al., 2021).

**Accounting and Investment Strategies:** Fair value accounting was meant to not tend to long-term equity investments, which synergize well with development, as they are necessary for sustainability. An alternative approach in measurement systems increases the change of optimizing long-term investment strategies, linking it to goals of sustainability (Palea, 2021).

**Resource Efficiency and Funding:** Thus, sustainable investment decisions are expected to be reflected in the fact that environmentally strategic investments in resource efficiency are positively related to the financial stability of long-term funding (Sun et al., 2024). As sustainable investing continues to advance over time, its adoption in long-term financial planning is reflective of its growing relevance and longevity. On that basis, the next section addresses the new trends that are defining the future of sustainable which are changing the very nature of how sustainability is integrated into 21st Century investment portfolios.

## 3. EMERGING TRENDS IN SUSTAINABLE INVESTING

Sustainable investing has gained significant traction, driven by the integration of Environmental, Social, and Governance (ESG) factors across various asset classes, the rise of green and sustainability-linked bonds, and the growth of impact investing. This evolution reflects a broader recognition of the financial implications of sustainability, influencing investment strategies and market dynamics.

## ESG Integration Across Asset Classes

ESG considerations are becoming more prevalent across a range of asset classes, such as equities, fixed income and property (Mariz, 2022). A survey has shown that 73% of investment professionals now take ESG factors into account, which signifies a culture shift in investment practice. The size of the global sustainable investment market is $21.4 trillion or 30.2% of professionally managed assets, with the most growth in Asia (Pizzani, 2015).

## Rise of Green and Sustainability-Linked Bonds

There was a record US$883 billion of sustainable bond issuance, including green, social, and sustainability-linked bonds, in 2021, an increase of 112% from 2020. These bonds are used to finance sustainable projects, such as environmental or social projects, and the leading market in this area is Europe (Mariz, 2022).

## Impact Investing Growth

Impact investing is concerned with generating measurable social and environmental benefits along with financial returns, so it has attracted investors who want to align their investments with their personal values (Xiao et al., 2023) (Yadav, 2024). This trend marks a notable shift in investors understanding that financial performance and sustainability are connected, as well as their growing desire to invest in opportunities that genuinely benefit society (Beisenbina et al., 2022).

## Climate-Focused Investing

Climate-focused investing prioritizes investments that build climate resilience and sustainability. It also entails, but not limited to, impact investing, which aims to generate both measurable social and environmental benefits and financial return (Xiao et al., 2023). The raising awareness of climate change has led to a growing demand for green finance initiatives including sustainability bonds (Yadav, 2024).

## Advancements in ESG Data and Analytics

Advanced technologies, including machine learning and artificial intelligence, are improving ESG data analytics (Marín-Rodríguez et al., 2025). Improvement of data quality and transparency is important for investors to accurately understand the impact of their investments (Zhong, W. (2023). Regulations are changing to improve ESG reporting standards to satisfy reported issues of standardization and transparency (Xiao et al., 2023).

## Sustainable ETFs and Index Funds

Sustainable exchange traded funds (ETFs) are a part of the conversation, as they provide diversified options to comply with ESG criteria. They perform relatively well during periods of market volatility, and also represent an opportunity for sustainability-focused strategies in investment vehicles (Marín-Rodríguez et al., 2025). The move away from traditional investment tools and towards green instruments illustrates that many ESG investment strategies are moving from socially responsible investment (SRI) to wider opting-in to socially responsible concepts by a diversity of exchange traded instruments (Beisenbina et al., 2022).

## Circular Economy Investments

Investments towards realizing a closed-loop system and reducing as much waste as possible by utilizing resources again if and when they may not be useable. There are promises of substantial cost savings and resources efficiency in such acquisitions that advocate sustainable economic growth (Yadav, 2024). Companies that take on circular practices as it engages recycling options or sustainable product design, will engage investor focus (Manaswi et al., 2023).

## Biodiversity and Natural Capital Investing

To achieve sustained longevity as a component of future financial value, solidifying ecosystems and natural resources are paramount. The ways in which this can be achieved includes funding conservation projects or sustainable land use, which can reward with ecological returns AND financial returns (Beisenbina et al., 2022). The literature describes the bedrock of research developing on the financial upside of investing in biodiversity, including an increase in scholarly work (Singhania et al., 2023).

## Social and Inclusive Investing

Aims to address social inequalities and promote inclusive growth through targeted investments in underserved communities. This includes impact investing, which seeks measurable social benefits alongside financial returns, and ESG integration in portfolio management (Cort, 2023). The rise of social impact bonds and community investment funds reflects a shift towards prioritizing social outcomes in investment decisions (Manaswi et al., 2023).

## The Growth of Impact Investing and Socially Responsible Investing (SRI)

Socially responsible investing (SRI) seems to be one of the fastest, growing areas in finance with instances growing globally from 2012 to 2015 by about 61% (Risalvato et al., 2018). Broadly, this investment approach embeds environmental, social and governance (ESG) issues in investment decision-making with a desire to harmonize education and a financial return (Mahn, 2016). More room for SRI also means more stakeholders around the world that are interested in scrutinizing the ESG practices of companies (Camilleri, 2020). Since the financial crisis in 2007, ethical indices, in general, have outperformed traditional indices (Risalvato et al., 2018). Much growth has occurred, yet there is little clarity in the academic literature in regards to understanding what drives investors to choose SRI strategies (Jun, 2013). Indeed, as investors analyze more and more other than financial performance with an emphasis on ESG credentials (Camilleri, 2020), one can expect the impact of sustainable investment on the global investment industry to record a massive jump within the next few years (Mahn, 2016).

## Technology and Digital Innovation in Sustainable Finance (e.g., Block Chain, AI-Driven ESG Analysis)

The new study shows how much the digital technologies are going to affect sustainable finance. In other words, AI, block chain, and big-data analytics are expected to improve decision-making processes, transparency, and effectiveness in sustainable investing (Zhao, 2024). This includes ESG compliance, risk management, and recognizing opportunities for sustainable growth (Zhao, 2024; Shkodina, 2024). Fintech innovations are helping democratize green investment opportunities and ESG reporting (Hasan et al., 2024). However, there are still issues, including regulatory fragmentation and cyber-security risks (Hasan et al., 2024). AI-driven "Alternative ESG ratings," in a way, are influencing sustainable investment methodology by providing benefits like greater standardization and real-time analytics, in comparison with traditional ESG ratings (Hughes et al., 2021). These technologies are creating a sustainable digital finance ecosystem that nurtures green initiatives geared toward achieving sustainable development goals (Shkodina, 2024; Hasan et al., 2024).

## Big Data Analytics in Assessing Sustainability Risks and Opportunities

Big data analytics capabilities (BDAC) give life to the assessment and mitigation of sustainability risks and opportunities in various sectors. In the supply chain, big data analytics capabilities can improve managers' responses to social, environmental, or economic changes affecting sustainability performance (Cetindamar et al., 2020). The so-called "sustainability presence" based on big data analytics allows generating cooperative frameworks interlinking finance, operations, marketing, and supply chain for enhanced sustainable consumption and production (Ongsakul& Sen, 2018). In manufacturing, big data analytics can predict social issues in the supply chain and thus contribute positively to environmental, economic, and social sustainability (Mani et al., 2017). Another area in environmental risk management involves analyzing and mitigating environmental aspects with a data-driven approach that uses advanced analytics, machine learning, and IoT applications: Stakeholders should intervene and government policies should support sharing data for sustainability projects (Gomes et al., 2024).

# 4. EMPOWERING INDIVIDUAL INVESTORS FOR GREEN DEVELOPMENT

Empowering individual investors for green development refers to providing the knowledge, skills, and motivations to make sustainable investment decisions. The goal of empowerment is critical in regard to accelerating the transition to a sustainable economy and enabling investors to act with the knowledge needed to pursue environmental objectives. Recent studies have been carried out that link investor empowerment and financial literacy to support sustainable development. Ringe (2023), refers to investor empowerment as a strategy to promote sustainability in capital markets. Research discusses the role of institutional investors and investor platforms for coordination in support of sustainability initiatives. Mittal (2023), examines the impact of financial literacy on university students' sustainable investment decisions, and outlines obstacles to students' sustainable investing decisions including a lack of knowledge about green financial products and calls for more financial literacy and education curriculum surrounding green finance. Rohith & Patil (2025), study the awareness of investors related to green finance initiatives, and finds that there is a strong consensus that it contributes to sustainable development through energy-efficient form of production and work toward clean energy. They highlight the role of supportive platforms, financial infrastructure to incentivize sustainability, and the importance of sustainability being integrated into an investor's portfolio. Overall,

all three studies contribute to the body of work focused on investor knowledge and empowerment through different lenses in support of sustainable economic change and reaching environmental climate goals.

## 4.1. Challenges Faced by Individual Investors in Sustainable Investing

Sustainable investing poses distinct challenges for individual investors as they grapple with effectively incorporating environmental, social, and governance (ESG) factors into their decision-making processes. These obstacles arise due to various factors: issues of data availability, exposure to green-washing, and variability in reporting frameworks. These are outlined in table 1.

*Table 1. Challenges Faced by Individual Investors in Sustainable Investing*

| Challenges | Description | Citation |
|---|---|---|
| The Perceived Inexistence of a "Business Case" | Many investors hesitate to commit to sustainable investments due to a lack of a clear business case, poor data quality, and undefined measurement standards. | Friede, 2019 |
| Behavioral Biases and Information Overload | Investors exhibit biases such as overconfidence and loss aversion. Additionally, excessive information makes it difficult for non-professionals to filter relevant sustainability data. | Friede, 2019; Hafenstein & Bassen, 2016 |
| Financial Literacy and Emotional Determinants | Higher financial literacy leads to greater investment in sustainable options. Emotional factors, like the "warm glow" effect, influence investment decisions based on personal values. | Gutsche et al., 2023 |

## 4.2. Strategies to Improve Knowledge and Accessibility on Sustainable Investments

There are several strategies to improve knowledge and accessibility to sustainable investments that focus on communication, regulatory processes and investor education, as discussed in table 2. These strategies hope to close the gap between sustainable investment possibilities and potential investors, thus creating a more inclusive investment environment.

*Table 2. Strategies to Enhance Accessibility and Knowledge on Sustainable Investments*

| Strategies | Description | Citations |
|---|---|---|
| Education and Training | Training of Financial Advisers: Enhancing advisers' knowledge of sustainable responsible investment (SRI) to better guide private investors. | Strauß, 2021 |
| | Academic Research: Universities can contribute to sustainable finance research, providing insights to investors and advisors for better decision-making. | Beisenbina et al., 2022; Joshipura et al., 2024 |
| Strategic Communication | Engagement Techniques: The 5A model of SRI decision-making helps financial advisers develop strategies to attract investors. | Strauß, 2021 |
| | Public Awareness Campaigns: More discussions on the benefits and performance of sustainable investments help draw in new investors. | Joshipura et al., 2024 |
| Policy Support | Regulatory Frameworks: Policies that create a supportive environment for sustainable investments encourage participation from issuers and investors. | Joshipura et al., 2024 |

## 4.3. Role of Financial Literacy, Government Incentives, and Regulatory

Sustainable investing, which integrates environmental, social and governance (ESG) factors into investment decisions, has gained considerable traction across the world. Drivers behind this trend include growing concerns over climate change, social justice, and the need for good corporate governance. Financial literacy, government support and sound regulation are necessary to develop and stimulate sustainable investing in this context.

### 4.3.1. Financial Literacy and Sustainable Investing

Financial literacy plays an important role in sustainable investing when it empowers the investors; enhances risk understanding of risk-taking behaviour; supports long-term thinking; and increases retail investors. Understanding financial concepts and knowledge of financial prediction models is necessary to make informed decisions in sustainable investing, especially with respect to investment encompassing environmental-related, social-related, and governance-related (ESG) facets of their investment. The following are the areas that drive sustainable investing:

### *Empowering Investors*

Financial literacy helps individuals acquire the knowledge or expertise needed to evaluate sustainable financial products, resulting in better decision-making (Filippini et al., 2024). Greater financial literacy level for sustainable finance is associated with a higher likelihood of engaging in sustainable investments, with a recent study indicating that for every unit of sustainable finance literacy improvement, there is a 4-5% increase in the probability of a sustainable investment, over measures of individual investor characteristics (Auzepy et al., 2024).

### *Risk Awareness*

It is essential to recognize financial risks, as low financial literacy leads to poor risk assessment, especially when considering sustainable investment (Dupuy, 2024). Knowing ESG issues will prepare investors to identify potential risk factors when faced with greenwashing and sustainability issues (Senaya, 2024).

### *Encouraging Long-Term Thinking*

Those who are financially literate are more apt to pursue long-term investment options that incorporate sustainable options and promote sustainable economic stability (Senaya, 2024). The awareness that many long-term investments have benefits in the future by way of sustainable investing can lead to the awareness of more financial planning and decision-making (Ahamed, 2025).

### *Increased Participation of Retail Investors*

Financial literacy can help close the knowledge gap on sustainable finance, and promote greater participation from retail investors in this expanding finance space (Filippini et al, 2024). Educational efforts that are designed to promote improved financial literacy have been shown to influence investment behaviours, especially among demographics with historically low participation rates in the sustainable finance space (Senaya, 2024).

## 4.3.2. Government Incentives for sustainability-linked Investors

Government incentives can encourage sustainable investments through tax breaks, subsidies, "green" bonds, public-private partnerships, sustainability-linked loans, and carbon credit markets. Government incentive programs can help reduce financial barriers to green projects and help complement economic growth to environmental sustainability.

### *Tax Breaks and Subsidies*

Some governments can provide investors tax breaks and subsidies to hedge against the initial upfront costs of green investments. These financial instruments provide equity and/or debt capital investment incentives, and they reduce capital costs for these investments allowing financial institutions to offer competitive preferential lending for green projects (Okeke et al, 2024).

### *Green Bonds and Public-Private Partnerships*

Green bonds are becoming a popular option to raise funding in support of environmentally friendly projects, making it possible for large investments in sustainable infrastructure and/or renewable energy (Eyo-Udo et al., 2024). Public-private partnerships effectively pool together resources and share risk, enabling green projects to flourish in emerging economies (Okeke et al., 2024).

### *Sustainability-Linked Loans and Carbon Credit Markets*

Sustainability-linked loans provided liquidity with certain fairly loose obligations, incentivizing borrowers to meet sustainability targets, while encouraging corporations to operate responsibly (Eyo-Udo et al., 2024). Carbon credit markets offer a financial reward, in the form of tradable credits, that can be bought and sold by companies who reduce or avoid greenhouse gas emissions (Andrada, 2015).

## 4.3.3. Approaches to Regulatory Frameworks for Sustainable Investments

Sustainable investments are increasingly under prescribed regulatory frameworks that are developing in order to meet the demand for transparency around Environmental, Social and Governance (ESG) decisions. Prescribed regulatory frameworks consist of ESG disclosures, sustainable investment standards, regulatory frameworks around corporate governance and green finance regulations.

### *ESG Disclosures*

Regulators are developing mandated ESG disclosures to help prescribe whether companies are transparently reporting their sustainability practices. For example, the European Union's Corporate Sustainability Reporting Directive (CSRD) requires ESG reporting for large companies and mandates them to provide more detailed ESG disclosures (Vorontsova et al., 2023). The disclosures help investors determine the risk associated with investing in companies that perform poorly on their ESG issues which rat's investors' ability to make things going forward (O'Sullivan, 2024).

### *Sustainable Investment Standards*

In addition, several international initiatives, like the Global Reporting Initiative (GRI) and the International Sustainability Standards Board (ISSB), are aiming to standardize and present ESG reports across the globe (Vorontsova et al., 2023). The joint use of established guidelines should assist the investor community in determining the comparability and reliability of the ESG data it needs to incorporate sustainability into its portfolio (Biswas & Gupta, 2023).

### *Stronger Corporate Governance Rules*

To guarantee that companies will prioritize ESG factors in their decision-making processes, new corporate governance rules are being implemented. This includes frameworks for accountability for the environmental and social consequences of company activities and aligning corporate strategy with sustainable development policy (Shah, 2024).

### *Green Finance Regulations*

Green finance regulations support investment and growth in environmentally sustainable projects. Recent regulations require financial institutions to recognize their clients' sustainability preferences to incorporate ESG factors into their financial products.

While financial awareness and government stimuli are important catalysts, it is policy and regulatory changes that shape the long-term investment environment. Over the last several years, the international regulatory environment has moved swiftly to establish various levels of responses to the growing demands for transparency, accountability, and standardization of green investment. These policy movements provide investors with more than just a recognised enabling environment; they will help to ensure the market remains viable by lowering the rate of greenwashing and enhancing investor confidence. These developments help to open up the alignment of financial markets with broad sustainability outcomes. In doing so, these developments begin to demonstrate a link between sustainability performance and financial performance, thus making sustainable investing a legitimate long-term pathway rather than a niche option.

## 5. POLICY AND REGULATORY DEVELOPMENTS SUPPORTING GREEN INVESTING

Green finance serves as a crucial instrument in addressing environmental challenges and fostering sustainable development (Abdel-aziem& Soliman, 2023).

Essentially, it involves financing both public and private green investments and enacting policies that stimulate green endeavours (Berensmann& Lindenberg, 2016). The regulatory environment of green finance consists of international initiatives, national policies, and the functions of primary regulatory authorities (Abdel-aziem& Soliman, 2023). On the other hand, impediments for market growth arise from regulatory loopholes, absence of unified definitions, and maturity mismatches between long-term green investments and short-term investor perspectives (Berensmann& Lindenberg, 2016; Abdel-aziem& Soliman, 2023). Experts have recommended strengthening regulatory structures, enhancing transparency, and increasing coordination between financial and environmental policies as means to promote green investments (Berensmann& Lindenberg, 2016; Kozlovska & Kirilieva, 2020). In addition, the strategic framework's adoption and ongoing application of policy are highly relevant for incentivizing commercial actors to contribute to greening the financial market (Kozlovska&Kirilieva, 2020).

## 5.1. Global and Regional Policies Driving Sustainable Finance Initiatives

The sustainability finance sector is being very much affected by global/regional policies in the framework set by China and the European Union (EU) as discussed in table 3. These laws aim at harmonizing financial systems with sustainable development goals, fostering corporate environmental liability, and addressing the most palpable environmental challenges. The key aspects of these very policies are touched upon in the following segments.

*Table 3. Global and regional policies for sustainable finance*

| Policy Aspect | Description | Citation |
|---|---|---|
| China as a Policy-setting Pioneer | Since 2015, China has led in green finance policy, creating an "Overton Window" for global green finance initiatives. | Larsen, 2022 |
| EU as a Standard Setter | The EU has focused on regulation, such as the SFDR, requiring financial system actors to disclose sustainability practices. | Bengo et al., 2022 |
| Corporate Environmental Responsibility | In China, Green Finance Reform and Innovation (GFRI) policy has strengthened corporate environmental responsibility, especially in high-pollution regions. | Yuan et al., 2024 |
| Macro-Financial Policy Integration | Integrating environmental factors into macro-financial policies enhances resilience in economic policymaking, addressing climate change and biodiversity loss. | D'Orazio et al., 2024 |

## 5.2. Impact of Green Taxonomies and Sustainable Reporting Frameworks (e.g., EU Green Taxonomy, TCFD, SFDR)

Green taxonomies and sustainability reporting frameworks, such as the EU Green Taxonomy, TCFD, and SFDR, significantly contribute to bringing about a change in the culture of sustainable finance and investment as shown in figure 2. Such frameworks help by providing format validation in such environmental performance assessment and disclosures for economic activities to enable the flow of capital towards the sustainable agenda.

**EU Green Taxonomy:** Even going further in the provisions of the EU Taxonomy Regulation, determining whether or not an activity is environmentally sustainable, according to the requirements, would increase transparency to investors (Brożek et al., 2024). It makes banks label investments as sustainable and builds confidence and clarity in the marketplace (Kirby et al., 2024). The regulation supports the convergence of financial flows on the European Green Deal towards climate-neutrality by 2050(Brożek et al., 2024).

**Sustainable Finance Disclosure Regulation (SFDR):** This sets out requirements for financial institutions to report on sustainability risks and impacts, giving room for accountability in the investments (Bengo et al., 2022). It should be the basis of a common platform for sustainability reporting, giving all investors the same figures to work with when making investment decisions (Bengo et al., 2022).

*Figure 2. Enhancing sustainability through green taxonomies and reporting frameworks*

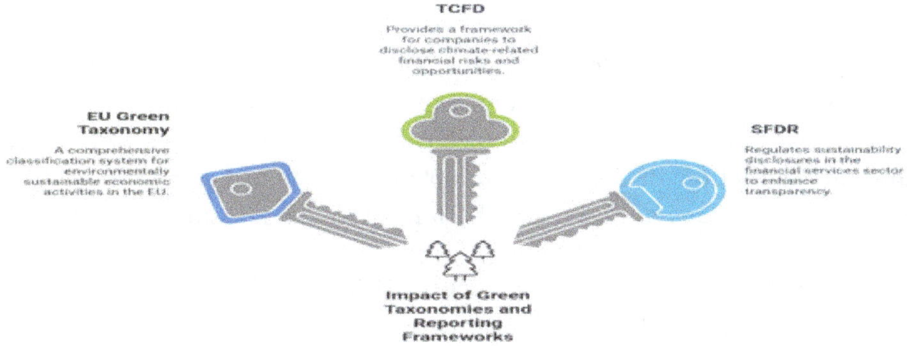


The building blocks of taxonomies and reporting templates of sustainable investment policies, it is the role of governments and international agencies to make the practice of sustainable investment systematic and captured in some formal way.

Governments and international agencies not only make regulations and implement them, they also catalyse further international coordination, technical assistance, finances, and goal alignment with respect to global sustainability objectives such as the Paris agreement and the UN "Sustainable Development Goals" (SDGs). Through policy leadership, multi-lateral collaboration, and harmonizing standards across countries, they create a unified and strong ecosystem that facilitates scaling up of sustainable finance both regionally and across sectors. By their involvement sustainable investing will seamlessly become part of the securities world's financial architecture rather than voluntary initiatives.

## 5.3. Role of Government and International Organizations in Fostering a Sustainable Investment Ecosystem

In building an investment ecosystem that promotes sustainability, governments and international organizations get involved through regulatory structures, collaboration with the private sector, and promoting responsible business conduct. Such entities are very instrumental in shaping the sustainable investment landscape, ensuring that both public and private actors play their roles in harmony with sustainable development goals. The following sections elaborate further on some key elements of this particular role.

**Regulatory frameworks:** Governments may change the financial regulations, for example, Basel III, so as to give incentives to banks for investing in assets that display environmental friendliness for the purpose of promoting sustainable investment (Triggs, 2023). International organizations like the UN could set guidelines and standards that would promote environmentally and socially responsible business practice in their core operations (Bule & Less, 2016).

**Collaboration with the Private Sector:** The rise of private sustainability governance (PSG) gives testimony to the significant role that public-private partnerships can play in achieving sustainability objectives. It is, therefore, possible for governments to bolster the PSG so as to promote innovation and effectiveness among sustainability interventions (Abbott, 2012). Institutional investment managers are now engaging in ESG stewardship, driven by a diverse global ecosystem consisting of other actors, such as NGOs and regulatory bodies, which help in shaping norms and practices for sustainable investments (Bowley & Hill, 2024).

**Promotion of Responsible Business Practices:** Governments and international organizations can promote responsible business conduct by establishing principles and standards that steer investments toward sustainable outcomes. This way, investment actions will bring positive benefits to society and the environment (Bule & Less, 2016).

Though regulatory frameworks, partnerships, and global standards have provided a solid ground for governments and international organizations, the future of green finance is both full of huge opportunities and some important challenges. The move towards a sustainable financial system is accelerating, promising the way to innovation, new markets, and value creation over the long term. Yet, these opportunities will be achieved by overcoming longstanding challenges like data inconsistency, greenwashing threats, regulatory fragmentation, and restricted access to green capital in emerging economies. Navigating and understanding this intricate terrain will be important for stakeholders that aim to deliver meaningful and inclusive growth through green finance.

## 6. OPPORTUNITIES AND CHALLENGES IN THE FUTURE OF GREEN FINANCE

It is emerging evidence that green finances form the backbone of successful sustainable business strategies that incorporate environmental values into investment decisions and do away with environmental risks (Lakasse et al., 2024). It indeed serves as a major bridge among the finance world, environmental improvement, and economic growth (Soundarrajan& Vivek, 2016). Even though green finance avails numerous opportunities for creating pathways toward environmentally sustainable innovations, various challenges remain, including insufficient public awareness, complexity in measuring environmental impacts, initial investments, data inadequacies, and constraints in resource availability (Lakasse et al., 2024). The other challenges include uncertainty of government's policies, little participation from financial suppliers, the short-term nature of financial instruments, and lack of knowledge about financing options available within companies (Falcone & Sica, 2019).

### 6.1 The Various Aspects of Opportunities in Green Finance

1) Technological Integration

**AI and Data Analytics:** AI is able to maximize resource utilization and enhance risk management in green investments, resulting in improved financial performance and environmental gains (Shajar et al., 2024).

**Fintech Innovations:** The use of financial technologies has the potential to make green finance processes seamless and accessible. It can further render green finance processes efficient (Sharma & Jain, 2024).

2) Policy and Regulatory Frameworks

**Government Support:** Increased funding and supportive policies across different government levels can make green infrastructure development and sustainable practices more viable (Ramakrishna, 2023).

**Regulatory Improvements:** Development of strong regulatory systems can counter problems like excessive transaction costs and insufficient awareness, providing a suitable climate for green finance (Sharma & Jain, 2024).

3) Collaborative Efforts

**Multi-Stakeholder Engagement:** Collaborative efforts among cities, provinces, and national governments are essential to fight environmental issues and support sustainable urban development (Ramakrishna, 2023).

**Research and Development:** Ongoing academic interest and study in green finance can discover novel opportunities and fuel innovation in sustainable practices (Miyan et al., 2024).

Though possibilities are interesting and keep evolving, it is also important to acknowledge the challenges that can restrict the complete potential of green finance. It is fresh evidence that green finances form the basis of successful sustainable business models that incorporate environmental values in investment decisions and cut out environmental risks.

## 6.2 Challenges in the Future of Green Finance

The future of green finance is threatened by a number of major challenges that may hamper its efficiency and expansion. These challenges are a result of a mix of regulatory, awareness, and market-related challenges that need concerted efforts from all stakeholders. It is important to understand these challenges in order to formulate strategies to improve green finance programs.

1). Regulatory Frameworks

**Inadequate Regulations:** Most nations do not have well-articulated regulatory systems that embrace green finance, and this causes inconsistency in policy implementation (Sharma & Jain, 2024) (Shi & Shao, 2024).

**Policy Coherence:** At both national and international levels, there is limited coordination of policies, making it difficult to provide a cohesive way of addressing green finance (Ozili, 2022)

2). Awareness and Education

**Low Awareness Levels:** One of the main obstacles is the overall lack of awareness regarding green finance among investors and the public, which constrains investment and participation in green projects (Sharma & Jain, 2024) (Ozili, 2022).

**Inconsistent Definitions:** The lack of a consistent and clear definition of what green finance is can create confusion and misalignment in investment strategies (Luurila, 2022).

3). Market Dynamics

**High Transaction Costs:** The transaction costs in green finance can be excessively high, discouraging investors from participating in green projects (Sharma & Jain, 2024).

**Profitability Concerns:** A common fear of unprofitability in green investments can discourage financial institutions from investing capital in these ventures (Shi & Shao, 2024) (Gupta et al., 2023).

## 7. CONCLUSION AND FUTURE OUTLOOK

Facilitating the empowerment of investors is central to building green and sustainable development. Human capital investment, particularly through the environment, education, and healthcare, is critical in building the knowledge and capacities that drive sustainability programs (Beisembina et al., 2023). Institutional investors have emerged as a primary force of empowerment, and therefore the empowerment of investors has been a central vehicle for building sustainability in capital markets (Ringe, 2023). Changing patterns in financial markets as well as rising common ownership trends have further enhanced the influence of institutional investors. Institutionalized investor platforms have emerged as an overbearing force to organize investor campaigns and allocate engagement burdens (Ringe, 2023). Discussion of environmental, social, and governance (ESG) matters can be a powerful force behind a more sustainable future, while regulatory measures have a mainly supporting role. All these measures together promote the empowerment of investors and green development (Ringe, 2023; Beisembina et al., 2022).

### 7.1 Key Messages on the Contribution of Individual Investors to Green Finance

The individual investor plays an important part in green finance as they champion sustainable investment patterns and drive market trends. Individual investor behavior is influenced by several factors such as environmental awareness, media, and policy settings. Understanding these factors is critical for developing more effective green investment schemes and ensuring greater sustainability in the financial market. Following are the key drivers:

### Key Driving Factors

**Environmental Consciousness:** More environmentally conscious individual investors tend to make green investments (Li et al., 2023).

**Influence of Media:** Communication of information through the media is an important driver of investor sentiment and behavior towards green finance (Li et al., 2023)

Government Policy Support: Support from government policies and incentives can play a major role in encouraging individual investors to invest in green initiatives (Li et al., 2023).

### Technological Innovations

**Emerging Technologies:** Technologies like block-chain and AI are promoting transparency and efficiency in green finance, making individual investors more proactive participants (Zhao 2024).

**Green Financial Products:** The availability of green financial products, such as green loans and sustainable insurance, brings personal finance into harmony with environmental concerns (Raji 2024).

## 7.2 Predictions for the Future of Sustainable Investing

Transforming the paradigm of future sustainable investment towards green development is to be topped by an alpine change with the growth of ESG frameworks, green finance mechanisms, and technology integration.

The future realm of sustainable investing relating to green development in a broader sense will be undergoing tremendous transformation, bringing along the developments in ESG frameworks and green finance mechanisms. Roy (2023) states that ESG-based credit rating models are gaining significance in identifying socially responsible borrowers and fostering long-term investment strategies. Thus, the increasing integration of ESG factors in investment decision-making is a key trend, with financial institutions being encouraged to align their portfolios to sustainable development objectives (Xiao et al., 2023). In terms of emphasizing topics of central concern to proceeds in scholarly discourse, bibliometric analysis identifies sustainability, the green economy, and investments as being valid, with China, the UK, and European countries taking the lead in terms of research contributions (Judijanto et al., 2024). Very rightly, the slow acceptance of green finance globally is traced to discrepancies in ESG frameworks and perceptions of the financial risks thereof (Judijanto et al., 2024). Credit rating models are, from the perspective of ESG, said to focus first on the financial bottom line, then on environmental impacts, social effects, and governance process (Roy, 2023). Such developments are important in the attainment of the global sustainability agenda and in promoting sustainable financial growth (Hai, 2024).

The increasing stakes of sustainable investments for the realization of global sustainability objectives usher into different trends.

**SG Integration and Credit Rating Models:** It becomes vital to find socially responsible borrowers from which long-term investors can get effective investment models by adopting ESG-based credit rating models (Roy, 2023). Such institutions could then be urged to adopt some of these models into their operations to realize more productive efficiency gains resulting from aligning a part of their portfolio with sustainable development objectives (Roy, 2023).

**Green Finance Dynamics:** Green finance and environmental sustainability have a rather complicated relationship, which is said to follow a nonlinear pattern across income levels in developing countries (Gul & Hussain, 2024). A need to adopt specific policies is imperative for maximizing the advantages accrued from green finance in middle-income countries where that connection is typically stronger (Gul & Hussain, 2024).

**Technological Innovations and Market Volatility:** Digital finance and AI convergence can futuristically develop green investments by upscaling their risk management and market dynamics (Mnif et al., 2024). Green stocks are driven by a lot of volatility because of how they are affected by geopolitical shocks and the measure of energy consumption by the investor. That calls for preparatory measures for investment strategies against unpredictable outcomes (Mnif et al., 2024).

## 7.3 Call to Action: Encouraging Active Participation in Sustainable Investment Initiatives for Green Development

As we progress towards green development, active participation in sustainable investment initiatives becomes imperative. The global need for sustainable infrastructures, particularly in developing countries, is estimated to demand $6 trillion/year for economic development and climate. While trust is an important motivation for retail investors to support sustainable companies, investment in green initiatives must be encouraged (Chan et al., 2022). Both public and private sectors play major roles in promoting the green economy. The private sector has different motives for investing in green projects, and the public sector uses incentives and regulations to steer the market toward sustainable development (Eskerkhanova et al., 2024).

Companies, policymakers, and investors must work together to raise awareness and drive green project investment (Chan et al., 2022). Though stakeholders are eager to partake, current investment volumes are way off from the requirements, compelling a call for action from governments, multilateral development banks, and investors to address the financing gap for sustainable infrastructure. Thus, the engagement of financial institutions, corporations, and communities can be catalyzed in numerous ways toward attaining a sustainable future:

**Financial Institutions and ESG Models:** Via ESG-based credit rating models, financial institutions can trace socially responsible borrowers, thereby establishing investment opportunities into projects of sustainable nature (Roy, 2023). The developed model confirms the accuracy of 84.31%, thus greatly influencing the distribution of capital between sustainable projects.

**Role of a Fin-tech in Corporate Investment:** Fin-tech innovations can greatly enhance corporate green investments by improving data-driven decision-making and information transparency (Tao & Chao, 2024). Through fin-tech solutions, energy sector companies can combine their sustainable development strategy with environmental goals.

**Community Engagement and Behavioral Change:** Breaking down the psychological inertia is vital for the encouragement of residents' participation in neighborhood regeneration projects (Fu et al., 2023). Stimuli, such as that concerning information acquisition and perceived government support, affect participation behavior and hence can often increase community involvement in sustainable initiatives.

While those strategies further accentuate that active participation is vital, others, such as the credibility of ESG data and a common approach to green investment assessment, remain critical (Meng 2023). Those issues must be addressed if sustainable investment initiatives are to work smoothly.

## REFERENCES


Abbott, K. W. (2012). Engaging the public and the private in global sustainability governance. *International Affairs*, *88*(3), 543–564. DOI: 10.1111/j.1468-2346.2012.01088.x

Abdel-Aziem, A. H., & Soliman, T. H. M. (2023). The Regulatory Landscape of Green Finance: An Improved Approach for Market Development. *Financial Technology and Innovation*, *2*(1), 26–34. DOI: 10.54216/FinTech-I.020103

Ahamed, A. J. (2025). Chapter-1 Financial Literacy. Social Science Research Network. DOI: 10.2139/ssrn.5084835

Alhejaili, M. O. (2024). Integrating Climate Change Risks and Sustainability Goals into Saudi Arabia's Financial Regulation: Pathways to Green Finance. *Sustainability (Basel)*, *16*(10), 4159. Advance online publication. DOI: 10.3390/su16104159

Ali, E., Anshari, M., Hamdan, M., Ahmad, N., &Surieshtino, Y. (2023). Green Finance for Sustainable Development: A Bibliographic Analysis. 46–49. DOI: 10.1109/SIBF60067.2023.10379915

Amram, M., & Kulatilaka, N. (2009). The Invisible Green Hand: How Individual Decisions and Markets Can Reduce Greenhouse Gas Emissions. *California Management Review*, *51*(2), 194–218. DOI: 10.2307/41166486

Andrada, I. (2015). Incentives for financing sustainable development. Annals - Economy Series, 1(2), 312–317. https://www.utgjiu.ro/revista/ec/pdf/2015-02/45_Moldovan.pdf

Auzepy, A., Bannier, C. E., & Gärtner, F. (2024). Looking beyond ESG preferences: The role of sustainable finance literacy in sustainable investing. Social Science Research Network. DOI: 10.2139/ssrn.4773211

Azad, S., & Devi, S. L. T. (2024). Sustainable development and investor confidence: The safe-haven appeal of green-bond issuing firms. *Sustainable Development*. Advance online publication. DOI: 10.1002/sd.3172

Bai, X. (2024). Post-2030 global goals need explicit targets for cities and businesses. *Science*, *385*(6714), eadq4993. Advance online publication. DOI: 10.1126/science.adq4993

Beisembina, A., Gizzatova, A., Kunyazov, Y., Ernazarov, T., Mashrapov, N., & Dontsov, S. (2023). Investing in human capital for green and sustainable development. *Journal of Environmental Management and Tourism*, *14*(5), 2300. DOI: 10.14505/jemt.v14.5(69).11

Beisenbina, M., Fabregat-Aibar, L., Barberà-Mariné, M. G., & Sorrosal-Forradellas, M. T. (2022). The burgeoning field of sustainable investment: Past, present and future. *Sustainable Development (Bradford)*, *31*(2), 649–667. DOI: 10.1002/sd.2422

Bengo, I., Boni, L., & Sancino, A. (2022). EU financial regulations and social impact measurement practices: A comprehensive framework on finance for sustainable development. *Corporate Social Responsibility and Environmental Management*, *29*(4), 809–819. DOI: 10.1002/csr.2235

Berensmann, K., & Lindenberg, N. (2016). Green Finance: across the universe. In WorldScientific eBooks (pp. 305–332). DOI: 10.1142/9789811206887_0011

Bhattacharyya, R. (2021). Green finance for energy transition, climate action and sustainable development: Overview of concepts, applications, implementation and challenges. *Green Finance*, *4*(1), 1–35. DOI: 10.3934/GF.2022001

Bhattacherjee, P., Mishra, S., Bouri, E., & Wee, J. B. (2024). ESG, clean energy, and petroleum futures markets: Asymmetric return connectedness and hedging effectiveness. *International Review of Economics & Finance*, *94*, 103375. DOI: 10.1016/j.iref.2024.103375

Biswas, B., & Gupta, R. P. (2023). Global ESG Regulatory Framework and Sustainability: Issues and Prospects (pp. 20–32). DOI: 10.31674/book.2023srdsi003

Bowley, T., & Hill, J. G. (2024). The Global ESG Stewardship Ecosystem. *European Business Organization Law Review*, *25*(2), 229–268. Advance online publication. DOI: 10.1007/s40804-024-00316-7

Brown, P. (2018). Environmental Sustainability Factors Impact on Financial Performance in Materials Industry. *Journal of International Business and Economics*, *18*(4), 49–53. DOI: 10.18374/JIBE-18-4.5

Brożek, J., Kożuch, A., Wieruszewski, M., Jaszczak, R., & Adamowicz, K. (2024). Taxonomy Regulation as a New Instrument for the Sustainable Management of the Forest Environment in Europe. *Sustainability (Basel)*, *16*(20), 8799. DOI: 10.3390/su16208799

Brühl, V. (2022). Green Financial Products in the EU — A Critical Review of the Status Quo. *Inter Economics*, *57*(4), 252–259. DOI: 10.1007/s10272-022-1057-2

Bule, T., & Less, C. T. (2016). Promoting sustainable development through responsible business conduct. *Diseases of the Colon and Rectum*, ●●●, 119–136. DOI: 10.1787/dcr-2016-12-en

Busch, T., Bauer, R., & Orlitzky, M. (2015). Sustainable development and financial markets. *Business & Society*, *55*(3), 303–329. DOI: 10.1177/0007650315570701

Cai, X., & Song, X.-F. (2022). Towards sustainable environment: Unleashing the mechanism between green finance and corporate social responsibility. 0958305X2211332. DOI: 10.1177/0958305X221133258

Caldecott, B. (Ed.). (2018). *Ullahtranded assets and the environment: Risk, resilience and opportunity*. Routledge. DOI: 10.4324/9781315651606

Camilleri, M. A. (2020). The market for socially responsible investing: A review of the developments. *Social Responsibility Journal*, *17*(3), 412–428. DOI: 10.1108/SRJ-06-2019-0194

Cetindamar, D., Shdifat, B., & Erfani, S. (2020). Assessing big data analytics capability and sustainability in supply chains. Proceedings of the . . . *Annual Hawaii International Conference on System Sciences/Proceedings of the Annual Hawaii International Conference on System Sciences*. DOI: 10.24251/HICSS.2020.026

Chala, V., & Demidov, B. (2024). Theoretical Aspects of Green Financing for Providing Sustainable Development. *Economic Scope*, *193*(193), 37–45. DOI: 10.30838/EP.193.37-45

Chan, K. H., Chong, L. L., Ng, T. H., & Ong, W. L. (2022). A model of green investment decision making for societal well-being. *Heliyon*, *8*(8), e10024. DOI: 10.1016/j.heliyon.2022.e10024

Chua, F., & Ho, J. (2023). Assessing the potential of green finance in supporting environmental sustainability. *International Journal of Geography Geology and Environment*, *5*(1), 266–269. DOI: 10.22271/27067483.2023.v5.i1c.271

Clark, G. L., Feiner, A., & Viehs, M. (2015). From the stockholder to the stakeholder: How sustainability can Drive financial Outperformance. SSRN Electronic Journal. DOI: 10.2139/ssrn.2508281

Cort, T. L. (2023). The Pragmatist's Guide to ESG. *Environment*, *65*(4), 10–17. DOI: 10.1080/00139157.2023.2205346

D'Orazio, P., Schäfer, D., & Stephan, A. (2024). *Macro-financial policy at the crossroad: addressing climate change, biodiversity loss, and environmental degradation - introduction to the special issue*. Eurasian Economic Review., DOI: 10.1007/s40822-024-00265-z

de Mariz, F. (2022). The Promise of Sustainable Finance: Lessons from Brazil. *Georgetown Journal of International Affairs*, *23*(2), 185–190. DOI: 10.1353/gia.2022.0030

Dimmelmeier, A. (2023). Expanding the politics of measurement in sustainable finance: Reconceptualizing environmental, social and governance information as infrastructure. Environment And Planning C: Politics and Space. DOI: 10.1177/23996544231209149

Dordi, T., Gehricke, S. A., Naef, A., & Weber, O. (2022). Ten financial actors can accelerate a transition away from fossil fuels. *Environmental Innovation and Societal Transitions*, *44*, 60–78. DOI: 10.1016/j.eist.2022.05.006

Dupuy, P. (2024). Finance literacy and sustainable finance literacy. Bankers, Markets, Investors/RB Bankers, Markets. *Investors*, *178*(3). 0031.doi.org/10.54695/bmi.178.0031

Eskerkhanova, L. T., Zaripova, R. S., & Mitrofanov, S. V. (2024). Sustainable development and investment in the green economy: The role of the private and public sectors. *Ekonomikaiupravlenieproblemyresheniya*, *3/4*(144), 85–91. DOI: 10.36871/ek.up.p.r.2024.03.04.011

Eyo-Udo, N. L., Agho, M. O., Onukwulu, E. C., Sule, A. K., & Azubuike, C. U. (2024). Advances in green finance solutions for combating climate change and ensuring sustainability. 2(6), 338–375. DOI: 10.51594/gjabr.v2i6.53

Falcone, P. M., & Sica, E. (2019). Assessing the Opportunities and Challenges of green finance in Italy: An analysis of the biomass production sector. *Sustainability (Basel)*, *11*(2), 517. DOI: 10.3390/su11020517

Filippini, M., Leippold, M., &Wekhof, T. (2024). Sustainable Finance Literacy and the Determinants of Sustainable Investing. DOI: 10.1016/j.jbankfin.2024.107167

Friede, G. (2019). Why don't we see more action? A meta synthesis of the investor impediments to integrate environmental, social, and governance factors. *Business Strategy and the Environment*, *28*(6), 1260–1282. DOI: 10.1002/bse.2346

Fu, X., Qian, Q. K., Liu, G. R., Zhuang, T., Visscher, H., & Huang, R. (2023). Overcoming inertia for sustainable urban development: Understanding the role of stimuli in shaping residents' participation behaviors in neighborhood regeneration projects in China. *Environmental Impact Assessment Review*, *103*, 107252. Advance online publication. DOI: 10.1016/j.eiar.2023.107252

Fuerst, F. (2015). The Financial Rewards of Sustainability: A Global Performance Study of real estate investment trusts. SSRN Electronic Journal. DOI: 10.2139/ssrn.2619434

Gao, Z., Luo, Y., Tian, G., & Yang, H. (2023). Green preference, green investment. SSRN Electronic Journal. DOI: 10.2139/ssrn.4655538

Ge, P., Liu, Y., Tang, C., & Zhu, R. (2024). Green bonds and corporate Environmental social and governance performance: Innovative approaches to identifying greenwashing in green bond markets. *Corporate Social Responsibility and Environmental Management*. Advance online publication. DOI: 10.1002/csr.3005

Gigliotti, M., Schmidt-Traub, G., & Bastianoni, S. (2019). The sustainable development goals. In Elsevier eBooks (pp. 426–431). DOI: 10.1016/B978-0-12-409548-9.10986-8

Gomes, A., Islam, N. M., & Karim, M. R. (2024). Data-Driven Environmental Risk Management and Sustainability Analytics. *Non-Human Journal.*, *1*(01), 100–113. DOI: 10.70008/jmldeds.v1i01.46

Gonzalez-Arcos, C., Meath, C., Leszczyc, P. P., Haruvy, E., & An, J. (2023). Fostering sustainable investments through micro-investing platforms. *Scientific Reports*, *13*(1), 21194. Advance online publication. DOI: 10.1038/s41598-023-48452-3

Gul, R., & Hussain, S. (2024). Unlocking sustainable futures: Exploring the nonlinear linkages between green finance and environmental sustainability in developing countries. *Journal of Environmental Management*, *370*, 122971. 122971.doi.org/10.1016/j.jenvman.2024.122971. DOI: 10.1016/j.jenvman.2024.122971

Gupta, S., Kaur, G., Kumari, I., & Kalra, D. S. (2023). *Exploration of Opportunities and Challenges in Green Finance*. IGI Global., DOI: 10.4018/979-8-3693-1388-6.ch018

Gutsche, G., Wetzel, H., & Ziegler, A. (2023). Determinants of individual sustainable investment behavior - A framed field experiment. *Journal of Economic Behavior & Organization*, *209*, 491–508. DOI: 10.1016/j.jebo.2023.03.016

Hachigian, H., & McGill, S. M. (2012). Reframing the governance challenge for sustainable investment. *Journal of Sustainable Finance & Investment, 2*(3-4), 166–178. DOI: 10.1080/20430795.2012.742632

Hafenstein, A., & Bassen, A. (2016). Influences for using sustainability information in the investment decision-making of non-professional investors. *Journal of Sustainable Finance & Investment, 6*(3), 186–210. DOI: 10.1080/20430795.2016.1203598

Haggag Kotb Kholaif, M. M. N., & Tang, X. (2024). The role of green finance to achieve sustainability through green supply chain management and innovative technologies. *Sustainable Development*. Advance online publication. DOI: 10.1002/sd.3176

Hai, W. (2024). Development and Future Trends of Green Finance from an ESG Perspective. *Frontiers in Business, Economics and Management, 16*(1), 351–354. DOI: 10.54097/0hkacp17

Hasan, M. H., Hossain, M. Z., Hasan, L., & Dewan, M. A. (2024). FinTech and Sustainable Finance: How is FinTech Shaping the Future of Sustainable Finance? European Journal of Management, Economics and Business. 1(3), 100–115.doi.org/10.59324/ejmeb.2024.1(3).09

Hughes, A., Urban, M. A., & Wójcik, D. (2021). Alternative ESG Ratings: How Technological Innovation is reshaping Sustainable investment. *Sustainability (Basel), 13*(6), 3551. DOI: 10.3390/su13063551

Hunt, K. J. (2022). Sustainable Finance. *Review of Finance, 26*(6), 1309–1313. DOI: 10.1093/rof/rfac069

Janicka, M. (2016). Financial markets and the challenges of sustainable growth. *Comparative Economic Research Central and Eastern Europe, 19*(2), 27–41. DOI: 10.1515/cer-2016-0011

Jednak, D., & Jednak, S. (2019). Socially responsible financial markets. In *Palgrave studies in impact finance* (pp. 103–125). DOI: 10.1007/978-3-030-16522-2_5

Johnson, L., Sachs, L., & Lobel, N. (2019). Aligning International Investment Agreements with the Sustainable Development Goals. SSRN Electronic Journal. DOI: 10.2139/ssrn.3452070

Joshipura, M., Mathur, S., & Kedia, N. (2024). Sustainable investing and financing for sustainable development: A hybrid review. *Sustainable Development (Bradford), 32*(5), 4469–4485. Advance online publication. DOI: 10.1002/sd.2912

Judijanto, L., Yoga, T., & Wijayanti, I. O. (2024). Bibliometric analysis of green finance and sustainable investment strategies. *West Science Social and Humanities Studies*, *2*(12), 1965–1980. DOI: 10.58812/wsshs.v2i12.1487

Jun, N. H. H. (2013). Investing Well by Investing for good? Exploring the motivations of socially responsible investors. *Asian International Studies Review*, *14*(1), 29–56. DOI: 10.1163/2667078X-01401002

Kirby, D., MacMahon, C. H., & Thompson, S. E. (2024). *The co-evolution of sustainable finance stakeholders under the EU taxonomy for sustainable activities: an exploratory study of Irish disclosure experiences*. Sustainability Accounting, Management and Policy Journal., DOI: 10.1108/SAMPJ-11-2023-0842

Kozlovska, A., & Kirilieva, A. (2020). Formation of an Effective Policy of "Green" Investment as A Priority Direction Of Sustainable Development of National Economy. *Pryazovskyi Economic Herald*, (2(19)). Advance online publication. DOI: 10.32840/2522-4263/2020-2-30

Kruse, T., Mohnen, M., & Sato, M. (2023). Do Financial Markets Respond to Green Opportunities? *Journal of the Association of Environmental and Resource Economists*. Advance online publication. DOI: 10.1086/727370

Lakasse, S., Amril, A., Syamsuri, H., & Jusman, I. A. (2024). The Role of Green Finance in Sustainable Business Strategies: Opportunities and Challenges for Business Organizations. *JurnalPenelitianInovatif*, *4*(2), 665–672. DOI: 10.54082/jupin.379

Langford, M. (2016). Lost in transformation? The politics of the sustainable development goals. *Ethics & International Affairs*, *30*(2), 167–176. DOI: 10.1017/S0892679416000058

Larsen, M. L. (2022). Driving Global Convergence in Green Financial Policies: China as Policy Pioneer and the EU as Standard Setter. *Global Policy*, *13*(3), 358–370. DOI: 10.1111/1758-5899.13105

Li, C., Zhang, Y., Hou, G., & Ma, M. (2023). Analysis of Driving Factors and Action Path of Green Investment Behavior of Individual Investors. Highlights in Business. *Economics and Management*, *9*, 33–43. DOI: 10.54097/hbem.v9i.7767

Lindenberg, N. (2014). Definition of Green Finance. Environmental Anthropology eJournal.

Luurila, K. (2022). Green finance research around the world: A review of literature. *International Journal of Green Economics*, *16*(1), 56. DOI: 10.1504/IJGE.2022.125554

Mahmood, S., Sun, H., Iqbal, A., Alhussan, A. A., & El-kenawy, E.-S. M. (2024). Green finance, sustainable infrastructure, and green technology innovation: Pathways to achieving sustainable development goals in the Belt and Road Initiative. *Environmental Research Communications*, *6*(10), 105036. Advance online publication. DOI: 10.1088/2515-7620/ad898f

Mahn, K. D. (2016). The impact of sustainable investment strategies. *Journal of Investing*, *25*(2), 96–102. DOI: 10.3905/joi.2016.25.2.096

Manaswi, K., Singh, A., & Gupta, V. (2023). Building a Better Future with Sustainable Investments: Insights from Recent Research. *Indian Journal of Human Development*, *17*(2), 320–343. DOI: 10.1177/09737030231194836

Mani, V., Delgado, C., Hazen, B., & Patel, P. (2017). Mitigating Supply Chain Risk via Sustainability Using Big Data Analytics: Evidence from the Manufacturing Supply Chain. *Sustainability (Basel)*, *9*(4), 608. DOI: 10.3390/su9040608

Marín-Rodríguez, N. J., González-Ruíz, J. D., & Botero-Botero, S. (2025). Towards New Strategies for Investing: Insights on Sustainable Exchange-Traded Funds (ETFs). *WORLD (Oakland, Calif.)*, *6*(1), 8. DOI: 10.3390/world6010008

Marín-Rodríguez, N. J., González-Ruiz, J. D., & Valencia-Arias, A. (2023). Incorporating Green Bonds into Portfolio Investments: Recent Trends and Further Research. *Sustainability (Basel)*, *15*(20), 14897. Advance online publication. DOI: 10.3390/su152014897

Markina, T. A. (2022). Defining a sustainable development target space for 2030 and 2050. *One Earth*, *5*(2), 142–156. DOI: 10.1016/j.oneear.2022.01.003

Meng, X. L., & Shaikh, G. M. (2023). Evaluating Environmental, Social, and Governance Criteria and Green Finance Investment Strategies Using Fuzzy AHP and Fuzzy WASPAS. *Sustainability (Basel)*, *15*(8), 6786. DOI: 10.3390/su15086786

Mittal, H. (2023). Exploring How Financial Literacy Affects University Students' Sustainable Investment Decisions. Educational Administration: Theory and Practice.

Miyan, M., Cheong, C. W. H., Sharif, A., & Afshan, S. (2024). Three Decades of Green Finance: The State of the Art and Way Forward. *International Journal of Energy Economics and Policy*, *14*(6), 88–105. DOI: 10.32479/ijeep.16718

Mnif, E., Jarboui, A., & Mouakhar, K. (2024). Strategic insights into carbon markets, digital finance and geopolitical risks for advancing green sustainability investments. *Management of Environmental Quality*, *35*(7), 1622–1649. Advance online publication. DOI: 10.1108/MEQ-10-2023-0369

Nile, I. V. E., Udo, E. S., Jack, A. E., & Abner, I. P. (2024), Green Finance and Sustainable Development Nexus in Sub-Saharan Africa. FWU Journal of Social Sciences, 78–90. DOI: 10.51709/19951272/Summer2024/8

O'Sullivan, N. (2024). *Sustainable investment.* Edward Elgar Publishing., DOI: 10.4337/9781800880344.ch39

Okeke, N. I., Bakare, O. A., &Achumie, G. O. (2024). Integrating policy incentives and risk management for effective green finance in emerging markets. International Journal of Frontiers in Science and Technology Research, 7(1), 076–088. DOI: 10.53294/ijfstr.2024.7.1.0050

Ongsakul, V., & Sen, S. K. (2018). Creating shared value through big-data analytics: a aleResearch, 12(04). DOI: 10.24052/JBRMR/V12IS04/ART-10

Owadally, I., Mwizere, J., Kalidas, N., Murugesu, K., & Kashif, M. (2021). Long-Term sustainable investment for retirement. *Sustainability (Basel), 13*(9), 5000. DOI: 10.3390/su13095000

Ozili, P. K. (2022). Green finance research around the world: A review of literature. *International Journal of Green Economics, 16*(1), 1. DOI: 10.1504/IJGE.2022.10048432

Palea, V. (2021). Accounting for sustainable finance: Does fair value measurement fit for long-term equity investments? *Meditari Accountancy Research, 30*(1), 22–38. DOI: 10.1108/MEDAR-07-2020-0965

Pizzani, L. (2015). Expanding ESG Coverage. *CFA Institute Magazine, 26*(6), 30–31. DOI: 10.2469/cfm.v26.n6.12

Pramitasari, D. A. (2024). ESG Investing: Evaluating the financial performance of sustainable portfolios. [EJME]. *Equator Journal of Management and Entrepreneurship, 12*(4), 332–340. DOI: 10.26418/ejme.v12i4.82793

Qadri, H. M. U. D., Ali, H., Abideen, Z. U., & Jafar, A. (2024). Mapping the evolution of green finance research and development in emerging green economies. *Resources Policy, 91*, 104943. DOI: 10.1016/j.resourpol.2024.104943

Raji. (2024). Sustainable Finance in Action: Exploring Green Loans in Promoting Environmental Responsibility. Kristu Jayanti Journal of Management Sciences (KJMS), 14–25. DOI: 10.59176/kjms.v2i1.2348

Ramakrishna, D. (2023). *Emerging Trends of Green Finance in India: Challenges and Opportunities.* International Journal for Multidisciplinary Research., DOI: 10.36948/ijfmr.2023.v05i05.7224

Raman, R., Ray, S., Das, D., & Nedungadi, P. (2025). Innovations and barriers in sustainable and green finance for advancing sustainable development goals. *Frontiers in Environmental Science, 12*, 1513204. Advance online publication. DOI: 10.3389/fenvs.2024.1513204

Richardson, B. J. (2014). The Evolving Marketscape of Climate Finance. *Climate Law*, *4*(1-2), 94–106. DOI: 10.1163/18786561-00402008

Ringe, W. (2023). Investor Empowerment for sustainability. *Review of Economics*, *74*(1), 21–52. DOI: 10.1515/roe-2023-0016

Risalvato, G., Venezia, C., & Maggio, F. (2018). Social Responsible Investments and performance. *International Journal of Financial Research, 10*(1), 10. DOI: 10.5430/ijfr.v10n1p10

Rohith, N. R., & Patil, N. H. (2025). Awareness of investors toward green finance initiatives. [PEN]. *Periodicals of Engineering and Natural Sciences*, *13*(2), 337–348. DOI: 10.21533/pen.v13.i2.283

Roy, P. K. (2023). Enriching the green economy through sustainable investments: An ESG-based credit rating model for green financing. *Journal of Cleaner Production*, *420*, 138315. DOI: 10.1016/j.jclepro.2023.138315

Schoenmaker, D., & Schramade, W. (2019). Investing for long-term value creation. *Journal of Sustainable Finance & Investment*, *9*(4), 356–377. DOI: 10.1080/20430795.2019.1625012

Senaya, N. G. M.Glenda M Senaya. (2024). Financial literacy and its role in promoting sustainable investment. *World Journal of Advanced Research and Reviews*, *24*(1), 212–232. DOI: 10.30574/wjarr.2024.24.1.2986

Shah, D. (2024). Sustainable Finance and ESG Investing. *International Journal for Research in Applied Science and Engineering Technology*, *12*(2), 412–416. Advance online publication. DOI: 10.22214/ijraset.2024.58346

Shajar, S. N., Kashif, M., George, J., & Nasir, S. (2024). *The Future of Green Finance*. IGI Global., DOI: 10.4018/979-8-3693-1878-2.ch013

Sharma, H., & Jain, S. (2024). Navigating the Green Finance Landscape: Trends, Challenges, and Future Directions in the Banking Sector. 344–348.doi.org/10.1201/9781003543633-55

Shi, Z., & Shao, T. (2024). *The Development Status*. Challenges and Problems of Green Finance in Different Countries., DOI: 10.54097/j8jyvd42

Sikken, B. J. (2011). Accelerating the transition towards sustainable investing - strategic options for investors, corporations, and other key stakeholders. SSRN Electronic Journal. DOI: 10.2139/ssrn.1891834

Singhania, M., Bhan, I., & Chadha, G. K. (2023). Sustainable investments: A scientometric review and research agenda. *Managerial Finance*, *50*(1), 266–294. DOI: 10.1108/MF-04-2023-0238

Sinha, A., Mishra, S., Sharif, A., & Yarovaya, L. (2021). Does green financing help to improve environmental & social responsibility? Designing SDG framework through advanced quantile modelling. *Journal of Environmental Management*, *292*, 112751. DOI: 10.1016/j.jenvman.2021.112751

Soundarrajan, P., & Vivek, N. (2016). Green finance for sustainable green economic growth in India. [ZemědělskáEkonomika]. *Zemedelská Ekonomika*, *62*(1), 35–44. DOI: 10.17221/174/2014-AGRICECON

Stafford Smith, M., Cook, C., Sokona, Y., Elmqvist, T., Fukushi, K., Broadgate, W., & Jarzebski, M. P. (2018). Advancing sustainability science for the SDGs. *Sustainability Science*, *13*(6), 1483–1487. DOI: 10.1007/s11625-018-0645-3

Strauß, N. (2021). Communicating Sustainable Responsible Investments as Financial Advisors: Engaging Private Investors with Strategic Communication. *Sustainability (Basel)*, *13*(6), 3161. DOI: 10.3390/su13063161

Tao, Z., & Chao, J. (2024). Investing in green, sustaining the planet: The role of fintech in promoting corporate green investment in the Chinese energy industry. *Journal of Environmental Management*, *370*, 122990. DOI: 10.1016/j.jenvman.2024.122990

Triggs, A. (2023). Promoting sustainable investment through financial architecture reform. *Oxford Review of Economic Policy*, *39*(2), 267–282. DOI: 10.1093/oxrep/grad009

Trukhachev, V., & Dzhikiya, M. (2023). Development of environmental economy and management in the age of AI based on green finance. *Frontiers in Environmental Science*, *10*, 1087034. Advance online publication. DOI: 10.3389/fenvs.2022.1087034

Ullah, A., Liu, X., Zeeshan, M., & Shah, W. U. (2024). Evaluating growth and crisis risk dynamics of sustainable climate Exchange-Traded Funds. *Sustainability (Basel)*, *16*(22), 10049. DOI: 10.3390/su162210049

Urwin, R. (2010). Sustainable Investing Practice: Simplified complexity. SSRN Electronic Journal. DOI: 10.2139/ssrn.1656988

Valadkhani, A., & O'Mahony, B. (2024). Sustainable investing in extreme market conditions: Doing well while doing good. *Journal of Economics*. Studies.doi.org/10.1108/jes-11-2023-0626

Vorontsova, A., Agafonova, E. O., & Bilan, S. A. (2023). *Directions of regulatory coordination of responsible (esg) investment in the world: fragmentation or unification?* Economics & Law., DOI: 10.15407/econlaw.2023.03.091

Wadhwani, D., & Malpani, P. (2023). United Nations Sustainable Goals: Global to local Need of the hour. SSRN Electronic Journal. DOI: 10.2139/ssrn.4426147

Xiao, R., Deng, J., Zhou, Y., & Chen, M. (2023). Analyzing contemporary trends in sustainable finance and ESG investment. *Law And Economy*, *2*(11), 44–52. DOI: 10.56397/LE.2023.11.06

Xu, D., Corbet, S., Lang, C., & Hu, Y. (2024). Understanding dynamic return connectedness and portfolio strategies among international sustainable exchange-traded funds. *Economic Modelling*, *141*, 106864. DOI: 10.1016/j.econmod.2024.106864

Yadav, A. P. (2024). Changing Dynamics of Sustainable Investing: Emerging Trends. Journal of Informatics Education and Research. DOI: 10.52783/jier.v3i2.467

Yu, R., & Li, J. (2024). Does fintech influence sustainable development under natural resource constraints: Insights from 270 Chinese cities. *Resources Policy*, *91*, 104924. Advance online publication. DOI: 10.1016/j.resourpol.2024.104924

Yuan, X., Shang, L., & Xu, J. (2024). Green Financial Policy, Resource Allocation and Corporate Environmental Responsibility. *Sustainability (Basel)*, *16*(15), 6273. DOI: 10.3390/su16156273

Yumnam, G., Gyanendra, Y., & Ibohal Singh, C. (2024). A Systematic Bibliometric Review of the Global Research Dynamics of United Nations Sustainable Development Goals 2030. *Sustainable Futures : An Applied Journal of Technology, Environment and Society*, *7*, 100192. Advance online publication. DOI: 10.1016/j.sftr.2024.100192

Zairis, G., Liargovas, P., & Apostolopoulos, N. (2024). Sustainable Finance and ESG Importance: A Systematic Literature Review and Research Agenda. *Sustainability (Basel)*, *16*(7), 2878. Advance online publication. DOI: 10.3390/su16072878

Zakari, A., & Khan, I. (2021). *The introduction of green finance: a curse or a benefit to environmental sustainability?* Energy Research Letters., DOI: 10.46557/001c.29977

Zhang, Y., & Umar, M. (2023). Examining the interconnectedness of green finance: An analysis of dynamic spillover effects among green bonds, renewable energy, and carbon markets. *Environmental Science and Pollution Research International*, *30*(31), 1–17. DOI: 10.1007/s11356-023-27870-w

Zhao, Y. (2024). Empowering Sustainable finance: The convergence of AI, blockchain, and big data analytics. *Advances in Economics Management and Political Sciences*, *85*(1), 267–273. DOI: 10.54254/2754-1169/85/20240925

Zhong, W. (2023). An analysis of focusing on ESG investment. *Highlights in Business Economics and Management*, *17*, 8–13. DOI: 10.54097/hbem.v17i.11016

Zhu, H., Feng, T., & Li, X. (2024). Green finance, green development and decarbonization of the energy consumption structure. PLOS ONE, 19. e.0300579DOI: <ALIGNMENT.qj></ALIGNMENT>10.1371/journal.pon

Zioło, M., Bąk, I., & Spoz, A. (2024). The Role of Financial Markets in Energy Transitions. *Energies*, *17*(24), 6315. DOI: 10.3390/en17246315

# Chapter 3
# Green Finance:
## Trailblazing Towards Sustainable Growth in Renewable Energy Investments

**Satya Ratnakaram**
https://orcid.org/0000-0002-8908-302X
*Bahrain Polytechnic, Bahrain*

**Qasim Albaqali**
*Bahrain Polytechnic, Bahrain*

**Huda Najjar**
https://orcid.org/0009-0006-8298-3160
*Bahrain Polytechnic, Bahrain*

**Hani Hamaidan**
https://orcid.org/0009-0005-8047-199X
*Bahrain Polytechnic, Bahrain*

**Devi Manikeswari**
https://orcid.org/0000-0002-5014-9423
*Bahrain Polytechnic, Bahrain*

## ABSTRACT

*This chapter explores the burgeoning field of green finance and its crucial role in propelling the renewable energy revolution. It defines green finance, outlines its key components, and emphasizes the symbiotic relationship between green finance and renewable energy development. The study details various financial instruments driving this relationship, including green bonds and green loans. An analysis of global*

DOI: 10.4018/979-8-3373-8287-6.ch003

it © 2026, IGI Global Scientific Publishing. Copying or distributing in print or electronic forms without written permission of IGI Global Scientific Publishing is prohibited. Use of this chapter to enerative artificial intelligence (AI) technologies is expressly prohibited. The publisher reserves all rights to license its use for generative AI training and machine learning model development.

*and regional investment trends reveals record investments in the energy transition, although disparities exist across regions. The chapter also examines the risk and return profiles of renewable energy investments and the pivotal role of government policies and public sector support. While challenges such as standardization and greenwashing persist, significant opportunities for future growth in green finance for renewable energy are highlighted, paving the way for a sustainable future.*

## INTRODUCTION

Advancement in the today's world is occurring at an unprecedented pace, transforming nearly every aspect known to humans. Transformation on every level and walk of life has become imperative for both individuals and organizations. This, however, is not without challenges, the most critical being environmentally in nature. Fossil fuels are facing significant challenges, including resource depletion, supply security issues, and their contribution to climate change (Morirarty & Honnery, 2016). The most significant threat posed by environmental degradation lies in its long-lasting and potentially irreversible ecological consequences. The neglect of these consequences could ultimately lead to the collapse of the entire ecosystem. Therefore, environmentalists and governments are actively working to address these concerns. Despite stricter environmental regulations and efforts to promote environmental awareness within organizations, the effective implementation of environmental management (EM) strategies in daily operations, however, remains uncertain (Al-Swidi et al., 2024). The concept of sustainability gained significant traction following the release of the Brundtland Report in the late 1980s. Organizational sustainability, primarily focused within for-profit companies, encompasses a wide range of concerns, including environmental protection, social responsibility, and the harmonious integration of economic activities with both the natural and social environments. "Greening" an organization necessitates a holistic approach, impacting various aspects such as supply chain management, production processes, waste management, organizational culture, values, strategies, and employee behaviors.

### 1.1 The Green Imperative and the Renewable Energy Promise

The growing demand for sustainability has significantly impacted businesses worldwide, regardless of their location or development level. This has spurred a global movement towards adopting greener practices. In today's competitive market, businesses must not only be efficient and deliver value but also demonstrate environmental responsibility. Driven by increasing global environmental concerns, companies are increasingly adopting environmentally friendly practices. This shift towards sustainability can provide a significant competitive advantage, enabling companies to become "green and competitive" (Yong et al., 2019).

### 1.1.1 Renewable Energy as the Cornerstone of Sustainability

Among the ground-breaking sustainability trends, Renewable Energy (RE) has gained unparalleled demand at both communal and individual level. The impending perils brought about by climate change, over-dependence on external parties for energy sources, depleting natural resources etc., have led to an enhanced fervor globally for RE. The RE sources present a promising long-term solution for overcoming such potential threats to the future generations (Morirarty & Honnery, 2016). Despite such significant demand, the RE sector faces a critical challenge: ensuring its sustainability goes beyond environmental concerns. Contrary to the simplistic view that innovation solely relies on scientific and technological advancements, a more nuanced understanding reveals that 'institutional factors' play a significantly larger role, contributing roughly 75% to practical developments. This is particularly crucial for RE, a relatively new field with critical implications for climate change mitigation. RE organizations come in many forms, each with its own unique mission and focus. While Industry Associations represent companies and individuals within specific RE sectors, non-governmental organizations are non-profit and focused on environmental protection and sustainability. Others include Research and Development organizations such as National Renewable Energy Laboratory (NREL), Lawrence Berkeley National Laboratory and Fraunhofer Institute for Solar Energy Systems work towards developing and improving renewable energy technologies. There are also important Government agencies such as the International Renewable Energy Agency (IRENA) and Solar Energy Industries Association (SEIA) that play a pivotal role in advancing the interests of the RE sector (Derrick, 2024). On a micro level, there exist Renewable energy Cooperatives (RE Cooperatives) which are grassroots initiatives driven by local communities and citizens who play a crucial role in promoting the production and consumption of renewable energy. These decentralized efforts, often independent of government or large corporations, empower communities to take charge of their energy future (Heras-Saizarbitoria et al., 2018). Among the notable players in the RE sector are companies like Canadian Solar Inc., Siemens Gamesa Renewable Energy SA, Vestas Wind Systems A/S and JinkoSolar Holding Co. Ltd., that support the switch from fossil fuels to renewable energy by championing innovation (Swallow, 2022).

*Figure 1. Showing the share of renewable energy in the primary energy consumption continent-wise*

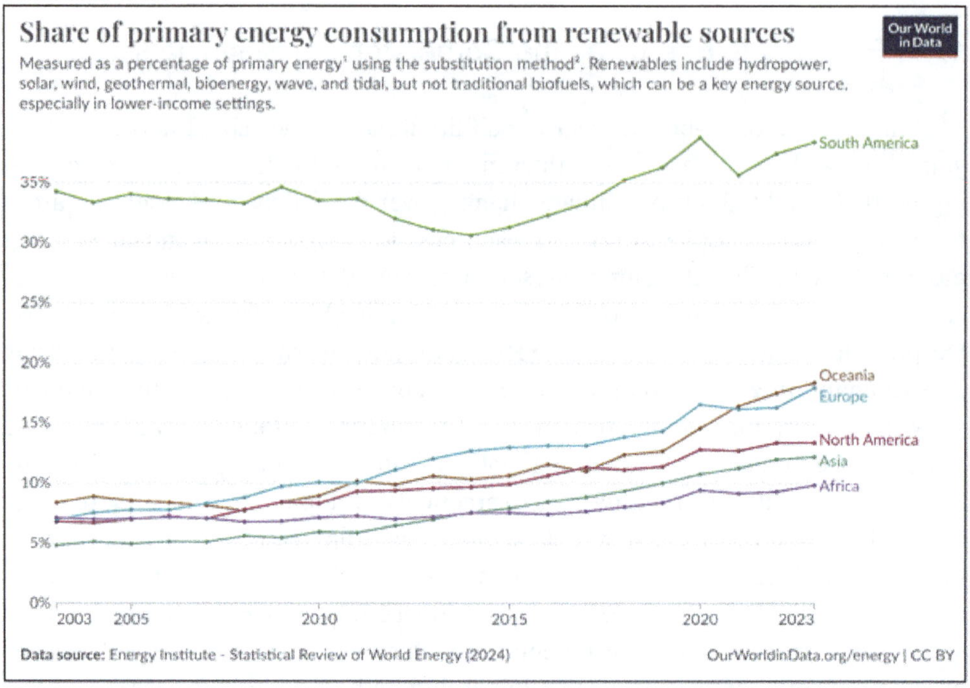


**Data source:** *Energy Institute - Statistical Review of World Energy (2024) OurWorldinData.org/energy*

Figure 1 above shows a clear upward trend in the share of renewable energy sources in primary energy consumption across various regions. From 2003 to 2023, the share of renewables has steadily increased in all regions, albeit at varying rates. South America has seen the most significant growth, with its renewable energy share reaching close to 35% in 2023. Europe and Oceania have also experienced notable increases, surpassing 15%. North America and Asia have shown moderate growth, while Africa's share remains the lowest but has also seen a steady increase. This trend highlights the growing global commitment to renewable energy sources and their increasing role in the energy mix.

The International Energy Agency (IEA) forecasts a significant increase in RE consumption across the power, heat, and transport sectors between 2024 and 2030. This growth is projected to nearly double, with RE's share in final energy consumption rising from 13% in 2023 to nearly 20% by 2030 (IEA, 2024). To effectively foster innovation in this area, it's essential to recognize the influence of diverse stakeholders, including politicians, planners, financiers, lawyers, social scientists, the media, and the public. Ethical, religious, and cultural values also shape these 'institutional factors' through the perspectives of artists, authors, theologians, and philosophers. Successful innovation in RE requires a broader understanding of these societal influences. Scientists and engineers can significantly enhance their impact by actively engaging with and participating in these broader societal and cultural spheres (Twidell, 2021).

### 1.1.2 Green Finance: A Catalyst for Change

One key motivator for companies to adopt sustainable practices is the need to comply with international treaties and regulatory frameworks. These frameworks, driven by organizations like the United Nations, encourage and promote global efforts to mitigate environmental and social impacts (Raut, et al., 2017). The process to adapt sustainable business practices, however, is not without challenges, one of them being difficulty accessing finance for green projects (Rasoulinezhad & Taghizadeh-Hesary, 2022).

Sustainable finance, which integrates environmental, social, and governance (ESG) factors into investment decisions, has become a cornerstone of modern finance. This shift is driven by a confluence of factors: companies with strong ESG practices often demonstrate superior financial performance, attracting customers, talent, and investment. Additionally, investors, particularly those managing long-term portfolios like pension funds, recognize the societal and environmental impact of their investments, seeking to align their portfolios with their values. Finally, a growing preference among investors for "green" stocks further fuels the demand for sustainable investments (Edmans & Kacperczyk, 2022). The accurate assessment of a company's sustainability performance poses a significant challenge in sustainable finance. This hurdle can be overcome through standardized data collection and reporting, third-party verification, technology-driven solutions, stakeholder engagement and continuous improvement of ESG strategies. These measures enhance the credibility and comparability of ESG data, enabling investors to make more informed decisions and drive sustainable business practices.

Green finance (GF) refers to organized financial efforts focused on supporting positive environmental results. It involves various financial tools like loans, bonds, and investments that are specifically intended to fund environmentally sound projects and greatly reduce the negative effects of human actions on the climate (World Economic Forum, 2020).

The World Bank emphasizes that green finance is essential for funding projects that aim to lessen the negative impacts of climate change and to help communities, especially in poorer nations, adapt to the unavoidable changes. This commitment became official in 2008 with the introduction of the "Strategic Framework for Development and Climate Change." This initiative was created to encourage and coordinate climate action from both government and private sectors. A key example of the innovative financial tools promoted by this framework is the World Bank Green Bond program. This program raises money from investors who buy fixed-income securities, and these funds are used to support projects that demonstrably reduce carbon emissions (World Bank Treasury, 2024).

The International Monetary Fund (IMF) sees green finance as a key part of the overall plan to tackle the economic and social consequences of climate change. They support the use of market-based methods, particularly the buying and selling of green bonds and sustainability-linked bonds – types of debt designed to fund climate-friendly and environmental initiatives (International Monetary Fund, n.d.)

The definitions from key institutions consistently show that green finance is about intentionally directing financial resources towards projects with positive environmental impacts. While sustainable finance covers more ground, green finance is a crucial element dedicated to environmental challenges. The increasing number of green financial products and the active participation of global bodies emphasize the growing recognition and importance of green finance in dealing with critical environmental issues.

With the intent of bridging the gap between the corporate sector and the road to sustainability, it is essential that GF and all inherent activities are bound by principles that allow consistency and accountability. Following are the key principles that GF operates in line with:

- **Environmental Integrity:** GF projects must demonstrate clear environmental benefits, such as reduced greenhouse gas emissions, improved energy efficiency, or protection of biodiversity. This principle emphasizes the importance of rigorous environmental assessments and transparent reporting of environmental impacts (UNEP Finance Initiative, 2023).
- **Social and Governance Considerations:** GF initiatives should address social and governance factors, including fair labor practices, respect for human rights, and responsible corporate governance. This ensures that environmental sustainability is achieved in a manner that is equitable and just (UN Principles for Responsible Investment, 2023).
- **Transparency and Disclosure:** Clear and consistent disclosure of environmental, social, and governance information is crucial for building trust and accountability in the green finance market. This allows investors to make informed decisions and track the environmental and social impact of their investments (International Capital Market Association, 2023).
- **Long-Term Sustainability:** Green finance initiatives should be designed to deliver long-term environmental and social benefits, while also ensuring financial viability and resilience. This requires careful consideration of risks

and opportunities associated with climate change and other environmental challenges (World Bank Group, 2023).

- **Innovation and Collaboration:** Continuous innovation and collaboration among stakeholders, including governments, businesses, investors, and civil society, are essential for advancing the field of green finance and achieving sustainable development goals (Global Green Growth Institute, 2023).

By adhering to these principles, GF can play a vital role in addressing global environmental challenges and creating a more sustainable and equitable future.

Prior research in green finance underscores the crucial role of financing in achieving sustainability goals. Drawing upon the resource-based view, Taghizadeh-Hesary and Yoshino (2020) emphasized the significance of green finance in overcoming obstacles to environmentally sound and sustainable projects. Similarly, Ng and Tao (2016) highlighted the necessity of addressing the funding deficit for renewable energy projects in Asia to secure sustainability. [3] However, the scarcity of long-term financing options and low investment returns continue to be major impediments to the widespread adoption of renewable energy sources (Taghizadeh-Hesary & Yoshino, 2020). This chapter attempts to bring to light the transformative role of green finance as a pioneering force driving sustainable growth and accelerating investments within the renewable energy sector, thereby paving the way for a low-carbon future.

## 1. DEFINING THE GREEN FINANCE FRONTIER FOR RENEWABLE ENERGY

GF plays a crucial role in driving the growth of the renewable energy sector by providing the necessary capital for the development and deployment of renewable energy projects. This includes various financial instruments such as green bonds, sustainable loans, and impact investments, which channel funds towards projects that promote environmental sustainability, including renewable energy sources like solar, wind, and hydropower (UNEP FI, 2023). It also helps overcome the initial high capital costs associated with renewable energy technologies, making them more economically viable and competitive with traditional fossil fuel-based energy sources. By reducing the financial barriers to entry, green finance encourages private sector investment in renewable energy projects, fostering innovation and technological advancements in the sector (IRENA, 2023).

Moreover, GF promotes the development of sustainable energy infrastructure, including smart grids and energy storage systems, which are essential for integrating renewable energy sources into existing energy systems and ensuring grid stability. By supporting the development of a robust and resilient energy infrastructure, green finance contributes to the long-term growth and sustainability of the renewable energy sector (WB, 2023).

Lee, Wang & Chang (2023) investigated the impact of green finance on renewable energy development in China using provincial data from 2001 to 2019. The findings indicated that green finance directly fosters renewable energy adoption and indirectly supports it by stimulating research and development, increasing market openness, and strengthening the overall economy. Notably, green finance has a more significant effect on promoting new renewable energy sources compared to traditional ones, and its marginal impact on renewable energy grows as the sector develops. Additionally, their study revealed a positive spatial spillover effect, where green finance in one province encourages renewable energy in neighboring provinces, with this spillover effect often exceeding the direct impact within the originating province.

In summation, GF is a critical enabler of the renewable energy transition, providing the financial resources and incentives needed to accelerate the deployment of clean energy technologies and build a sustainable energy future.

## 1.1 Navigating the Green Finance Landscape

Sustainable finance is a wider concept where financial resources are used to significantly help achieve the UN's Sustainable Development Goals (SDGs) (Ratnakaram, Et.al, 2025) In practice, it means funding projects through bonds or loans that follow established international guidelines like the Green Bond Principles (GBP) and Green Loan Principles (GLP). By the first half of 2021, the total value of outstanding green, social, and sustainability (GSS) bonds was a substantial $2.1 trillion, showing the market's large size. Within this, green finance specifically follows the GBP or GLP and focuses on environmental goals by carefully tracking how the funds are used.

GF is a broad area that involves directly funding environmentally positive investments in both the public and private sectors. This supports a wide array of projects focused on preventing, reducing, or offsetting environmental harm, as well as fostering environmentally friendly products and services. It also includes funding government policies that encourage environmentally protective, mitigating, or adaptive projects. Furthermore, the financial system contains specific entities like green banks and funds dedicated to green initiatives. The main financial tools used are debt and equity, including green bonds (for sustainable projects) and green loans (typically smaller and private). Sustainable investments that specifically take environmental, social, and governance (ESG) factors into account are also a vital part of GF (Martin, 2023).

The green finance market is a dynamic space with a wide array of participants, from major global financial players to specialized green investment firms. Well-established institutions like Citigroup, Goldman Sachs, HSBC, and JP Morgan Chase are increasingly offering green financial products such as green bonds and loans (Market Research Future, 2025).

The European Union, the United States, and China are at the forefront of global green investments, each with its own distinct approach shaped by their political and economic contexts. The EU is a leader through significant renewable energy investments and green bond issuances, supported by regulations like the Green Taxonomy and the European Investment Bank's Green Bond Program. The US market is growing rapidly, fueled by initiatives like the Clean Energy Investment Initiative and the Inflation Reduction Act, alongside strong private sector involvement in sustainability-linked financing. China has become a major force with substantial investments in clean energy, electric vehicles, and green infrastructure, driven by consistent government policies and local initiatives (Saliou, Muller & Rocha, (2025).

Beyond these leading regions, numerous other major financial institutions globally are actively participating in green finance, including BNP Paribas, Mitsubishi UFJ Financial Group, Société Générale, Deutsche Bank, ICBC, ING Group, Morgan Stanley, Royal Bank of Canada, Standard Chartered, UBS, Agricultural Bank of China, Bank of America, and Crédit Agricole. These institutions offer diverse green financial products and services, contributing to the market's expansion. Multilateral development banks, such as the World Bank Group and its arm, the International Finance Corporation (IFC), play a crucial role in green finance. The IFC is a leading provider of green loans and supports clients in issuing green bonds, often as a key investor. Mizuho Financial Group also actively participates in green finance, using its project finance expertise to fund renewable energy projects (MRF, 2025).

In essence, the development of GF is driven by government regulations, the strategic moves of major financial institutions, and the increasing desire of investors to put their money into sustainable ventures. The diverse strategies and focuses seen across different parts of the world and within various organizations underscore the constantly changing and critically important nature of this field.

## 1.2 The Symbiotic Relationship: Green Finance and Renewable Energy

Basically, green finance and renewable energy go hand-in-hand, helping each other grow and become more sustainable. Research shows that green finance helps boost the amount of renewable energy available in the long run and also makes energy use more efficient. It does this by making it easier to fund new renewable energy technologies and helping industries become more environmentally friendly. Interestingly, studies suggest that green finance becomes even better at supporting the development of renewable energy technology once that technology reaches a certain level of advancement (Alharbi et al., 2023; Shi & Shi, 2025).

Essentially, GF is super important because it offers reliable and affordable money for renewable energy projects, which usually cost a lot to get started. It also helps bring more diverse investors and more money into the renewable energy market overall. Plus, green finance gives investors smart ways to handle the potential risks of investing in renewables, like special insurance and credit guarantees. On top of that, GF is key to speeding up the use of new renewable energy technologies. It encourages different groups – like companies, universities, and researchers – to work together. It directly supports the research and development of new ideas and helps build pilot projects, which pushes technological innovation in renewable energy forward. By bringing together money, technology, skilled people, and other innovative elements, green finance helps create a strong environment for the advancement of renewable energy technology. GF really helps renewable energy projects deal with money problems. It often provides long-term loans with better interest rates, which makes things easier financially for the people developing these projects and helps keep renewable energy technology moving forward. Furthermore, by putting money into environmentally friendly, low-carbon projects, green finance helps green industries grow and pushes traditional industries to become more efficient and modern. As industries get greener and more people want eco-friendly products, the demand for renewable energy and other green technologies increases, which then encourages even more technological innovation in these areas (Shi & Shi, 2025).

Investing in renewable energy through GF helps countries become less dependent on fossil fuels, which boosts their energy security and speeds up the use of green technologies. It also encourages investment in making energy use more efficient, which helps renewable energy compete even better. The effect of GF on how much renewable energy is produced can be especially strong when "green bonds" are specifically used to fund these alternative energy projects. Plus, if a country already has strong technological capabilities, GF can have an even bigger and longer-lasting impact on its renewable energy production (Alharbi et al., 2023).

## 2. TRAILBLAZING INSTRUMENTS: FINANCING THE RENEWABLE ENERGY REVOLUTION

GF utilizes a variety of tools to channel funds towards environmentally beneficial projects. These instruments include green bonds and loans specifically for eco-friendly initiatives, green funds that pool investments in sustainable assets, carbon finance mechanisms focused on emission reduction, Sharia-compliant green sukuk, blended finance that combines public and private capital, green insurance for environmental risk mitigation, and dedicated climate funds supporting developing nations. Together, these diverse instruments play a crucial role in funding the transition to a greener economy across various sectors and have been discussed below.

## 2.1 Green Bonds: Debt Instruments for a Sustainable Future

Essentially, green bonds are a type of investment where the money raised is specifically used to fund projects that are good for the environment or help with climate change. So, unlike regular bonds, you know the money is going towards things like renewable energy, making things more energy efficient, preventing pollution, and protecting nature (Jain, Gangopadhyay & Mukhopadhyay, 2022)

Rasoulinezhad & Taghizadeh-Hesary (2022) advocate for green bonds to have proven to be an effective tool for encouraging the development of green energy projects and achieving substantial reductions in CO2 emissions. However, they also point out that the data indicates that this positive impact is not immediately apparent in the short term, suggesting a longer timeframe is needed to observe the direct causal relationship between green bond issuance and these environmental outcomes.

The Green Bond Principles (GBP), created by the International Capital Market Association (ICMA), are like a set of helpful, voluntary rules for the green bond market. They encourage openness and clear communication to build trust. The main goal of the GBP is to help those issuing green bonds fund projects that are good for the environment and contribute to a world with net-zero emissions, while also protecting the environment. By suggesting that issuers report on how the green bond money is used, the GBP make it easier to see where the funds are going and understand their potential environmental benefits (ICMA, 2023).

For example, the World Bank issues Green Bonds to gather money from investors who want a steady income. This money then goes towards the World Bank's projects that aim to reduce climate change or help people deal with its effects. These projects are carefully checked by the World Bank's experts and must meet specific standards for activities that lower carbon emissions. The fact that the World Bank has issued over USD 20 billion worth of Green Bonds since 2008 shows how important these bonds are in bringing together funds for climate solutions through a reliable investment option (World Bank Treasury, 2024).

Essentially, the main goal of green bonds is to direct investment money towards projects that support environmental sustainability and the shift to a low-carbon economy. By offering a specific way to fund environmentally friendly projects, green bonds are key to speeding up the adoption of renewable energy and other sustainable efforts. They help overcome funding challenges and allow important projects to move forward. Green bonds have become a popular way to finance the growth and implementation of various renewable energy projects, including solar farms, rooftop solar panels, onshore and offshore wind farms, hydroelectric power stations, and biomass energy facilities. The money raised from selling these bonds is specifically used to fund the development, building, and operation of these renewable energy projects.

## 2.2 Green Loans and Sustainability-Linked Finance

Green loans are a type of funding specifically created for projects that benefit the environment, like renewable energy projects that lower $CO_2$ emissions or the development of eco-friendly technologies and services. A key difference from green bonds is that green loans tend to be smaller in size and are usually agreed upon privately between a lender and someone borrowing the money, rather than being larger and potentially traded on a public exchange. For a loan to be officially recognized as a green loan, it needs to follow the Green Loan Principles (GLP). These principles are an international set of guidelines built on four main ideas: how the money will be used, the process for evaluating and choosing projects, how the money will be managed, and how the borrower will report on its use. The GLP clearly state that all of the borrowed money must be used only for qualifying green projects that have obvious environmental advantages, and the borrower needs to assess, measure, and report on these benefits (World Bank Group, 2021).

Across the world, green loans are being used to fund many different kinds of renewable energy projects. For example, Nordea offers green loans to companies that are building solar farms and to support the expansion of businesses that develop water purification technology. This shows how widely green loans can be applied within the renewable energy and clean technology industries (Nordea, 2023).

The International Finance Corporation (IFC) has played a key role in setting up and bringing together funding for major renewable energy projects through green loans. For instance, in Mexico, the IFC arranged a $541 million green loan with a 15-year term for Infrastructura Energetica Nova (IEnova). This supported the building of five solar power plants with a total capacity of 526 MW. These projects are predicted to replace more polluting thermal power generation, leading to significant yearly decreases in $CO_2$ emissions. Furthermore, the IFC provided a €73.5 million green loan to fund the construction of a wind power project in Georgia, helping the country move towards cleaner energy sources (World Bank Group, 2021).

Green loans provide several attractive benefits for renewable energy. One key advantage is that borrowers might get better financing deals, like lower interest rates, as a direct reward for working on environmentally positive projects. This can really improve the financial success of renewable energy projects, making them more appealing to developers and investors. Also, taking out a green loan can boost a borrower's reputation, showing stakeholders, customers, and investors that they are serious about environmental sustainability and responsible business practices. This positive image can be really valuable in today's eco-conscious market (Kerr & Avendano 2020).

From the lender's side, offering green loans can help them lower the emissions associated with their investments, aligning their portfolios with wider sustainability goals and potentially improving their own environmental reporting. It also allows banks and financial institutions to be more involved in tackling climate change and supporting sustainable growth. In some situations, green loans might even offer larger loan amounts to help cover the potentially higher initial costs of energy-efficient and renewable energy technologies.

## 2.3 Carbon Markets and Pricing Mechanisms: Internalizing Environmental Costs

There are two main ways to put a price on carbon emissions, and both help encourage the use of and investment in renewable energy: carbon taxes and cap-and-trade systems (Abrell & Kosch 2021). A carbon tax works by directly charging a fee based on the amount of carbon in fossil fuels. This makes energy sources that produce a lot of carbon, like coal, oil, and natural gas, more expensive. Because renewable energy sources produce little to no carbon emissions when they're running, this price increase makes them a more financially attractive option (Digitemie & Ekemezie, 2024). Essentially, both carbon taxes and cap-and-trade systems are really important government tools for making sure that the environmental costs of carbon emissions are factored into the price of energy. This, in turn, makes renewable energy a more financially sound and appealing choice for both investment and producing power.

The carbon pricing mechanisms aim to address the negative externalities associated with greenhouse gas emissions by assigning an economic value to carbon pollution (Yun & Hu, 2024). By internalizing these environmental costs, they create financial incentives for businesses and individuals to reduce their carbon footprint and invest in cleaner alternatives, including renewable energy technologies.

The way putting a price on carbon emissions is approached has slowly but surely moved towards using market-based solutions to tackle global climate change. From the initial ideas to setting up international carbon markets and the increasing number of carbon pricing efforts around the world, the development of carbon pricing has involved new ideas, tried different approaches and worked together. When carbon pricing systems, like taxes or emissions trading, are announced and put into place, they change how competitive companies are. These new rules can be seen as an unexpected event that adds to production costs and could potentially create extra income, as has happened to some extent with the European Union Emissions Trading System (Nippa et al., 2021).

## 3. CHARTING THE COURSE: INVESTMENT TRENDS AND MARKET DYNAMICS IN RENEWABLE ENERGY

The global landscape of energy is undergoing a profound transformation, driven by the urgent need to decarbonize economies and mitigate the escalating impacts of climate change. At the heart of this transition lies the burgeoning renewable energy sector, attracting unprecedented levels of investment and experiencing dynamic market shifts. This evolution is characterized by technological advancements, evolving policy frameworks, and increasing cost competitiveness, all contributing to a reshaping of energy portfolios worldwide. Understanding the intricate interplay of investment trends and market dynamics within renewable energy is crucial for stakeholders navigating this rapidly evolving landscape and for realizing a sustainable energy future.

### 3.1 Global and Regional Investment Landscapes

In 2024, the world poured an unprecedented $2.1 trillion into the shift towards low-carbon energy – that's a solid 11% jump from the year before! This huge increase was mainly driven by big investments in things like electric vehicles, renewable power sources, and making our electricity grids better, all of which saw record levels of funding. Out of all that energy transition investment in 2024, a significant $728 billion was specifically channeled into renewable energy technologies. This includes a wide variety of sources like wind power (both on land and at sea), solar energy, biofuels, energy from biomass and waste, marine energy, geothermal energy, and small-scale hydropower.

Interestingly, mainland China was the biggest single investor in the energy transition globally, attracting a whopping $818 billion in 2024. That's a significant 20% jump from their 2023 investment and made up two-thirds of the entire global increase in energy transition spending for the year. The United States also showed a strong dedication to clean energy, keeping their investments steady at a substantial $338 billion in 2024. This funding supported significant additions to their renewable power capacity, especially big solar and wind projects.

On the other hand, both the European Union and the United Kingdom saw a dip in their energy transition investments in 2024, with the EU reaching $375 billion and the UK $65.3 billion (BloombergNEF, 2025).

Globally, investment in renewable energy is clearly on the rise, with solar power taking the lead. However, most of this money is flowing into China and developed countries. Developing economies outside of China are still struggling to attract enough investment for their clean energy transitions. This uneven distribution highlights the need for specific plans to help these regions secure the funding they need to meet global climate targets.

## 3.2 Risk and Return Profiles of Renewable Energy Investments

Financial markets are increasingly focused on climate change due to the underperformance of carbon-intensive company stocks compared to others, and a trend of individual investors selling off shares in these high-emission firms (Choi et al., 2020). Investors view the issuance of green bonds by EU nations as a positive action that increases value and lowers risk. Furthermore, long-term and institutional investors are increasingly prioritizing Environmental, Social, and Governance (ESG) factors, considering climate change risk a crucial element in their investment decisions and company valuations (Krueger et al., 2020).

Investing in renewable energy projects comes with its own set of risks that investors need to think about carefully. Usually, these projects require a lot of money upfront to develop and build facilities like solar farms and wind turbines (Ottinger & Bowie, 2014). Another thing to consider is the risk of not getting paid, for example, if the company buying the electricity under a power purchase agreement (PPA) can't meet their obligations. Also, it can be tough to get funding, especially for projects that are just starting out. Finally, changes or uncertainties in government policies, like new regulations or the removal of support programs, can make investing in renewable energy seem riskier (Bassey, Aigbovbiosa & Agupugo 2024). However, once these renewable energy projects are operational, they usually have low ongoing operating costs because their main fuel sources – like the sun, wind, and water – don't cost anything.

## 3.3 The Pivotal Role of Policy and Public Sector Support

Government policies and public sector initiatives are indispensable catalysts in accelerating the transition to a sustainable energy future. By establishing clear regulatory frameworks, offering financial incentives, and fostering research and development, the public sector plays a pivotal role in de-risking investments, leveling the playing field for renewable energy technologies, and driving their widespread adoption. This support is crucial in overcoming market barriers, stimulating innovation, and creating the enabling environment necessary for the renewable energy sector to flourish and contribute effectively to climate change mitigation and energy security goals (Lv, 2023).

To foster sustainable economic growth while addressing environmental concerns, governments should adopt consistent, long-term supportive policies aimed at increasing private sector investment in green energy projects. This is particularly crucial during and after the COVID-19 pandemic, a period when green initiatives may face greater challenges in securing financing. By creating a stable and encouraging policy environment, governments can incentivize private participation and drive the necessary capital towards environmentally beneficial energy projects, contributing to both economic recovery and long-term sustainability (Rasoulinezhad & Taghizadeh-Hesary, 2022). Furthermore, a robust economy and strong government support are crucial for this positive influence (Lee, Wang & Chang, 2023). Also, the role of banks is crucial. The banking sector is the linchpin of the financial system, acting as a vital intermediary that facilitates transactions, mobilizes savings, and provides crucial credit to individuals, businesses, and governments. By efficiently allocating capital and managing risk, banks drive economic growth, implement monetary policy, and ensure financial stability. This makes them indispensable for the smooth functioning and development of the overall economy (Kumar & Sheela, 2024).

From an economic standpoint, nations with a greater reliance on carbon-intensive activities are expected to implement more proactive institutional changes. These adjustments would involve policies aimed at decreasing emissions from power generation, restructuring electricity markets, and incentivizing investments in low-carbon technologies to lower their overall carbon intensity. Consequently, it is proposed that the impact of GF on the generation of renewable energy will be more pronounced in countries with higher initial carbon emission intensity compared to those with lower intensity. Following this logic, it is also argued that the effect of GF on renewable energy production will likely be greater in countries that have established low-carbon emission policies or set net-zero targets than in those without such commitments (Alharbi et al., 2023).

A study conducted by Wang et al., (2023) examined how GF and renewable energy affect energy efficiency within the E-7 economies, considering both non-linear and asymmetric relationships. Utilizing data from 1985 to 2017 and employing NARDL and 2SLS methodologies, the research reveals variations in green finance development across the E-7, with China leading (0.61) and Mexico (0.37) having the lowest level. Although the paper states Russia's Gini coefficient was highest in 2019 (0.57), followed by Turkey, other sources indicate a different value for Russia. The empirical findings suggested that a primary obstacle to improved green energy efficiency in these nations is insufficient private and public investment in the energy sector, hindering efforts to enhance power access, energy security, and environmentally sustainable economic growth. The study concludes that while renewable energy and energy efficiency deployment in the E-7 countries shows promise, it remains vulnerable, emphasizing the need to address limitations in green financing and renewable energy policies to fully leverage the funding potential for energy efficiency.

The trajectory of renewable energy development and deployment is inextricably linked to the proactive and strategic involvement of governments and the public sector. Through well-designed policies, consistent financial support, and a commitment to fostering innovation, the public sector can effectively mitigate risks, attract private capital, and create stable market conditions conducive to the sustained growth of renewable energy. This enabling environment is not only essential for achieving ambitious climate targets and enhancing energy security but also for unlocking the significant economic opportunities inherent in the global transition towards a clean energy future.

## 4. NAVIGATING THE HEADWINDS AND SEIZING THE OPPORTUNITIES

Investing in renewable energy comes with a mix of risks and rewards. On one hand, once projects are running and under contract, they tend to have stable long-term operating costs and income. On the other hand, they can be vulnerable to things outside their control, like changes in government policies, the availability of sun or wind, and shifts in the energy market. Because of this, it's really important for investors in this area to carefully assess and plan for these potential risks. Even though investing in renewable energy usually looks like it will provide good returns, especially with the world moving towards cleaner energy and technology getting cheaper, the actual profit you make on any specific project depends on a lot of different things that are all connected. So, if investors want to get the best possible returns in this changing industry, they really need to understand and carefully consider all these different factors.

### 4.1 Overcoming the Challenges in Scaling Green Finance for Renewable Energy

Getting enough green finance to meet the huge investment needs of renewable energy faces several challenges. A major problem is the lack of consistent ways to measure and define ESG (environmental, social, and governance) factors. Without a set of universally agreed-upon standards for reporting on these factors, investors struggle to compare different green finance options and truly understand their impact. This makes it harder to allocate money efficiently and creates openings for companies to falsely present themselves as environmentally friendly (greenwashing).

Greenwashing itself is a big obstacle, as companies might overstate or lie about their sustainability efforts to attract environmentally aware investors. This damages trust in the green finance market and can lead to money going to projects that don't really offer significant environmental benefits (Zioło, Bak, Spoz, 2024).

Another key issue is the limited availability and quality of data on green finance, especially when it comes to the environmental impact of projects. Without trustworthy and comparable data, it's tough to accurately evaluate risks, set prices for financial instruments, and track how well green investments are working. Finally, many renewable energy projects, especially in developing countries, are seen as riskier and potentially less profitable compared to traditional investments. This can discourage private companies from getting involved and limit the overall amount of green finance available.

The amount and type of finance are crucial to successfully implementing climate mitigation and adaptation strategies (Wang et al., 2023). The growth of the green bond market is being held back by a few key issues. These include a lack of established official structures, a weak local bond market, a still-developing overall bond market with not much involvement from private companies, and the absence of international standards to certify green bonds (Jain, Gangopadhyay & Mukhopadhyay, 2022).

The fact that financial markets often focus on quick profits can make it hard for renewable energy projects, which usually take longer to pay off, to get steady funding because investors tend to prioritize investments that show immediate returns. To truly expand green finance for renewable energy and overcome the current hurdles, a focused, collaborative effort is needed. This includes creating consistent standards, making things more transparent, developing effective ways to manage risks, having steady and supportive government policies, improving how we collect and share data, strengthening the organizations involved and encouraging a long-term view on investments. Tackling these challenges is essential to fully unlock the potential of green finance so it can drive the renewable energy transition at the speed and scale required to meet global climate goals.

## 4.2 Unlocking the Potential: Opportunities for Future Growth

Strengthening capital markets, similar to what we see in developed countries, would make it easier to attract both local and international investors. This would also help align with global efforts to tackle climate change (Jain, Gangopadhyay & Mukhopadhyay, 2022).

Despite the current challenges, the future of green finance for renewable energy looks incredibly bright, with significant potential for growth and impact. A major driving force is the increasing demand for sustainable investments from a growing number of environmentally conscious investors. As people become more aware of climate change and its risks, more investors want their money to support sustainable and responsible (ESG-compliant) assets, creating a strong market for green financial products that back renewable energy.

Advances in renewable energy technology, energy storage, and managing power grids are constantly creating new and more appealing investment opportunities. These innovations are bringing down costs, improving efficiency, and making renewable energy systems more reliable, making them more competitive with traditional energy sources and thus more attractive to investors.

Government support and policies around the world are playing a crucial role in directing money towards renewable energy through green finance. Ambitious goals, financial incentives, and regulations like the US Inflation Reduction Act and the EU Green Deal are strongly encouraging investment in clean energy technologies and infrastructure (WEF, 2024).

The vast potential for deploying renewable energy in developing countries presents a huge area for green finance to grow. These regions, with their increasing energy needs and abundant renewable resources, offer unique opportunities for sustainable development and clean energy transitions, which will require significant green financial support (Feng et al., 2024).

## 5. CONCLUSION: FORGING A SUSTAINABLE FUTURE THROUGH GREEN FINANCE INNOVATION

GF is essential for the global shift to sustainable energy, particularly for renewables. It includes various financial tools like green bonds and loans, all directing investment towards eco-friendly projects and innovation. A diverse group of stakeholders, including financial institutions, governments, and international bodies, are involved in this effort to decarbonize energy. While global renewable energy investment is at record highs, especially in solar and wind in regions like China, the US, and Europe, significant investment gaps persist in developing economies outside China, highlighting the need for greater financial mobilization there. Although renewable energy investments can be profitable long-term, they also carry risks related to markets, policies, technology, and project development, making risk management crucial for sustained investment. Government policies and support are vital for renewable energy growth via green finance, using incentives, regulations, and public investment to lower financial barriers and stimulate clean energy innovation. Despite progress, scaling green finance faces hurdles like a lack of unified ESG metrics, greenwashing concerns, high transition costs, regulatory uncertainties, and infrastructure limits. Overcoming these requires better transparency, robust standards, and stronger collaboration across finance and energy sectors. The future of green finance in renewables is promising, driven by demand for sustainable investments, technological advancements, supportive policies, and new financial solutions, indicating its potential to be a key driver for a global sustainable energy system.

To build a sustainable future through innovative green finance, several key actions are needed. First, we must establish globally standardized and compatible green finance classifications to provide investor clarity, reduce regulatory obstacles, and direct capital to genuinely environmentally beneficial projects. Second, stricter regulations and greater transparency in ESG reporting and verification are crucial to combat greenwashing, build investor confidence, and ensure green finance truly supports sustainability. Third, increased public-private partnerships and innovative blended finance tools are vital to combine public and private capital, de-risk renewable energy projects in emerging markets, and address issues like currency volatility and political instability. Fourth, governments should increase support through targeted incentives, grants, and loan programs to lower the high initial costs of renewable energy and improve its financial viability. Fifth, significant investment in modernizing grids and developing energy storage is necessary to tackle the intermittency of renewable sources and ensure a reliable clean electricity supply. Sixth, we must enhance capacity building and technical assistance in developing countries to improve their ability to structure and manage green finance and renewable energy projects, thereby reducing project risks and promoting a more equitable global energy transition. Seventh, fostering international cooperation and knowledge sharing among governments, financial institutions, and technology providers is essential for accelerating the global shift to sustainable energy through green finance innovation. Finally, we should continue to develop and adopt market-based solutions like green bonds that align with clear, science-based environmental goals, ensuring green finance remains a dynamic and effective tool for a sustainable future. Achieving a sustainable future through green finance innovation requires a global commitment to tackling current challenges and leveraging the vast opportunities in the renewable energy sector. By focusing on standardization, transparency, risk mitigation, policy support, infrastructure development, capacity building, and international collaboration, we can unlock the full potential of green finance to drive a transformative shift towards a clean and sustainable energy system for future generations.

## REFERENCES

Abrell, J., & Kosch, M. (2022). The impact of carbon prices on renewable energy support. *Journal of the Association of Environmental and Resource Economists, 9*(3), 531–563. DOI: 10.1086/717417

Al-Swidi, A. K., Al-Hakimi, M. A., & Al-Hattami, H. M. (2024). Fostering environmental preservation: Exploring the synergy of green human resource management and corporate environmental ethics. *The Bottom Line (New York, N.Y.), 37*(1), 1–26. DOI: 10.1108/BL-06-2023-0191

Alharbi, S. S., Al Mamun, M., Boubaker, S., & Rizvi, S. K. A. (2023). Green finance and renewable energy: A worldwide evidence. *Energy Economics, 118*, 106499. DOI: 10.1016/j.eneco.2022.106499

Bassey, K. E., Aigbovbiosa, J., & Agupugo, C. (2024). Risk management strategies in renewable energy investment. *International Journal of Novel Research in Engineering and Science, 11*(1), 138–148. DOI: 10.5281/zenodo.13311076

Bloomberg New Energy Finance. (2025). Global Investment in the Energy Transition Exceeded $2 Trillion for the First Time in 2024, BloombergNEF Report Retrieved from: https://about.bnef.com/blog/global-investment-in-the-energy-transition-exceeded-2-trillion-for-the-first-time-in-2024-according-to-bloombergnef-report/

Choi, D., Gao, Z., & Jiang, W. (2020). Attention to global warming. *Review of Financial Studies, 33*(3), 1112–1145. DOI: 10.1093/rfs/hhz086

Derrick, M. (2024). Top 10: Energy Industry Associations. *Energy Digital.* https://energydigital.com/top10/top-10-energy-industry-associations

Digitemie, W. N., & Ekemezie, I. O. (2024). Assessing the role of carbon pricing in global climate change mitigation strategies. *Magna Scientia Advanced Research and Reviews, 10*(2), 22-31. DOI: 10.30574/msarr.2024.10.2.0040

Edmans, A., & Kacperczyk, M. (2022). Sustainable Finance. *Review of Finance, 26*(6), 1309–1313. DOI: 10.1093/rof/rfac069

Feng, K., Yang, Z., Zhuo, Y., Jiao, L., Wang, B., & Liu, Z. (2024). Impact of Carbon Tax on Renewable Energy Development and Environmental–Economic Synergies. *Energies, 17*(21), 5347. DOI: 10.3390/en17215347

Global Green Growth Institute. (2023). Principles of Green Finance. Retrieved from https://gggi.org/

Heras-Saizarbitoria, I., Sáez, L., Allur, E., & Morandeira, J. (2018). The emergence of renewable energy cooperatives in Spain: A review. *Renewable & Sustainable Energy Reviews*, *94*, 1036–1043. DOI: 10.1016/j.rser.2018.06.049

International Capital Market Association. (2023). Green Bond Principles. Retrieved from https://www.icmagroup.org/sustainable-finance/the-principles-guidelines-and-handbooks/green-bond-principles-gbp/

International Energy Agency. (2024), *Renewables 2024*, IEA, Paris, Retrieved from: https://www.iea.org/reports/renewables-2024

International Monetary Fund. (n.d.). *Climate Finance Indicators.* Retrieved from: https://climatedata.imf.org/pages/climate-finance

International Renewable Energy Agency. (2023). Renewable Energy. Retrieved from https://www.irena.org/

Jain, K., Gangopadhyay, M., & Mukhopadhyay, K. (2022). Prospects and challenges of green bonds in renewable energy sector: Case of selected Asian economies. *Journal of Sustainable Finance & Investment*, *14*(3), 708–731. DOI: 10.1080/20430795.2022.2034596

Kerr, T. M., & Avendano, F. (2020). Green loans and multinational corporations. *Natural Resources and Environment*, *35*(2), 46–49. https://www.jstor.org/stable/e27010659

Krueger, P., Sautner, Z., & Starks, L. T. (2020). The importance of climate risks for institutional investors. *Review of Financial Studies*, *33*(3), 1067–1111. DOI: 10.1093/rfs/hhz137

Kumar, R. S. P., & Sheela, P. (2023). Can Islamic banks be sustainable with a simultaneously strong conventional banking counterpart? A comparative study of the financial performance of Islamic and conventional banks in Bahrain. *International Journal of Business Excellence*, *30*(2), 133–159. DOI: 10.1504/IJBEX.2023.132063

Lee, C. C., Wang, F., & Chang, Y. F. (2023). Does green finance promote renewable energy? Evidence from China. *Resources Policy*, *82*, 103439. Advance online publication. DOI: 10.1016/j.resourpol.2023.103439

Li, B. (2023). The role of financial markets in the energy transition: An analysis of investment trends and opportunities in renewable energy and clean technology. *Environmental Science and Pollution Research International*, *30*(43), 97948–97964. DOI: 10.1007/s11356-023-29014-6 PMID: 37599346

Lv, Y. (2023). Transitioning to sustainable energy: Opportunities, challenges, and the potential of blockchain technology. *Frontiers in Energy Research, 11*, 1258044. DOI: 10.3389/fenrg.2023.1258044

Market Research Future. (2025). *Global Green Finance Market Overview* Retrieved from: https://www.marketresearchfuture.com/reports/green-finance-market-24469]

Martin, V. (2023). Green Finance: Regulation and Instruments. *Journal of Central Banking Theory and Practice.* DOI: 10.2478/jcbtp-2023-0019

Moriarty, P., & Honnery, D. (2016). Can renewable energy power the future? *Energy Policy, 93*, 3–7. DOI: 10.1016/j.enpol.2016.02.051

Ng, T. H., & Tao, J. Y. (2016). Bond financing for renewable energy in Asia. *Energy Policy, 95*, 509–517. https://doi.org/10. DOI: 10.1016/j.enpol.2016.03.015

Nippa, M., Patnaik, S., & Taussig, M. (2021). MNE responses to carbon pricing regulations: Theory and evidence. *Journal of International Business Studies, 52*(5), 904–929. DOI: 10.1057/s41267-021-00403-8

Nordea (2023). What are green loans? Retrieved from: https://www.nordea.com/en/news/what-are-green-loans

Ottinger, R. L., & Bowie, J. (2014). Innovative Financing for Renewable Energy. *Academy of Environmental Law Colloquium.* DOI: 10.2139/ssrn.2497175

Rasoulinezhad, E., & Taghizadeh-Hesary, F. (2022). Role of green finance in improving energy efficiency and renewable energy development. *Energy Efficiency, 15*(2), 14. DOI: 10.1007/s12053-022-10021-4 PMID: 35529528

Ratnakaram, S., Manikeswari, D., Babu, M., & Paluri, S. (2025). *Islamic Banking, Environmental Social Governance (ESG) Ingredients for Enhanced Sustainability in the Banking Sector.* Digital Transformation and Sustainability of Business. DOI: 10.1201/9781003606185-49

Raut, R. D., Narkhede, B., & Gardas, B. B. (2017). To identify the critical success factors of sustainable supply chain management practices in the context of oil and gas industries: ISM approach. *Renewable & Sustainable Energy Reviews, 68*, 33–47. DOI: 10.1016/j.rser.2016.09.067

Saliou, P., Muller, V., & Rocha, F. (2025). Green Finance: The role of the EU, US and China, and how Securitization can unlock the market potential. *Ernest & Young.* Luxembourg. Retrieved from: https://www.ey.com/en_lu/insights/securitization/green-finance-the-role-of-the-eu-us-china

Shi, X., & Shi, D. (2025). Impact of Green Finance on Renewable Energy Technology Innovation: Empirical Evidence from China. *Sustainability (Basel)*, *17*(5), 2201. DOI: 10.3390/su17052201

Swallow, T. (2022). Top 10: largest renewable energy organisations in the world. *Sustainability Magazine*. https://sustainabilitymag.com/renewable-energy/10-largest-renewable-energy-organisations-in-the-world

Taghizadeh-Hesary, F., & Yoshino, N. (2020). Sustainable solutions for green financing and investment in renewable energy projects. *Energies*, *13*(4), 788. DOI: 10.3390/en13040788

Twidell, J. (2021). *Institutional and Economic Factors. Renewable energy resources* (4th ed.). Routledge. DOI: 10.4324/9780429452161

UN Principles for Responsible Investment. (2023). The Six Principles for Responsible Investment. Retrieved from https://www.unpri.org/

United Nations Environment Programme Finance Initiative. (2023). Principles for Responsible Banking. Retrieved from https://www.unepfi.org/banking/bankingprinciples/

Wang, Z., Peng, M. Y. P., Anser, M. K., & Chen, Z. (2023). Research on the impact of green finance and renewable energy on energy efficiency: The case study E– 7 economies. *Renewable Energy*, *205*, 166–173. DOI: 10.1016/j.renene.2022.12.077

World Bank. (2023). Green Finance. Retrieved from https://documents1.worldbank.org/curated/zh/148291573020848322/pdf/Executive-Summary.pdf

World Bank Documents and Reports the basic green finance reference guide -, accessed April 16, 2025. Retrieved from: https://documents1.worldbank.org/curated/en/099126011232333546/pdf/IDU132f9c75017b0314d0e1bedb16cb861caace2.pdf

World Bank Group. (2021). *What You Need to Know About Green Loans.* Retrieved from: https://www.worldbank.org/en/news/feature/2021/10/04/what-you-need-to-know-about-green-loans

World Bank Treasury. (2024). *Green Bonds* Retrieved from https://treasury.worldbank.org/en/about/unit/treasury/ibrd/ibrd-green-bonds

World Economic Forum. (2020). *What is green finance and why is it important?* (Green Horizon Summit: The Pivotal Role of Finance). Cologny, Switzerland. https://www.weforum.org/stories/2020/11/what-is-green-finance/

World Economic Forum. (2024). *3 financing trends to watch that can propel a clean energy revolution in the Global South.* Retrieved from: https://www.weforum.org/stories/2024/12/3-financing-trends-to-watch-that-can-propel-a-clean-energy-revolution-in-the-global-south/

Yong, J. Y., Yusliza, M., Ramayah, T., Chiappetta Jabbour, C. J., Sehnem, S., & Mani, V. (2019). Pathways towards sustainability in manufacturing organizations: Empirical evidence on the role of green human resource management. *Business Strategy and the Environment.* Advance online publication. DOI: 10.1002/bse.2359

Yun, X., & Hu, Y. (2024). An Overview of the Evolution in the Research Landscape of Green Finance. *WORLD (Oakland, Calif.)*, *5*(4), 1335–1366. DOI: 10.3390/world5040068

Zioło, M., Bąk, I., & Spoz, A. (2024). Literature review of greenwashing research: State of the art. *Corporate Social Responsibility and Environmental Management*, *31*(6), 5343–5356. DOI: 10.1002/csr.2842

# Chapter 4
# Carbon Credits and Biodiversity Credits:
## Opportunities, Risks, and Global Perspectives of a Market-Based Environmental Policy

**Silvio Andrae**
https://orcid.org/0000-0002-8586-7812
*Independent Researcher, Germany*

## ABSTRACT

*In light of global environmental crises, market-based instruments such as carbon and biodiversity credits are gaining importance. This chapter examines their functioning, opportunities, and risks based on a theoretical analysis and international case studies (Brazil, Indonesia, Kenya) to provide a comprehensive picture of the effectiveness and challenges of both approaches. Carbon credits are established worldwide and primarily aim to finance emission reductions through reforestation projects. Biodiversity credits promote the protection and restoration of ecosystems but are more difficult to quantify and less standardized. The analysis reveals synergies in projects that combine carbon sequestration and biodiversity but also conflicting goals. The findings underscore the importance of local participation, transparency, and regulatory clarity, and inform recommendations for improving the governance of both instruments and their integrated use to advance climate goals and biodiversity protection.*

DOI: 10.4018/979-8-3373-8287-6.ch004

© 2026, IGI Global Scientific Publishing. Copying or distributing in print or electronic forms without written permission of IGI Global Scientific Publishing is prohibited. Use of this chapter to [g]enerative artificial intelligence (AI) technologies is expressly prohibited. The publisher reserves all rights to license its use for generative AI training and machine learning model development.

## 1. INTRODUCTION

The world is currently grappling with an urgent and escalating ecological crisis. The man-made climate change and the rapid loss of biodiversity are not just significant challenges, but they are also immediate threats. The rising average temperatures, more frequent extreme weather events, and the disappearance of habitats are causing irreversible damage to natural ecosystems and posing a direct threat to human societies' economic and social foundations. Despite numerous international agreements and political initiatives, the progress in climate protection and biodiversity conservation has not matched the urgency of the situation or the goals set by the international community. The Paris Climate Agreement and the Kunming-Montreal Global Biodiversity Framework have set a path to achieve the global vision of 'living in harmony with nature' by 2050. However, the financing needs for climate protection, adaptation, and biodiversity are significantly high (Seidl et al., 2024), and the time to act is now.

Amidst this crisis, there is a ray of hope in the form of innovative and practical instruments that combine ecological goals with economic incentives. Market-based mechanisms, particularly tradable environmental goods such as carbon credits and biodiversity credits, have emerged as promising approaches. They have the potential to efficiently distribute the costs of emission reductions and nature conservation measures and to mobilize investment in sustainable projects. The creation of markets for the reduction of greenhouse gas emissions or the preservation of biodiversity leads to an economic valuation and traceability of ecological services. Both policymakers and businesses are increasingly embracing this concept, offering hope for a more sustainable future.

However, it should be noted that these market-based approaches are the subject of heated debate. Critics point to potential risks such as 'greenwashing' or 'carbonwashing' (In & Schumacher, 2021), a practice where an organization presents itself as more environmentally friendly than it actually is, lack of transparency, ineffective incentives, and social inequalities, which poorly designed markets could exacerbate. In addition, the fundamental question of whether ecological values such as climate and biodiversity should be subject to market logic is increasingly being debated.

In this context, this paper aims to systematically analyze the potential, limitations, and global perspectives of market-based environmental policy using the examples of carbon credits and biodiversity credits. The study focuses on the following research questions: What opportunities do market-based approaches offer for climate protection and biodiversity conservation? The potential risks and side effects of monetizing ecological services must be discussed. The question arises of under what conditions environmental markets can contribute to a genuinely sustainable transformation rather than merely masking existing problems.

The study will use a combination of theoretical analysis and empirical research to answer these questions. This paper first discusses carbon and biodiversity markets' theoretical functioning and logic. It then highlights their similarities and differences and discusses key economic and ecological challenges. Empirically, the paper draws on selected case studies from different regions of the world—including projects in Brazil, Indonesia, and Africa—to shed light on practical experiences, success factors, and problem areas of specific initiatives.

The world is undergoing a period of profound ecological change. Climate change is currently considered one of the most significant global challenges, with consequences that are not only ecological but also social and economic. Since the beginning of industrialization, a significant increase in the concentration of greenhouse gases in the atmosphere has been observed, leading to a continuous rise in global average temperatures. The increase in extreme weather events such as droughts, floods, and heat waves is significant in frequency and intensity. This results in substantial damage to infrastructure, agriculture, and human health.

At the same time, biodiversity loss is progressing at an alarming rate. According to the Global Assessment Report of the World Biodiversity Council (IPBES), around one million species are threatened with extinction, with a significant proportion of these species likely to be wiped out within a few decades. The loss of biodiversity undermines the stability of ecosystems and impairs vital functions such as pollination, water purification, and climate regulation. Climate change and biodiversity loss are not isolated phenomena but reinforce each other: climate change accelerates species loss, while the degradation of ecosystems, in turn, reduces the Earth's ability to store $CO_2$.

The world is undergoing a period of profound ecological change. Climate change is currently considered one of the most significant global challenges, with not only ecological but also social and economic consequences. Since the beginning of industrialization, a significant increase in the concentration of greenhouse gases in the atmosphere has been observed, leading to a continuous rise in global average temperatures. The increase in extreme weather events such as droughts, floods, and heat waves is significant in frequency and intensity. This results in substantial damage to infrastructure, agriculture, and human health.

At the same time, biodiversity loss is progressing at an alarming rate. According to the Global Assessment Report of the World Biodiversity Council (IPBES), around one million species are threatened with extinction, with a significant proportion of these species likely to be wiped out within a few decades. The loss of biodiversity undermines the stability of ecosystems and impairs vital functions such as pollination, water purification, and climate regulation. Climate change and biodiversity loss are not isolated phenomena but reinforce each other: climate change accelerates species loss, while the degradation of ecosystems, in turn, reduces the Earth's ability to store $CO_2$.

Despite the existence of many international agreements—from the United Nations Framework Convention on Climate Change (UNFCCC) and the Convention on Biological Diversity (CBD) to the Paris Agreement—the progress has not met the targets set. Global emissions are on a steady rise, and measures to restore ecosystems and halt species extinction often remain local and underfunded. The need for effective and innovative solutions has, therefore, become more pressing than ever. This situation underscores the importance of each individual's role in finding and implementing these solutions.

In light of this, market-based instruments are becoming increasingly relevant as complementary to traditional regulatory instruments. Making ecological services such as emission reductions or biodiversity protection tradable is based on the assumption that markets can enable more efficient allocation and additional investment. Instead of relying solely on government regulation or voluntary commitments, economic incentives that integrate climate and nature protection into market-based processes should be created.

Carbon credits, which certify and make tradable savings or reductions in CO2 emissions, have established themselves as one of the best-known instruments in this context. They are used in mandatory emissions trading systems, such as the EU ETS, and voluntary markets. In addition, similar concepts are becoming increasingly relevant in biodiversity protection. Biodiversity credits aim to mobilize investment in measures to preserve or restore biological diversity while delivering precise, measurable environmental results.

Market-based approaches promise several advantages: On the one hand, they could activate significant private financial resources for environmental and climate protection. On the other hand, they could enable flexible and cost-effective solutions and stimulate innovation. At the same time, however, they are associated with considerable risks. Lack of transparency, inadequate regulation, greenwashing, and the risk of social injustice, especially in countries in the Global South, pose significant challenges. In addition, further research is needed on the extent to which markets are suitable for adequately reflecting complex, non-monetary environmental values.

This article pursues several key research questions arising from this tension.

- What structural opportunities and limitations do carbon and biodiversity credits offer for environmental and climate protection?
- What risks and conflicts of interest arise from the monetization of ecological goods?
- Under what conditions can market-based instruments contribute to sustainable transformation rather than exacerbating existing environmental problems?

This article aims to analyze the potential of market-based approaches in a differentiated manner and show how carbon and biodiversity markets can be designed to combine ecological effectiveness, economic efficiency, and social justice. In this process, both theoretical concepts and practical experience are taken into account to develop a well-founded and practice-oriented picture of the topic. Particular attention is paid to the interactions between carbon and biodiversity markets and to the question of how synergies can be maximized and conflicts of interest minimized.

In terms of methodology, the article combines a theoretical and conceptual analysis with an empirical examination of case studies. The first step systematically elaborates on the theoretical foundations of carbon and biodiversity credits, including their history, mechanisms, incentive structures, and challenges. This process integrates environmental economics, political science, and sustainability research findings.

In the second step, empirical case studies reflecting concrete experiences from different regions of the world are evaluated. The present study considers case examples such as a reforestation project in Brazil, biodiversity conservation measures in Indonesia, and multifunctional ecosystem projects in Africa. It examines their ecological effectiveness, social impacts, and economic efficiency. The aim is to identify success factors and obstacles and draw conclusions for the future design of market-based environmental instruments.

The article combines theoretical reflection and empirical evidence to provide an analytical assessment and concrete impetus for politics, business, and civil society. The goal is to responsibly and effectively unleash the transformative power of environmental markets.

This article aims to contribute to the scientific and political debate on the role of market-based instruments in global environmental management. To this end, a structured approach has been chosen. In this context, particular emphasis is placed on presenting both the theoretical foundations and the practical challenges in a differentiated manner and deriving concrete recommendations for action for the design of sustainable environmental markets.

The following section begins with an overview of how carbon markets work and their importance for climate protection (Section 2), followed by an analysis of biodiversity markets' specific mechanisms and challenges (Section 3). Section 4 discusses the synergies and conflicts between the two approaches. Section 5 uses case studies to provide in-depth insights into practical implementation. Section 6 brings together the institutional prerequisites and equity issues that underpin biodiversity and carbon markets, linking governance design with political feasibility. Finally, Section 7 discusses ethical, political, and regulatory implications before summarizing key findings and formulating concrete recommendations for action (Section 7).

## 2. CARBON MARKETS: HOW THEY WORK, OPPORTUNITIES AND CHALLENGES

### 2.1 Basic Principles of Carbon Credits

Carbon credits are tradable certificates that confirm that a certain amount of greenhouse gas emissions—usually measured in tons of carbon dioxide equivalent ($tCO_2e$)—have been saved, avoided, or sequestered. The underlying principle is based on the premise that emissions generated in one place can be offset by reductions elsewhere. The underlying logic is the global nature of climate change. Since greenhouse gases are distributed evenly in the atmosphere, it is initially irrelevant from a climatic viewpoint where emission reductions occur.

Carbon credits typically arise from projects that either avoid emissions (e.g., through the expansion of renewable energies) or sequester carbon (e.g., through reforestation). After successful verification, these services are certified as certificates and traded on markets. Buyers of carbon credits can either fulfill legal emission obligations or enter into voluntary climate protection commitments.

The central promise of carbon markets lies in their efficiency. They are intended to open up more cost-effective reduction options and direct investment to where it will have the most significant impact. In addition, they offer companies a flexible way to meet emission targets or credibly underpin their climate strategies.

### A Simple Model of a Carbon Credit

According to the definition, a carbon credit represents one ton of carbon dioxide equivalents ($CO_2$ equivalents) that have either been avoided or sequestered. The central idea behind this analysis is to compare a project's actual emissions with hypothetical emissions without the project.

Formally, a carbon credit can be modeled as follows:

$$carbon\ credit = baseline\ emissions - actual\ emssions$$

where:

- Baseline emissions ($E_{\text{base}}$): the emissions that would be generated without the project
- Actual emissons ($E_{\text{actual}}$): the emissions that are actually generated by the project

$$CC = E_{base} - E_{actual}$$

A carbon credit (CC) is awarded when:

$$CC \geq 1\ tCO2e$$

In a simple example, it is assumed that without a reforestation project, 500 tons of $CO_2e$ would be released annually (e.g., through degradation, lack of sequestration). The project results in an emission reduction of only 200 tons of $CO_2e$ or the sequestration of carbon.

This results in:

$$CC = 500\, tCO2e - 200\, tCO2e = 300\, tCO2e$$

The project can generate 300 carbon credits.

In real certifications, other factors are often taken into account:

- Leakage factor ($L$): Emissions displaced outside the project area
- Buffer factor ($B$): Safety margins for risks (e.g., forest fires)
- Durability ($D$): Reduction if the sequestration is only temporary.

The formula then becomes more complex:

$$CC_{adj} = (E_{base} - E_{actual})\,(1 - L)\,(1 - B)$$

Example with factors:

- Leakage: 10% ($L = 0.1$)
- Buffer: 20% ($B = 0.2$)

Then:

$$CC_{adj} = 300\,(1 - 0.1)\,(1 - 0.2) = 300\ 0.9\ 0.8 = 216\, tCO2e$$

The project could issue 216 carbon credits.

Jones et al. (2024) have made a significant contribution to our understanding of carbon sequestration through nature conservation measures, particularly in the Dorset region (United Kingdom). Their empirical findings demonstrate that the cost per additional ton of carbon sequestered varies significantly depending on the nature conservation project. On average, the cost of this offsetting in the nature conservation projects we examined is £80 per ton of CO2e, with a range of £120 to £0 depending on the project and the availability of existing biodiversity grants. However, this figure is based on the adaptation and refinement of existing nature conservation projects. It does not consider costly factors such as land purchase, which make prices potentially unrealistic, particularly in the context of the Global North. Combining this approach with biodiversity credits or other credit programs could make the higher costs more attractive to potential buyers (Section 3.1).

## 2.2 Certification and Trading Mechanisms

Carbon credits, a crucial tool in the fight against climate change, are not created automatically. They must undergo a rigorous certification process to ensure their credibility and effectiveness. This process is a key step in the creation of carbon credits. When it comes to carbon markets, two main types can be distinguished: mandatory (compliance markets) and voluntary (voluntary markets).

The term' mandatory markets' is defined in the relevant literature by legal frameworks. A prominent example is the European Emissions Trading System (EU ETS), where companies are allocated fixed emission caps, which are the maximum amount of greenhouse gases they are allowed to emit. Companies can buy or sell emission allowances, which are permits that allow them to emit a certain amount of greenhouse gases. They can also use certified carbon credits from recognized projects to fulfill part of their obligations, for example, through mechanisms such as the Clean Development Mechanism (CDM) under the Kyoto Protocol.

Voluntary Carbon Markets (VCMs) provide a platform for companies, organizations, and individuals who are committed to climate protection beyond legal requirements. These entities can take proactive steps to offset their emissions by purchasing voluntary carbon credits (VCCs). This not only helps them meet their climate protection commitments but also contributes to the global effort to reduce greenhouse gas emissions.

VCCs are issued globally by various certification bodies, known as 'carbon standards.' These bodies are subject to specific regulations, such as the requirement that CO2 reduction projects must demonstrate that the reductions or removals of greenhouse gases are real, measurable, permanent, additive, independently verified, unique, and traceable. In addition, proof must be provided that adequate safeguards are in place to evaluate and mitigate potential environmental or social impacts of the project. Projects are assessed using the methodology established by the respective certification body. Once a project has been certified, tradable VCCs are issued for each tCO2e reduced or removed, which are then sold on the open market (Koumpli, 2024).

Certification processes usually comprise several stages:

- Project design and methodology selection,
- Independent validation,
- Monitoring and reporting,
- Independent verification of results, and
- Issuance and trading of credits.

VCCs are recorded in central registration systems—known as 'registries'—subject to different rules. The registry tracks the creation, issuance, transfer, withdrawal, and deletion of VCCs. Since VCCs are issued for a specific project with specific characteristics, such as the type of emission reduction, the location of the project, and the social and environmental benefits it provides, these factors directly impact the quality of the resulting VCCs and the price at which they are marketed. According to Koumpli (2024), a VCC is permanently delisted after it has been canceled or withdrawn. Therefore, trading in the VCC and using it to offset further emissions is no longer possible.

The quality of a carbon credit depends heavily on the rigor of the processes implemented, particularly the criteria of additionality, permanence, and avoidance of double counting (Section 2.4). Avoidance of double counting is a principle that ensures the same emission reduction is not counted more than once. This is important to maintain the integrity of the carbon market and to accurately reflect the actual emissions reductions achieved.

The commercialization of emission allowances, which is essential for reducing emissions, requires accurate forecasts of the carbon price. These forecasts must consider the significant impact of climate change and extreme weather events on the demand for energy and emission allowances (Xie et al., 2022). The more we understand and anticipate these impacts, the better we can plan and manage our emissions reduction strategies.

## 2.3 Examples of Applications

Carbon credit projects are characterized by a high degree of content diversity. The present study covers the following typical applications in terms of content and location.

Given global warming, the afforestation and reforestation of forests, whose importance for carbon sequestration and preserving biodiversity is becoming increasingly evident, is gaining importance. These projects involve sequestering carbon dioxide ($CO_2$) by planting new forests or restoring degraded areas. Projects such as REDD+ (Reducing Emissions from Deforestation and Forest Degradation) typically combine carbon sequestration with biodiversity protection and social development. In Japan, however, where around 40 percent of the land area consists of production forests, this situation is an exception. The economic basis for forest management is under threat in the regions concerned. On the one hand, it is due to the decline in demand for wood and, on the other hand, to increasing competitive pressure from imports. It results in a reduction in the maintenance function of forests and an increased risk of disasters. Akita and Ohe (2021) use Japan as an example to analyze the potential of carbon credits to finance a conservation approach in which degraded production forests are converted into ecologically more valuable environmental forests. The analysis of carbon stocks shows that investments in conservation measures pay for themselves in the long term, even at low certificate prices, with a break-even point after around 30 years. This finding underscores the potential of carbon credits to not only enhance ecological value but also ensure economic viability, offering a hopeful outlook for the future of sustainability.

This study focuses on renewable energy projects and energy efficiency measures. Expanding wind, solar, and hydroelectric power plants is an important measure for replacing fossil fuel sources and contributing to reducing $CO_2$ emissions. These projects are particularly important in developing and emerging countries, where they are seen as a fundamental bridge to a sustainable energy supply. Initiatives such as improved cooking stoves and building efficiency programs reduce energy demand and, thus, emissions, paving the way for a more sustainable future.

Carbon capture and storage (CCS) technologies are crucial for reducing residual emissions. They include methods for directly removing $CO_2$ from the atmosphere and for industrial capture and underground storage of the resulting gas. Such projects can generate carbon credits, and while they are still in the early stages of scaling up and cost calculation, their potential for significant emission reduction is promising.

The diversity of projects demonstrates the flexibility of carbon markets but also creates challenges. Lininger and Lave (2024) doubt whether carbon credits for river corridors would meet market requirements for quickly generated, stable, and simple credits. The argument is based on the premise that biophysical and political-economic uncertainties call into question the validity of carbon credits for the restoration of river corridors. The present study examines the spatial-temporal patterns of verified emission credit projects.

This analysis examines verified emission credit projects' spatial and temporal patterns from 2004 to 2022. The Gold Standard Foundation's registry provides the data for this analysis. Empirical evidence shows that South Asia and East Africa are significantly relevant for emission credit projects. The primary epicenters shifted from China, Brazil, Peru, Panama, and Cambodia (2004–2016) to India, Kenya, Rwanda, and Uganda (2017–2022), with Turkey remaining a hotspot. The analysis provides evidence of spatial clustering of projects.

## 2.4 Key Challenges

Carbon market programs serve as a tool for project developers to obtain carbon credits by reducing carbon dioxide emissions through emission reduction projects. However, concerns have also been raised about environmental integrity. Many individual studies conclude that in many voluntary climate protection projects, the actual emission reductions are either greatly overestimated or no measurable reductions can be demonstrated. West et al. (2023) analyzed the impact of 27 forest protection projects in six countries and found that most projects did not reduce deforestation. In addition, the reductions were significantly lower than those claimed by the projects. Others point out that disclosures can serve as a form of carbon and greenwashing when companies deliberately or selectively communicate information that does not correspond to the actual environmental impact (In & Schumacher, 2021).

Probst et al. (2024) conducted a pivotal overview study that examined the actual compensation effect of CO2 certificates across a wide range of common project types. Their comprehensive analysis of 64,000 potentially relevant studies identified 65, from which quantitative data on actual emission reductions were extracted and analyzed. The studies considered in this paper are all based on rigorous experimental or observation-based methods. The authors examine both specific CO2 compensation projects and emission reduction measures without focusing on the issuance of certificates. The studies were selected based on specific quality criteria.

Projects must also be classified as 'additional,' a crucial classification that ensures the emission reductions achieved by the certificate are realized exclusively through its sale. The term 'additionality' describes the condition that emission reductions may only be credited if they would not have occurred without financing from the carbon market. If additionality is lacking, the purchase of credits does not improve climate protection but merely legitimizes existing emissions ('greenwashing'). Verifying additionality is methodologically challenging and subject to uncertainty. The criterion can be estimated more reliably using statistical methods developed in economics and healthcare over many decades. In this context, it is essential to eliminate discrepancies in estimating the counterfactual scenario, i.e., the hypothetical development without intervention.

This study focuses on the aspect of permanence. Finally, the CO2 credit system requires more robust methods to account for the volatility of carbon in vegetation and soils. The risk of a possible revision of emission reductions must be addressed. One example of a potential scenario is the cancellation of CO2 credits generated from forest protection measures due to a forest fire. Projects based on natural sinks such as forests are particularly exposed to potential risks such as fires, pest infestation, or illegal deforestation. Such events can lead to previously stored emissions being rereleased, potentially jeopardizing the long-term climate impact. Insurance solutions, risk buffers, and long-term monitoring are intended to mitigate these risks but have not yet been implemented across the board (Fiegenbaum, 2024). Current certification methods aim to ensure the longevity of credits by providing a shared pool of non-tradable credits that can be drawn upon in the event of reversals. However, this system does not incentivize future actors to prevent carbon releases after issuing credits.

Under the current rules, double counting is prohibited. It means that each carbon credit can only be used by one party. An emission reduction cannot be credited to the buyer of the credit and to the greenhouse gas balance of the country of origin to avoid double counting. An example of possible double counting would be if both the country of origin of a project and the purchaser of a carbon credit claim the same reduction for themselves. International initiatives, such as the 'corresponding adjustments' under Article 6 of the Paris Agreement, aim to prevent double counting.

Regarding resource allocation, there is uncertainty about the distribution of costs and benefits of CO2 offset projects among stakeholders and decision-making. Furthermore, it should be noted that Indigenous peoples or local communities have rarely or insufficiently been integrated into the process (Antonelli et al., 2024).

Probst et al. (2024) analysis covers about one-fifth of the total amount of CO2 certificates issued globally, corresponding to nearly one billion tons of CO2 emissions. The offset achievement ratio compares the number of certificates issued with estimates from independent studies. An offset achievement ratio of 100 percent means that a certificate for one ton of CO2 has avoided that amount of greenhouse gas; at a rate of 50 percent, only half was avoided. The evaluation of many offset projects, which exceeded the 2,000 mark, revealed that less than 16 percent of the CO2 certificates analyzed represent actual emission reductions. The analysis showed that the lowest avoidance rates were recorded in wind power projects and improved forestry. However, no statistically significant emission reductions could be demonstrated for either type of project (offset achievement ratio of 0%). The analysis showed that none of the project types examined could demonstrate actual emission reductions on average equal to the certificates issued. The projects examined in this context, which are dedicated to wind power and improved forestry, did not produce any measurable results. In contrast, industrial measures to reduce the greenhouse gas HFC-23 achieved the best results, with an avoidance rate of 68 percent.

Trencher et al. (2024) analyzed twenty companies that withdrew the most offsets from the voluntary CO2 market between 2020 and 2023. The analysis is based on a dataset at the company level to measure quality and climate benefits using four dimensions: (1) use of offsets from low/high-risk project types; (2) age of projects and credits; (3) price of credits; and (4) country of implementation. It was found that companies predominantly purchased offsets in low-quality and low-cost forms. It was found that 87 percent of the projects examined are at high risk of not achieving significant additional emission reductions. Analysis of the offsets revealed that most of these payments are from forest protection and renewable energy projects.

The debate on the quality of CO2 certificates often overlooks that heterogeneous quality and uncertainty are inherent characteristics of CO2 projects. CO2 certificates are intangible goods whose accounting must be considered imperfect. The success of CO2 offset markets depends partly on accepting this imperfection rather than concealing or ignoring it. Cabiyo and Field (2025) propose that CO2 offset markets need new mechanisms considering iterative methodological improvements in allocating CO2 certificates. The authors of this paper believe that potential measures could include various insurance-like mechanisms, guarantees, and ex-post adjustment mechanisms. Such instruments act as guarantors that the credits issued deliver on their promises. This principle has already been applied to credit registries' withdrawal of carbon credits. In practice, corresponding solutions exist in insurance products, buffer pools, or discounted credit portfolios.

The study's results suggest significant quality problems with CO2 certificates and that the information on climate neutrality and net-zero targets based on these certificates is highly likely inaccurate. An analysis of the available data shows that several systemic problems can be traced back to the following leading causes (Probst et al., 2024):

- Unrealistic assumptions: Project developers make assumptions that overestimate actual emission reductions.
- Outdated or selective data: Outdated or selected data to maximize the number of credits issued is used.
- Methodological weaknesses: Incorrect calculations and insufficient verification lead to incorrect emission reduction results.

In addition, the procedures for issuing emission credits need to be optimized to consider the risk of increased emissions elsewhere adequately. The analysis shows that initiating a CO2 compensation project can prevent the production of food or wood. As a result, this production and its CO2 impact can be shifted to another location. Most assessments of this 'displacement' of CO2 emissions focus on rough estimates of smaller displacements and significantly neglect or underestimate the longer-term displacement of production. There is little evidence that current practices to combat displacement effects are practical. In this context, Filewod and McCarney (2023) present empirical evidence suggesting that the effects of displacement are significantly underestimated in business practice. The critics' argument is based on the assumption that current efforts to improve accounting methods will not provide the necessary accuracy. They, therefore, propose an alternative approach to avoid displacement effects from the outset. This approach is based on a new conceptual framework for understanding displacement effects in nature-based measures. Recently, new methods have been developed to optimize the consideration of displacement effects and to adequately evaluate temporary storage (Balmford et al., 2023).

Market programs, in particular, are called upon to improve the quality of certificates. The methodology for reviewing projects and calculating emission reductions is recommended to be significantly optimized. It is important here that conservative assumptions are made and that the latest scientific findings serve as a basis. In addition, independent review mechanisms are needed to increase the credibility and effectiveness of the measures.

## 2.5 Current Regulatory Approaches and Reform Proposals

In view of these challenges, various efforts are being made to optimize the design of carbon markets in terms of robustness, transparency, and effectiveness. At the international level, Article 6 of the Paris Agreement establishes a new framework for international trade in emission reductions. This framework aims to ensure both the integrity of the markets and the national climate targets (Nationally Determined Contributions, NDCs). It includes, in particular, requirements to avoid double counting, increased transparency requirements, and robust accounting rules.

Simultaneously, the role of standard-setters such as Verra, Gold Standard, and others is gaining significance. These entities are developing increasingly stringent project requirements, instilling a sense of confidence in the credibility of the carbon market. New initiatives like the Integrity Council for the Voluntary Carbon Market (ICVCM) are developing global quality standards and benchmarks to professionalize the voluntary market and prevent greenwashing, further enhancing the market's integrity.

Government regulations are also becoming increasingly relevant. Countries such as Colombia, South Korea, and New Zealand are pursuing hybrid approaches that integrate voluntary and mandatory markets and set national minimum standards for carbon credits. As part of revising climate policy in the European Union, discussions are underway on how voluntary compensation measures can be integrated into a coherent overall system.

Future reforms will need to focus primarily on the following areas:

- Stricter and more uniform requirements for additionality, permanence, and avoidance of double-counting;
- Improved transparency and traceability through digital technologies such as blockchain;
- Integration of social and environmental co-benefits into the assessment and pricing of carbon credits, and
- Stronger integration of voluntary markets with government climate strategies.

Analysis of the available data underscores a critical point: only a comprehensive reform program, implemented with urgency, will enable carbon markets to realize their full potential as an effective tool for climate protection.

# 3. BIODIVERSITY MARKETS: CONCEPTS, POTENTIAL, AND CHALLENGES

## 3.1 Basic Principles of Biodiversity Credits

Biodiversity credits are a mechanism highlighted in the Global Biodiversity Framework that could help generate private funds and ensure that these funds are used for verifiable nature conservation and restoration outcomes. Biodiversity credits are a mechanism highlighted in the Global Biodiversity Framework that could help generate private funds and ensure that these funds are used for verifiable conservation and restoration outcomes. The purchase of these credits by companies enables achieving the following goals: It is hypothesized that companies, regardless of their own activities, could contribute to improving global biodiversity. It could lead to a strengthening of the company's profile and marketing. Secondly, after assessing their environmental impact and taking all measures to avoid or minimize damage, companies could compensate for any remaining damage similarly. This means the credits they purchase would have to finance remediation measures in the exact location and ecosystem where the damage occurred. Finally, organizations can invest in measures to increase biodiversity and resilience in their supply chains (Antonelli et al., 2024).

The underlying mechanisms are similar. Projects that demonstrably increase biodiversity—whether through the restoration of destroyed habitats or the protection of endangered species—are recognized through certification. The credits generated in this way can then be traded on a virtual market. Buyers of these credits thereby offset negative impacts on biodiversity, for example, in the context of construction projects or agricultural use (Antonelli et al., 2024).

Biodiversity credits can take three different forms. A central approach to managing biodiversity-related interventions is known as no-net-loss systems. These are based on the principle that equivalent measures must fully offset losses in biodiversity caused by economic or infrastructural measures. The aim is to maintain biodiversity at a stable level despite growing land use demands from settlement construction, agriculture, or infrastructure projects. In practice, this means that project developers are obliged to offset biodiversity losses—such as those caused by habitat destruction or species decline—through protection, restoration, or replacement measures elsewhere. The equivalence and permanence of the measures are key requirements: the compensated habitats must be as close as possible to the original habitat in terms of quality, extent, and ecological function and be secured in the long term. Critics argue that true equivalence is often difficult to guarantee, especially when complex or rare ecosystems are involved. Nevertheless, no-net-loss systems provide an important regulatory basis for keeping anthropogenic pressure on natural habitats within controllable limits.

Net gain programs go one step further: they require project developers to preserve biodiversity and actively improve it. A prominent example is the UK's Biodiversity Net Gain program, introduced in February 2024, which requires all new construction projects to achieve at least a 10 percent net improvement in biodiversity. The assessment is based on standardized ecological criteria such as the size, type, and quality of the habitats affected and their strategic importance—for example, in terms of species richness or conservation value. The UK is thus setting new standards for the mandatory integration of biodiversity targets into spatial planning and demonstrating that ambitious policy frameworks can play a key role in strengthening nature-based approaches. In February 2024, for example, the UK government introduced a program called 'Biodiversity Net Gain,' which requires all new construction projects to achieve a net gain in biodiversity of 10 percent (measured by the size, type, condition, and strategic importance of the habitats affected, based on information such as species richness and rarity).

Another format is 'Payments for Ecosystem Services' (PES). In this context, 'market-based incentive systems' refer to rewarding land users for maintaining ecosystem services. This study examines the issue of the amount of revenue from the sale of credits that flows to rights holders. Currently, some biodiversity credit systems guarantee that 60–80 percent of the profits from the sale of credits flow back to the rights holders, while other systems do not specify such a percentage. The present findings suggest that precise wording is needed to substantiate buyers' claims regarding the 'high integrity' of credits and to ensure a mutually agreed fair return for rights holders (Clifton & Schwerdtner Mánez, 2025).

It is essential to remember that biodiversity credits are always linked to local or regional ecological conditions. This leads to significantly greater complexity in terms of transferability and standardization compared to carbon markets.

## A Simple Model of a Biodiversity Credit

$$BC = B = B_{actual} - B_{base}$$

where:

- $B_{base}$: Biodiversity index at the beginning (e.g., species diversity, habitat quality)
- $B_{actual}$: Biodiversity index after implementation of the project
- $B$: Net improvement in biodiversity

The hypothesis is that a project's biodiversity can be measured using a biodiversity index such as the Shannon index or a simple species count.

- Before the project $B_{base}$: 30 Arten
- After the project $B_{actual}$: 45 Arten

Then:

$B = 45 - 30 = 15$

Depending on the system, you could then define, for example:

- 1 BC = Net increase of 1 species
- Or more complex: 1 BC = increase by x points on a biodiversity index

Here, the project would generate 15 biodiversity credits.

In many projects, biodiversity is not only measured by the number of species, but also weighted according to:

- Threat status (e.g., red list species count more)
- Functional importance (e.g., pollinator species are more important than others)
- Habitat quality

The formula can then be expanded to:

$$BC = \sum_{i=1}^{n} w_i (B_{i\,actual} - B_{i\,base})$$

with:

- $w_i$ for weighting factor for species/habitat
- $B_i$ for species/habitat status

It is possible to prioritize improvements for endangered species more than for common species.

The challenge lies in biodiversity encompassing a wide range of factors (number of species, genetic diversity, habitat quality), making it necessary to develop indicators or indices for quantification. The definition of a biodiversity credit depends on the measure chosen for biodiversity. Projects are often required to achieve a minimum value, such as 'no net loss.' Monitoring and verification are crucially important, as natural fluctuations occur.

## 3.2 Comparison with Carbon Credits

The predominant focus on carbon sequestration, a key objective of most carbon-oriented credit and offset commitments, often leads to the establishment of non-native, fast-growing monocultures. These monocultures can be detrimental to biodiversity and soil-related ecosystem services, a significant contributor to global biodiversity and home to traces of above-ground organisms (Tedersoo et al., 2024).

To ensure that biodiversity credits direct the necessary financial flows into nature conservation and restoration and that the work on the ground is practical, governments and companies establishing biodiversity credit markets must ensure that the problems arising in emissions credit markets are avoided. In addition, it is essential to ensure the conditions for biodiversity credit markets to function effectively. For companies purchasing biodiversity credits, purchasing biodiversity credits should be a way to channel funds into long-term conservation and restoration initiatives rather than as a quick sale to generate profits. An example of this type of sale is cap-and-trade systems, in which a limited supply of carbon credits can become valuable commodities (Antonelli et al., 2024).

It is essential to understand that the impact of one ton of CO2 is consistent regardless of its release location, whereas the effects of biodiversity damage can vary significantly depending on the specific location. For instance, if a company causes damage to a rainforest in Borneo, any biodiversity credits it purchases to offset this damage must fund equivalent protection and restoration measures in the same ecosystem. This local impact and responsibility are crucial in biodiversity credit markets (Antonelli et al., 2024).

Carbon credits are based on a globally uniform, physically clearly defined unit (one ton of $CO_2e$), whereas biodiversity is a multidimensional, difficult-to-quantify asset. Differences arise in several aspects:

- It should be noted that $CO_2$ emissions can be measured with high precision and that continuous monitoring is also possible. Biodiversity, conversely, encompasses aspects such as species diversity, genetic diversity, functional ecosystem services, and complex interactions that are difficult to standardize.
- The carbon market benefits from internationally recognized protocols and standards. However, in the field of biodiversity, there are currently no globally uniform standards. Projects are usually based on local ecological assessments and individual objectives.
- Temporal stability is an essential aspect to consider when analyzing $CO_2$ storage. While $CO_2$ storage is theoretically measurable in the long term, gains in biodiversity can be much more dynamic. Population dynamics are subject to natural fluctuations that can be influenced by external factors such as climate

change or the spread of invasive species. This can impair the effectiveness of protective measures.

- Carbon credits are evaluated economically through market mechanisms. The assessment of $CO_2$ as a pollutant contributes to a consistent evaluation. On the other hand, biodiversity's economic value is highly context-dependent and difficult to convert into monetary value.

*Table 1. Comparison of carbon credits vs. biodiversity credits*

| Criterion | Carbon credits | Biodiversity credits |
|---|---|---|
| Objectives | Reduction or offsetting of greenhouse gas emissions | Preservation and restoration of biological diversity |
| Measurability | Highly standardizable ($CO_2$ equivalents) | Complex, multidimensional measurement (number of species, habitats, indices) |
| Standardization | Well established (e.g., Verra, Gold Standard, EU ETS) | Still inconsistent, fragmented approaches |
| Market types | Mandatory and voluntary markets | Mainly voluntary markets and compensation schemes |
| Project examples | Reforestation, renewable energies, CCS | Habitat restoration, species protection, nature-friendly agriculture |
| Verification/certification | Predominantly standardized and verified by third parties | Inconsistent, often context-dependent |
| Additionality measurable? | Relatively easy to assess | More difficult to verify |
| Long-term impact | Dependent on the permanence of $CO_2$ storage | Dependent on ecosystem dynamics and management |
| Risks | Greenwashing, carbonwashing, double counting, temporary $CO_2$ storage | Ecological ineffectiveness, social conflicts, measurement problems |
| Price dynamics | Comparatively well developed, volatile | Little price transparency, highly context-dependent |
| Synergy potential | High for nature-based solutions (NbS) | High if biodiversity measures also sequester carbon |
| Typical actors | Energy companies, airlines, financial investors | Nature conservation organizations, NGOs, foundations, public authorities |
| Regulatory framework | EU ETS, CORSIA, national climate policies | Pilot projects, biodiversity banking, sectoral regulations |
| Future prospects | Growing importance due to climate targets and $CO_2$ pricing | Growing interest, but still in institutional development |

The biodiversity market is currently more fragmented, less standardized, and more complex in its operational implementation than the carbon market (Table 1).

## 3.3 Typical Projects

Significantly, research findings by Clifton and Schwerdtner Mánez reveal that the majority (93%) of biodiversity credit projects are concentrated on terrestrial ecosystems. In contrast, only 5 percent are dedicated to marine ecosystems, with the remaining 2 percent focusing on both terrestrial and marine ecosystems.

An exemplary instance of biodiversity credits in action is the orangutan conservation program in Borneo. This program not only secures the habitat of these endangered species but also promotes their genetic preservation, thereby serving as a model for other conservation projects.

Research is focusing, in particular, on restoring degraded ecosystems. Various measures are being taken to this end, including the renaturation of wetlands, the reforestation of near-natural forests, and the recultivation of fallow land. These measures not only contribute to improving biodiversity but also strengthen ecosystem services such as water retention, soil protection, and pollination.

Innovative biodiversity projects integrate conservation goals into existing agricultural systems, for example, through agroecology, mixed cropping, or extensive grazing management. In this context, biodiversity is promoted without jeopardizing the economic basis of local communities. A prominent example is promoting traditional farming systems such as the dehesa in Spain, which combine economic use with high biodiversity.

Marine ecosystems hold immense potential for providing carbon and biodiversity credits. The high carbon sequestration rates of mangroves and seagrass, coupled with the importance of reversing biodiversity decline in crucial ecosystems such as coral reefs and mangroves, present inspiring opportunities for the future (Shefy et al., 2025).

## 3.4 Problem Areas

Five aspects must be taken into account when establishing biodiversity credits. It is up to the stakeholders to measure biodiversity and nature in order to select providers of credits or other instruments, set standards, or determine which standards should be adopted. Measuring biodiversity is proving to be much more complex than measuring CO2 emissions. The term encompasses various aspects, including genetic, taxonomic, functional, evolutionary, and ecosystem diversity. It should be noted that these aspects can be assessed in different ways. Taxonomic diversity is assessed by counting the number of species in an area or, more narrowly, the number of genera. To date, more than 570 measures of biodiversity have been proposed, and standards for monitoring biodiversity continue to be discussed at the international and national levels. It should also be noted that human assessment of biodiversity depends on the species or ecosystem in question and the geographical and cultural context. Another aspect that complicates the situation is that habitat regeneration can take several decades. This makes it difficult to measure a project's actual or potential impact. However, the reassurance comes from the fact that long-term monitoring is not just needed, but a necessary part of the process. It is possible to balance technical precision and practical applicability (Antonelli et al., 2024).

The most important decisions in this process are (WEF & McKinsey, 2024):

- Should practices or results be measured?
- What type(s) of metrics should be used?
- How aggregated should the metrics be?
- How should changes in metrics be quantified?

One of the biggest challenges is to measure biodiversity reliably and quantify changes robustly. Various approaches exist:

- Species indicators: Counting or monitoring key species or species diversity (e.g., bird counts).
- Habitat quality: Assessment of the quality and extent of habitats.
- Ecosystem services: Indirect measurement via functions such as pollination or water filtration.

Biodiversity manifests itself as a spatially heterogeneous and temporally variable phenomenon. Selecting appropriate indicators and implementing robust reference values ('baselines') are essential but difficult to achieve.

The metrics presented below are currently used in the biodiversity credit markets. Burgess et al. (2024) identified 573 biodiversity-related metrics, indicators, indices, and levels in a database that address aspects of genetic diversity, species, and ecosystems. A significant proportion of the findings were found to be relevant beyond the scope of credits. This is because the analysis focuses on measuring nature and biodiversity rather than the credits themselves. This study identifies three metrics-based models (WEF & McKinsey, 2024).

The comprehensive aggregate model uses composite metrics based on various direct measurements. The aim is to capture a holistic and accurate picture of biodiversity, which is summarized in a single metric or a few metrics. Static or dynamic base values can be used. In the present study, for example, the change in the average long-term global survival probability of species is used as a metric, as described by Rossberg et al. (2024).

The second model, the 'critical indicator model,' also uses direct measurements. Unlike the first model, which aims to create a composite, the critical indicator model relies on fewer discrete metrics. These metrics are representative of overall biodiversity. The focus is on using static baseline values.

The mosaic compilation model is an approach that uses multiple measurements and metrics to capture biodiversity or other factors such as pollutants and socioeconomic factors. The goal is to create a customized and comprehensive picture of an ecosystem and its environment (including neighboring societies). Static or dynamic baseline values can be used.

These models are not exhaustive but serve to segment the space and facilitate discussion. The three models were derived from surveying 32 methods for capturing biodiversity credits. The methods were defined by project developers who measure biodiversity for their credits or by (prospective) credit standard setters.

Ecosystem services and biodiversity are typically measured using field-level indicators. However, it should be noted that various significant agricultural and economic factors and agroecological measures operate at higher levels. As a result, field-level indicators need to be scaled up. In this paper, Klaus et al. (2024) present a range of options for scaling up ecosystem services and biodiversity indicators from the field to the farm level. These options are discussed and debated in a detailed analysis. The proposals focus on making field-level data available for aggregation at the farm level. Such aggregation must take into account the relationship between the supply of ecosystem services and the resulting benefits, i.e., the supply-benefit relationship, which describes how a change in supply affects the resulting benefits for farmers and/or society. The argument is based on the premise that this relationship can also be transferred to biodiversity, whereby the benefit of a field or farm for biodiversity conservation is considered the decisive factor. Since the benefits often do not increase continuously with supply but may exhibit breakpoints defined by supply thresholds, the supply-benefit relationship varies between ecosystem services and biodiversity components. For the upscaling of biodiversity indicators, for example, a conservation value must be taken into account that considers that the conservation benefit may not change linearly with supply, i.e., the quality and quantity of habitats, and becomes marginal below certain thresholds. Considering such potential thresholds is a prerequisite for selecting a suitable upscaling approach from those presented in this paper. The definitions provided here are a fundamental prerequisite for accurately determining biodiversity credits.

While carbon credits are typically established for 20 to 100 years, biodiversity protection is an even longer-term endeavor. Biodiversity gains can be lost if protected areas are abandoned or management measures are discontinued. Therefore, mechanisms for long-term financing and monitoring are not just necessary, but crucial. Trust funds or commitments to follow-up measures over several decades can be established for this purpose, ensuring the sustainability of biodiversity protection.

Biodiversity projects often raise questions about land rights, resource use, and local populations' traditional ways of life. Inadequate involvement can lead to conflicts, displacement, or inequalities. Therefore, successful projects are characterized by early and fair participation, recognition of traditional land rights, equitable distribution of benefits and compensation, and cultural sensitivity. In this context, Indigenous communities can be seen both as important partners and as potentially disadvantaged groups in biodiversity projects (Schwerdtner Mánez & Clifton, 2025).

The Biodiversity Credit Market (BCM), which is currently in the development phase, aims to promote biodiversity financing but reflects the inconsistencies of the carbon credit market. To ensure its success, it is essential that it primarily uses dynamic reference values with control sites and that credits are awarded through an independent, transparent, and cost-efficient validation process (Mitchell Aide, 2024).

## 3.5 Regulatory Framework and Need for Reform

The regulation of biodiversity credits, a system that quantifies the value of biodiversity in a given area, is in its early stages of development and varies considerably from region to region. Some key approaches are discussed below: The New South Wales Biodiversity Offsets Scheme has been identified as one of the most advanced systems in Australia. It sets precise requirements for compensation measures and the generation of biodiversity credits. In the United States, California has Habitat Conservation Plans and Mitigation Banking. These measures link biodiversity conservation with economic development. As part of the 2030 Biodiversity Strategy, the European Union is discussing the possibility of making the integration of biodiversity offsets mandatory in environmental regulations.

However, continuing barriers to expansion include the persistent lack of high-return investment opportunities and the multitude of risks faced by investors, including political, environmental, and reputational risks, which impact the supply and demand for investment opportunities. Public policy plays a crucial role in creating and hindering these mechanisms. Policy can create natural markets and investment opportunities, while agricultural subsidies and poor coordination between public funding sources undermine the supply of return-oriented investment opportunities. Investors demand risk mitigation for their investments, which is sometimes caused by policy uncertainties. These markets urgently require decisive government intervention to enable expansion while achieving positive environmental outcomes. Without significant policy changes and public investment, an expansion of private investment is unlikely (Ermgassen et al., 2025).

Despite the progress made, there is still a significant need for reform. Standardization, the basis for developing uniform methodologies and clear criteria for measuring and verifying biodiversity gains, must be a priority. Mechanisms for securing protection measures in the long term must be expanded. Existing disclosure, monitoring, and reporting requirements must be strengthened to ensure the desired level of transparency. Most importantly, the consideration of local interests and rights must be established as a mandatory and integral component of all projects, making all stakeholders feel included and valued.

Furthermore, the ongoing discussion about the potential integration of biodiversity credits into international environmental and climate policies, such as the Post-2020 Global Biodiversity Framework, is gaining momentum. The prospect of a globally coordinated biodiversity market, while requiring high institutional and methodological standards, holds significant potential for the future of biodiversity conservation.

# 4. SYNERGIES AND CONFLICTS BETWEEN CARBON AND BIODIVERSITY CREDITS

## 4.1 Projects That Combine Carbon Sequestration and Biodiversity Protection

The potential of the link between carbon and biodiversity markets is not just significant, but also promising. In many cases, measures to sequester carbon and protect biodiversity have a synergistic effect. Natural ecosystems such as forests, moors, mangroves, and savannas act as effective carbon sinks and are also hotspots of biodiversity. Projects to preserve or restore these ecosystems can deliver a double benefit. Climate protection and biodiversity conservation are not just essential goals, but also achievable ones.

Nature-based solutions (NbS) are an example of such synergies. Suitable measures include reforestation with near-natural tree species, renaturation of wetlands, and protection of primary forests. Such projects not only enable large amounts of carbon to be stored in biomass and soil pools but also create habitats for numerous species, improve water quality, increase landscape diversity, and promote resilience to the impacts of climate change. However, it should be borne in mind that the NbS concept is often applied in isolation from the social and economic drivers of these societal challenges. These include, in particular, the ubiquitous focus on market-based mechanisms and the imperative of economic growth. In light of this, Chausson et al. (2023) draw on recent research on the effectiveness, governance, and practice of NbS to highlight the key limitations and pitfalls of a narrow focus on natural capital markets. Natural capital markets refer to the economic value of natural resources and ecosystems, and the authors of the paper propose developing complementary financing mechanisms in parallel. Financial instruments and market-based mechanisms play an important role in closing the biodiversity financing gap and reducing dependence on public funds. However, it has been found that they are not a panacea for the expansion of non-motorized roads (NbS).

It should be noted that projects aimed at obtaining so-called ‘high integrity carbon credits’ deserve special attention. These projects do not focus exclusively on carbon storage but also explicitly consider biodiversity and social inclusion criteria. 'High integrity carbon credits' are a type of carbon credit that is issued for projects that not only reduce carbon emissions but also have positive impacts on biodiversity and local communities. Examples include initiatives such as REDD+ (Reducing Emissions from Deforestation and Forest Degradation), which aim to reduce emissions while protecting biodiversity and combating poverty.

This study concludes that integrated projects could play a central role. By linking carbon and biodiversity credits, these projects have the potential to address multiple environmental goals simultaneously through a single commitment. This is not just attractive for ESG-oriented investors, but also inspiring for all those who are committed to sustainability.

## 4.2 Modeling Conflicting Goals

Despite these promising synergies, significant conflicts exist between carbon sequestration and biodiversity conservation. These tensions, which are complex and multifaceted, can lead to measures considered sensible from a climate policy perspective being problematic from a biodiversity perspective—and vice versa. The development of a mathematical model forms the starting point for the study. Individual specific areas of tension are discussed in more detail below.

### Mathematical model

1. Basic assumptions and target values

There are two ecosystem services:

- C = amount of CO2 emissions bound (in tons of CO2)
- B = measure for biodiversity conservation (e.g., index value 0-1)

A project P generates both outputs with certain intensities:

- $\alpha$ = Carbon sequestration efficiency
- $\beta$ = Efficiency of biodiversity conservation

A project with a budget R (resources: e.g., space, financing)
Functions:
$C = \alpha R$
$B = \beta R$
The parameters α and β are not always complementary. There is often a trade-off: increasing α (e.g., through monoculture plantations) decreases β (less biodiversity)—and vice versa.

2. Modeling synergies and conflicts

We introduce a trade-off parameter $\theta$:

- $\theta \in [-1, 1]$
- $\theta > 0$ ; Synergy between carbon sequestration and biodiversity conservation
- $\theta = 0$ ; no interaction
- $\theta < 0$ ;conflict between carbon sequestration and biodiversity conservation

Modified functions:
$C = \alpha(1 + \theta) R$
$B = \beta(1 + \theta) R$
Interpretation:

- If $\theta > 0$ the output of both functions increases (e.g., in near-natural reforestation)
- In the case of $\theta < 0$, an increase in one output inhibits the other (e.g., monocultures promote $C$ but harm $B$).

3. Optimization problem of a project developer

A rational project developer wants to maximize revenue:

4. Sale of CC: price pC per ton of CO2
5. Sale of BC: price pB per unit of biodiversity

Target function:

$$max \prod(R) = p_C C + p_B B - k(R)$$

with:

- $\prod(R)$ = profit function
- $k(R)$ = cost function (e.g., linear or convex, such as $k(R) = k_0 R)$

When used, the result is:

$$\prod(R) = p_C \alpha(1+\theta)R + p_B \beta(1+\theta)R - k(R)$$
$$= (p_C\alpha + p_B\beta)(1+\theta)R - k(R)$$

6. Interpretation of the model

Positive synergies ($\theta > 0$) automatically increase the overall profitability of projects, as both markets can be served simultaneously.

Negative synergies ($\theta < 0$) lead to difficult trade-offs: The project manager must decide whether to focus on carbon or biodiversity services, depending on which market price ($p_C$ vs $p_B$) is more attractive.

Regulatory interventions (e.g., minimum standards for biodiversity protection) could be introduced to prevent a 'race to the bottom' in β.

**Case study: Brazilian reforestation project—model application**

A reforestation project in Brazil's Mata Atlântica region has two objectives: firstly, to sequester carbon (CC) by reforesting degraded land, and secondly, to protect biodiversity by restoring the natural forest structure with native species.

**Step 1**: Parameterization of the model

The aforementioned model is used:

$$C = \alpha(1+\theta)\,R$$

Parameters determined in a field study:

- Resource input: $R = 100$ ha
- Carbon efficiency $\alpha = 5$ (tCO2/ha)
- Biodiversity index $\beta = 0.4$ (Index/ha)
- Synergy parameter $\theta = +0.3$ (positive interaction through near-natural reforestation)

**Step 2**: Calculating the outputs

$$C = 5(1+0.3)\,100 = 5\;1.3\;100 = 650\;tCO2$$
$$B = 0.4(1+0.3)\,100 = 0.4\;1.3\;100 = 52 \text{ biodiversity units}$$

**Step 3**: Monetary valuation

- Market price CC: $p_C$=20 US$/t CO2
- BC (hypothetically): $p_B$ = 100 US$/unit

Revenues:

$E_C = 650\ 20 = 13,000\ US\$$
$E_B = 52\ 100 = 5,200\ US\$$

Total revenues:

$E_{sum} = E_C + E_B = 18,200\ US\$$

**Step 4**: Comparison with conflict-oriented scenario

What if the project focused on rapid carbon sequestration through monoculture plantations?

New values:

- $\theta = -0.4$ conflicting goals—biodiversity suffers
- $\alpha = 6, \beta = 0.1$ Monoculture: a lot of C, hardly any B

$C = 6(1 + 0.4)\ 100 = 6\ 0.6\ 100 = 360\ tCO2$
$B = 0.1(1 + 0.4)\ 100 = 0.1\ 0.6\ 100 =$ 6 biodiversity units
$E_C = 3600\ 20 = 7,200\ US\$$
$E_B = 6\ 100 = 600\ US\$$

Total proceeds in the event of a conflict of objectives:

$E_{sum} = E_C + E_B = 7,800\ US\$$

*Table 2. Conclusion of the model application*

| Project strategy | Synergy project | Conflict project (monoculture) |
|---|---|---|
| Carbon sequestration (tCO2) | 650 | 360 |
| Biodiversity value | 52 | 6 |
| Total revenue (US$) | 18,200 | 7,800 |
| Ecological sustainability | High | Low |

This study underscores the potential benefits of synergy projects, highlighting their ecological and economic advantages. It emphasizes that the existence and profitability of both markets are crucial for their success.

Webb et al. (2025) use Australia as an example to illustrate the potential of creating a joint system for CO2 and biodiversity credits/offsets. This system could not only help maximize returns in both areas but also avoid the adverse effects of separation. The application of a joint credit/offset system for carbon and biodiversity on marginal agricultural land at low prices for carbon offsets offers a hopeful prospect for financial gains. Integrating these systems could significantly contribute to refocusing attention on the global scale of biodiversity loss, an area that has been neglected compared to the mitigation of carbon emissions.

In this paper, Tedersoo et al. (2024) develop a system for jointly crediting carbon and biodiversity. This system is based on evidence-based criteria for selecting potential conservation and restoration areas. The authors combine field surveys, remote sensing, soil maps, and machine learning algorithms to develop the system. A co-crediting system can mitigate biodiversity loss by encouraging industry and governments to consider biodiversity more rigorously, explicitly, and equitably in carbon sequestration projects. This emphasis on biodiversity could help prioritize protection over restoration and promote more socially and environmentally sustainable land management, making the audience more aware of the potential impact of their work on the environment.

## Monetization of carbon vs. biodiversity priorities

A key trade-off is the different ways carbon and biodiversity can be monetized. Carbon can be standardized, quantified, and marketed with relatively little effort. On the other hand, biodiversity's economic valuation and actionability are more limited. This asymmetry results in project design primarily focused on maximizing carbon sequestration, while biodiversity goals are often neglected.

Market mechanisms favor projects that generate as many carbon credits as possible at the lowest possible cost. This can lead to aspects of biodiversity that are difficult to convert into monetary units, which play a subordinate role in the planning and evaluation of projects. In such cases, biodiversity becomes an unnoticed side effect or, worse still, collateral damage of pure carbon projects.

The following example illustrates this issue: A particularly striking example of this conflict is the establishment of monoculture plantations, for example, with fast-growing exotic tree species such as eucalyptus or acacia. Due to their high capacity to bind large amounts of $CO_2$ in a short period of time, these plants are considered attractive investment targets for carbon credit projects.

From an ecological perspective, however, such plantations are highly problematic:

- It can be observed that the areas in question are only very limitedly suitable as habitats for native species.
- Invasive tendencies may develop, which could damage local ecosystems.
- It has been observed that water consumption and soil degradation are higher in many cases than in near-natural forests.
- In the long term, such systems generally show lower resilience to climate stressors such as droughts or fires.

Therefore, from the perspective of the carbon market, this can be considered a ‘success’ as high carbon sequestration is achieved. However, from the perspective of biodiversity ecology, a loss of species richness and ecological functionality can be observed.

### Tensions between global markets and local ecosystems

Another conflict arises from the discrepancy between the logic of global markets and the needs of local ecosystems and communities. Carbon and biodiversity credits are usually traded on international markets, with buyers in industrialized countries financing projects in developing countries.

This creates the risk that projects will be primarily geared toward internationally accepted standards and accounting systems while local ecological and social contexts are given too little consideration. The functionality of ecosystems is primarily viewed as a carbon sink. However, this can devalue their multifunctional roles (Yan et al., 2024).

Furthermore, the transfer of responsibility (known as 'offsetting') may lead companies or countries to neglect real emissions reductions or measures to preserve biodiversity in their own countries while purchasing supposedly cheap offsets abroad.

Empirical studies show that projects involving local communities at an early stage, respecting Indigenous groups' rights, and integrating local knowledge systems achieve more sustainable and robust results—both for carbon and biodiversity targets.

## 4.3 Case Studies of Successful and Problematic Combinations

The Yurok Tribe Forest Carbon Project in California, USA, is a shining example of successful forest management, thanks to its key success factors. The Yurok tribe in northern California has initiated an innovative project that generates carbon and biodiversity credits. The acquisition and sustainable management of traditional tribal lands leads to a significant reduction in $CO_2$ emissions and contributes to preserving endangered species and strengthening cultural identity. The project's success can be attributed to several key factors: The implementation of a unique blend of traditional ecological knowledge systems and modern certification, the preservation of near-natural, species-rich forests, the fostering of inclusive governance and local value creation, and the establishment of transparent monitoring and reporting procedures for carbon and biodiversity indicators. These success factors underscore the importance of integrated approaches in promoting both ecological and social resilience, and serve as a guide for future forest management projects.

The eucalyptus plantations in Chile, on the other hand, are a problematic example. In the 1990s and 2000s, large areas of degraded land in Chile were planted with fast-growing eucalyptus trees. This measure aimed to sequester carbon and produce wood products. Although these plantations were prosperous regarding carbon balance, they had significant negative impacts. These include a decline in local biodiversity (only a few specialized species used the monocultures), the displacement of native plant and animal species, high water consumption, which led to conflicts with the local population, and increased susceptibility to forest fires. For instance, the high water consumption of eucalyptus trees led to a decrease in water availability for local communities and agriculture, exacerbating existing social and economic disparities. This example demonstrates that focusing on a single environmental goal, such as carbon sequestration, without considering other ecological factors can be counterproductive in the long term.

## 5. EMPIRICAL CASE STUDIES: EXPERIENCES FROM DIFFERENT REGIONS

The theoretical discussion about carbon and biodiversity credits only gains practical relevance when it is reflected upon using concrete case studies. Regional projects illustrate the potential and the systemic challenges of market-based environmental instruments. This section provides an exemplary analysis of three projects from Brazil, Indonesia, and Kenya. The aim is to identify success factors and risk areas to derive lessons for future initiatives.

### 5.1 Case Study 1: Brazil

In scientific literature, Brazil is described as a potential market leader in the global market for emission certificates (Alves et al., 2024). In Pará, numerous reforestation projects have emerged to generate carbon credits by restoring degraded land in recent years. A prominent example is the 'Projeto Reflorestar,' which focuses on reforestation with native tree species. This sequesters carbon in the forest ecosystem in the long term and strengthens additional ecological functions. Reforestation positively affects soil quality, water regulation, and the creation of new habitats for various animal species.

The project uses the 'voluntary carbon market', a market where carbon credits are bought and sold voluntarily, particularly the 'Verified Carbon Standard (VCS)', a widely used standard for certifying carbon credits, and targets international buyers who want to offset their emissions. This offers promising opportunities: potential sources of income are created for landowners, ecological restoration becomes more economically attractive, and international climate protection goals can be supported through market-based mechanisms.

The project uses the voluntary carbon market, particularly the Verified Carbon Standard (VCS), and is aimed at international buyers who want to offset their emissions. The opportunities this offers are promising: potential sources of income are created for landowners, ecological restoration becomes more economically attractive, and international climate protection goals can be supported through market-based mechanisms.

At the same time, however, it should be noted that the model involves considerable risks. In many cases, the land earmarked for reforestation competes with other forms of land use, particularly small-scale farming. In some cases, local communities feel disadvantaged or dispossessed by the projects, leading to social tensions. Another aspect that has been criticized is additionality. In certain areas, it is questionable whether CO2 sequestration is only achieved through the project or whether the areas would have been reforested even without targeted measures, such as natural succession. Another problem arises with long-term security: although income is already generated from the sale of carbon credits, the carbon sequestered remains in the forest for decades and is therefore vulnerable to risks such as forest fires, illegal logging, or future land use changes.

The Projeto Reflorestar example shows that reforestation projects in tropical regions can make an important contribution to climate protection, provided they are carefully planned, ecologically viable, socially accepted, and secure over long periods of time. However, ecological goals will be missed without integrating local interests and reliable governance, and social conflicts will be exacerbated.

## 5.2 Case Study 2: Indonesia

In Indonesia, biodiversity conservation is becoming increasingly important, particularly through market-based instruments such as biodiversity credits. A particularly outstanding example is the Rimba Raya Biodiversity Reserve Project in Central Kalimantan Province on the island of Borneo. The project takes an integrated approach by combining measures to prevent deforestation under the REDD+ mechanism with an explicit focus on biodiversity conservation. The focus is on protecting the natural habitat of the endangered orangutan. These conservation measures are complemented by various sustainable development programs, including reforestation initiatives, the development of ecotourism offerings, and educational projects for the local population.

In Indonesia, biodiversity conservation is becoming increasingly important, particularly through market-based instruments such as biodiversity credits. A particularly outstanding example is the Rimba Raya Biodiversity Reserve Project in Central Kalimantan Province on the island of Borneo. The project takes an integrated approach by combining measures to prevent deforestation under the REDD+ mechanism with an explicit focus on biodiversity conservation. The focus is on protecting the natural habitat of the endangered orangutan. These conservation measures are complemented by various sustainable development programs, including reforestation initiatives, the development of ecotourism offerings, and educational projects for the local population.

The project offers promising synergies: conserving extensive, untouched forests is crucial for long-term carbon sequestration and preserving endangered species. Rimba Raya has been certified according to the internationally recognized Verra standard and meets additional requirements under the CCB standards. It should be noted that the involvement of local communities in decision-making processes is particularly positive. They benefit not only from alternative income sources but also from social infrastructure improvements.

However, this approach is associated with significant challenges. In Indonesia, regulating land ownership and usage rights is often unclear or conflictual. In Rimba Raya, there have also been disputes over the legal definition of project boundaries, which can undermine confidence in the legitimacy of the measures. In addition, the strong dependence on the international market must be identified as a structural risk. The volatility of prices for biodiversity credits poses a risk to the long-term financial viability of the conservation measures. Another problem is the only partial control of surrounding land use: although positive effects have been achieved within the project area, monoculture plantations, especially for oil palms, continue to expand in neighboring regions. These developments not only counteract biodiversity goals but also pressure carbon sequestration capacity.

The Rimba Raya Biodiversity Reserve illustrates that market-based approaches to biodiversity conservation can be highly effective, especially when social participation, clear legal frameworks, and ecological multifunctionality are considered. The project shows that sustainable impact can only be guaranteed with long-term stable financing and a coherent political environment.

## 5.3 Case Study 3: Kenia

In Africa, an increasing number of projects aim to combine carbon sequestration, biodiversity conservation, and rural development within an integrated framework. A particularly pioneering example is the Kasigau Corridor REDD+ Project in Kenya. The project aims to protect an important wildlife corridor between Tsavo East and Tsavo West National Parks, a region of high ecological and conservation importance. The goal is to prevent deforestation of the dry forest while promoting social development measures. These measures include promoting education, ensuring medical care, and creating alternative sources of income for the local population.

The project is an excellent example of the multifunctionality of market-based environmental instruments: it protects over 500,000 acres of dry forest, helps to sequester millions of tons of $CO_2$, and provides a habitat for a variety of endangered species, including elephants and lions. A key element of the project design is the participation of the local population: Around 30 percent of the income from the sale of carbon credits is invested directly in community projects, including the construction of schools and health stations and the financing of microcredit programs for small businesses. Certification according to internationally recognized standards, such as the VCS and the Climate, Community, and Biodiversity (CCB) Standards, increases the project's credibility and international marketability.

Nevertheless, the project also faces significant risks. Dry forests' vulnerability to droughts and fires threatens long-term carbon storage. In addition, the market for emission allowances is volatile, which means that revenues from the sale of carbon credits are subject to strong fluctuations, and therefore, the financing of social measures cannot always be reliably guaranteed. Furthermore, political uncertainties and regional conflicts can impair the effectiveness of protective measures or even render them completely ineffective.

The Kasigau Corridor REDD+ Project demonstrates that market-based environmental instruments can have significant ecological and social impacts, especially provided that revenues are distributed transparently and local interests are consistently taken into account. At the same time, the project clearly shows that long-term effectiveness can only be guaranteed if appropriate risk management strategies are implemented to cushion external shocks such as climate risks or market instability.

## 5.4 Lessons Learned

The analysis of the three case studies highlights key success factors and structural challenges in dealing with carbon and biodiversity credits. Projects that pursue both ecological and social goals in an integrated manner are particularly sustainable. The simultaneous pursuit of biodiversity conservation, climate protection, and local development not only enhances the ecological effectiveness of the projects but also their social acceptance and long-term stability. A key success factor here is local communities' early and substantial involvement. Recognizing traditional land use rights and the participatory design of project measures contribute significantly to legitimacy, conflict avoidance, and resilience to external influences.

Transparency and systematic monitoring play a crucial role in the success of carbon and biodiversity projects. The implementation of independent verification, transparent reporting, and the use of clearly defined indicators to measure climate and biodiversity effects are key in strengthening the credibility of projects and promoting their market opportunities. Furthermore, projects that integrate climatic, political, and economic risks into their planning are more resilient to external disruptions. Therefore, forward-looking risk analysis and appropriate adaptation strategies are essential for sustainable project architecture (Table 3).

*Table 3. Comparison of case studies*

| Criterion | Brazil: Reforestation project | Indonesia: Biodiversity conservation project | Kenia: Kasigau Corridor Projekt |
|---|---|---|---|
| Region | Brazil (Pará) | Indonesia (Borneo) | Kenia (Kasigau Corridor) |
| Objectives | Carbon sequestration through reforestation Prevention of deforestation, biodiversity protection | Prevention of deforestation, biodiversity protection | Prevention of deforestation, protection of wildlife corridors |
| Primary markets | Voluntary Carbon Standard (VCS) | REED+, voluntary biodiversity market | Voluntary Carbon Standard (VCS) |
| Additional social measures | Limited social programs | Education. Ecotourism, alternative sources of income | School construction, health centers, microcredits |
| Local participation | Partial, conflicts with land use | Strong local involvement | Very strong local involvement |
| Main problems | Land use conflicts, additionality | Land use rights, market volatility | Climate vulnerability, political uncertainties |
| Certification | VCS | VCS + CCB standards | VCS + CCB standards |
| Long-term risks | Fires, illegal logging | Price fluctuations, plantation expansion | Drought, fire, political instability |

It's crucial to understand that biodiversity credits present a more intricate challenge than carbon credits. The conversion of goods that lack consistent measurement is a complex task. Unlike carbon emissions, biodiversity cannot be encapsulated by a single indicator. In ecology, a variety of measures are employed to document species abundance and diversity. These measures, such as indices, are contingent on the local context. A species that holds paramount importance in one ecosystem can be found across the globe. As Law (2025) points out, condensing local biodiversity into a set of tradable numbers inevitably leads to biodiversity loss.

The loss of unique and irreplaceable ecosystem elements is an inevitable consequence of biodiversity loss. Attempting to compensate for losses in one location with gains in another is not a feasible strategy. This principle is similar to the global attempts to offset CO2 emissions. For instance, the reforestation of forests in Malaysia cannot adequately substitute for the extinct species in Peru. The subjectivity of the verification process, which involves determining which species and how much habitat should be classified as relevant, often leads to conflicts of interest that are even more serious than those already present in carbon markets. While robust market design could address some concerns, governance alone cannot resolve them.

## 6. GOVERNANCE, POLICY DESIGN, AND INDIGENOUS RIGHTS IN BIODIVERSITY AND CARBON MARKETS

This section brings together the institutional prerequisites and equity issues associated with biodiversity and carbon markets, linking them to governance design and political feasibility. Subsection 6.1 provides a comparative analysis of the political framework conditions in countries with successful and unsuccessful implementations, and derives key success factors and sources of error from this analysis. Subsection 6.2 focuses on the rights architectures of indigenous and local communities (especially in the Global South) and translates them into operational safeguards such as FPIC, benefit sharing, and co-determination.

### 6.1 Comparative Analysis of Political Framework Conditions

This section summarizes the political and regulatory conditions that make biodiversity and carbon markets viable—and where they fail. It builds on the programs and countries mentioned in Chapter 1 (the UK/BNG, NSW/Australia, California/USA, EU debates, hybrid approaches in Colombia, South Korea, and New Zealand, as well as the case studies of Brazil, Indonesia, and Kenya). It derives comparative determinants (see Table 4).

*Table 4. Comparative analysis*

| Country/Instrument | Political approach | What works | Where are the sticking points/risks | Takeaway |
|---|---|---|---|---|
| **UK – Biodiversity Net Gain (BNG)** | Mandatory: ≥ 10% net gain for new construction; standardized habitat metrics | Clear, binding target; mainstreaming in planning | Implementation capacities and monitoring over decades | Binding nature and standardized rules/metrics generate demand, acceptance, and speed of implementation |
| **NSW (AUS) – Biodiversity Offsets Scheme** | Precise offsetting rules and credit generation | Detailed framework, predictability | 'True' equivalence and long-term security are challenging | Strict rules help, but they are no substitute for good baselines |
| **California (USA) – HCP & Mitigation Banking** | Links protection and development via banking | Institutionalized compensation; market signal | Equivalence/follow-up obligations vary | Institutions and banking infrastructure = scaling |

continued on following page

*Table 4. Continued*

| Country/Instrument | Political approach | What works | Where are the sticking points/risks | Takeaway |
|---|---|---|---|---|
| **EU – Biodiversity/ Climate Framework** | Taxonomy/ debate on offsets, integration VCM | System coherence and minimum standards in sight | Still fragmented in practice | EU coherence can raise quality in the internal market |
| **Colombia, South Korea, New Zealand (hybrid approaches)** | Interlinking of voluntary and mandatory markets, national minimum standards | Minimum quality and connection to NDCs | High implementation and data requirements | Hybrid systems curb 'cheap credits' |
| **Brazil (Reflorestar, ...)** | VCM-driven; reforestation | Potential for climate and ecosystem services | Land use conflicts, additionality, long-term risks (fire/ deforestation) | Without land rights and governance, there is a risk of backlash and greenwashing |
| **Indonesia (Rimba Raya)** | REDD+ and biodiversity focus; CCB safeguards | Strong co-benefits and community programs | Unclear boundaries/ rights; price volatility | Social standards and clear rights are key |
| **Kenya (Kasigau Corridor)** | REDD+ with community revenue share | High ecological and social impact | Drought/fire risks, volatile revenues | Risk buffers are needed for climate risks and price fluctuations |

A comparison of individual countries reveals that biodiversity and carbon markets are most sustainable when clear targets, legal certainty, and social safeguards work in tandem. The UK's Biodiversity Net Gain (BNG) regime illustrates the leverage effect of commitment and standardization: The legal minimum requirement for net biodiversity gain in new construction projects, supported by a uniform habitat metric, creates predictable incentives, anchors biodiversity in municipal planning practice, and contributes to market demand for high-quality measures. The key challenge lies less in formulating the target value than in long-term implementation capacity: monitoring over decades, the permanent securing of compensation areas, and operational quality assurance determine whether initial success can be sustained.

The Biodiversity Offsets Scheme in the Australian state of New South Wales operates similarly, relying on detailed rules to generate credits and establish ecological equivalence. Although the precise regulatory framework promotes investment security and transparency, it also reveals the limits of technical fine-tuning: Even strict assessment formulas cannot compensate for a poor starting point or insufficient permanence. In California, habitat conservation plans and mitigation banking have established themselves as institutionalized infrastructure for compensating for environmental impacts. The combination of protection and development logic enables scaling and professionalization. However, it requires consistent follow-up in terms of the equivalence of measures and fulfillment of follow-up obligations over extended periods of time.

At the European level, a coherent regulatory framework is emerging that brings the areas of taxonomy, minimum standards, and market supervision closer together. In practice, however, implementation remains fragmented, with quality assurance, MRV (monitoring, reporting, and verification) requirements, and integration with nature conservation and planning legislation at varying stages of development. In this context, hybrid approaches in countries such as Colombia, South Korea, and New Zealand, which combine voluntary and mandatory mechanisms, are interesting. National minimum standards, links to climate targets, and the recognition of selected voluntary standards can help identify high-quality projects and increase their attractiveness; however, this comes with higher data and governance requirements.

Case studies from the Global South show that ecological potential is quickly undermined without robust governance. In Brazil, reforestation offers significant benefits for climate and biodiversity, but land use conflicts, unresolved rights, and long-term risks, such as fire or deforestation, jeopardize its additionality and permanence. In Indonesia, REDD+ projects with strong social and biodiversity criteria show how co-benefits can be generated for local communities – provided that land rights and responsibilities are clear and price and regime volatilities are reduced through buffer and hedging mechanisms. In Kenya, community-based models show that revenue sharing and participatory monitoring can stabilize both ecological and social impacts, provided that climate risks (e.g., droughts) and fluctuating market revenues are cushioned countercyclically.

Six overarching determinants can be derived from these cases. First, binding target architectures (e.g., net gain quotas or strictly defined equivalence rules) are a strong driver of demand and quality. Second, clarified land and usage rights are a fundamental prerequisite, because without a clear title, there is a risk of conflicts, double-counting, and legitimacy deficits. Third, strict quality standards and MRV systems must reliably demonstrate the criteria of additionality, permanence, and avoidance of double counting. Fourth, social safeguards, including early and fair participation and contractually secured benefit sharing, are not an additional service but are fundamental to effectiveness and acceptance. Fifth, long-term financing, buffer, and insurance mechanisms make projects resilient to natural and market volatility. Sixth, policy coherence—including the interlinking of voluntary and mandatory instruments and embedding in national biodiversity and climate strategies—stabilizes quality incentives and reduces arbitrage.

## 6.2 Framework Conditions for Indigenous Rights in Biodiversity Markets

Indigenous and locally rooted communities are key players in ecological protection and restoration services, yet they are also particularly vulnerable to market- and project-induced interventions. In biodiversity markets, the quality of the rights architecture determines whether projects are legitimate, can be sustained over time, and distribute benefits equitably. In practice, three clusters of problems regularly emerge:

(1) unclear or unrecognized traditional land and usage rights,
(2) formally existing but materially inadequate participation processes, and
(3) fragile or non-transparent financing and governance arrangements that do not secure benefit flows sustainably.

A robust protection and participation framework can be summarized as a 'safeguard stack.' The first step is to clarify rights: customary tenure must be identified, mapped, and reconciled with government cadastral data. Overlapping claims must be moderated and documented in a publicly verifiable manner prior to the project's commencement. It is followed by an FPIC (Free, Prior and Informed Consent) process that is worthy of its name: a free decision without pressure, made in good time before irreversible measures are taken, informed about opportunities, risks and alternatives, moderated by independent third parties and with the possibility of conditioning or revoking consent. FPIC must be understood not as a one-off formality, but as an ongoing process of negotiation and learning.

Financial and institutional participation is specified in a contractually fixed benefit-sharing agreement, which includes a clearly defined share of revenues and co-financing secured over several years. Transparent payment channels (e.g., via local trust funds) and joint control over the use of funds strengthen the incentive and the sense of fairness. In addition, co-determination in project management is a standard practice: representatives of rights holders should be given voting or veto rights in steering committees for measures that have a high cultural or habitat impact. Community-based monitoring of biodiversity and social indicators increases accountability and data quality.

Long-term safeguards are essential, particularly in the Global South, where climate and market risks accumulate. Permanence and risk buffers, insurance against natural hazards, price floors, or multi-year purchase agreements stabilize community income and protect against investment and acceptance failures. Equally important is alignment with recognized social and biodiversity standards. Minimum requirements for participation, rights, and benefit sharing should serve as eligibility criteria for the recognition of credits and for access to registries and markets—not as a voluntary quality label.

Another principle applies to biodiversity offsets: the locality and equivalence principle ensures that compensation occurs in the same or an ecologically equivalent system. It protects culturally and ecologically particular areas from 'long-distance trade' in biodiversity, which can exacerbate local loss and conflict situations. Finally, every system needs robust complaint and reversal mechanisms, i.e., low-threshold, independent dispute resolution and clearly defined consequences for safeguard violations – from adjustment requirements and share increases to project pauses or terminations.

Experience shows that where rights are clarified at an early stage, the right to free, prior, and informed consent (FPIC) is substantially implemented, benefits are shared fairly, and governance is jointly supported, ecological and social outcomes reinforce each other. Where, on the other hand, rights, participation, and benefit sharing remain unclear, trust and sustainability erode – even if ecological indicators are convincing in the short term. For the Global South, this is not only a question of project ethics, but of the systemic stability of biodiversity markets as a whole. Without credible foundations for rights and participation, high-quality biodiversity remains difficult to monetize, and markets fail to achieve their development and conservation goals.

## 7. ETHICS, POLITICS, AND REGULATION: THE FUTURE OF ENVIRONMENTAL MARKETS

The carbon and biodiversity credits markets are increasingly caught between pragmatic compensation and the demand for more profound transformation. Critical voices emphasize that environmental markets often legitimize 'business as usual' instead of necessary systemic changes. Companies and governments have the option of 'offsetting' their emissions or interventions in nature by purchasing certificates without fundamentally changing their production and consumption patterns. A particular problem arises in cases where the credits do not meet strict additionality criteria or are not effective in the long term. In this case, they create an illusion of sustainability while ecological crises continue to escalate. Critics use the term 'climate delay' to describe this phenomenon. Another term used in this context is 'biodiversity washing.'

This contrasts with the transformative vision of environmental markets: in this perspective, carbon and biodiversity credits are used as startup financing and incentives for comprehensive societal change—towards low-carbon, biodiversity-friendly economic systems. Therefore, It will be crucial to determine whether future markets are more firmly embedded in comprehensive decarbonization and biodiversity strategies or remain mere compensation instruments.

The effectiveness of emission credits must be evaluated for the desired emission reductions. Only if they lead to a significant reduction in emissions can the desired progress be achieved in the fight against climate change and preserving biodiversity. This study examines the potential risk of a trust problem arising from governments and companies using CO2 certificates to achieve their climate targets. The effectiveness of these credits is crucial, as failure could undermine trust in the offset markets, which are considered an essential tool for combating climate change.

Political and regulatory frameworks largely determine the functioning and integrity of environmental markets. With the Sustainable Finance Taxonomy, the European Union has created a binding framework that classifies economic activities according to their sustainability. Projects dedicated to carbon sequestration and biodiversity conservation are explicitly integrated into the overall concept. The taxonomy aims to prevent the misuse of certificates and provide investors with clear standards.

REDD+ (Reducing Emissions from Deforestation and Forest Degradation) is an international program that aims to reduce emissions from deforestation and the progressive deterioration of forest areas. The REDD+ program developed by the United Nations compensates countries in the Global South that avoid deforestation. It occupies a central position within the biodiversity and carbon markets but has been repeatedly criticized for its lack of transparency, problematic land use rights, and unclear additional effects.

The future development of the markets will depend mainly on the ability of national and international regulations to ensure harmonization, transparency, and an appropriate level of ambition. The most obvious conclusion that can be drawn from the analysis of carbon credit markets is that governments are obliged to develop and enforce clear and precise rules. These rules must clearly define the use of biodiversity credits, the necessary reporting requirements for sellers, the permissible statements about them, and other aspects. Implementing and enforcing these standards requires cooperation between governments and international supervisory authorities on the one hand and organizations that set standards (e.g., certification systems), Indigenous peoples, local communities, and international and national non-governmental organizations on the other. Governments should require developers who sell biodiversity credits to make project information publicly available. This includes the impact of projects on biodiversity and the benefits they provide to local communities. There is an opportunity for a new or existing body at the international level to support the development of ethical and trustworthy biodiversity markets. This could be done by developing standards and exchanging information and experiences from projects financed by biodiversity credits (Antonelli et al., 2024).

Designing robust and credible markets is a key challenge. Comprehensive reforms are needed to achieve such a transformation. These reforms concern transparency and standardization, the use of digital technologies, the avoidance of market distortions and misguided incentives, and the issues of speculation and greenwashing. Current syntheses show that standardized metrics and consistent rules promote the investability and scalability of compensation systems by reducing uncertainty and transaction costs. Conversely, the trend toward greater flexibility (looser equivalence rules, less precise valuation methods) can weaken ecological quality and enforceability. At the same time, the literature makes it clear that the power of actors throughout the policy cycle (agenda setting, policy formulation, implementation) is crucial. This should make the audience feel engaged and part of the process. The channels of influence range from lobbying and litigation to discursive shifts. Good governance opens up procedures to a diverse range of stakeholders, but at the same time shields them from narrow private interests (Barral et al., 2025).

Increasing the transparency of CO2 offsetting mechanisms through decisive measures requiring disclosure of the information is crucial to promptly fulfilling the promise of economically efficient mitigation. Establishing transparency is the first necessary step toward restoring the credibility of the VCM, but it is not sufficient (Delacote et al., 2024). Transparent project reports, uniform measurement methods, and clear disclosure standards are essential to strengthen trust in environmental markets. Initiatives such as the Integrity Council for the Voluntary Carbon Market (ICVCM) and the Biodiversity Credit Alliance are currently working to develop global minimum standards.

Blockchain technology and satellite monitoring offer additional opportunities for real-time verification and public documentation of project results. This technological advancement, as demonstrated by Saraji and Borowczak (2024), could establish an ecosystem for emission certificates using smart contracts in conjunction with blockchain technology. The aim is to optimize carbon markets for greater transparency, accessibility, liquidity, and standardization. The ecosystem comprises a tokenization mechanism for secure digitization with clearly defined protocols for issuance and burning, a transparent mechanism for token distribution, a free, automated market maker for trading carbon tokens, and mechanisms for involving all stakeholders, including the energy industry, project auditors, liquidity providers, NGOs, affected citizens, and governments.

Measures must be implemented to prevent market distortions and misguided incentives. Particular attention must be paid to the potential misguided incentives that market-based instruments can create. A one-sided focus on measuring carbon quantities could promote species-poor monocultures. Regulations ensure that qualitative criteria such as the preservation of intact ecosystems or social justice are systematically taken into account.

Furthermore, it is crucial to minimize the role of speculation. Projects should be based on real environmental performance and not primarily traded as financial derivatives.

This study concludes that greenwashing is one of the most significant challenges to the credibility of carbon and biodiversity credits. Companies could deliberately purchase inferior certificates in order to feign environmental compatibility.

Regulators could take several measures in this context:

- Strict definitions of 'high-quality' credits should be established.
- It should be investigated whether a ban or restriction on offset claims for questionable projects is necessary.
- It is paramount that all offset strategies be disclosed in sustainability reports.

Credibility and strict regulation of environmental markets are essential prerequisites for their significant contribution to ecological transformation. The implementation of strict regulations, as suggested by this study, will provide a sense of reassurance to the audience about the future integrity of environmental markets.

The treatment of carbon and biodiversity markets, which have often been separated up to now, does not reflect the complexity of ecological systems. Integrating both goals is, therefore, a key project for the future. Multi-benefit projects are an urban development tool that pursues several goals at once. It is recommended that projects should have a systematic approach to pursuing two goals. This includes both increasing carbon storage and protecting biodiversity. Examples include nature-based solutions such as mangrove protection or the renaturation of wetlands.

Establishing common standards is necessary. Developing new certification approaches could enable the integration of carbon and biodiversity credits, promote the avoidance of duplicate structures, and maximize synergy effects.

Support programs and market developments could also be designed to make investments in projects with combined climate protection and biodiversity benefits particularly attractive.

It is recommended that policies in climate protection, nature conservation, and the economy be more closely linked to achieve improved policy coherence. National strategies could include mandatory quotas for biodiversity-friendly climate projects.

A holistic approach that recognizes ecology's multidimensional nature and designs economic incentives accordingly is needed to develop environmental markets from a pure compensation instrument into a driver of genuine sustainability transformation.

## 8. CONCLUSION

An analysis of the markets for carbon credits and biodiversity credits reveals a promising potential for market-based instruments. These instruments, if designed effectively, can significantly support the urgent measures to combat climate change and biodiversity loss. They have the power to generate financial resources, create incentives for conservation and restoration projects, and enable innovative solutions, instilling a sense of hope and optimism in the fight against these pressing issues.

However, it should be borne in mind that these instruments are associated with certain risks. Although new monitoring technologies can help quantify biodiversity, there is a trade-off between simple metrics that enable liquid markets and more costly metrics that provide a more accurate picture of biodiversity (Wunder et al., 2025). In this context, the issues of additionality (the requirement that projects funded by carbon credits must result in emissions reductions that would not have occurred otherwise), transparency, carbonwashing, and long-term effectiveness are critical. A large number of case studies demonstrate that without clear regulatory guidelines, environmental markets run the risk of exacerbating social inequalities or remaining ecologically inefficient. Furthermore, market-based mechanisms pose significant governance challenges and can reinforce power asymmetries (Chausson et al., 2023).

The effectiveness of carbon markets is insufficient and does not meet the required standards. There is an urgent need for reform. The effectiveness of emissions credit systems is highly dependent on fundamental changes to the systems to ensure that climate change is reduced. Reforming these systems is paramount, as otherwise, there is a risk of failing to meet climate targets and enabling companies to present themselves as more environmentally friendly than they are. This aspect becomes particularly relevant when biodiversity markets come into focus. Biodiversity is a highly complex, multidimensional concept. The standardization and measurability of biodiversity credits pose a greater challenge. More robust benchmarks, standards, and governance arrangements are needed to design, implement, and impact assess biodiversity credits. It is to be expected that high-quality credits will incur higher costs than those where compromises are made in terms of integrity. This could dampen the expected boom in biodiversity credits (Wunder et al., 2025).

At the same time, synergies—for example, in nature-based solutions—open up enormous opportunities: projects dedicated to carbon sequestration and biodiversity protection offer not only ecological but also social and economic benefits. In the long term, the success of these markets will depend on whether they can move beyond mere compensation logic and promote genuine transformations of economic and land use systems.

At the same time, synergies—for example, in nature-based solutions—open up enormous opportunities: projects dedicated to carbon sequestration and biodiversity protection offer not only ecological but also social and economic benefits. In the long term, the success of these markets will depend on whether they can grow beyond mere compensation logic and promote genuine transformations of economic and land use systems.

Targeted recommendations for action by the various stakeholder groups are needed to ensure that environmental markets are designed effectively and fairly. Governments have a key role to play in this context. It is recommended that uniform and strict standards for carbon and biodiversity credits be established to ensure the quality and integrity of the markets. Implementing clear regulatory frameworks makes it possible to establish binding criteria such as additionality, permanence, and social compatibility. In addition, policy programs should specifically promote projects that integrate climate protection and biodiversity. Another key aspect is the protection of local rights: legal frameworks must ensure that local communities are involved in the planning and implementation of projects and receive a fair share of the benefits. Furthermore, implementing comprehensive transparency obligations for companies is of significant relevance. Environmental certificates require the disclosure of activities and their impacts, as well as standardized documentation.

Companies have a responsibility to be transparent in their communication. Offsetting emissions with certificates should never be a substitute for actual emission reductions. Environmental certificates should be seen as complementary to comprehensive, biodiversity-friendly business models. When selecting projects, companies should ensure that the underlying measures have measurable, lasting, and socially acceptable environmental impacts. Transparent communication is essential. Statements about climate neutrality or contributions to biodiversity protection must be comprehensible and verifiable to build trust among consumers and partners, providing reassurance and confidence in their actions.

Investors should integrate environmental criteria into their risk analyses systematically. When analyzing environmental market investments, it is essential to consider financial, ecological, and social risks. It is recommended to invest capital in projects referred to as 'multi-benefit' projects. These projects are characterized by the fact that they simultaneously sequester $CO_2$, promote biodiversity, and strengthen social structures, thereby providing a range of benefits and reducing the risk of negative environmental or social impacts. A long-term perspective is crucial here: those focusing exclusively on short-term returns neglect the goal of promoting sustainable transformation processes through environmental markets.

The future of environmental markets lies in an integrated, qualitative, and equity-oriented design:

- **Integrated certificates**: Developing standards that jointly measure carbon and biodiversity services could avoid duplication and maximize ecological added value.
- **Systemic transformation**: Environmental markets should be understood as part of a broader transition to sustainable economic models, such as promoting regenerative agriculture, nature-based urban planning, or biodiversity-friendly energy production.
- **Participation and empowerment of local communities**: The success of ecological projects depends mainly on the extent to which local actors are involved, respected, and economically empowered.
- **Making sensible use of technological innovations**: Modern technologies (e.g., blockchain, satellite monitoring, AI-supported biodiversity measurement) can improve transparency and efficiency but should be used in a socially and environmentally responsible manner.

In summary, carbon credits and biodiversity credits are not panaceas for environmental crises but essential tools for achieving a sustainable future. Their effectiveness will be measured by whether they enable real ecological progress and accompany social transformations rather than merely providing symbolic compensation.

# REFERENCES

Akita, N., & Ohe, Y. (2021). Sustainable forest management evaluation using carbon credits: From production to environmental forests. *Forests*, *12*(8), 1016. DOI: 10.3390/f12081016

Akrofi, M. M. (2025). Green hotspots? Unveiling global hotspots and shifting trends in carbon credit projects. *Sustainable Development (Bradford)*, *33*(2), 1782–1796. DOI: 10.1002/sd.3209

Alves, L. L. M., Angelo, H., Almeida, A. N., Silva, G. F., Matricardi, E. A. T., Nunes, A., & Souza Júnior, C. V. N. (2024). Strategic analysis of the forest carbon market in Brazil. *Sustainability (Basel)*, *16*(16), 6898. DOI: 10.3390/su16166898

Antonelli, A., Rueda, X., Calcagno, R., & Kalunda, P. N. (2024). How biodiversity credits could help to conserve and restore nature. *Nature*, *634*(8036), 1045–1049. DOI: 10.1038/d41586-024-03475-2 PMID: 39468324

Balmford, A., Keshav, S., Venmans, F., Coomes, D., Groom, B., & Madhavapeddy, A.. (2023). Realising the social value of impermanent carbon credits. *Cambridge Open Engage*. DOI: 10.33774/coe-2023-5v93l-v3

Barral, S., Ghosh, R., & Corbera, E. (2025). The politics of influence in biodiversity offsetting. *Nature Sustainability*, *8*(4), 350–357. DOI: 10.1038/s41893-025-01514-y

Burgess, N. D., Ali, N., Bedford, J., Bhola, N., Brooks, S., Cierna, A., Correa, R., Harris, M., Hargey, A., Hughes, J., McDermott-Long, O., Miles, L., Ravilious, C., Rodrigues, A. R., van Soesbergen, A., Sihvonen, H., Seager, A., Swindell, L., Vukelic, M., & Butchart, S. H. M. (2024). Global metrics for terrestrial biodiversity. *Annual Review of Environment and Resources*, *49*(1), 673–709. DOI: 10.1146/annurev-environ-121522-045106

Cabiyo, B., & Field, C. B. (2025). Embracing imperfection: Carbon offset markets must learn to mitigate the risk of over-crediting. *PNAS Nexus*, *4*(5), pgaf091. Advance online publication. DOI: 10.1093/pnasnexus/pgaf091 PMID: 40352644

Chausson, A., Welden, E. A., Melanidis, M. S., Gray, E., Hirons, M., & Seddon, N. (2023). Going beyond market-based mechanisms to finance nature-based solutions and foster sustainable futures. *PLOS Climate*, *2*(4), e0000169. DOI: 10.1371/journal.pclm.0000169

Clifton, J., & Schwerdtner Mánez, K. (2025). A framework based on payments for ecosystem services to support the delivery of high integrity carbon and biodiversity credits. *Ecosystem Services*, *73*, 101724. DOI: 10.1016/j.ecoser.2025.101724

Delacote, P., L'Horty, T., Kontoleon, A., West, T. A. P., Creti, A., Filewod, B., LeVelly, G., Guizar-Coutiño, A., Groom, B., & Elias, M. (2024). Strong transparency required for carbon credit mechanisms. *Nature Sustainability*, *7*(6), 706–713. DOI: 10.1038/s41893-024-01310-0

Fiegenbaum, H. (2024). Complementing carbon credits from forest-related activities with biodiversity insurance and resilience value. *arXiv*. DOI: 10.31219/osf.io/buvzy

Filewod, B., & McCarney, G. (2023). Avoiding carbon leakage from nature-based offsets by design. *One Earth*, *6*(7), 790–802. DOI: 10.1016/j.oneear.2023.05.024

In, S. Y., & Schumacher, K. (2021). Carbonwashing: A new type of carbon data-related ESG greenwashing. DOI: 10.2139/ssrn.3901278

Jones, E.-A., Paige, L., Smith, A., Worth, A., Betts, L., & Stafford, R. (2024). Potential for carbon credits from conservation management: Price and potential for multi-habitat nature-based carbon sequestration in Dorset, UK. *Sustainability (Basel)*, *16*(3), 1268. DOI: 10.3390/su16031268

Klaus, V. H., Schaub, S., Séchaud, R., Fabian, Y., Jeanneret, P., Lüscher, A., & Huguenin-Elie, O. (2024). Upscaling of ecosystem service and biodiversity indicators from field to farm to inform agri-environmental decision- and policy-making. *Ecological Indicators*, *163*, 112104. DOI: 10.1016/j.ecolind.2024.112104

Koumpli, V. (2024). EU ETS and voluntary carbon markets: Key features and current challenges. *Journal of World Energy Law and Business*, *17*(1), 87–93. DOI: 10.1093/jwelb/jwad034

Law, K. (2025). Biodiversity credits are more problematic than carbon credits. *Nature*, *637*(8045), 272. DOI: 10.1038/d41586-025-00017-2 PMID: 39774804

Lininger, K. B., & Lave, R. (2024). River restoration can increase carbon storage but is not yet a suitable basis for carbon credits. *Bioscience*, *74*(10), 717–724. DOI: 10.1093/biosci/biae083 PMID: 39444511

Manfrino, M. (2024). Beyond carbon: Navigating the path to biodiversity credits for climate action and ecosystem conservation. DOI: 10.2139/ssrn.4687255

Mitchell Aide, T. (2024). The Biodiversity Credit Market needs rigorous baseline, monitoring, and validation practices. *npj. Npj Biodiversity*, *3*(1), 30. DOI: 10.1038/s44185-024-00062-6

Probst, B. S., Toetzke, M., Kontoleon, A., Anadón, L. D., Minx, J. C., & Haya, B. K.. (2024). Systematic assessment of the achieved emission reductions of carbon crediting projects. *Nature Communications*, *15*(9562), 1–14. DOI: 10.1038/s41467-024-53645-z PMID: 39543137

Rossberg, A. G., O'Sullivan, J. D., Malysheva, S., & Shnerb, N. M. (2024). A metric for tradable biodiversity credits quantifying impacts on global extinction risk. *Journal of Industrial Ecology*, *28*(4), 1009–1021. DOI: 10.1111/jiec.13518

Saraji, S., & Borowczak, M. (2024). A Blockchain-based carbon credit ecosystem. *arXiv*.

Schwerdtner Mánez, K., & Clifton, J. (2025). *Biodiversity credits: A new currency to support nature conservation?* Fauna & Flora International. DOI: 10.1017/S0030605324001467

Seidl, A., Cumming, T., Arlaud, M., Crossett, C., & van den Heuvel, O. (2024). Investing in the wealth of nature through biodiversity and ecosystem service finance solutions. *Ecosystem Services*, *66*, 101601. DOI: 10.1016/j.ecoser.2024.101601

Shefy, D., Rossi, S., & Rinkevich, B. (2025). Not just carbon: Biodiversity credits for restoration of the marine animal forests. *Ecosystems and People (Abingdon, England)*, *21*(1), 2488350. DOI: 10.1080/26395916.2025.2488350

Tedersoo, L., Sepping, J., Morgunov, A. S., Kiik, M., Esop, K., Rosenvald, R., Hardwick, K., Breman, E., Purdon, R., Groom, B., Venmans, F., Kiers, E. T., & Antonelli, A. (2024). Towards a co-crediting system for carbon and biodiversity. *Plants, People, Planet*, *6*(1), 18–28. DOI: 10.1002/ppp3.10405

Trencher, G., Nick, S., Carlson, J., & Johnson, M. (2024). Demand for low-quality offsets by major companies undermines climate integrity of the voluntary carbon market. *Nature Communications*, *15*(1), 6863. DOI: 10.1038/s41467-024-51151-w PMID: 39127784

Webb, J., Fujii, H., Rowlings, D., Grace, P., Mundree, S., Managi, S., & Wilson, C. (2025). Prospects for integration of carbon and biodiversity credits: An Australian case study review. *Sustainability Science*. Advance online publication. DOI: 10.1007/s11625-024-01603-5

WEF & McKinsey. (2024). Biodiversity credits: Demystifying metrics for nature markets. https://www3.weforum.org/docs/WEF_Biodiversity_Credits_2024.pdf

West, T. A. P., Wunder, S., Sills, E. O., Börner, J., Rifai, S. W., Neidermeier, A. N., Frey, G. P., & Kontoleon, A. (2023). Action needed to make carbon offsets from tropical forest conservation work for climate change mitigation. *Science*, *877*(6660), 873–877. DOI: 10.1126/science.ade3535 PMID: 37616370

Wunder, S., Fraccaroli, C., Bull, J. W., Dutta, T., Eyres, A., & Evans, M. C.. (2025). Biodiversity credits: An overview of the current State, future opportunities, and potential pitfalls. *Business Strategy and the Environment.*

Xie, Q., Hao, J., Li, K., & Zheng, X. (2022). Carbon price prediction considering climate change: A text-based framework. *Economic Analysis and Policy*, *74*, 382–401. DOI: 10.1016/j.eap.2022.02.010

Yan, N., Liu, G., Ulgiati, S., & Yang, Z. (2024). Biodiversity conservation strategies from No Net Loss to Net Gain. A multidimensional accounting method. *Earths' Future, 12*(10), e2024EF004652. DOI: 10.1029/2024EF004652

zu Ermgassen, S. O. S. E., Hawkins, I., Lundhede, T., Liu, Q., Thorsen, B. J., & Bull, J. W. (2025). The current state, opportunities and challenges for upscaling private investment in biodiversity in Europe. *Nature Ecology & Evolution*, *9*(3), 515–524. DOI: 10.1038/s41559-024-02632-0 PMID: 39910373

# Chapter 5
# Green and Sustainability Sukuk for SDGs:
## Lesson From Saudi Arabia, UAE, Malaysia, and Indonesia

**Khairunnisa Musari**
https://orcid.org/0000-0003-0525-9903
*Kiai Haji Achmad Siddiq State Islamic University, Indonesia*

## ABSTRACT

*Green and Sustainability Sukuk issuance has maintained a strong growth momentum and marked a consecutive record of annual issuance since the market's inception in 2017. Saudi Arabia, the United Arab Emirates (UAE), Malaysia, and Indonesia are the top four Green and Sustainability Sukuk-issuing countries in the world. Saudi Arabia is the leading issuer within the Gulf region, followed by the UAE. If Malaysia is known as the world's first Green Sukuk issuer, Indonesia is known as the world's first sovereign Green Sukuk as well as the world's first retail Green Sukuk. Therefore, through a literature review by gathering data mainly sourced from the official publications of the related ministry and institutions, this chapter focuses on discussing: (1) Green and Sustainability Sukuk framework in Saudi Arabia, UAE, Malaysia, and Indonesia; (2) Green and Sustainability Sukuk performance for the four countries; (3) the impacts of their Green and Sustainability Sukuk for SDGs targets.*

## INTRODUCTION

The historical evolution of Islamic finance as a value-based system has long positioned Islamic finance as an ethical alternative to conventional finance, em-

DOI: 10.4018/979-8-3373-8287-6.ch005

ht © 2026, IGI Global Scientific Publishing. Copying or distributing in print or electronic forms without written permission of IGI Global Scientific Publishing is prohibited. Use of this chapter to generative artificial intelligence (AI) technologies is expressly prohibited. The publisher reserves all rights to license its use for generative AI training and machine learning model development.

phasizing transparency, social justice, and environmental stewardship. The global rise of interest in Environmental, Social, and Governance (ESG) investing and the mainstreaming of the Sustainable Development Goals (SDGs) have provided the convergence of Islamic finance principles with global ESG and SDG agendas and fertile ground for the emergence of Green and Sustainability Sukuk. These instruments align naturally with the huge funding needs to meet the Paris Agreement and SDG targets, as well as to realize the *maqasid al-shari'ah,* particularly to preserve the environment *(hifz al-bi'ah).* Post-2008 financial reforms and climate change imperatives further catalyzed demand for financial products that merge return generation with tangible environmental or social outcomes.

Urgent and decisive measures are required to address the severe and immediate threat that climate change poses to human welfare and ecological systems. Tackling this challenge necessitates a fundamental transformation toward a low-carbon, climate-resilient economic model, with the financial sector playing a pivotal role (Helali, 2024). Reflecting the persistent financing shortfall in meeting the goals of the Paris Agreement (Yu, 2016), the funding gap for achieving the SDGs in developing nations has expanded from USD 2.5 trillion to over USD 4 trillion annually between 2020 and 2025 (OECD, 2022). The Islamic Declaration on Climate Change, endorsed by prominent Islamic scholars, underscores a strong ethical obligation grounded in Islamic principles, urging Muslims and followers of all faiths to take immediate climate action (IISD, 2015). Within this framework, Green Sukuk have gained attention as a viable and ethically aligned alternative to conventional green financial instruments (Helali, 2024).

Green and Sustainability Sukuk are two of four types of Sustainable Sukuk (Finvizier, 2024), or two of six types of ESG Sukuk (Refinitiv, LSE, UKIFC, and GEFI, 2022). Sustainability aligns naturally with Islamic finance, offering a unique opportunity to channel funds toward sustainable development in a way that upholds Islamic principles and addresses global climate challenges (Hidayat, Musari, Masrohatin, and Smolo, 2024). Therefore, Green and Sustainability Sukuk are not only timely financial innovations but also tools for reorienting Islamic finance towards Islamic sustainable finance, fiscal sustainability, and sustainable economy impacts. Sustainable Sukuk market is projected to experience substantial growth in the coming years, driven by a mix of factors—growing demand in Islamic economies, fiscal requirements, climate and SDGs financing priorities, deeper capital market integration, and heightened investor awareness.

In simple terms, Green Sukuk can be explained as use-of-proceeds instruments specifically designed to finance or refinance eligible green projects that are both environmentally beneficial and Shari'ah-compliant, in alignment with the Green Bond Principles, which are issued with the sole purpose of funding initiatives that contribute positively to environmental sustainability (Refinitiv, LSE, UKIFC, and

GEFI, 2022; ICMA, IsDB, and LSEG, 2024). Meanwhile, Sustainability Sukuk are a widely adopted financial instrument in which the proceeds are exclusively allocated to a combination of Shari'ah-compliant green and social projects, in accordance with the Sustainability Bond Guidelines, which serve as a key financing tool by directing funds toward initiatives that support both environmental sustainability and positive social impact, while adhering to Islamic finance principles (Refinitiv, LSE, UKIFC, and GEFI, 2022; ICMA, IsDB, and LSEG, 2024).

Green and Sustainability Sukuk issuance has maintained a strong growth momentum and marked the consecutive record of annual issuance. Since 2018, an average of 82% of Green and Sustainability Sukuk have been issued in foreign currencies on international markets—compared to just 32% for traditional sukuk—indicating stronger global investor demand, a trend reinforced by the 2022 Refinitiv Sukuk Survey, which found that 54% of sukuk investors have incorporated ESG factors into their investment strategies (Refinitiv, LSE, UKIFC, and GEFI, 2022). Although ESG Sukuk still represents a relatively small segment, it is expanding rapidly. Issuance climbed from \$4.8 billion in 2020 to \$15.2 billion in 2024, signaling strong momentum, where this growth is expected to continue as ESG Sukuk strives to match the scale of the conventional ESG bond market, especially with increasing interest from Islamic countries in advancing the SDGs and financing climate initiatives (Kohli and Al Taitoon, 2025).

In 2025, the global ESG Sukuk market is projected to exceed \$50 billion in outstanding value, becoming a significant source of dollar-based funding in Islamic finance across key markets, mostly driven by Kingdom of Saudi Arabia ("Kingdom" or "Saudi Arabia"), the United Arab Emirates (UAE), Malaysia, and Indonesia (Fitch Ratings, 2025; Ho, 2025; Middle East Briefing, 2025; ZAWYA, 2025). Malaysia is known as the issuer of the first Green Sukuk in the world (Hadad-Zervos, 2017; Cho, 2023), and Indonesia is known as the issuer of the first Sovereign Green Sukuk as well as the world's first Retail Green Sukuk (MoF of Indonesia, 2019; UNDP Indonesia, 2020; UNDP in Asia and the Pacific, 2020; Musari and Hidayat, 2023; Musari, 2021, 2025), where the two rank as the second and third largest globally, following Saudi Arabia, as well as both nations have positioned themselves at the forefront of the growing movement toward sustainability within Islamic finance (BIX Malaysia, 2023).

In the Gulf region, Saudi Arabia has emerged as the leader in Sustainable Sukuk issuances, followed by the UAE (ZAWYA, 2024). Although the UAE was new to the Green Sukuk market, the UAE was the first to establish a Framework for Federal Bond and Sukuk issuances to help develop its primary and secondary financial markets in the Gulf region (Rahman, Musari, Mahsyar, and Kilinc-Ata, 2025) and its Green Sukuk was the first in Middle East and North Africa (MENA) Region (GGGI, 2023). In 2025, issuers from Saudi Arabia and the UAE are predicted to continue their leadership in the sustainable bond markets, with green initiatives continuing to play a significant role in support of national net-zero goals, especially in the clean energy sector, and Sustainable Sukuk are also predicted to emerge as a key area of growth (S&P Global, 2025).

Through literature review, particularly from the official publications of the Ministry of Finance - Republic of Indonesia (MoF of Indonesia), the Securities Commission Malaysia (SC), the MoF of Saudi Arabia, and the UAE Ministry of Climate Change and Environment (MOCCAE), this chapter focuses on three issues to describe: (1) Green and Sustainability Sukuk framework in Saudi Arabia, UAE, Malaysia, and Indonesia; (2) Green and Sustainability Sukuk performance for the four countries; (3) The impacts of their Green and Sustainability Sukuk for SDGs targets. As the book is positioned, this chapter presents a valuable information about Islamic green financing through Green and Sustainability Sukuk by taking case studies in Saudi Arabia, UAE, Malaysia, and Indonesia. As we believe, tackling climate change needs a strong political will and commitment. National efforts should include not just policy changes and supportive environments, but also financial investment.

The remaining part of the chapter is organized into five sections. The first to third section presents the framework, performance, and impacts for SDGs from Green and Sustainability Sukuk in Saudi Arabia, UAE, Malaysia, and Indonesia. The subsequent section concludes the entire chapter. Overall, this chapter is expected to have outcomes and impacts: (1) Enhance the integration of Islamic economics and finance in efforts to address climate change and support the achievement of SDG13, which urges immediate action to combat climate change and its effects; (2) Support economic financing while reducing reliance on foreign loans, interest-based debt, and conventional interest-bearing instruments; (3) Motivate governments in emerging and Muslim-majority countries to explore alternative development financing options by adopting Islamic sustainable finance principles to promote Islamic fiscal sustainability.

## GREEN AND SUSTAINABILITY SUKUK FRAMEWORK

To advance the SDGs, implement climate initiatives, and support recovery from the COVID-19 pandemic, financing will play a crucial role in driving progress. As Islamic financial instrument, Sukuk issuance typically necessitates an asset pool with a value equal to the issuance amount. Green Sukuk specifically require a sufficient number of environmentally focused or climate-related projects suitable for securitization, in contrast, Sustainability Sukuk encompass a broader scope, incorporating both green and climate-focused initiatives alongside projects aimed at social sector development (Iqbal, 2024). As the top four Green and Sustainability

Sukuk-issuing countries, the four— Saudi Arabia, UAE, Malaysia, and Indonesia— have national framework.

## Saudi Arabia

Besides having a comprehensive climate action strategy through the Saudi Vision 2030 and Saudi Green Initiative, the Kingdom of Saudi Arabia also has the financial resources and institutional capacity to issue Green Sukuk and other Islamic financial instruments at a significant scale. In 2024, global ESG sukuk issuance reached US$11.1 billion, up 3.8% (y-o-y), mostly driven 39% by Saudi Arabia, 22% by Malaysia, 20% by UAE, and 8% by Indonesia (Ho, 2025). Previously, Saudi Arabia developed its Green Financing Framework in line with the Green Bond Principles 2021, including Appendix 1, released in June 2022 by the International Capital Market Association (ICMA). This Framework enables the Saudi to issue Green Bonds or Sukuk. Following these Principles, the Kingdom commits to implementing the following measures for each Green Bond or Sukuk issued, as outlined in the Framework. Table 1 shows the key component of Saudi Arabia's SDGs Government Securities Framework.

*Table 1. Key Components of the SDGs Government Securities Framework in Saudi Arabia*

| SDGs Government Securities Framework | | | |
|---|---|---|---|
| **Use of Proceeds** | **Process for Project Evaluation and Selection** | **Management of Proceeds** | **Reporting** |
| An amount equivalent to the net proceeds from any Green Bond or Sukuk issued by the Kingdom of Saudi Arabia under this Green Financing Framework will be allocated—either partially or fully—to fund new projects or refinance existing ones that fall within the defined eligible green project categories. | To ensure that the proceeds from any Green Bond or Sukuk issued by the Kingdom are directed toward new or existing projects and expenditures that meet the eligibility criteria outlined in the Use of Proceeds section. To manage its green bond and sukuk issuances, the Kingdom has formed a Sustainable Financing Committee, supported by a Projects and Monitoring Committee that reports directly to it. | MoF of Saudi Arabia will oversee the issuance of Green Bonds or Sukuk. The net proceeds will be directed to eligible budgetary programs within the Kingdom's General Budget, to be allocated within two fiscal years following the issuance. The total spending on these eligible programs will be equal to or greater than the net proceeds from the Green Bonds or Sukuk. | An annual allocation report will be published within one year of each issuance, providing detailed information on how the net proceeds have been allocated. |

Source: MoF of Saudia Arabia (2024)

Following the completion of all processes outlined in the Framework, the next step is the External Review. Saudi Arabia is committed to maintaining the highest standards in reviewing its Green Financing Framework. Referring to MoF of Saudia Arabia (2024), the Kingdom adopts a two-step verification process. First, pre-issuance verification (second-party opinion) by engaging Moody's Investors Service to conduct an external review of its Green Financing Framework, confirming its alignment with the ICMA Green Bond Principles. The resulting Second-Party Opinion will be published on the MoF's website. Second, post-issuance external verification, where annual reports will undergo external verification by an independent reviewer to assess the compliance of financed assets with the eligibility criteria in the Use of Proceeds section, confirm the amounts allocated to eligible green projects, and verify the management of both allocated and unallocated proceeds. The auditor's report will also be publicly available on the MoF's website.

## UAE

To establish a comprehensive legal framework for Green Bonds and Sukuk, according to PME (2023), the UAE has made substantial progress in establishing a robust legal and regulatory framework for Green Bonds and Sukuk, offering greater clarity and support to both issuers and investors. First, the Securities and Commodities Authority (SCA) serves as the main regulator of the UAE's financial markets, overseeing the issuance of all securities, including Green Bonds and Sukuk. Second, the Dubai Financial Services Authority (DFSA) provides specific regulatory guidelines for entities operating within the Dubai International Financial Centre (DIFC), which has emerged as a key center for financial and sustainable investment activities in the UAE. Third, the Central Bank of the UAE contributes by regulating the country's banking and financial services sector, working alongside other regulatory institutions to maintain financial system stability.

In the UAE, Rahman, Musari, Mahsyar, and Kilinc-Ata (2025) highlighted that issuing Green Sukuk has emerged as a growing trend among corporations seeking to raise capital. In response, the UAE MOCCAE, in collaboration with the Global Green Growth Institute (GGGI), released guidelines to enhance awareness and understanding of Green Bond and Sukuk issuance aligned with international best practices. According to these guidelines, issuers must follow four key steps: defining the use of proceeds, establishing a process for project evaluation and selection, managing proceeds, and ensuring transparent reporting. The issuance of Green Sukuk falls under the same legal framework regulated by the Emirates Securities and Commodities Authority (ESCA), alongside additional requirements from MOCCAE and other relevant ministries to ensure environmental and social compliance. Table 2 shows the key component of the UAE's Green Sukuk Framework.

*Table 2. Key Components of the Green Sukuk Framework in the UAE*

| **Green Sukuk Framework** | | | |
|---|---|---|---|
| **Use of Proceeds** | **Process for Project Evaluation and Selection** | **Management of Proceeds** | **Reporting** |
| Issuers need to carefully choose projects that align with the eligibility requirements for green or sustainable financing, ensuring they support environmental protection and sustainability objectives. | Process to identify, evaluate and select eligible projects. Independent third-party certification is often necessary to confirm that proceeds from Green Bonds or Sukuk are allocated appropriately and for their intended environmental purposes. | A central element of the Use of Proceeds sukuk principles is the effective management and allocation of funds. Market trends now favor the simpler method of tracking "equivalent amounts" of net proceeds. To ensure transparency and accuracy, issuers are strongly advised to have an external auditor or third party verify the tracking and allocation of these funds. | To provide impact reporting and disclosure, issuers are expected to uphold transparency by clearly disclosing how funds are used and reporting regularly on the environmental outcomes and progress of funded projects. |

Source: GGGI (2023); PME (2023); ICMA, IsDB, and LSEG (2024), developed

Indeed, the commitment of the UAE to become a global hub for sustainability is also underpinned by its UAE Vision 2021 National Agenda, the Sustainable Finance Framework 2021, the Dubai Declaration on Sustainable Finance in 2016, and the Abu Dhabi Sustainable Finance Declaration in 2019 (MOCCAE, 2022; Rahman, Musari, Mahsyar, and Kilinc-Ata, 2025). When issuing Green Sukuk, PME (2023) noted that issuers must carefully select projects that align with green or sustainable financing criteria and contribute to environmental and sustainability goals. Ensuring proper use of proceeds often requires third-party certification and verification. Transparency is crucial, with issuers expected to provide clear disclosures on fund allocation and regularly report on the environmental impact and progress of funded projects. Additionally, Green Sukuk issuers must comply with Islamic finance principles, avoiding interest-based transactions and unethical investments.

## Malaysia

In 2014, the SC released the Sustainable and Responsible Investment (SRI) Sukuk Framework to foster an ecosystem that promotes sustainable and responsible investing for both SRI investors and issuers. Aligned with international standards and best practices, the Framework places strong emphasis on transparency through robust disclosure requirements. It aims to facilitate the financing of projects that support the United Nations SDGs. SRI Sukuk issuance also seeks to diversify the investor base by attracting those with SRI mandates to invest in green, social, and sustainable projects, including initiatives involving waqf properties and/or assets.

As of December 2020, RM5.4 billion in SRI sukuk had been issued under the SRI Sukuk Framework, which was rebranded in January 2021 and subsequently extended to 2025 as the SRI Sukuk and Bond Grant Scheme to also cover issuances under the ASEAN Green, Social, and Sustainability Bond Standards (MOCCAE, 2022). Table 3 shows the key component of Malaysia SRI Framework.

*Table 3. Key components of the SRI Sukuk Framework in Malaysia*

| **SRI Sukuk Framework** | | | |
|---|---|---|---|
| **Utilisation of Proceeds** | **Process for Project Evaluation and Selection** | **Management of Proceeds** | **Reporting** |
| Funds obtained from the issuance of the SRI sukuk are exclusively used to finance activities or transactions associated with the eligible SRI projects | Develop internal procedures to assess and choose qualified SRI projects. | Funds allocated to eligible SRI projects are either deposited into a designated account or monitored through an appropriate tracking method. | Annual reports should include details on the initial allocation for eligible SRI projects, the amount spent, any unutilised funds along with their interim placement or investment, and a list of funded projects with brief descriptions and their actual or anticipated impacts. |

Source: SC (2019)

Once all processes detailed in the Framework have been completed, the subsequent phase is the External Review. An external reviewer can be engaged to evaluate and report on the eligibility of SRI Projects or the issuer's adherence to the applicable requirements outlined in the SC's guidelines. The Eligible SRI Projects aim to achieve six key objectives: conserving energy usage, encouraging the adoption of renewable energy, enhancing the quality of life within society, reducing greenhouse gas emissions, safeguarding the environment and natural resources, and addressing or alleviating a specific social issue or promoting positive social outcomes (SC, 2019).

## Indonesia

In Indonesia, since 2015, the Government has made efforts to integrate climate change considerations into its planning and budgeting frameworks and introduced a budget tagging system to identify portions of the national budget associated with climate change impacts (MoF and UNDP Indonesia, 2018). This mechanism has enabled the Government to assess green financing requirements across various sectors and build on the success of the Green Sukuk Framework. In March 2018, the

Government launched its first sovereign Green Sukuk on the global market (MoF of Indonesia, 2019; MOCCAE, 2022; Musari and Hidayat, 2023; Musari, 2021, 2025; Balative, Hariyanto, Sholikhah, and Prayoga, 2025).

To support the issuance of Blue Sukuk, the Government of Indonesia updated the Green Sukuk Framework 2017, which previously incorporated the outcomes of climate budget tagging, into the SDGs Government Securities Framework in 2021 (Suminto, 2024; Musari, 2025). This also demonstrates the Government of Indonesia's commitment to issuing Green and SDGs Securities to finance projects that deliver environmental and social benefits, contributing to the country's 2030 sustainable development and climate change goals (MoF of Indonesia, 2023; Rahman, Musari, Mahsyar, and Kilinc-Ata, 2025).

Green and SDGs Securities issued under the Framework will be aligned to the respective applicable market standards: 2021 Green Bond Principles, 2021 Social Bond Principles, and 2021 Sustainability Bond Guidelines or as they may subsequently be updated, Green Bond Standards, Social Bond Standards, and Sustainable Bond Standards from the ASEAN Capital Markets Forum. Table 4 shows the key component of the Indonesia's SDGs Government Securities Framework.

*Table 4. Key components of the SDGs Government Securities Framework in Indonesia*

| **SDGs Government Securities Framework** | | | |
|---|---|---|---|
| **Use of Proceeds** | **Process for Project Evaluation and Selection** | **Management of Proceeds** | **Reporting** |
| The proceeds raised from Green Securities issued under this Framework will be allocated to designated Eligible SDGs Expenditures with a focus on Green and Blue initiatives. Meanwhile, proceeds from SDGs Securities will be directed primarily toward Eligible SDGs Expenditures with a Social focus and may also be optionally used for expenditures with Green and Blue focus. | To ensure that proceeds from Green and SDGs Securities are allocated to Eligible Expenditures, as defined in the Framework. Two tagging methods are used to identify suitable projects for funding through these securities. | Proceeds from each Green and SDGs Security will be managed through the Government's general account following prudent treasury practices. Upon request, funds will be transferred to designated accounts of relevant Line Ministries to finance projects aligned with the Framework. | MoF of Indonesia will provide annual reports for each Green and SDGs Security issued, with the first report to be released within one year of the issuance date. Each Green and SDGs Securities report will include, at a minimum: a list and brief overview of the funded projects and expenditure types; the amount of proceeds allocated to each project; and details on SDGs alignment and impact. When feasible, the MoF will provide information on the environmental and/ or social outcomes linked to the Eligible Expenditures supported by the net proceeds of the Green and SDGs Securities. |

Source: Republic of Indonesia SDGs Government Securities Framework 2021

Thus, Indonesia's SDG Securities Framework consists of four key components: Use of Proceeds, directing funds to eligible Green, Blue, and Social-focused projects; Project Evaluation and Selection, using two tagging methods to identify qualifying projects; Management of Proceeds, with funds managed through the government's general account and allocated to ministries as needed; and Reporting, requiring annual updates detailing fund allocation, project types, SDG alignment, and, when possible, the environmental and social impacts.

## GREEN AND SUSTAINABILITY SUKUK PERFORMANCE

In 2024, as reported by Bennett and Coyle (2025), sukuk issuances totaled around $180 billion, with the market steadily progressing toward an outstanding total of $1 trillion within the next few years, and Green Sukuk is playing a crucial role in expanding the market. It is explained that Green Sukuk and Bonds share several similarities, such as their emphasis on how proceeds are used and reliance on independent verification—Shariah boards for sukuk and third-party reviewers for green bonds. Both appeal to investors seeking ethical investments that also generate financial returns. The rise of green sukuk has bridged the gap between these two instruments, with green and sustainable sukuk now making up about 10% of the total sukuk market. Despite their shared features, sukuk and green bonds continue to operate largely within separate investor communities and regional markets.

Regarding Sustainable Sukuk, in 2024, as reported by Damak, Jagtiani, Lescova, and Ozyavuz (2025), the issuance reached $11.9 billion, slightly up from $11.4 billion in 2023, and represented roughly 25% to 30% of all sustainable issuances in the Middle East. Unless there is a significant push toward net-zero commitments by key Islamic finance nations or new regulatory measures, issuance levels are expected to remain steady at around $10–12 billion in 2025. Saudi Arabia led the market, accounting for 38% of total sustainable sukuk issuances, driven largely by its banking sector. Indonesia followed, fueled by sovereign issuances. Although the UAE saw a 60% drop in volume compared to 2023, when COP28 activities boosted issuance, it still contributed 15% to the total.

Further, Bamgbose (2024) notified in the Global Ethical Finance Initiative (GEFI) Insight Series that Sustainable and Green Sukuk issuances rose to nearly US$4.0 billion in the first quarter of 2024, marking a 17% increase compared to the same period in 2023. According to the London Stock Exchange Group (LSEG), this growth was largely driven by Sustainability Sukuk issued by banks in the Gulf Cooperation Council (GCC) region. According to Refinitiv, LSE, UKIFC, and GEFI (2022), there are six types of ESG Sukuk, namely Green Sukuk, Social Sukuk, Sustainability Sukuk, Sustainability-or SDGs-Linked Sukuk, Transition Sukuk, and Blue Sukuk. Table 5 shows the issuance of Green Sukuk and other types of ESG Sukuk during 2017 to Q1 2024.

*Table 5. Green and Other Typed of ESG Sukuk Issuance during 2017 to Q1 2024 ($ Million)*

| Year | Green Sukuk | % Green Sukuk to Total ESG Sukuk | Other Types of ESG Sukuk | % Other Types of ESG Sukuk to Total ESG Sukuk | Total |
|---|---|---|---|---|---|
| 2017 | 421 | 95.25 | 21 | 4.75 | 442 |
| 2018 | 1,358 | 92.76 | 106 | 7.24 | 1,464 |
| 2019 | 3,537 | 98.74 | 44 | 1.23 | 3,582 |
| 2020 | 2,517 | 52.34 | 2,291 | 47.64 | 4,809 |
| 2021 | 1,714 | 26.34 | 4,794 | 73.66 | 6,508 |
| 2022 | 3,422 | 36.35 | 5,993 | 63.65 | 9,415 |

continued on following page

*Table 5. Continued*

| Year | Green Sukuk | % Green Sukuk to Total ESG Sukuk | Other Types of ESG Sukuk | % Other Types of ESG Sukuk to Total ESG Sukuk | Total |
|---|---|---|---|---|---|
| 2023 | 7,772 | 58.10 | 5,606 | 41.90 | 13,378 |
| Q1 2024 | 249 | 6.24 | 3,741 | 93.76 | 3,990 |

Source: LSEG Workspace, in Bamgbose (2024), modified and developed

Table 1 illustrates the growth of ESG Sukuk, which was initially dominated by Green Sukuk, then slowly dominated or balanced with other types of ESG Sukuk. Green Sukuk issuance experienced a decline in issuance in 2020 and 2021, which then returned to positive growth in the following years. The growth of ESG Sukuk itself consistently shows a positive trend. Although there is no data available in the table, Bamgbose (2024) stated that Green Sukuk and Sustainability Sukuk are the most dominant instruments issued in the composition of ESG Sukuk types. GEFI (2024) also highlighted that impressive growth in the issuance of Green and Sustainability Sukuk, which reached $11 billions by the third quarter of 2024. Previously, LSEG Data & Analytics, LSE, UKIFC, & GEFI (2023) mentioned that demand for Green and Sustainability Sukuk has been higher than for traditional sukuk, which reflecting strong interest from global investors.

Further, Figure 1 strengthens that Green Sukuk and Sustainability Sukuk are the most dominant instruments issued in the composition of ESG Sukuk types. The figure illustrates the issuance of Sustainable Sukuk by ESG Type as of Q1 2024, where the value of Green Sukuk and Sustainability Sukuk to the total value of Sustainable Sukuk is 48% and 50%, respectively. This is followed by Sustainability-Linked Sukuk (2%) and Social Sukuk (0.004%), the value of which is still very small.

*Figure 1. Sustainable Sukuk Issuance by ESG Type as of Q1 2024 (% of Value of Sukuk issued)*

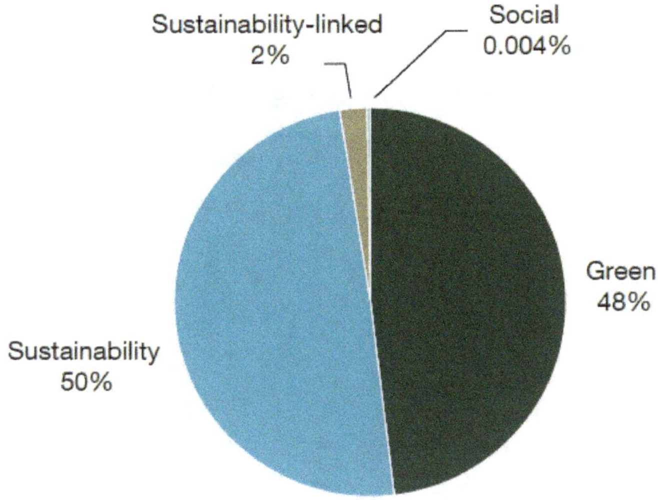


*Source: ICMA, IsDB, and LSEG (2024)*

Then, Figure 2 shows the value of Sustainable Sukuk issuance by country as of the first quarter of 2024, where Sustainable Sukuk issuance has been dominated by Malaysia, Indonesia, the UAE, and Saudi Arabia, which together accounted for 83% of the total cumulative issuance (ICMA, IsDB, and LSEG, 2024). However, even though it remains mastered by these four countries, the composition of its value at the end of 2024 has changed. The ESG sukuk issuance in 2024 overall mostly dominated by 39% by Saudi Arabia, 22% by Malaysia, 20%by the UAE, and 8% by Indonesia (Ho, 2025).

*Figure 2. Sustainable Sukuk Issuance by Country as of Q1 2024 (% of Value of Sukuk issued)*

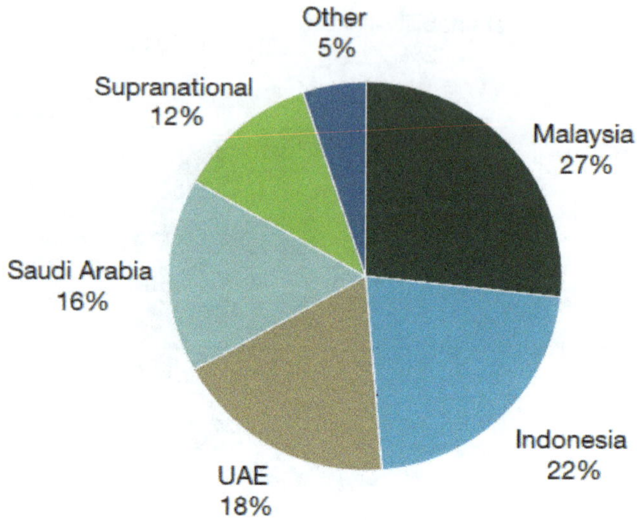


*Source: ICMA, IsDB, and LSEG (2024)*

Although the issuances of ESG Sukuk remain concentrated in a handful of countries, Sukuk is now a key ESG funding tool in emerging markets, with growth expected amid sustainability initiatives, funding needs and a favourable funding environment (Ho, 2025). The growth of the ESG sukuk market is driven by initiatives in standardization, ecosystem development, and improved transparency, although it still faces potential risks from geopolitical instability, fluctuating oil prices, evolving Shariah requirements affecting credit risk, and declining momentum in sustainability efforts within key markets (Finvizier, 2024). Although investors generally react positively to announcements of green sukuk and green bond issuances, however, the response is somewhat stronger for corporate green sukuk announcements than for corporate green bonds, with investors deriving slightly greater benefits from green sukuk issuances compared to green bonds (Riaz, Selamat, Nor, and Hassan, 2024).

## THE IMPACTS ON SDGS

In recent years, many countries around the world have integrated environmental priorities into their national agendas. However, sustainable development continues to require a careful balance between environmental resilience and the pursuit of economic and human progress, even after the achievement of the SDGs (Musari and Khan, 2023). The complex relationship between economic growth and environmental sustainability remains a topic of intense debate (ElMassah & Hassanein, 2023). In response, there is a growing need to strengthen the reliance on sustainable finance—an approach that integrates ESG factors into financial decision-making to support long-term investments in environmentally and socially responsible projects (Hidayat, Musari, Masrohatin, and Smolo, 2024). COP28 reaffirmed the global commitment to $100 billion in annual climate finance through 2025, highlighting Islamic finance as a promising, values-driven source of capital that aligns with sustainability and ESG principles (GEFI, 2024).

## Saudi Arabia

In its Green Financing Framework 2024, Saudi Arabia is firmly dedicated to ensuring a sustainable future for the next generations and achieving long-term national economic growth. Aligned with the Paris Agreement, the Kingdom has initiated extensive and transformative reforms across its public sector, economy, and society under Vision 2030. These reforms are aligned in ambition and purpose with the United Nations SDGs, reflecting their shared focus on sustainable development. Vision 2030 serves as a strategic framework that supports the realization of the SDGs, with both sets of targets being interconnected and mutually reinforcing—progress in one area contributing to advances in the other. Table 6 shows the Saudi Arabia's Green Financing Framework and its impacts on SDGs to reach the Vision 2030.

*Table 6. Green Financing Framework and Its Impacts on SDGs*

| **GREEN FINANCING FRAMEWORK**<br>**Green Bond Principles Project Category** | **SDGs** |
|---|---|
| Environmentally sustainable management of living natural resources and land use | 12, 13, 15 |
| Energy efficiency | 7, 11, 13 |
| Renewable energy | 7, 13 |
| Clean transportation | 11, 13 |
| Pollution prevention and control | 7, 12, 13 |
| Sustainable water and wastewater management | 6 |
| Climate change adaptation | 11, 13, 15 |
| Terrestrial and aquatic biodiversity | 14 |

Source: MoF of Saudi Arabia (2024)

As a note, to explore the challenges and sustainability potential of Green Sukuk in Saudi Arabia within the context of Vision 2030, focusing on their role in financing environmentally friendly projects, also reviews the Saudi Electricity Company's (SEC) framework for advancing a low-carbon and circular economy, community empowerment, and responsible business practices, a study by Shalhoob (2023) found several obstacles to Green Sukuk issuance, such as unclear definitions, limited awareness, lack of standardized measurement, insufficient institutional capacity, and lengthy legal processes. The research highlights the need for clear definitions and standardized metrics and offers valuable insights for stakeholders—including researchers, governments, policymakers, industries, investors, and regulators—on advancing Green Sukuk development.

## UAE

In its UAE Sustainable Finance Framework 2021-2031, it has been acknowledged that because of the UAE's environmental and climate change challenges, the government has made the green economy—focused on environmental sustainability, resource efficiency, and social inclusion—a strategic priority over the past decade. In response, both federal and local authorities have introduced a range of initiatives, including the UAE Vision 2021, the National Green Agenda 2015–2030, and the National Climate Change Plan 2017–2050, along with various sectoral and emirate-level strategies. Together, these efforts have established a solid policy and regulatory foundation to support the country's transition toward a green economy.

Further, in 2023, Emirates News Agency – WAM (2023) reported that the UAE Green Agenda 2030 has been updated to support the nation's SDGs and the long-term vision outlined in UAE Centennial 2071. Between 2023 and 2030, the UAE plans to launch various initiatives and projects aimed at advancing the green economy, including raising GDP by 4% to 5%, boosting exports by approximately AED 24 to 25 billion, and cutting emissions from 430 kilowatt-hours in 2013 to below 100 kilowatt-hours by 2030. Table 7 shows the main environmental priorities of the policy within the General Policy for the Environment in the UAE to support the implementation of the SDGs.

*Table 7. Main Environmental Priorities and Its Impacts on SDGs*

| MAIN ENVIRONMENTAL PRIORITIES | SDGs |
|---|---|
| Integrated waste management | 11, 12 |
| Promoting environmentally sound management of chemicals | 3, 6, 12 |
| Mitigating the effects of climate change to support the country's economic development priorities | 8, 13 |
| Promoting and ensuring the safety of food products and diversifying their sources | 2, 12 |

continued on following page

*Table 7. Continued*

| MAIN ENVIRONMENTAL PRIORITIES | SDGs |
|---|---|
| Preserving natural environment | 11, 14, 15 |
| Sustaining local livestock production and optimizing local natural resource | 2, 12, 15 |
| Enhancing air quality | 3, 11, 13 |
| Sustaining local agricultural production and preserving its resources | 2, 12, 15 |

Source: MOCCAE (2020), developed

Thus, the main environmental priorities within the UAE's General Policy for the Environment are closely aligned with key SDGs 2, 3, 6, 11, 12, 13, and 15. These initiatives not only reflect the nation's commitment to responsible environmental stewardship but also directly support the ambitions of Vision 2030 and the UAE Centennial 2071 by fostering sustainable economic growth and environmental resilience. In this context, the development of Green Sukuk emerges as a vital financing mechanism, enabling the mobilization of Shari'ah-compliant capital toward projects that contribute to these national and global sustainability objectives, while reinforcing the UAE's position as a regional leader in Islamic sustainable finance.

## Malaysia

To support the financing of projects aligned with the United Nations SDGs, SRI Sukuk are issued with proceeds designated exclusively for funding activities or transactions connected to eligible SRI Projects. The goals of issuing SRI Sukuk include promoting energy conservation, enhancing societal well-being, safeguarding the environment and natural resources, encouraging the use of renewable energy, reducing greenhouse gas emissions, and addressing specific social challenges or striving for positive social impact. Table 8 shows the eligible SRI Projects to support the implementation of the SDGs.

*Table 8. Eligible SRI Projects and Its Impacts on SDGs*

| ELIGIBLE SRI PROJECTS | SDGs |
|---|---|
| GREEN | |
| Renewable energy | 3, 7, 8, 9, 11, 12, 13 |
| Energy efficiency | |
| Pollution prevention and control | 3, 11, 12 |

continued on following page

*Table 8. Continued*

| ELIGIBLE SRI PROJECTS | SDGs |
|---|---|
| **GREEN** | |
| Environmentally sustainable management of living natural resources and land use | 2, 6, 11, 12, 14, 15 |
| Terrestrial and aquatic biodiversity conservation | |
| Clean transportation | 11 |
| Sustainable water and wastewater management | 6, 11, 12 |
| Climate change adaptation | 1, 2, 13 |
| Eco-efficient and/or circular economy adapted products, production technologies and processes | 8, 11, 12 |
| Green buildings which meet regional, national or internationally recognized standards or certifications | 11 |
| **SOCIAL** | **SDGs** |
| Affordable basic infrastructure | 2, 3, 6, 7, 9, 11 |
| Access to essential services | 1, 2, 3, 4, 5, 8, 9 10 |
| Affordable housing | 1, 11 |
| Employment generation including the potential effect of SME financing and microfinance | 8, 9 |
| Food security | 2, 12 |
| Socioeconomic advancement and empowerment | 1, 2, 4, 5, 8, 10, 11,14 |
| **WAQF PROPERTIES AND/OR ASSETS** | **SDGs** |
| Development of waqf properties or assets | 1, 3, 4,7, 8, 9, 10, 11 |

Source: SC (2019)

Eligible SRI projects encompass a broad range of initiatives that align with environmental, social, and ethical objectives. Additionally, SRI Sukuk may fund integrated green and social projects, as well as waqf-based initiatives focused on the development of waqf properties or assets to advancing the United Nations SDGs. This diverse scope highlights the flexibility and impact potential of SRI Sukuk in supporting sustainable development across multiple sectors. Green projects support goals such as affordable and clean energy (SDG 7), sustainable cities and communities (SDG 11), climate action (SDG 13), and responsible consumption and production (SDG 12) by promoting renewable energy, pollution control, biodiversity conservation, and climate resilience. Social projects directly address goals like no poverty (SDG 1), zero hunger (SDG 2), good health and well-being (SDG 3), quality education (SDG 4), decent work and economic growth (SDG 8), and reduced inequalities (SDG 10) through enhanced infrastructure, access to services, affordable housing, job creation, and financial inclusion. Combined green-social initiatives and waqf-based developments further strengthen community empowerment and sustainable resource use, reinforcing the role of SRI Sukuk as a powerful instrument in achieving holistic and inclusive sustainable development.

## Indonesia

Indonesia has demonstrated its commitment to achieving the 2030 Sustainable Development Agenda by establishing a legal foundation and forming an inclusive coordination team to support SDG implementation. Integrating the SDGs into national development planning provides a solid base for their effective execution. Each SDG goal is linked to specific programs, designated government ministries, participating non-state actors, and allocated state funding. Additionally, the SDGs Government Securities Framework outlines how Indonesia plans to issue Green and SDGs-linked securities, including Green Sukuk, to finance projects that generate environmental and social benefits, reinforcing the country's efforts to meet its 2030 targets. Table 9 shows the sector focus of Green and SDGs Securities to support the implementation of the SDGs.

*Table 9. SDGs Government Securities Framework and Its Impacts on SDGs*

| SECTOR<br>GREEN AND BLUE FOCUS | SDGs |
|---|---|
| Renewable Energy | 7, 8, 9, 11, 13, 14 |
| Energy Efficiency | 7, 8, 9, 11, 13, 14 |
| Waste to Energy and Waste Management | 7, 11, 12, 13, 14 |
| Sustainable Transport | 7, 8, 9, 11, 13 |
| Sustainable Management of Natural Resources on Land | 13, 15 |
| Sustainable Water and Wastewater Management | 6, 13 |
| Sustainable Management of Natural Resources on Ocean | 13, 14 |
| Green Tourism | 8, 13, 14, 15 |
| Green Building | 9, 11, 13 |
| Resilience to Climate Change for Highly Vulnerable Areas and Sectors/Disaster Risk Reduction | 3, 5, 6, 8, 9, 10, 11, 13, 14, 15 |
| **SOCIAL FOCUS** | **SDGs** |
| Employment Generation including through the Potential Effect of SME Financing and Microfinance Socioeconomic Advancement and Empowerment | 1, 5, 8, 10 |
| Food Security and Sustainable Food Systems | 2 |

continued on following page

*Table 9. Continued*

| SECTOR | SDGs |
|---|---|
| **GREEN AND BLUE FOCUS** | |
| Access to Essential Services | 3, 4 |
| Affordable Basic Infrastructure | 6, 9, 11 |

Source: Republic of Indonesia SDGs Government Securities Framework 2021; MoF of Indonesia (2024); Musari and Hidayat (2023), developed

Many countries are actively seeking innovative financing mechanisms to meet the SDGs and fulfill commitments under the Paris Agreement. However, these ambitions place considerable pressure on the already limited resources of developing nations, a situation worsened by the COVID-19 pandemic, which has further constrained the availability of funds for long-term sustainable development, leading many countries to increase their debt levels (OECD, 2022). While the SDGs serve as valuable reference points for fiscal planning and donor engagement, standard cross-country cost estimations can often be inaccurate or misleading (Vorisek and Yu, 2020). To address funding gaps, engaging the private sector through blended finance has become increasingly vital (Brunnhuber, 2023), as it enables greater risk-sharing in SDG-related investments (UNCTAD, 2014) and has evolved from a niche strategy into a powerful tool for mobilizing development finance (Mutambatsere and Schellekens, 2020), also will play in addressing global inequalities (Dial, 2025).

Indeed, blended finance serves as a tool to catalyze the strategic development finance to attract additional funding for sustainable development, especially by engaging the private sector (DFI, 2023) as well as leveraging public and philanthropic resources into projects that generate both social impact and financial returns (OECD, 2021), particularly for projects aligned with the SDGs, including those focused on nature-based solutions (Blended Finance Taskforce, 2017), in developing countries (OECD, 2018). Likewise, Islamic blended finance refers to the funding of sustainable development, aligned with shari'ah principles, by integrating Islamic commercial finance with Islamic social finance to generate both financial returns as well as positive societal and environmental outcomes (Musari, 2025). As governments face growing fiscal constraints, blended finance offers a means to fill financing gaps while also supporting sustainable management of natural resources and biodiversity (Brears, 2022). Multilateral development banks and development finance institutions are pivotal in this process, including a broader array of stakeholders like philanthropic foundations, banks, venture capital firms, private equity, hedge funds, corporations, as well as institutional and commercial investors (OECD, 2018, 2021).

In the realm of Islamic commercial finance, sukuk is widely used to support climate-related and sustainability goals. Expanding on this, new sukuk variants are being explored, including Yellow Sukuk (Ergun, 2023), White Sukuk, Blue Sukuk, and Catastrophe Sukuk (Buana and Musari, 2020; Musari, 2020a, 2020b, 2025). On the social finance side, Islamic instruments such as w*aqf, infaq, sadaqa, hiba,* and *zakat* are commonly utilized to advance social welfare (Musari, 2025). Although limited research exists on using *zakat* specifically for environmental initiatives, evidence from Malaysia shows that *zakat* can contribute to green economic growth in the short term (Hamid et al., 2019) and holds significant potential to support equitable economic development while addressing environmental risks (Kurniawan, Nastiti, and Ali, 2024).

In response to the revealing question, whether Green and Sustainability Sukuk are more profitable for investors than Green Bonds, the results of the study by Lee, Kim, and Lee (2025) can serve as empirical evidence. By taking the data of Malaysia, the study reveals that Green Sukuk offer significantly higher returns than Green Bonds, suggesting a more attractive option for yield-seeking investors in the green finance market. Importantly, the lack of a causal relationship between green sukuk and green bonds implies that they operate independently, so this offers diversification benefits. For investors, Green Sukuk provide both higher returns and ethical investment opportunities, while for issuers—especially those in non-Islamic finance countries—they present a means to access new capital by attracting Shari'ah-compliant investors. Policymakers are urged to develop distinct strategies for each instrument, supporting investor access through tax incentives, mutual funds, and educational programs, while encouraging domestic firms to issue green sukuk internationally to fund environmental initiatives and broaden the investor base.

Further, Green and Sustainability Sukuk also still have some risk challenges. Table 10 shows five types of Green and Sustainability Sukuk's risk challenges.

*Table 10. Risk Challenges of Green and Sustainability Sukuk*

| Type of Risks | Description |
|---|---|
| Pricing and Market Risks | • Unexplained pricing disparity, where discrepancy between green and non-green financial instrument prices remains unresolved, impacting valuation transparency;<br>• Adverse selection risk, where the issuers may opportunistically choose between green and non-green instruments, leading to inefficiencies in sustainable capital allocation;<br>• Inadequate risk premium, where the current sukuk pricing structures often do not reflect environmental risks, suggesting the need for environmental risk premiums;<br>• Ambiguity in contract pricing and market development, where lack of harmonization make inconsistent ESG standards across jurisdictions. |
| Environmental Risks | • Environmental degradation, where financing might unintentionally support harmful projects, increasing pollution and waste;<br>• Systemic environmental risk, where severe environmental harm can escalate into systemic financial risks impacting global markets. |
| Reputational Risks | • Greenwashing and mislabeling, where misuse of 'green' labels by issuers may lead to loss of trust in green sukuk instruments;<br>• Reputation damage in crisis, where non-green sukuk holders may face reputational damage during systemic environmental crises;<br>• Underrepresentation of diverse regional scholars in standard setting organizations (SSOs) leads to low legitimacy and adoption of global Islamic finance standards. |

continued on following page

*Table 10. Continued*

| Type of Risks | Description |
|---|---|
| Structural and Operational Risks | • Late market entry, where Islamic finance entered the green finance space later than conventional finance, affecting competitiveness;<br>• Complex Shari'ah compliance, where additional requirements for Shari'ah compliance increase complexity in structuring green sukuk;<br>• Inefficient issuance process, where Green and Sustainability Sukuk lead to longer issuance timelines and increased transaction costs, higher transaction and reporting costs, where the ESG verification and Shari'ah governance processes elevate costs relative to conventional green bonds;<br>• Client readiness, where the issuers and investors often lack the readiness to adhere to rigorous ESG covenants, where capacity & awareness gaps emerge because limited investor education and institutional awareness about sustainability in Islamic finance;<br>• Irregular issuance frequency, where Green and Sustainability Sukuk issuance remains sporadic due to a limited pipeline of eligible green projects as underlying assets;<br>• Lack of cross-jurisdictional harmonization, where divergent Shari'ah interpretations across countries lead to structural and operational inconsistencies; |
| Legal, Regulatory, Standardization, Governance, and Harmonization Risks | • Regulatory fragmentation hinders the unified implementation of Green and Sustainability Sukuk frameworks, where the absence of standardized regulatory frameworks for Islamic sustainable finance, where differing national regulations for Shari'ah compliance, ESG criteria, and financial disclosures;<br>• Insufficient representation in SSOs, where lack of inclusive representation from diverse jurisdictions in standard-setting bodies hinders the creation of widely acceptable Green and Sustainability Sukuk instruments, where the existence of SSOs often prefer domestic standards, creating asymmetry in financial reporting, governance, and auditing; where varied opinions among scholars and use of local Shari'ah standards create uncertainty in contract validity and recognition of Green and Sustainability Sukuk structures across borders;<br>• Weak governance standards, where inconsistent governance protocols across jurisdictions lead to questions regarding the authenticity of Shari'ah compliance in Green and Sustainability Sukuk issuances. |

Source: Compiled from Sasongko and Sakti (2020), Musari and Hidayat (2023), BIX Malaysia (2023), Hidayat, Musari, Masrohatin, and Smolo (2024), and Author's Own

Thus, the comprehensive typology of the risks associated with Green and Sustainability Sukuk illustrates the multifaceted and systemic nature of barriers impeding their effective development and deployment. Key issues span across five critical domains---pricing and market risks; environmental risks; reputational risks; structural and operational risks; as well as legal, regulatory, standardization, governance, and harmonization risks. Each contributes distinct yet interconnected risks. Addressing these structural deficiencies requires urgent and coordinated efforts among standard-setting bodies, regulators, scholars, and financial institutions to foster a more inclusive, efficient, and innovation-driven system. Addressing these interrelated risks requires a holistic and coordinated strategy involving regulatory unification, enhanced institutional capacity, and inclusive stakeholder engagement to support a resilient and credible Islamic sustainable finance ecosystem. Overall,

Green and Sustainability Sukuk can also be a gateway to finding innovative sustainable financing instruments to diversify risks through Islamic public borrowing.

Last but not least is to answer the question 'how to measure the success of Green and Sustainability Sukuk?'. Of course, the measure of success of sustainable financial instruments is unique and must have an impact on the environment. To ensure that the Green Sukuk investment generates sustainable environmental and/or social outcomes alongside financial returns, by referring to Indonesia Green Sukuk Allocation and Impact Report 2019-2024 (MoF of Indonesia, 2019, 2020, 2024), at least the standard measure of success of Green and Sustainability Sukuk can use indicators for the mitigation of annual greenhouse gas (GHG) emission avoided, in carbon dioxide (CO2). The methodology employed for calculating GHG emissions adheres to the methods established by the Intergovernmental Panel on Climate Change (IPCC) Guidelines, specifically the IPCC Guidelines 2006 (MoF of Indonesia, 2024). It can also be added with other indicators for the direct impact of the green projects, such as the achievement of social/SDGs or the national vulnerability index.

## CONCLUSION

Green and Sustainability Sukuk have proven to be effective instruments for aligning Islamic finance with global sustainable development objectives, particularly in advancing the United Nations SDGs and fulfilling the Paris Agreement commitments. The experiences of Saudi Arabia, the UAE, Malaysia, and Indonesia demonstrate how comprehensive national frameworks, supported by clear regulatory guidelines and strategic alignment with national visions, can mobilize Shari'ah-compliant capital to finance environmentally and socially impactful projects. These sukuk not only support environmental initiatives such as renewable energy, climate adaptation, clean transportation, and biodiversity conservation but also address social priorities like affordable housing, food security, and employment generation, thereby reinforcing their dual utility and multidimensional impact.

The performance of the ESG Sukuk market, with issuance volumes reaching over $15 billion in 2024 and projections exceeding $50 billion in 2025, reflects a strong global appetite for ethical, purpose-driven investments. Green and Sustainability Sukuk, in particular, dominate the ESG Sukuk segment, accounting for nearly 98% of the market in early 2024. This growth has been largely driven by the leadership of the four focus countries, which collectively represent over 80% of total global sustainable sukuk issuances. However, despite their remarkable progress, challenges remain, such as limited market penetration, regulatory gaps, and the need for standardization and increased institutional capacity. Addressing these barriers is critical to broadening the impact and accessibility of Islamic green finance.

Ultimately, the integration of green and sustainability sukuk into national financing strategies offers a powerful model for climate-resilient and socially inclusive development. These instruments exemplify the potential of Islamic finance not only as an ethical alternative to conventional finance but also as a strategic enabler of global sustainability agendas. Moving forward, strengthening partnerships between governments, the private sector, and international organizations while expanding innovative models such as Islamic blended finance will be essential to scaling up investment and ensuring that sustainable finance plays a central role in achieving both national development priorities and global SDGs.

## REFERENCES


Balative, M. I., Hariyanto, E., Sholikhah, A., & Prayoga, R. G. (2025). A closer look at Indonesia's experience in developing green sukuk. In Taghizadeh-Hesary, F., Thaker, H. M. T., Bhatti, M. I., & Thaker, M. A. M. T. (Eds.), *Islamic finance and sustainability: A research companion* (pp. 441–464). Routledge. DOI: 10.4324/9781003518617-23

Bamgbose, O. (2024, June 24). Bridging faith and sustainability: Unlocking Islamic sustainable finance. *Global Ethical Finance Initiative (GEFI) Insights Series,* https://www.globalethicalfinance.org/2024/06/26/bridging-faith-and-sustainability-unlocking-islamic-sustainable-finance/

Bennett, M., & Coyle, H. (2025, March 4). State of the sukuk market and prospects for growth. *World Bank,* https://blogs.worldbank.org/en/allaboutfinance/state-of-the-sukuk-market-and-prospects-for-growth

Blended Finance Taskforce. (2017). *Better finance, better world.* Consultation paper of the Blended Finance Task Force in partnership with the Business & Sustainable Development Commission and SYSTEMIQ. http://s3.amazonaws.com/aws-bsdc/BFT_BetterFinance_final_01192018.pdf

Brears, R. (2022). *Financing nature-based solutions: Exploring public, private, and blended finance models and case studies*. Springer International Publishing AG. DOI: 10.1007/978-3-030-93325-8

Brunnhuber, S. (2023). *Financing our anthropocene: How wall street, main street and central banks can manage, fund and hedge our global commons*. Springer. DOI: 10.1007/978-3-031-23285-5

Buana, G. K., & Musari, K. (2020, December 28). A new sphere of sukuk: Linking pandemic to Paris agreement. *The World Financial Review,* November-December Edition, Islam Finance, pp. 59-61. https://worldfinancialreview.com/a-new-sphere-of-sukuk-linking-the-pandemic-to-the-paris-agreement/

Cho, K. Q. (2023, December 1). Malaysia's progress in green sukuk. *Phillip Invest,* Finance, Investments, https://www.phillipinvest.com.my/malaysias-progress-in-green-sukuk/

Damak, M., Jagtiani, S., Lescova, T., & Ozyavuz, A. (2025, January 13). Sukuk market: Strong performance set to continue in 2025. *S&P Global,* https://www.spglobal.com/ratings/en/research/articles/250113-sukuk-market-strong-performance-set-to-continue-in-2025-13377916

DFI. (2023). *DFI working group on blended concessional finance for private sector projects*. Joint Report, March. https://idbinvest.org/en/publications/dfi-working-group-blended-concessional-finance-private-sector-projects-2023

Dial, A. (2025, March 31). Blended finance & impact investing in the global south. *Yale School of Management,* https://som.yale.edu/story/2025/blended-finance-impact-investing-global-south

ElMassah, S., & Hassanein, E. A. (2023). Economic development and environmental sustainability in the GCC countries: New insights based on the economic complexity. *Sustainability (Basel)*, *15*(10), 7987. DOI: 10.3390/su15107987

Emirates News Agency – WAM. (2023, February 6). *UAE foreign trade achieved AED2.233 trillion in 2022 with growth rate of 17%: Mohammed bin Rashid.* https://www.wam.ae/en/details/1395303125677

Ergun, H. (2023). Yellow sukuk unveiled: Harnessing agricultural commodity trade for islamic finance and paradigm shift in commodity exchanges. *Al Qasimia University (AQU). Journal of Islamic Economics*, *3*(1), 81–114. DOI: 10.52747/aqujie.3.1.229

Finvizier. (2024). *Sustainable sukuk: Global trends and market overview.* https://www.finvizier.com/wp-content/uploads/2024/07/sustainable-sukuk-global-trends-and-market-overview-upd.pdf

Fitch Rating. (2025, January 21). *ESG sukuk to cross usd50 billion in 2025: Key ESG funding role in emerging markets.* https://www.fitchratings.com/research/non-bank-financial-institutions/esg-sukuk-to-cross-usd50-billion-in-2025-key-esg-funding-role-in-emerging-markets-21-01-2025

GEFI. (2024). Green and sustainability sukuk report 2024: Crossing borders. *Global Ethical Finance Initiative (GEFI),* https://www.globalethicalfinance.org/2024/11/28/green-and-sustainability-sukuk-report-2024-crossing-borders

GGGI. (2023). Role of green bonds and sukuk in unlocking climate finance in Arab countries: International experiences in issuing green bonds and policy implications. *Global Green Growth Institute (GGGI),* https://climate2023.arabfund.org/wp-content/uploads/2023/08/163INT1.pdf

Hadad-Zervos, F. (2017, July 31). Malaysia launches the world's first green Islamic bond. *World Bank,* Blog, https://blogs.worldbank.org/en/eastasiapacific/malaysia-launches-the-worlds-first-green-islamic-bond?

Hamid, N. A., Muda, R., Alam, M. M., Omar, N., & Nadzri, F. A. A. (2019). Contribution of Islamic social capital on green economic growth in Malaysia. *International Journal of Business and Management Science*, *9*(2), 239–256.

Helali, L. (2024, May 2). Green sukuk as an alternative to green bonds – opportunities and challenges. *Islamic Business and Financial Law,* https://blogs.helsinki.fi/islamic-business-financial-law/2024/05/02/green-sukuk-as-an-alternative-to-green-bonds-opportunities-and-challenges/

Hidayat, S. E., Musari, K., Masrohatin, S., & Smolo, E. (2024). The future of Islamic finance. In Smolo, E., & Raheem, M. M. (Eds.), *The future of Islamic finance: From shari'ah law to fintech* (pp. 221–242). Emerald Publishing Limited. DOI: 10.1108/978-1-83549-906-120241014

Ho, J. (2025, January 22). Global ESG sukuk market to surpass US$50 bil in 2025. *Singapore News Yahoo,* https://sg.news.yahoo.com/global-esg-sukuk-market-surpass-140000332.html

ICMA, IsDB, & LSEG. (2024). *Guidance on green, social and sustainability sukuk.* International Capital Market Association (ICMA), the Islamic Development Bank (IsDB), and the London Stock Exchange Group (LSEG).

IISD. (2015). Islamic climate change declaration calls for zero emissions strategy. *International Institute for Sustainable Development (IISD),* https://sdg.iisd.org/news/islamic-climate-change-declaration-calls-for-zero-emissions-strategy/

Indonesia, U. N. D. P. (2020, November 11). Pioneering the green sukuk in Indonesia. *United Nations Development Programme (UNDP),* https://www.undp.org/content/undp/en/home/stories/pioneering-the-green-sukok-in-indonesia.html

Iqbal, Z. (January 23, 2024). Islamic Development Bank | Expert Insights | The Knowledge Portal. https://ukifc.com/2024/01/23/islamic-development-bank-expert-insights-the-knowledge-portal/

IsDB. (2020). Annual Impact Report on IsDB Debut Green Sukuk. Islamic Development Bank (IsDB), https://www.isdb.org/publications/annual-impact-report-on-isdb-debut-green-sukuk-dec-2020

Kohli, S., & Al Taitoon, J. (2025, February 17). Why ESG sukuk has the wind in its sails. *London Stock Exchange Group (LSEG) Insights,* https://www.lseg.com/en/insights/why-sustainable-sukuk-has-wind-in-its-sails

Kurniawan, E., Nastiti, H. M., & Ali, R. A. (2024). Zakat environment: A bibliometric analysis. *Indonesian Conference of Zakat - Proceedings,* 398-405. DOI:DOI: 10.37706/iconz.2023.587

Lee, E., Kim, J. Y., & Lee, Y. (2025). A comparative analysis of green sukuk and green bonds. *International Journal of Islamic and Middle Eastern Finance and Management*. .DOI: 10.1108/IMEFM-12-2024-0609

LSEG Data & Analytics, LSE, UKIFC, & GEFI. (2024). *Green and sustainability sukuk update 2023: Financing a sustainable future.* Refinitiv, London Stock Exchange Group (LSEG) Data & Analytics, London Stock Exchange (LSE), Islamic Finance Council United Kingdom (UKIFC), and the Global Ethical Finance Initiative (GEFI).

Malaysia, B. I. X. (2023, January 3). *The state of Islamic sustainable finance in Malaysia and Indonesia, according to the legal community.* https://www.bixmalaysia.com/learning-center/articles-tutorials/the-state-of-islamic-sustainable-finance-in-malaysia-and-indonesia,-according-to-the-legal-community

Middle East Briefing. (2025, January 23). ESG Sukuk to Cross US$50 Billion in 2025, Key Funding Tool in Emerging Markets. https://www.middleeastbriefing.com/news/esg-sukuk-to-cross-usd50-billion-in-2025-key-global-funding-tool/

MOCCAE. (2020, December 16). Ministry of Climate Change and Environment Launches UAE Environmental Policy. https://www.moccae.gov.ae/en/media-center/news/16/12/2020/ministry-of-climate-change-and-environment-launches-uae-environmental-policy.aspx#page=1

MOCCAE. (2021). *UAE sustainable finance framework 2021-2031.* United Arab Emirates (UAE) Ministry of Climate Change and Environment (MOCCAE), https://www.moccae.gov.ae/assets/24b84d14/UAE_Sustainable_framework_21.pdf.aspx

MOCCAE. (2022). *UAE green bond and sukuk program development situation analysis report.* United Arab Emirates (UAE) Ministry of Climate Change and Environment (MOCCAE), https://www.moccae.gov.ae/assets/download/a36ce910/UAE%20Green%20Bond%20and%20Sukuk%20Program%20Development.pdf.aspx

MoF & UNDP Indonesia. (2018). *Indonesia's green bond & green sukuk initiative.* Ministry of Finance Republic of Indonesia (MoF of Indonesia), Jakarta.

MoF of Indonesia. (2019). *Green sukuk, allocation and impact report – February 2019.* Ministry of Finance Republic of Indonesia (MoF of Indonesia), Jakarta.

MoF of Indonesia. (2020). *Green sukuk, allocation and impact report – March 2020.* Ministry of Finance (MoF), Republic of Indonesia, Jakarta.

MoF of Indonesia. (2024). Green sukuk, allocation and impact report 2024. Ministry of Finance Republic of Indonesia (MoF of Indonesia), Jakarta.

MoF of Saudi Arabia. (2024). *Kingdom of Saudi Arabia Green Financing Framework March 2024.* Ministry of Finance Kingdom of Saudi Arabia (MoF of Saudi Arabia).

Musari, K. (2020a, January 7). Measuring the opportunities of white sukuk for SDGs. *Bisnis Indonesia,* Opini, 2.

Musari, K. (2020b, April 14). Pandemic and catastrophe sukuk. *Bisnis Indonesia,* Opini, 2.

Musari, K. (2021). Green sukuk, Islamic green financing: A lesson learned from Indonesia. In Olarewaju, O. M., & Ganiyu, I. O. (Eds.), *Climate change and the sustainable financial sector* (pp. 1–16). IGI Global. DOI: 10.4018/978-1-7998-7967-1.ch001

Musari, K. (2025). Towards the perpetual sustainable sukuk through Islamic blended finance: Lesson from green sukuk and blue sukuk in Indonesia. In de Pablos, P. O., Lytras, M., & Malik, S. (Eds.), *Securing sustainable futures through blue and green economies* (pp. 381–402). IGI Global. DOI: 10.4018/979-8-3693-7893-9.ch015

Musari, K., & Hidayat, S. E. (2023). The role of green sukuk in maqasid al-shariah and SDGs: Evidence from Indonesia. In Jumat, Z. H., Khateeb, S. H., & Ali, S. N. (Eds.), *Islamic finance, fintech, and the road to sustainability: Reframing the approach in the post-pandemic era* (pp. 181–203). Palgrave CIBFR Studies in Islamic Finance. Palgrave Macmillan. DOI: 10.1007/978-3-031-13302-2_9

Musari, K., & Khan, T. (2023). *Sustainable development and circular economy in the GCC countries.* A paper was presented at the Workshop "Circular Economy and Sustainable Development Model: It's Role in the GCC States' National Visions" held by Gulf Research Centre Cambridge (GRCC), University of Cambridge, Cambridge – United Kingdom, July, 11th -13th

Mutambatsere, E., & Schellekens, P. (2020). *The why and how of blended finance.* A Discussion Paper of International Finance Corporation (IFC) World Bank Group, November

OECD (2018), *Making Blended Finance Work for the Sustainable Development Goals*. Organisation for Economic Co-operation and Development (OECD) Publishing. DOI: 10.1787/9789264288768-en

OECD. (2021). The OECD DAC blended finance guidance. Organisation for Economic Co-operation and Development (OECD) Development Co-operation Directorate, Paris

OECD. (2022). *Global outlook on financing for sustainable development 2023: No sustainability without equity.* Organisation for Economic Co-operation and Development (OECD) Publishing. DOI: 10.1787/fcbe6ce9-en

PME. (2023, November 7). *Green bonds and sukuk in the UAE: Legal framework and considerations.* Prudential Middle East (PME) Global LLC, https://www.linkedin.com/pulse/green-bonds-sukuk-uae-legal-framework-znmff/

Rahman, M. P., Musari, K., Mahsyar, N. M., & Kilinc-Ata, N. (2025). Towards a sustainable future: Evaluating green sukuk in Indonesia and the UAE. In Taghizadeh-Hesary, F., Thaker, H. M. T., Bhatti, M. I., & Thaker, M. A. M. T. (Eds.), *Islamic finance and sustainability: A research companion* (pp. 487–507). Routledge. DOI: 10.4324/9781003518617-25

Refinitiv, LSE, UKIFC, & GEFI. (2022). *Green and sustainability sukuk report 2022.* Refinitiv, London Stock Exchange (LSE), Islamic Finance Council United Kingdom (UKIFC), and the Global Ethical Finance Initiative (GEFI).

Riaz, T., Selamat, A. I., Nor, N. M., & Hassan, A. F. S. (2024). Do investors get benefits from corporate green sukuk issuance. *Journal of Islamic Monetary Economics and Finance*, *10*(3), 445–470. DOI: 10.21098/jimf.v10i3.1944

Sasongko, A., & Sakti, A. (2020). *Sovereign green sukuk: Environmental risk model development.* Working Paper of Bank Indonesia Number WP/2/2020, https://publication-bi.org/repec/idn/wpaper/WP022020.pdf

SC. (2019). *Sustainable and responsible investment sukuk framework: An overview.* Securities Commission (SC) Malaysia. S&P Global. (2025, March 25). *Sustainability insights: Sustainable bond outlook 2025: Middle east issuance to remain high.* https://www.spglobal.com/ratings/en/research/articles/250304-sustainability-insights-sustainable-bond-outlook-2025-middle-east-issuance-to-remain-high-13424912

Shalhoob, H. (2023). Green sukuk in Saudi Arabia: Challenges and potentials of sustainability in the light of Saudi Vision 2030 . *Journal of Governance & Regulation*, *12*(4), 351–360. DOI: 10.22495/jgrv12i4siart15

Suminto. (2024). Preface. In Musari, K. (Ed.), *Series 3 of IAEI east java writes: Searching for the opportunity of Islamic sustainable financing* (pp. iii-vii). Jakad Media Publishing.

The UAE's Government portal. (2024). The UAE's Green Agenda – 2030. https://u.ae/en/about-the-uae/strategies-initiatives-and-awards/strategies-plans-and-visions/environment-and-energy/the-uaes-green-agenda-2030

UNCTAD. (2014). World investment report 2014 - Investing in the SDGs: An action plan. *United Nations Conference on Trade and Development (UNCTAD)*, New York & Geneva.

UNDP in Asia and the Pacific. (2020, November 9). Footing the bill: Innovative financing for climate action in Indonesia and the pioneering of green sukuk. *United Nations Development Programme Indonesia (UNDP) in Asia and the Pacific.* https://undpasiapac.medium.com/footing-the-bill-innovative-financing-for-climate-action-in-indonesia-and-the-pioneering-of-green-bbee3262047

Vorisek, D. L., & Yu, S. (2020). *Understanding the cost of achieving the sustainable development goals.* World Bank Policy Research Working Paper No. 9164. https://ssrn.com/abstract=3545657

Yu, Y. (2016). *Climate finance in and beyond the Paris agreement: Implementing climate finance commitments in Asia and the Pacific.* A Discussion Paper of Macroeconomic Policy and Financing for Development Division at First High-Level Follow-up Dialogue on Financing for Development in Asia and the Pacific, March 30$^{th}$-31$^{th}$, Incheon.

ZAWYA. (2024, September 25). Saudi Arabia leads GCC in sustainable sukuk issuances. https://www.zawya.com/en/economy/islamic-economy/saudi-arabia-leads-gcc-in-sustainable-sukuk-issuances-smnx5ezs

ZAWYA. (2025, January 21). ESG sukuk to cross $50bln in 2025: Key ESG Funding Role in Emerging Markets. https://www.zawya.com/en/press-release/research-and-studies/esg-sukuk-to-cross-50bln-in-2025-fo768f6h

## ADDITIONAL READING

Khazzam, E. R. (March 23, 2015). How Islamic Finance Facilitates Green Investment. https://www.ifac.org/knowledge-gateway/discussion/how-islamic-finance-facilitates-green-investment

Musari, K. (2019). The evolution of waqf and sukuk toward sukuk-waqf in modern Islamic economy. *IJUS | International Journal of 'Umranic Studies,* 2(1), 45-54. DOI: 10.59202/ijus.v2i1.567

Musari, K. (2021). Esham, the origin of sukuk for facing the crisis: Historical experience. *Iqtishoduna: Jurnal Ekonomi Islam*, *10*(1), 45–58. DOI: 10.36835/iqtishoduna.v10i1.945

Musari, K. (2022). A comparative study of Islamic fiscal instrument securitization in history to modern ages: *esham*, sukuk, cash *waqf* linked sukuk (CWLS). In Akkaya, Ş., & Ergüder, B. (Eds.), *Handbook of Research on Challenges in Public Economics in the Era of Globalization* (pp. 397–418). IGI Global. DOI: 10.4018/978-1-7998-9083-6.ch021

Musari, K. (2022). Integrating green sukuk and cash waqf linked sukuk, the blended Islamic finance of fiscal instrument in Indonesia: A proposed model for fighting climate change. *International Journal of Islamic Khazanah, 12*(2), 133–144. DOI: 10.15575/ijik.v12i2.17750

Musari, K. (2025). Between esham and cash waqf linked sukuk to fiscal and development sustainability: Comparative analysis. In Başbay, M. M. (Ed.), *Islamic economics, growth, and development* (pp. 119–140). Routledge. DOI: 10.4324/9781003312864-10

## KEY TERMS AND DEFINITIONS

**Green Sukuk:** One of the sukuk variants to finance environmentally friendly or climate-related projects, which usually they are called eligible green sectors; an Islamic financial instrument that combines the principles of sukuk with the goals of green finance, which focuses on environmental sustainability; Shari'ah-compliant financial instruments based on the use-of-proceeds model, designed to fund or refinance environmentally friendly projects, which follow the Green Bond Principles, with eligible projects typically including areas such as renewable energy, energy efficiency, pollution reduction, sustainable land and resource management, biodiversity protection, and clean transportation; designed to finance projects with clear environmental benefits, such as renewable energy, eco-friendly transportation, carbon reduction initiatives, and sustainable water or wastewater management.

**Islamic Blended Finance:** A financing mechanism that integrates Islamic commercial finance and Islamic social finance; a strategic utilization of development finance for the mobilization of additional finance towards sustainable development based on the Shari'ah principle; the creation of financial mechanisms that utilize philanthropic or public development funds for the mobilization of capital from the additional external private commercial finance for SDG-related investments; an approach of Islamic finance to combining capital seeking market-rate returns with risk-tolerant capital to address social and environmental issues; a scheme of Islamic finance for fascinating commercial capital towards projects that merit society while also providing investors a financial gain.

**Shari'ah:** Sometimes also written Sharia, Sharī'ah, Shari'a, or Shariah; Islamic law; refers to the set of of Islamic law that governs both the religious and worldly aspects of a Muslim's life. Commonly, though somewhat redundantly, called "Shari'ah law," it represents the legal framework of Islamic practice; a body of religious law that forms a part of the Islamic tradition based on scriptures of Islam; The core religious principle in Islam, representing God's divine guidance for how humans should live in accordance with His will.

**Social Sukuk:** Similar to green sukuk in their use-of-proceeds structure, are dedicated to financing or refinancing Sharia-compliant social initiatives that align with the Social Bond Principles. Commonly supported areas include affordable infrastructure, healthcare and education access, low-cost housing, and programs that promote socioeconomic development; are aimed at supporting projects with positive social outcomes, including affordable infrastructure, low-cost housing, job creation, and promoting workplace diversity.

**Sukuk:** An Arabic term; a plural of the word *sakk* which means 'certificate'; certificates of equal value representing undivided shares in ownership of tangible assets, usufruct and services; an Islamic financial certificate that represents ownership in a tangible asset; Islamic financial certificates similar to bonds but structured to comply with Shari'ah.

**Sustainability- or SDG-Linked Sukuk:** Are tied to the issuer's commitment to achieving specific ESG goals. While the funds can be used for general purposes, the issuer must meet predefined targets—failure to do so typically results in higher coupon payments as a financial penalty.

**Sustainability Sukuk:** Blend elements of both green and social sukuk, enabling the funding of a combination of green and social projects within a single issuance. These sukuk are structured in line with both the Green Bond Principles and Social Bond Principles, thereby supporting a wide range of sustainability-related objectives; allocate proceeds exclusively to a mix of eligible green and social initiatives, combining environmental and social impact under a single issuance.

**Sustainability-Linked Sukuk:** A type of sukuk which are not tied to specific projects but to broader sustainability performance targets set by the issuer. These general-purpose sukuk are structured so that their financial terms may adjust depending on the issuer's success in meeting those targets, making them results-oriented instruments.

**Sustainable Sukuk:** Islamic finance instruments that support initiatives with environmental or social benefits. They merge Shari'ah principles with sustainability goals, and are frequently aligned with the United Nations SDGs.

**Transition Sukuk:** Are issued to support a company's efforts in reducing its environmental footprint, particularly in lowering carbon emissions during the transition to more sustainable practices.

Chapter 6

# The Role of Green Bonds in Financing Climate Resilience Projects

**Pedro Pinheiro Gomes**
https://orcid.org/0009-0005-4996-4534
*Secretary General for Environment, Portugal*

**Tiago Cardoso**
https://orcid.org/0009-0008-5223-2299
*Secretary General for Environment, Portugal*

## ABSTRACT

*Green bonds play a key role in financing climate resilience and sustainable development by directing investments toward projects with measurable environmental benefits, such as renewable energy and climate-resilient infrastructure. These bonds align capital flows with global sustainability goals, leveraging transparency and adherence to frameworks like the Green Bond Principles to attract investors. However, challenges like high issuance costs, inconsistent standards, and greenwashing risks limit their adoption. This study explores green bonds' opportunities, challenges, and policy implications, analyzing market trends, innovative practices, and regulatory frameworks. The findings highlight the need for harmonized standards, capacity-building initiatives, and technological tools to enhance green bonds' impact in driving sustainability.*

DOI: 10.4018/979-8-3373-8287-6.ch006

...t © 2026, IGI Global Scientific Publishing. Copying or distributing in print or electronic forms without written permission of IGI Global Scientific Publishing is prohibited. Use of this chapter to ...enerative artificial intelligence (AI) technologies is expressly prohibited. The publisher reserves all rights to license its use for generative AI training and machine learning model development.

## 1. INTRODUCTION

The escalating impacts of climate change have underscored the critical need for robust adaptation and mitigation strategies. With increasing frequency and intensity of climate-related disasters such as floods, hurricanes, and heatwaves, economies, ecosystems, and human livelihoods face unprecedented threats. These challenges, exacerbated by rising greenhouse gas emissions and unsustainable development practices, necessitate immediate and substantial action. The Intergovernmental Panel on Climate Change (IPCC, 2021) highlights that addressing these risks requires a multifaceted approach, with climate resilience emerging as a cornerstone of sustainable development. Climate resilience refers to the capacity of systems—be they natural, social, or economic—to absorb and recover from climate-induced shocks, minimizing long-term damage and fostering sustainability.

However, achieving resilience on a global scale presents a significant financial challenge. Implementing large-scale adaptation measures often requires capital well beyond the reach of governments, particularly in developing countries and vulnerable regions. According to the Global Commission on Adaptation (2019), an estimated $1.8 trillion in investments is required by 2030 to adequately address climate impacts. While the benefits of these investments could exceed $7 trillion, mobilizing the necessary funds remains a critical barrier.

In this context, green bonds have emerged as a transformative financial instrument capable of bridging the funding gap. Introduced by the European Investment Bank (EIB) in 2007, green bonds were initially designed to fund renewable energy and energy efficiency projects (Climate Bonds Initiative, 2023). Over time, their scope has expanded significantly, now encompassing a wide range of sustainability initiatives such as sustainable agriculture, disaster risk reduction, and climate-resilient infrastructure. By 2024, the global issuance of green bonds surpassed $2 trillion, reflecting the growing convergence of investor interest and regulatory support for sustainable finance (Nasir & Ahmed, 2024).

## The Role of Green Bonds

Green bonds are unique in their emphasis on transparency and accountability. Issuers are required to earmark proceeds exclusively for environmentally beneficial projects, and they must provide periodic impact reports to ensure compliance. This feature distinguishes green bonds from conventional bonds and has contributed to their growing popularity among socially conscious investors. Moreover, frameworks such as the International Capital Market Association's (ICMA) Green Bond Principles provide standardized guidelines for issuance and reporting, further enhancing market credibility and investor confidence (Tang et al., 2024).

Green bonds not only enable issuers to access dedicated financing for climate resilience projects but also create a ripple effect by attracting additional investment to the sustainable finance ecosystem. For instance, municipal governments can use green bonds to fund urban resilience initiatives such as flood defenses, sustainable water management systems, and green infrastructure. Private entities, too, leverage green bonds to align their financial strategies with sustainability objectives, often achieving lower borrowing costs due to investor preferences for environmentally responsible investments.

## Bridging the Funding Gap

Despite their rapid growth, green bonds account for only a small portion of the funding needed to meet global climate resilience goals. The market's current scale, while significant, falls short of the estimated $1.8 trillion required annually by 2030. Bridging this gap necessitates innovative approaches, including blended finance models that combine public and private capital to de-risk investments in high-impact but high-risk regions. Initiatives like the African Development Bank's Green Bond Program demonstrate how targeted interventions can enable developing economies to access green finance, addressing both financial and technical barriers (Adisa et al., 2024).

## Objectives of the Chapter

This chapter aims to provide a comprehensive analysis of the role of green bonds in financing climate resilience projects. It explores their potential to address the growing demand for sustainable investment while overcoming the challenges associated with market access, risk perceptions, and regulatory inconsistencies. By examining opportunities, challenges, and emerging trends, the chapter offers actionable insights for policymakers, investors, and stakeholders interested in leveraging green bonds to achieve global climate goals.

## Chapter Structure

The chapter is organized into the following sections:

1. **Section 2**: Defines the conceptual framework of green bonds, detailing their principles, issuance mechanisms, and relevance to climate resilience. This section

also explores the historical evolution of green bonds and their alignment with global sustainability frameworks such as the Paris Agreement.

2. **Section 3**: Highlights the economic and environmental opportunities offered by green bonds. This section examines their ability to reduce borrowing costs for issuers, attract ESG-conscious investors, and fund projects that yield measurable environmental benefits.
3. **Section 4**: Discusses the challenges hindering the widespread adoption of green bonds. Topics include market barriers such as high transaction costs, the lack of standardized frameworks, risk perceptions among investors, and the threat of greenwashing, which undermines market credibility.
4. **Section 5**: Explores policy measures needed to scale the use of green bonds. This section emphasizes the importance of regulatory harmonization, capacity-building initiatives, and innovative financial mechanisms like blended finance to broaden market access and enhance effectiveness.
5. **Section 6**: Presents emerging trends and the future outlook for green bonds. It discusses the integration of technologies like blockchain and AI to improve transparency and accountability, as well as the increasing regional diversification of green bond markets.
6. **Section 7**: Concludes with key findings and recommendations, highlighting actionable steps for stakeholders to strengthen the role of green bonds in financing climate resilience projects.

Green bonds represent a powerful tool for mobilizing capital toward climate resilience and sustainable development. By addressing financial gaps and aligning investments with global climate goals, they offer a viable solution to some of the most pressing challenges of our time. However, realizing their full potential requires coordinated efforts from governments, financial institutions, and international organizations. With targeted interventions and innovative practices, green bonds can become a cornerstone in the global response to climate change.

## 2. CONCEPTUAL FRAMEWORK

### 2.1 What Are Green Bonds?

Green bonds, introduced by the European Investment Bank (EIB) in 2007, have become a cornerstone of sustainable finance, offering an innovative way to align capital markets with global sustainability objectives. These financial instruments are uniquely designed to raise funds for projects that deliver measurable environmental benefits, bridging the gap between financial returns and ecological responsibility.

By channeling investments into initiatives that address climate risks, protect ecosystems, and build resilience, green bonds play a critical role in advancing the global transition to a low-carbon economy.

## The Concept and Scope of Green Bonds

Green bonds are structured to support a broad spectrum of environmentally beneficial projects. Their scope extends across various sectors, including renewable energy generation, sustainable agriculture, energy efficiency, biodiversity conservation, and the development of climate-resilient infrastructure. For instance, green bonds have been instrumental in financing wind and solar farms, constructing flood defenses, improving urban wastewater systems, and restoring degraded ecosystems. By addressing diverse sustainability challenges, these bonds contribute to both climate mitigation—reducing greenhouse gas emissions—and adaptation—enhancing the capacity of systems to withstand climate shocks.

What sets green bonds apart is their adaptability to both developed and emerging markets. In developed economies, they are primarily used to fund energy transition and carbon reduction projects, reflecting the region's advanced infrastructure and high carbon footprint. In emerging economies, green bonds have been vital in addressing pressing vulnerabilities such as water scarcity, food insecurity, and extreme weather events. Maltais and Nykvist (2020) emphasize that green bonds have been particularly impactful in mobilizing resources for infrastructure projects in developing regions, benefiting local communities and ecosystems while fostering sustainable development.

## Frameworks Governing Green Bonds

The credibility and transparency of green bonds are underpinned by globally recognized frameworks, the most prominent being the International Capital Market Association's (ICMA) Green Bond Principles (GBP). These principles are designed to ensure that green bonds are issued and managed in a way that aligns with sustainability objectives. They focus on four key components:

1. **Use of Proceeds**: Green bond proceeds must be exclusively allocated to projects with clear environmental benefits, ensuring that funds are directed toward impactful initiatives.
2. **Process for Project Evaluation and Selection**: Issuers are required to outline how eligible projects are identified, evaluated, and selected, emphasizing the assessment of their environmental impacts.

3. **Management of Proceeds**: To maintain accountability, funds must be tracked and managed separately, ensuring they are used only for their intended purposes.
4. **Reporting**: Issuers must provide periodic updates on the allocation of funds and the environmental impact of the financed projects, fostering transparency and investor confidence.

Certifications from independent bodies, such as the Climate Bonds Initiative, add an additional layer of assurance by verifying compliance with stringent environmental standards. These certifications are increasingly important as they enhance market trust and reduce the risk of greenwashing, where projects falsely claim environmental benefits.

## The Appeal to ESG-Oriented Investors

Green bonds have become a preferred investment vehicle for those seeking to integrate Environmental, Social, and Governance (ESG) principles into their portfolios. The growing demand for sustainable investments has been a driving force behind the consistent annual growth of the green bond market. According to the Climate Bonds Initiative (2023), green bonds have expanded their geographical reach and diversified the sectors benefiting from green finance, appealing to institutional and retail investors alike.

A defining financial characteristic of green bonds is the "greenium," a premium investors often pay to hold environmentally focused assets. This premium results in lower borrowing costs for issuers, incentivizing the development of environmentally friendly projects. Zerbib (2019) and Ehlers and Packer (2017) highlight how this positive feedback loop between investor demand and project development has accelerated the adoption of green bonds across sectors and regions.

## Innovations and Challenges in the Green Bond Market

As the market matures, innovative solutions are being explored to enhance the efficiency and transparency of green bonds. Technologies like blockchain are gaining traction for their potential to revolutionize fund tracking and reporting. Kreibich and Ossenbrink (2021) argue that blockchain's immutable ledger capabilities provide real-time, verifiable data on fund allocation and environmental impacts, addressing concerns about greenwashing and enhancing investor confidence.

However, challenges persist. High issuance costs and complex certification processes can discourage smaller issuers, particularly in emerging economies where financial and technical resources are limited. The absence of universally accepted global standards further complicates cross-border investments, creating inconsistencies that hinder the market's scalability. Policy harmonization, capacity-building initiatives, and the integration of digital tools are crucial to overcoming these barriers and ensuring the inclusivity of the green bond market.

Green bonds are a transformative tool in the global effort to combat climate change and achieve sustainable development. By channeling capital into projects with measurable environmental benefits, they bridge the gap between ecological needs and financial returns. While the market faces challenges such as high issuance costs, inconsistent standards, and the risk of greenwashing, innovations and evolving frameworks are steadily addressing these issues. As the demand for sustainable finance grows, green bonds will remain a vital instrument for governments, corporations, and investors seeking to align their activities with global climate goals. In a world increasingly vulnerable to climate risks, green bonds represent a scalable, impactful solution for building a more sustainable and resilient future.

## 2.2 Climate Resilience

Climate resilience refers to the capacity of social, ecological, and economic systems to absorb, adapt, and recover from the adverse effects of climate change. This concept encompasses strategies that enable societies to withstand both sudden disruptions, such as hurricanes and floods, and long-term environmental shifts, such as rising sea levels and desertification (Folke et al., 2010). Resilience-building involves enhancing the adaptive capacity of systems through the integration of sustainable practices, technological innovation, and robust policy frameworks.

Key strategies for fostering climate resilience include investments in climate-smart infrastructure, such as flood barriers, stormwater management systems, and drought-resistant agriculture (Rockström et al., 2009). These measures not only mitigate the immediate impacts of climate change but also provide co-benefits, such as improved biodiversity and increased food security. For instance, coastal protection measures like mangrove restoration not only shield communities from storm surges but also contribute to carbon sequestration and habitat preservation (Spalding et al., 2014).

The financial requirements for implementing these strategies are substantial. According to the United Nations Environment Programme (UNEP, 2021), annual adaptation costs in developing countries alone are projected to reach $140–300 billion by 2030. Bridging this financing gap necessitates innovative funding mechanisms, with green bonds emerging as a key solution. These instruments channel investments into projects that enhance climate resilience while ensuring accountability and transparency in fund allocation (Carney, 2015).

Building climate resilience also involves addressing systemic vulnerabilities, particularly in low-income and marginalized communities that are disproportionately affected by climate risks. Enhanced early warning systems, sustainable urban planning, and decentralized renewable energy systems are critical interventions that can reduce exposure and increase adaptive capacity (Solecki et al., 2017). Additionally, international cooperation, such as through multilateral development banks and global climate funds, plays a pivotal role in supporting resilience initiatives in vulnerable regions (Pelling et al., 2015).

Moreover, the integration of technology into resilience planning is gaining prominence. Advances in remote sensing, artificial intelligence, and blockchain are enabling more precise climate modeling, efficient resource allocation, and enhanced monitoring of resilience projects (Kreibich & Ossenbrink, 2021). These innovations are reshaping the landscape of climate adaptation, providing tools for more effective decision-making and impact assessment.

In conclusion, climate resilience is a multifaceted approach that demands coordinated efforts across financial, technological, and policy domains. By leveraging innovative instruments such as green bonds and integrating resilience strategies into development planning, societies can better equip themselves to navigate the challenges posed by a changing climate.

Green bonds have established themselves as a critical instrument in the nexus of sustainable finance and climate resilience. By channeling investments into projects that address climate adaptation and disaster risk reduction, green bonds serve not only as a financing mechanism but also as a catalyst for innovation and commitment toward sustainability. Their role in mitigating climate risks and fostering resilience highlights their importance in achieving global sustainability goals.

## Supporting Climate Resilience through Infrastructure

Green bonds have proven invaluable in financing adaptive infrastructure, which is critical for communities vulnerable to climate-induced shocks. Cities prone to flooding, for instance, have utilized green bonds to fund the construction of resilient urban drainage systems, seawalls, and stormwater management solutions. The Global Commission on Adaptation (2019) underscores the effectiveness of such investments, noting that infrastructure designed to manage flood risks can save lives, protect livelihoods, and reduce economic losses.

Urban areas, particularly in low-lying regions, are increasingly relying on green bonds to address climate vulnerabilities. Projects funded through green bonds have enhanced the durability of transport systems, retrofitted buildings for energy efficiency, and expanded renewable energy networks. By integrating resilience into infrastructure design, these projects not only mitigate risks but also contribute to long-term sustainability.

## Enhancing Urban Planning for Sustainability

Green bonds enable municipalities to embed climate resilience into urban planning processes, addressing both present and future challenges. In rapidly urbanizing regions, such as parts of Africa and Asia, these bonds have financed projects that integrate green spaces, improve energy efficiency, and enhance water management systems. Adisa, Ilugbusi, and Obi (2024) highlight how green bonds have been utilized to develop sustainable housing projects in Africa, incorporating solar panels, efficient water systems, and heat-resistant designs to withstand extreme weather.

In developed nations, green bonds are increasingly funding initiatives aimed at decarbonizing urban centers. Cities in the United States, for example, have used green bonds to support smart city projects that integrate renewable energy grids and efficient public transportation. These projects enhance urban sustainability while addressing climate risks, demonstrating the versatility of green bonds in various contexts.

## Disaster Risk Reduction and Nature-Based Solutions

Green bonds also play a pivotal role in funding nature-based solutions (NBS) for disaster risk reduction. Coastal restoration projects, such as mangrove reforestation and wetland rehabilitation, exemplify the dual benefits of NBS: ecological protection and economic resilience. Spalding et al. (2014) emphasize that such initiatives mitigate the impacts of hurricanes and tsunamis while preserving biodiversity and supporting local livelihoods.

In addition to coastal ecosystems, green bonds have funded reforestation projects that stabilize soils, reduce flood risks, and sequester carbon. Pelling, O'Brien, and Matyas (2015) argue that by integrating NBS with traditional engineering approaches, green bonds create more holistic strategies for disaster management and climate adaptation.

## Synergies with Global Financial Markets

The impact of green bonds extends beyond individual projects, influencing global financial markets and fostering innovation. As noted by Tang et al. (2024), the rise of fintech solutions such as blockchain platforms has enhanced the transparency and accountability of green bond issuance. Blockchain technology allows real-time tracking of funds and outcomes, ensuring that investments are directed toward verified sustainability projects.

The integration of such technologies has strengthened investor confidence, attracting a broader pool of participants to the green bond market. Additionally, the alignment of green bonds with Environmental, Social, and Governance (ESG) criteria has amplified their appeal, further expanding their market reach and potential for driving sustainable development.

## Challenges and Opportunities

Despite their promise, green bonds face challenges that hinder their broader adoption. The absence of universally accepted standards creates inconsistencies in reporting and certification, making it difficult for investors to assess the authenticity of environmental claims. High issuance costs further limit access for smaller issuers, particularly in developing regions. Maltais and Nykvist (2020) argue that addressing these barriers requires international cooperation to establish robust governance frameworks and streamline certification processes.

Opportunities, however, abound. The Climate Bonds Initiative (2023) reports a surge in global green bond markets, with growing investor demand and regulatory support fueling expansion. Innovations such as blended finance models—combining public and private capital—can further enhance market access, particularly in regions with limited financial capacity. By aligning green bonds with comprehensive climate policies, governments and financial institutions can maximize their impact on global adaptation and mitigation goals.

## Future Directions

To fully realize their potential, green bonds must integrate seamlessly into global climate strategies. Carney (2015) advocates for embedding climate resilience into financial systems, encouraging investors to prioritize assets that align with long-term sustainability goals. This requires not only market incentives but also regulatory measures that ensure accountability and transparency.

Initiatives like those outlined by the IPCC (2021) call for an integrated approach that addresses both climate mitigation and adaptation challenges. By coordinating efforts across sectors and geographies, green bonds can contribute to a unified global response to climate change. Furthermore, innovations in technology and policy will continue to enhance the effectiveness and accessibility of green bonds, ensuring that they remain a cornerstone of sustainable finance.

## 3. OPPORTUNITIES

### 3.1 Growth of the Green Bond Market

Since their inception in 2007, the green bond market has seen extraordinary growth, fueled by increasing awareness of the environmental and financial benefits they offer. By 2024, cumulative issuance had exceeded $2 trillion globally, marking a significant shift in investment patterns toward sustainability-focused financial instruments. This growth is supported by investor demand for greater transparency and the ability of green bonds to align financial returns with environmental impact.

#### Expansion Across Sectors and Regions

The green bond market has expanded beyond traditional sectors like renewable energy to include agriculture, water resource management, and climate-resilient infrastructure. Flammer (2021) noted that corporate green bonds have become an essential part of sustainability strategies for private companies, reflecting a broader adoption of green finance principles. Additionally, Tang et al. (2024) highlighted the role of green finance in ASEAN economies, emphasizing its integration with fintech to ensure transparency and scalability in bond issuance.

Europe remains the leader in green bond issuance, with the European Union's Sustainable Finance Taxonomy providing a robust framework for investments. According to Maltais and Nykvist (2020), Europe's regulatory leadership has set a global precedent for developing standards and certifications, which bolster investor confidence and market growth.

#### Innovations Driving Market Expansion

Technological advancements are also fueling market growth. Kreibich and Ossenbrink (2021) explored the transformative role of blockchain in green bond issuance, which ensures transaction transparency and facilitates real-time tracking of funds. Similarly, Ehlers and Packer (2017) emphasized the importance of certification and third-party verification in enhancing the credibility of green bonds, a factor that has significantly influenced investor participation.

#### Responding to Climate Commitments

Green bonds are instrumental in meeting global climate commitments, such as those outlined in the Paris Agreement. United Nations Environment Programme (2021) reported that green bond financing is crucial for bridging the adaptation finance gap, enabling countries to fund necessary transitions to low-carbon economies. Moreover, Zerbib (2019) found that green bonds generally trade at a premium, reflecting strong investor preferences for environmentally friendly financial products.

### Challenges and Opportunities Ahead

Despite its rapid growth, the green bond market faces challenges such as the lack of standardized reporting frameworks and the high costs of certification. However, organizations like the Climate Bonds Initiative (2023) are actively working to address these issues by advocating for global standards and streamlining the certification process. These efforts not only lower barriers to entry for issuers but also enhance the market's integrity, encouraging further investment.

Looking ahead, there is immense potential for growth in emerging markets. Adisa, Ilugbusi, and Obi (2024) observed that African nations are increasingly leveraging green bonds to fund projects like renewable energy and sustainable urban development, demonstrating that these instruments can play a transformative role in regions most vulnerable to climate change.

## 3.2 Economic and Environmental Benefits

Green bonds have proven to be an effective financial instrument that combines economic benefits with measurable environmental impact. As a form of debt financing, these bonds allow issuers to raise funds for environmentally sustainable projects while appealing to investors seeking both financial returns and a positive ecological footprint.

The economic advantages of green bonds are underscored by their ability to lower the cost of capital for issuers. Recent studies, such as Intonti et al. (2025), reveal that green bonds often trade at favorable rates due to heightened demand from investors prioritizing Environmental, Social, and Governance (ESG) factors. This preference creates a “greenium,” allowing issuers to secure financing at lower yields compared to conventional bonds. Municipalities, in particular, have leveraged green bonds to fund projects that not only enhance urban infrastructure but also drive local economic activity.

Environmentally, green bonds enable the financing of projects with significant ecological benefits. Kythreotis (2024) highlighted their dual impact, illustrating how funds are channeled into renewable energy, energy efficiency, and sustainable transportation projects, reducing greenhouse gas emissions while creating economic value. For instance, investments in public transit systems and urban green spaces improve air quality and reduce urban heat islands, directly contributing to healthier living conditions.

Another notable aspect of green bonds is their role in fostering innovation in green technology. Cui et al. (2025) emphasized that green finance mechanisms, including bonds, are critical to accelerating research and development in renewable energy technologies and other sustainable solutions. By providing the necessary capital, these bonds help bridge the gap between innovation and large-scale implementation.

Moreover, green bonds serve as a catalyst for private-sector involvement in sustainability. Research by Sule et al. (2024) indicates that these financial tools incentivize private companies to incorporate ESG principles into their operations. By offering an avenue for businesses to align financial goals with sustainability, green bonds encourage a more inclusive approach to addressing global environmental challenges.

Despite these advantages, challenges such as the lack of uniform standards and the complexities of impact measurement persist. However, the adoption of blockchain technology in green bond issuance, as noted by Ragazou et al. (2024), offers a promising solution. Blockchain ensures transparency and traceability, enhancing investor confidence and ensuring that funds are allocated to their intended environmental projects.

Looking forward, the continued growth and standardization of the green bond market will likely amplify their economic and environmental impact. Collaborative efforts among governments, financial institutions, and private investors are essential to unlocking the full potential of green bonds in fostering a more sustainable global economy.

## Regional Case Studies of Successful Green Bond Applications

Practical evidence of the effectiveness of green bonds can be seen across different regions. In Europe, France's sovereign green bonds have financed projects ranging from renewable energy integration to climate-resilient transport, setting a precedent for national-level commitments (Agence France Trésor, 2025).

Germany has also emerged as a leader, directing green bond proceeds into energy-efficient building programs and biodiversity protection (Climate Bonds Initiative, 2023). In North America, municipal green bonds have been successfully employed in cities such as New York and San Francisco to enhance flood resilience, upgrade public transit systems, and finance sustainable water management (Climate Bonds Initiative, 2017).

In emerging economies, the African Development Bank's Green Bond Program has enabled investments in renewable energy and urban adaptation projects, particularly in Sub-Saharan Africa, where conventional financing channels remain limited (African Development Bank, 2024).

China, now the largest global issuer of green bonds, has demonstrated the scalability of this instrument by funding large-scale renewable energy projects and sustainable urbanization initiatives, supported by targeted government incentives (OECD, 2021). These examples highlight the adaptability of green bonds across diverse contexts, reinforcing their potential as a global tool for climate resilience.

## 3.3 International Support

International support has been instrumental in fostering the growth, credibility, and inclusivity of the green bond market. Multilateral development banks (MDBs) play a central role in these efforts, leveraging their financial strength, expertise, and partnerships to create an enabling environment for green finance. Their leadership not only funds transformative projects but also catalyzes private sector involvement and market development, especially in emerging economies.

### The Role of MDBs as Market Creators

MDBs such as the World Bank, the Asian Development Bank (ADB), and the African Development Bank (AfDB) have taken the lead in issuing green bonds, demonstrating their viability as a sustainable financing tool. These institutions use their high credit ratings and financial expertise to raise capital for large-scale projects addressing climate resilience, renewable energy, and sustainable infrastructure. Huang and Xu (2024) emphasize that MDBs act as market creators, showcasing the profitability and scalability of green finance to attract private sector participation.

For example, the World Bank's green bonds have financed renewable energy projects, such as solar and wind farms, while also supporting energy efficiency upgrades in schools, hospitals, and public buildings. Similarly, the ADB has funded sustainable urban transport and water management systems, reducing emissions and improving resilience in rapidly urbanizing regions. These efforts meet immediate sustainability needs while building investor confidence in the green bond market.

### Enhancing Governance and Standards

MDBs play a critical role in shaping the frameworks and standards that govern green bond issuance. By promoting rigorous certification and reporting processes, they enhance the transparency and integrity of the market. According to Espagne (2024), MDBs' leadership in governance has established green bonds as a credible financial instrument, bridging the gap between environmental objectives and investor expectations.

MDBs have also contributed to the development of global standards, such as the Green Bond Principles (GBP) and Climate Bonds Standard, ensuring that funds are allocated to projects with verifiable environmental benefits. This leadership has encouraged issuers and investors to adopt best practices, fostering trust and scalability in the green bond market.

## Supporting Emerging Economies

Emerging economies face unique challenges in accessing green finance, including weak regulatory frameworks, limited technical expertise, and high certification costs. MDBs address these barriers by providing technical assistance, capacity-building programs, and financial support. Initiatives like the Climate Investment Funds (CIFs), supported by the AfDB, have enabled African countries to finance infrastructure projects that address both mitigation and adaptation challenges.

For instance, MDB-backed green bonds have funded projects aimed at increasing access to clean energy and promoting climate-resilient agriculture. Anyiam-Osigwe and Ibrahim (2024) highlight that such interventions not only address pressing developmental needs but also help countries transition to low-carbon pathways, aligning with global climate goals.

## Partnerships for Market Development

Collaboration between MDBs, local governments, and financial institutions is crucial for expanding market access and fostering sustainability in developing regions. Through partnerships, MDBs help build local capacity to issue green bonds, creating self-sustaining mechanisms for financing sustainable projects. Fareniuk (2024) notes that these collaborations often include training programs, knowledge sharing, and co-financing arrangements that enhance local expertise and market readiness.

These partnerships also address the financing gap in underserved regions by blending public and private capital to de-risk investments. For example, MDBs often provide guarantees or concessional financing, making green projects more attractive to private investors. This blended finance approach has been particularly effective in regions with high investment risks, such as Sub-Saharan Africa and Southeast Asia.

## Encouraging Innovation in Green Finance

The demonstration effect of MDB-led green bond programs has encouraged other public and private entities to adopt green finance. By showcasing successful projects and innovative financing models, MDBs act as anchors in green finance ecosystems, paving the way for new financial products that address global climate challenges. Sruthi (2024) argues that MDBs' leadership has inspired the development of sustainability-linked bonds and social impact bonds, which complement traditional green bonds by broadening the scope of sustainable investments.

Furthermore, MDBs have integrated technological innovations into their green finance initiatives. Blockchain platforms, for example, are being explored to enhance transparency and ensure accountability in fund allocation. These advancements not only build investor confidence but also improve the efficiency of green bond issuance and management.

## 4. CHALLENGES

### 4.1 Market Barriers

Despite its rapid growth and increasing adoption, the green bond market faces persistent barriers that hinder its full potential, particularly in emerging and developing economies. These challenges stem from structural inefficiencies, regulatory hurdles, and a lack of standardization across different markets.

A significant challenge in the green bond market is the high cost associated with certification and compliance. Issuers often need to undergo rigorous evaluation processes to ensure that their projects meet the green bond criteria, which can be financially prohibitive for smaller entities. Karumanchi (2024) discusses how these financial barriers disproportionately affect smaller issuers in developing countries, limiting their access to green finance and stalling critical sustainable projects.

Additionally, inconsistent standards across different regions create confusion and discourage investment. The absence of a universal framework leads to varying definitions of what constitutes a "green" project. According to Khoa and Anh (2024), this lack of uniformity complicates cross-border investments and increases the risk perception for international investors, thereby reducing market liquidity and accessibility.

In emerging economies, low financial literacy and limited market infrastructure exacerbate the challenges. Asimiyu (2024) highlights that many local issuers and investors are unfamiliar with the concept of green finance, which hampers their ability to participate effectively in the market. This knowledge gap underscores the need for capacity-building initiatives and awareness campaigns to promote understanding and adoption of green bonds.

Another critical issue is market volatility and regulatory unpredictability, which discourage long-term investments. Ojukwu and Osundare (2024) argue that inconsistent policy environments, particularly in developing regions, deter potential issuers and investors from engaging with green bond markets. This challenge is further compounded by currency risks and a lack of hedging instruments, making green bonds less attractive in volatile economic climates.

Emerging technologies like blockchain have been proposed as solutions to enhance transparency and reduce transaction costs, but their adoption remains limited. Panfilov et al. (2024) suggest that integrating digital tools into the green bond market could address some of the barriers by providing real-time tracking and reporting mechanisms. However, these innovations require substantial upfront investment and technical expertise, which are often lacking in less developed regions.

Lastly, there is a clear disparity between the availability of green bonds in developed markets and their accessibility in emerging economies. Shaheen et al. (2024) emphasize that advanced economies dominate the green bond market, while many developing countries struggle to issue bonds due to insufficient institutional support and financial infrastructure. Bridging this gap will require coordinated efforts from international organizations, multilateral development banks, and local governments.

## 4.2 Risk Perceptions

Risk perceptions are a significant barrier to the widespread adoption of green bonds, especially for projects targeting climate resilience. These perceptions stem from uncertainties about financial returns, long payback periods, and unstable regulatory environments. Investors are often hesitant to commit to green projects due to a combination of perceived and actual risks.

One key aspect influencing risk perceptions is the lack of consistent performance data for climate resilience projects. Pokhrel and Dangi (2024) highlight that green finance-related products, including green bonds, are relatively new and lack the historical data needed to validate their financial viability. This uncertainty often leads investors to prioritize more traditional, lower-risk financial instruments.

The regulatory environment also plays a critical role in shaping investor attitudes. Cheteni et al. (2025) argue that policy inconsistencies and unstable governance frameworks in some regions exacerbate the risk associated with green bond investments. For instance, sudden changes in environmental policies or financial regulations can impact project outcomes, further discouraging potential investors.

In addition to regulatory risks, investors are concerned about the technical and operational risks inherent in many green projects. Dahlgren and Santesson (2024) note that complex projects like renewable energy plants or urban resilience infrastructure often face delays, cost overruns, and other implementation challenges, which increase the perception of financial risk.

Emerging markets face unique challenges in attracting green bond investors. Lone et al. (2024) found that currency volatility and limited access to hedging mechanisms are significant deterrents for foreign investors considering green bond issuances in developing economies. These factors contribute to higher risk premiums, making it more expensive for issuers to attract investment.

Finally, there is a psychological dimension to risk perception. Nevatia (2024) asserts that the novelty of green bonds and their association with emerging sustainability goals can create skepticism among traditional investors. Educating investors and improving the transparency of green bond markets are essential to mitigating these psychological barriers.

Efforts to address risk perceptions are underway. For example, the integration of innovative financial mechanisms such as blended finance, where public funds are used to de-risk private investments, has shown promise in reducing perceived risks. Similarly, improved reporting standards and third-party verification processes are helping to build investor confidence, as noted by Malgaonkar (2024).

## 4.3 Greenwashing Concerns

The risk of "greenwashing" presents a significant challenge to the credibility and effectiveness of the green bond market. Greenwashing occurs when issuers misrepresent or exaggerate the environmental benefits of their projects, undermining investor confidence and the market's overall impact.

The lack of standardized definitions and frameworks for green bonds is a key factor contributing to greenwashing. Bortz (2024) highlights that inconsistent taxonomies across jurisdictions make it difficult to verify whether projects financed by green bonds meet genuine environmental criteria. This ambiguity allows some issuers to market bonds as "green" despite minimal environmental impact, eroding trust in the market.

Transparency is another critical issue. Chauhan (2024) emphasizes that insufficient disclosure of project details and outcomes exacerbates greenwashing concerns. Investors often lack access to robust data on the environmental performance of green bond-funded projects, making it challenging to assess their true impact. This gap in transparency not only fuels skepticism but also dissuades potential investors from engaging with the market.

In emerging markets, greenwashing risks are particularly acute. Li et al. (2024) observe that the absence of rigorous certification processes and third-party audits in many developing countries increases the likelihood of false environmental claims. This issue is further complicated by the high costs associated with obtaining credible green certifications, which can deter smaller issuers from pursuing stringent oversight mechanisms.

Technological innovations such as blockchain have been proposed as solutions to mitigate greenwashing. Muniasamy (2024) argues that blockchain can enhance transparency and accountability by enabling real-time tracking of funds and environmental outcomes. However, the adoption of such technologies remains limited due to technical and financial barriers, particularly in less developed regions.

To address these challenges, regulatory bodies and international organizations are working to establish clearer guidelines and standards. For instance, the proposed European Union Green Bond Standard (EuGBS) aims to provide a harmonized framework for green bond issuance. Camilleri (2024) highlights that initiatives like the EuGBS could significantly reduce greenwashing by setting stringent criteria and requiring regular reporting on environmental outcomes.

Despite these efforts, greenwashing remains a pervasive concern that threatens to undermine the green bond market's credibility. Building investor confidence will require continued progress in standardizing green finance frameworks, enhancing transparency, and promoting third-party verification mechanisms.

### Examples of Contested Green Bond Issuances

Despite their potential, green bonds have also faced criticism when projects financed failed to meet rigorous environmental standards. For example, some early Chinese green bonds directed funds to "clean coal" projects, which, while framed as transitional, were criticized by international observers for undermining climate goals (OECD, 2021).

Similarly, several corporate green bonds in developed markets have faced scrutiny due to limited disclosure on environmental outcomes, raising concerns about their actual impact. These cases illustrate how insufficient transparency and weak certification processes can erode investor confidence. By acknowledging such controversies, the market can better identify governance gaps and strengthen safeguards against greenwashing.

## 5. POLICY IMPLICATIONS

### 5.1 Enhancing Regulatory Frameworks

The development of robust and harmonized regulatory frameworks is critical to scaling the green bond market and ensuring its long-term sustainability. Regulatory clarity and consistency provide investors and issuers with the confidence needed to engage in green finance, while also mitigating risks such as greenwashing and market fragmentation.

Standardization is at the heart of these efforts. The European Union's Green Bond Standard (EuGBS), as noted by Nasir and Ahmed (2024), is a leading initiative aimed at creating a uniform set of guidelines for green bond issuance. By defining clear eligibility criteria for projects, the EuGBS enhances transparency, enabling investors to compare bonds across jurisdictions and ensuring that funds are directed toward verifiable environmental outcomes.

Beyond Europe, global organizations such as the International Capital Market Association (ICMA) have developed principles that serve as voluntary guidelines for green bond issuances. These principles, including the Green Bond Principles (GBP), have been widely adopted and are increasingly shaping national regulatory policies. However, Ehlers and Packer (2017) emphasize that while such frameworks have brought significant progress, their voluntary nature leaves gaps in enforcement and accountability.

Emerging markets face unique challenges in adopting and implementing regulatory standards. In many developing countries, regulatory infrastructure is still nascent, and financial institutions often lack the capacity to align with international frameworks. Adisa et al. (2024) highlight the importance of capacity-building initiatives to support these markets, suggesting partnerships between multilateral development banks and local regulators as a way to facilitate the adoption of harmonized policies.

Digital technologies, including blockchain, are being explored to complement regulatory frameworks. Kreibich and Ossenbrink (2021) argue that blockchain can enhance transparency and compliance by providing immutable records of fund allocation and environmental impact. Integrating such technologies into regulatory systems could reduce monitoring costs and increase trust among investors.

Policy harmonization efforts must also address the cost of compliance. Dahlgren and Santesson (2024) note that smaller issuers, particularly in low-income regions, are often deterred by the high costs of adhering to certification and reporting requirements. Subsidies, public-private partnerships, and simplified certification processes could lower these barriers and encourage broader participation.

Finally, addressing investor concerns about greenwashing requires stringent oversight and enforcement mechanisms. Camilleri (2024) suggests that mandatory reporting and independent third-party verification should become standard practices, ensuring that green bonds deliver on their promised environmental benefits. This approach would not only safeguard market integrity but also attract a more diverse and robust pool of investors.

As green bonds continue to play a pivotal role in financing the transition to a sustainable economy, enhancing regulatory frameworks will be crucial for their success. Coordinated global efforts, coupled with regional adaptations, will be key to creating a trusted and efficient green bond market.

## 5.2 Financial Incentives

Governments play a crucial role in fostering the growth of the green bond market by implementing incentives that make green bond issuance more attractive to both issuers and investors. These incentives reduce financial and regulatory burdens, enabling broader participation and accelerating the transition to sustainable finance.

Tax exemptions are among the most effective tools for incentivizing green bonds. By waiving or reducing taxes on green bond interest income, governments make these instruments more appealing to investors seeking tax-efficient investment options. For example, the United States offers tax credit bonds, such as the Clean Renewable Energy Bonds (CREBs), which provide tax benefits for investors, thus encouraging investments in renewable energy projects.

Subsidies and guarantees are additional mechanisms used to lower the financial risks associated with green bond issuance. Subsidies can offset the high costs of certification and compliance, while guarantees reduce the perceived credit risk of issuers. In developing countries, multilateral organizations often collaborate with governments to offer partial guarantees for green bonds, thereby attracting foreign investment. According to Adisa et al. (2024), such strategies have been particularly effective in Africa, where local issuers face significant challenges in accessing green finance.

China's Green Bond Guidelines are a prominent example of how government policies can incentivize the green bond market. As noted by Tang et al. (2024), these guidelines include preferential policies such as access to lower interest rates and streamlined approval processes for green projects. These measures have positioned China as a global leader in green bond issuance, with a substantial portion of its bonds funding renewable energy, pollution control, and sustainable infrastructure projects.

Additionally, governments can encourage green bond issuance by establishing regulatory frameworks that provide clarity and standardization. Nasir and Ahmed (2024) highlight the importance of such frameworks in reducing market entry barriers and building investor confidence. For instance, the European Union's Sustainable Finance Taxonomy provides detailed criteria for green projects, which has significantly boosted green bond activities across member states.

Public awareness campaigns and capacity-building initiatives also play a role in fostering market growth. Governments can partner with financial institutions and industry bodies to educate potential issuers and investors about the benefits and processes associated with green bonds. Such efforts can demystify the market and expand its reach to smaller issuers and less experienced investors.

By combining financial incentives with supportive policies and frameworks, governments can catalyze the expansion of the green bond market, driving investments toward environmentally sustainable projects and contributing to global climate goals.

## 5.3 Capacity Building

Capacity-building initiatives are essential for the sustained growth and inclusivity of the green bond market. These efforts aim to bridge knowledge gaps, enhance technical capabilities, and empower stakeholders to effectively participate in the market, whether as issuers, investors, or regulators.

For issuers, technical assistance is critical in developing high-quality projects and ensuring compliance with green bond standards. Banga and Afzal (2025) highlight that targeted training programs can help issuers understand complex reporting and certification requirements, ultimately improving the credibility and marketability of their bonds. These programs often focus on project design, environmental impact assessment, and the development of robust monitoring systems to track progress.

Investors also benefit from awareness campaigns and educational initiatives. Many potential investors are unfamiliar with the mechanics of green bonds or their environmental and financial benefits. Capacity-building efforts aimed at this group can demystify green finance, thereby expanding the investor base. For example, Nasir and Ahmed (2024) suggest that workshops and informational materials tailored to institutional and retail investors can significantly enhance market participation.

Regulators and policymakers require capacity-building to create and implement effective frameworks. In many emerging markets, regulatory institutions lack the expertise to align national policies with international green finance standards. Tang et al. (2024) emphasize the importance of multilateral partnerships in providing technical assistance to regulators, helping them establish transparent and efficient regulatory environments that support green bond issuance.

Technology also plays a role in capacity-building. Digital tools, such as blockchain and AI-driven analytics, can simplify reporting processes and enhance transparency. However, their effective implementation requires training for stakeholders. According to Kreibich and Ossenbrink (2021), integrating such technologies into the green bond ecosystem can reduce costs, improve oversight, and build trust among investors, provided stakeholders are equipped with the necessary technical knowledge.

Moreover, regional and international collaboration is key to successful capacity-building. Programs organized by multilateral development banks and international organizations often provide tailored support to countries or regions, addressing specific challenges they face in adopting green bonds. For instance, the World Bank has conducted workshops in Africa and Asia to train issuers on designing projects that meet global standards, as noted by Adisa et al. (2024).

In conclusion, capacity-building initiatives are vital for overcoming barriers to market entry and ensuring the green bond market's inclusivity and sustainability. By equipping issuers, investors, and regulators with the necessary knowledge and tools, these efforts can drive meaningful progress toward global climate and sustainability goals.

# 6. FUTURE OUTLOOK

## 6.1 Emerging Trends

The green bond market is poised for significant evolution, driven by emerging trends that promise to enhance efficiency, inclusivity, and impact. Among these trends, technological advancements, particularly blockchain, are expected to play a transformative role in addressing long-standing challenges and fostering investor confidence.

Blockchain technology offers the potential to enhance transparency and accountability in the green bond market. By providing an immutable ledger for transactions, blockchain can ensure that funds raised through green bonds are allocated exclusively to projects with verifiable environmental benefits. According to Tang et al. (2024), this capability can address greenwashing concerns by enabling real-time tracking of fund allocation and environmental outcomes, significantly increasing market trust and integrity.

Another emerging trend is the integration of artificial intelligence (AI) in the green bond ecosystem. AI-driven tools can analyze vast datasets to assess the environmental performance of projects, predict market trends, and identify risks. These insights can guide both issuers and investors in making informed decisions, as noted by Kreibich and Ossenbrink (2021). Additionally, AI can automate the monitoring and reporting processes, reducing compliance costs and making green bonds more accessible to smaller issuers.

Sustainability-linked bonds (SLBs) are also gaining traction as a complement to traditional green bonds. Unlike green bonds, which are tied to specific projects, SLBs are linked to the overall environmental performance of issuers. This flexibility enables a broader range of organizations to participate in the market, including those with diverse sustainability objectives. Adisa et al. (2024) highlight that SLBs have been particularly successful in encouraging private sector participation in sustainability initiatives.

Emerging markets are expected to play a larger role in the future of green finance. Governments in these regions are increasingly recognizing the potential of green bonds to attract foreign investment and fund critical infrastructure projects. Nasir and Ahmed (2024) emphasize that international partnerships and capacity-building initiatives will be crucial in unlocking the green finance potential of emerging economies, addressing barriers such as regulatory gaps and high issuance costs.

Furthermore, regulatory developments are shaping the future outlook of the green bond market. The introduction of standardized frameworks, such as the European Union's Green Bond Standard (EuGBS), is setting a global benchmark for transparency and accountability. Camilleri (2024) suggests that similar initiatives in other regions could harmonize global markets, making it easier for investors to allocate funds across borders while ensuring environmental integrity.

Lastly, investor preferences are shifting toward a more holistic view of sustainability. Environmental, Social, and Governance (ESG) factors are increasingly being integrated into investment strategies, leading to greater demand for financial instruments that align with these principles. Flammer (2021) observes that the alignment of green bonds with ESG criteria enhances their attractiveness to institutional investors, further driving market growth.

In conclusion, the future of the green bond market is marked by technological innovation, regulatory advancements, and expanding global participation. These trends hold the promise of addressing existing challenges, such as greenwashing and high compliance costs, while unlocking new opportunities for sustainable finance. As these developments unfold, the green bond market is expected to play an even more pivotal role in achieving global climate and sustainability goals.

### Fintech as a Driver of Market Integrity

Fintech innovations are increasingly shaping the green bond market by enhancing efficiency and reducing transaction costs. Blockchain platforms, beyond offering immutable fund-tracking, are being piloted by multilateral banks to automate verification processes and lower certification costs for smaller issuers (BBVA, 2019).

Artificial intelligence applications are also gaining traction in monitoring environmental impact by processing satellite and sensor data, providing real-time evidence of project performance (Huang & Xu, 2024).

These tools have the potential to address two persistent challenges—greenwashing and high issuance costs—by making impact reporting both cheaper and more reliable. Nevertheless, the deployment of fintech solutions is uneven, with high initial investment requirements and technical expertise acting as barriers in emerging economies (OECD, 2021). This suggests that while fintech can enhance transparency and accountability, its full integration will require targeted capacity-building and regulatory alignment.

## 6.2 Expanding Market Access

Expanding market access is a critical component of fostering an inclusive and sustainable green bond market. By addressing barriers that limit participation, particularly for smaller issuers and entities in emerging economies, global efforts can democratize green finance and amplify its impact on climate action and sustainable development.

Support for smaller issuers is a key aspect of market expansion. Smaller organizations often face significant challenges, including high costs of certification, complex regulatory requirements, and limited expertise in green finance. Programs aimed at reducing these barriers, such as subsidized certification processes or simplified issuance frameworks, can enable broader participation. Nasir and Ahmed (2024) emphasize that tailored financial products and capacity-building initiatives for small and medium-sized enterprises (SMEs) can empower them to leverage green bonds for sustainability projects.

Emerging economies represent a significant opportunity for market growth but are often constrained by weak regulatory environments and limited investor confidence. Initiatives like the African Development Bank's (AfDB) Green Bond Program have been instrumental in addressing these challenges. According to Adisa et al. (2024), the AfDB program not only provides funding for critical infrastructure projects but also offers technical assistance to local issuers, enhancing their ability to meet international green bond standards.

Blended finance mechanisms are also gaining traction as a means to support market access in developing regions. By combining public and private capital, these mechanisms de-risk investments in green projects, making them more attractive to private investors. Karumanchi (2024) highlights that blended finance has been particularly effective in funding renewable energy and sustainable agriculture projects in South Asia and Sub-Saharan Africa.

Technology plays a pivotal role in democratizing the green bond market. Digital platforms and fintech innovations can streamline the issuance process, reduce transaction costs, and provide access to a wider pool of investors. Tang et al. (2024) observe that blockchain technology, for instance, enhances transparency and simplifies fund tracking, which can be especially beneficial for smaller issuers in emerging markets.

Collaboration between international organizations and local governments is crucial for creating an enabling environment for green bond issuance. Fareniuk (2024) suggests that partnerships between multilateral development banks and national financial institutions can help align local policies with global best practices, ensuring that emerging markets can attract international capital while maintaining transparency and accountability.

Public awareness campaigns are another essential strategy for expanding market access. These campaigns can educate potential issuers and investors about the benefits and requirements of green bonds, reducing knowledge gaps and fostering greater participation. Adisa et al. (2024) recommend that such initiatives be tailored to regional contexts to maximize their effectiveness.

In conclusion, expanding access to the green bond market requires a multi-faceted approach that includes financial incentives, regulatory reforms, technological integration, and capacity-building efforts. By addressing the unique challenges faced by smaller issuers and emerging economies, these efforts can drive inclusive growth and ensure that the benefits of green finance are distributed equitably across the globe.

## 6.3 Regional Perspectives

The green bond market is evolving across different regions, each characterized by unique opportunities and challenges. While Europe and North America continue to dominate the global market, Asia, Africa, and Latin America are emerging as important players, driven by growing environmental awareness, government initiatives, and international support. Tailored strategies that reflect regional priorities and challenges are essential for maximizing the impact and inclusivity of green bonds.

### Europe: Setting the Benchmark

Europe remains the leader in green bond issuance, supported by robust regulatory frameworks such as the European Union's Sustainable Finance Taxonomy and the Green Bond Standard (EuGBS). These initiatives have set global benchmarks for transparency, accountability, and environmental performance. Camilleri (2024) emphasizes that the strong regulatory environment in Europe has fostered investor confidence, driving significant investments in renewable energy, energy efficiency, and climate adaptation projects. Furthermore, countries like Germany and France have issued sovereign green bonds, demonstrating national commitments to sustainability.

### North America: Municipal and Corporate Leadership

North America, particularly the United States, has leveraged its well-established municipal bond market to support green finance. Municipal green bonds have been instrumental in funding local infrastructure projects, such as renewable energy installations and sustainable water management systems. According to Flammer (2021), corporate green bonds are also gaining traction in North America, enabling private companies to integrate sustainability into their financial strategies. However, the absence of a unified regulatory framework, as seen in Europe, poses a challenge for scaling the market further.

## Asia: A Fast-Growing Hub

Asia is rapidly emerging as a significant player in the green bond market, with China leading the way. China's Green Bond Guidelines and government-backed incentives have made it the world's largest green bond issuer. Tang et al. (2024) note that the majority of funds in China are directed toward pollution control, renewable energy, and sustainable urbanization. In Southeast Asia, the ASEAN Green Bond Standards have facilitated cross-border investments, enabling countries like Indonesia, Thailand, and Malaysia to attract international capital for climate-resilient projects.

Japan and South Korea are also notable contributors, with a focus on technological innovations and energy transition. For example, Japan has directed green bond proceeds toward energy-efficient housing and electric vehicle infrastructure, reflecting its national priorities for reducing carbon emissions.

## Africa: Unlocking Potential

Africa's green bond market is still in its infancy but holds immense potential. With pressing climate adaptation needs, green bonds provide a viable solution for financing renewable energy, water management, and agricultural resilience projects. The African Development Bank (AfDB) has played a crucial role in supporting the region's green finance efforts. Adisa et al. (2024) highlight that the AfDB's Green Bond Program has provided not only funding but also technical assistance, enabling local issuers to meet international standards.

However, Africa faces challenges such as weak regulatory frameworks, high issuance costs, and limited market infrastructure. Addressing these barriers requires international partnerships, capacity-building programs, and innovative financing mechanisms like blended finance.

## Latin America: Leveraging Natural Assets

Latin America has gradually expanded its green bond activities, leveraging its rich natural resources for sustainable development. Countries like Brazil, Mexico, and Chile are at the forefront, issuing green bonds to finance renewable energy, reforestation, and climate adaptation projects. Fareniuk (2024) suggests that strengthening regional cooperation and harmonizing standards with global frameworks could unlock further potential, attracting both local and international investors.

## Emerging Trends and Opportunities

Technology is playing an increasingly significant role in regional green bond markets. Blockchain and AI are being integrated to enhance transparency, reduce transaction costs, and build investor trust. Kreibich and Ossenbrink (2021) argue that these innovations are particularly beneficial for regions with limited financial infrastructure, as they simplify compliance and reporting processes.

Moreover, international organizations such as the World Bank and the United Nations are promoting green bond issuance in underrepresented regions. These efforts include technical assistance, knowledge sharing, and financial guarantees, all of which contribute to building local capacity and reducing barriers to entry.

In conclusion, while Europe and North America currently dominate the green bond market, emerging regions like Asia, Africa, and Latin America are poised for significant growth. Tailored strategies that address regional challenges, coupled with international cooperation and technological integration, will be key to ensuring that green bonds become a truly global instrument for sustainable development.

# 7. CONCLUSION

Green bonds have emerged as a transformative tool for financing climate resilience and advancing global sustainability goals. By channeling capital toward projects that mitigate environmental risks and promote sustainable practices, green bonds bridge the critical gap between investment needs and the urgent demands of climate action. Their ability to mobilize both public and private sector resources underscores their significance in the broader framework of sustainable development.

Despite their potential, green bonds face notable challenges, including high transaction costs, complex certification requirements, and the risk of greenwashing. These barriers, particularly pronounced in developing economies and among smaller issuers, limit market accessibility and undermine confidence in the environmental integrity of projects. However, targeted policy interventions, such as harmonized regulatory frameworks and financial incentives, can address these obstacles. The European Union's Green Bond Standard serves as a prime example of how robust regulations can enhance transparency, accountability, and investor confidence.

Technological advancements further promise to revolutionize the green bond market. Innovations such as blockchain and artificial intelligence offer solutions to persistent issues of transparency and inefficiency. By enabling real-time tracking of fund allocation and environmental impacts, these technologies can reduce the risk of greenwashing while simplifying compliance processes for issuers. Integrating these tools into green finance ecosystems is crucial for building trust and expanding market participation.

As climate risks intensify, the role of green bonds in building resilience becomes even more critical. Projects financed through green bonds—ranging from renewable energy and sustainable urban infrastructure to nature-based solutions—are vital for reducing vulnerability to climate change while fostering economic growth. Their dual focus on environmental and financial outcomes makes them a cornerstone of climate adaptation strategies worldwide.

Moreover, the global expansion of green bond markets offers an inclusive path forward. Tailored approaches that address regional challenges and leverage local opportunities can unlock untapped potential in emerging economies, ensuring that the benefits of green finance reach the most vulnerable populations. Initiatives led by multilateral development banks and international organizations have already demonstrated the viability of such approaches, particularly in Africa, Asia, and Latin America.

Green bonds represent more than just a financial instrument; they are a symbol of the intersection between economic prosperity and environmental stewardship. By addressing existing challenges through policy innovation, capacity building, and technological integration, green bonds can unlock unprecedented opportunities for sustainable development. As the world grapples with escalating climate risks, their role as a tool for resilience and sustainability will only grow in importance, solidifying their place as a key strategy for a sustainable future.

## REFERENCES


Adisa, O., Ilugbusi, B. S., & Obi, O. C. (2024). Green bonds in climate finance: A review of USA and African initiatives. *International Journal of Science and Development.*

African Development Bank. (2024). Climate Change and Green Growth at the African Development Bank, Annual Report 2022 https://www.afdb.org/fr/documents/climate-change-and-green-growth-2022-annual-report

Agence France Trésor. (2025). *Green OATs overview*. https://www.aft.gouv.fr/en/green-oat

Anyiam-Osigwe, T., & Ibrahim, S. E. (2024). Across the boards: Corporate governance and access to climate finance. *Academy of Management Proceedings*. Retrieved from https://journals.aom.org

Asimiyu, Z. (2024). Fintech solutions to overcome financing constraints in corporate green innovation. *ResearchGate*. Retrieved from https://www.researchgate.net

BBVA. (2019). *BBVA issues the first blockchain-supported structured green bond for MAPFRE.* https://www.bbva.com/en/sustainability/bbva-issues-the-first-blockchain-supported-structured-green-bond-for-mapfre/

Bortz, P. G. (2024). Green and sustainable taxonomies: Dimensions, challenges, and difficulties. *UNSAM*. Retrieved from https://www.unsam.edu.ar

Camilleri, L. (2024). The EU's green agenda: An analysis of green finance efforts to date and expectations for the new EU Green Bond Standard. *UM Theses*. Retrieved from https://www.um.edu.mt

Carney, M. (2015). Breaking the tragedy of the horizon—Climate change and financial stability. *Bank of England Speech*. Retrieved from https://www.bankofengland.co.uk

Chauhan, R. (2024). Sustainable finance and green investing: Navigating the future of ethical capital markets. *ITM University*. Retrieved from https://mis.itmuniversity.ac.in

Cheteni, P., Matsongoni, H., & Umejesi, I. (2025). South Africa's green bond market: Financing sustainable development. *Cogent Economics & Finance*. Retrieved from https://www.tandfonline.com

Climate Bonds Initiative. (2017). Green bond highlights 2017. https://www.climatebonds.net/resources/reports/green-bond-highlights-2017

Climate Bonds Initiative. (2023). Green bond market summary. Retrieved from https://www.climatebonds.net

Cui, H. D., Rokicki, B., & M'Barek, R. (2025). *European green bonds, carbon tax, and crowding-out: The economic, social, and environmental impacts of the EU's green investments under different scenarios. Renewable and Sustainable Energy Reviews*. Retrieved from ScienceDirect.

Dahlgren, H., & Santesson, P. (2024). Lost in translation: Bridging the gap between climate change and municipal bonds. *Diva Portal*. Retrieved from https://www.diva-portal.org

Ehlers, T., & Packer, F. (2017). Green bond finance and certification. *BIS Quarterly Review*. Retrieved from https://www.bis.org

Flammer, C. (2021). Corporate green bonds. *Journal of Financial Economics*, *142*(2), 499–516. DOI: 10.1016/j.jfineco.2021.01.010

Folke, C., Carpenter, S. R., Walker, B., Scheffer, M., Chapin, T., & Rockström, J. (2010). Resilience thinking: Integrating resilience, adaptability and transformability. *Ecology and Society*, *15*(4), art20. Advance online publication. DOI: 10.5751/ES-03610-150420

Global Commission on Adaptation. (2019). *Adapt now: A global call for leadership on climate resilience*. Retrieved from https://gca.org

Huang, Y., & Xu, J. (2024). Public development banks and green bond market development. *SSRN*. Retrieved from https://papers.ssrn.com DOI: 10.2139/ssrn.4972418

Intonti, M., De Leonardis, M., & Starace, G. (2025). *Enhancing circular practices in olive oil production: The role of green finance. Sustainability*. MDPI.

IPCC. (2021). *The physical science basis*. Sixth assessment report of the Intergovernmental Panel on Climate Change. Retrieved from https://www.ipcc.ch

Karumanchi, L. (2024). The role of green financing in accelerating sustainable economic development in emerging economies. *International Journal of Trade and Business Management*. Retrieved from https://ijtbm.com

Khoa, D. D., & Anh, D. N. (2024). Integrating green finance for sustainable agricultural practices and economic diversification in rural Vietnam. *Organizational Committee Proceedings*. Retrieved from https://duan.edu.ua

Kreibich, N., & Ossenbrink, J. (2021). The role of blockchain in the sustainable development goals: A case study of green bond issuance. *Journal of Cleaner Production*, *303*, 127015. DOI: 10.1016/j.jclepro.2021.127015

Lone, F. A., Aggarwal, S., & Jain, S. (2024). Retail investors' perception towards green bonds in advancing sustainability: Evidence from India. *Asia-Pacific Financial Markets*. Retrieved from https://link.springer.com

Maltais, A., & Nykvist, B. (2020). Understanding the role of green bonds in advancing sustainability. *Environmental Innovation and Societal Transitions*, *27*, 1–8. DOI: 10.1016/j.eist.2017.10.003

Muniasamy, I. G. (2024). Digital platform dynamics: Governance, market design and AI integration. *Purdue University*. Retrieved from https://hammer.purdue.edu

Nasir, N., & Ahmed, W. (2024). *Green finance initiatives and their potential to drive sustainable development*. Springer. DOI: 10.1007/978-3-031-56419-2_1

Nevatia, V. (2024). Sovereign green bonds: Reducing climate capital costs in emerging markets. *SSRN*. Retrieved from https://papers.ssrn.com DOI: 10.2139/ssrn.4983252

OECD. (2021). *Mobilising Bond Markets for a Low-Carbon Transition*. https://www.oecd.org/en/publications/mobilising-bond-markets-for-a-low-carbon-transition_9789264272323-en.html

Panfilov, M. A., Nikishova, N. V., & Logutenkov, A. V. (2024). Impact of green bond issuance on the company's efficiency. In *Creation of green finance frameworks*. Springer. DOI: 10.1007/978-3-031-70962-3_21

Pelling, M., O'Brien, K., & Matyas, D. (2015). Adaptation and transformation. *Climatic Change*, *133*(1), 113–127. DOI: 10.1007/s10584-014-1303-0

Rockström, J., Steffen, W., Noone, K., Persson, Å., Chapin, F. S., Lambin, E., & Schellnhuber, H. J. (2009). A safe operating space for humanity. *Nature*, *461*(7263), 472–475. DOI: 10.1038/461472a PMID: 19779433

Solecki, W., Leichenko, R., & O'Brien, K. (2017). Climate change adaptation strategies and disaster risk reduction in cities: Connections, contentions, and synergies. *Current Opinion in Environmental Sustainability*, *19*, 1–7. DOI: 10.1016/j.cosust.2015.08.001

Spalding, M. D., Ruffo, S., Lacambra, C., Meliane, I., Zeitlin, H., & Hale, L. Z. (2014). The role of ecosystems in coastal protection: Adapting to climate change and coastal hazards. *Ocean and Coastal Management*, *90*, 50–57. DOI: 10.1016/j.ocecoaman.2013.09.007

Sruthi, S. (2024). The role of financial institutions in promoting green finance for sustainable development. *Redshine Archive*. Retrieved from https://chapters.redshine.in

Tang, P., Ma, H., Sun, Y., & Xu, X. (2024). *Exploring the role of Fintech, green finance and natural resources towards environmental sustainability: A study on ASEAN economies. Resources Policy*. Retrieved from Elsevier.

United Nations Environment Programme (UNEP). (2021). *Adaptation gap report 2021: The gathering storm*. UNEP. Retrieved from https://www.unep.org

Zerbib, O. D. (2019). The effect of pro-environmental preferences on bond prices: Evidence from green bonds. *Journal of Banking & Finance*, *98*, 39–60. DOI: 10.1016/j.jbankfin.2018.10.012

# Chapter 7
# Green Finance: Unlocking Sustainable Development and Navigating the Greenwashing Challenges

**Y. Adarsha**
https://orcid.org/0009-0009-3197-8048
*Dayananda Sagar College of Engineering, India*

**Ganesha K. S.**
https://orcid.org/0000-0001-8181-2411
*Dayananda Sagar College of Engineering, India*

## ABSTRACT

*Green finance is fast becoming a key tool for solving global issues such as climate change, natural resource scarcity, and social inequality. Green finance mobilizes financial resources as investments with environmental benefits that contribute and activate investments based on sustainable development goals (SDGs) to help steer the economy into one focusing on long-term ecological, social wellbeing. This chapter investigates the role of green finance for sustainable development, more specifically which financial instruments help shaping a more sustainable economic model. Globally, the use of green bonds and sustainability linked instruments have picked up in both developed and emerging economy jurisdictions indicating a universal commitment to deliver the sustainability objectives. This chapter indicates that firms which issue green bonds tend to see a financial benefit as investors realign themselves to meet the needs of portfolio responsibilities.*

DOI: 10.4018/979-8-3373-8287-6.ch007

ht © 2026, IGI Global Scientific Publishing. Copying or distributing in print or electronic forms without written permission of IGI Global Scientific Publishing is prohibited. Use of this chapter to generative artificial intelligence (AI) technologies is expressly prohibited. The publisher reserves all rights to license its use for generative AI training and machine learning model development.

## INTRODUCTION

Green finance continues to expand as a primary sustainable development force because of mounting global issues including environmental change together with diminishing resources and social inequality. Financial capital used deliberately to fund projects with environmental benefits can accurately be described as green finance (Rahman et al., 2024). Sustainable Development Goals of the United Nations and a sustainable world economic growth toward ecological and social excellence rely heavily on this approach (Van Niekerk, 2024). The study addresses the role of green finance towards sustainable development in considering critical financial instruments guiding economic transformation to sustainability (Selvakumar & Manjunath, 2025). Green bonds and sustainability-linked instruments are now becoming a popular feature in developed and emerging economies as they show global commitment towards sustainability objectives (Banga & Afzal, 2025). The increasing interest among investors in green portfolios compels companies to issue green bonds that allow them to attain favorable financial performance as per research studies. Regulatory systems for green finance framed by the European Union promote investment in the market by means of effective structures (Alves, 2023).

The path toward green finance consists of multiple substantial challenges. The practice of false environmental claims about financial products called greenwashing endangers the integrity of the market (Dempere et al., 2024). Green finance markets lose their legitimacy when deceptive practices deceive investors thus diminishing their trust in the industry (Dempere et al., 2024). Financial product environmental impact evaluation becomes difficult for investors and policymakers because they lack standardized sustainability disclosure and impact assessment frameworks to accurately assess these products (da Cunha et al., 2025). The chapter outlines major financial resources alongside regulatory instruments which propel green investments during sustainable development initiatives (Triggs, 2023). The text examines how the combination of green bonds and sustainability-linked products and carbon pricing and fintech developments helps achieve a low-emission economy transition (Heine et al., 2019). Green finance finds its main acceleration through the fintech revolution (Hasan et al., 2024). Traditionally outdated financial systems were revitalized by both blockchain-based carbon trading (Kharche & Kudal, 2024) and AI tools for ESG risk evaluation. The chapter explores both regulatory aspects of green finance alongside the mandate for transparency and the development of investor trust together with the obstacles created by greenwashing practices (Steuer & Tröger, 2022).

## FINTECH AND DIGITAL INNOVATION: REVOLUTIONIZING GREEN FINANCE FOR A SUSTAINABLE FUTURE

The world of green finance is quickly changing as a result of various fintech and digital innovations, and it is streamlining processes within the industry by making it more efficient, transparent and accessible (Singh, 2022; Wang et al., 2019). Digital tools are proving to be effective in fighting environmental issues on a global scale by directing marketable skills and resources towards sustainable investments (Wang et al., 2022). Fintech innovations are changing traditional ways of offering financial services, especially in green finance, by developing new instruments and methods designed to promote green finance (Volz, 2018). Carbon markets are improving with the use of blockchain technology for carbon credit transactions which results in greater transparency and security for the buying and selling of carbon credits (Espelage et al., 2022). AI technologies are important in the doing ESG risk assessments by providing analytical insights on the huge database concerning the sustainability performance of companies and investments, thereby assisting investors in making better decisions by reducing the chances for greenwashing(Sari et al., 2025). Digital technologies allow the sustainable parameters of an investment to be monitored as it is being implemented towards its goals so that measurement can begin during the process (Binder & Wade, 2024). This monitoring greatly enhances transparency of the actual impacts of the investment and progress towards the sustainability goals. Security against fraud is improved with the help of technology as it preventing fraudulent green finance transactions (Abd Aziz et al., 2025). Self-directing compliance reporting is automated, improving performance accountability and efficiency in green finance (Nasis et al., 2025). The fact that fintech is able to widen financial inclusion is of utmost importance, as it provides greater access to financial services to more stakeholders and broadens participation in the green economy (Mhlanga, D, 2024). Fintech also assists the expansion of green consumer finance, as personal finance management applications now have carbon footprint trackers and ESG investment options which enable users to reduce their environmental impact through their spending and investing decisions (Khan & Wahab, 2025). To sum up, fintech and other forms of digital inovation are transforming green finance for the better by increasing its efficiency, transparency, and convenience (Puaschunder, 2023). Such developments are needed in order to enable funds for sustainable investments and accelerate the shift towards a greener and more sustainable economy (Lee, 2020). With the progress of technology, its impact on the future of green finance will only become more significant (Sonavane, 2024).

## GREEN FINANCE

The quick ascent of green finance as a vital solution for worldwide sustainability problems is blocked by major obstacles that researchers must solve to maximize its power (Nadkarni, P, 2024). Market trust and authority suffer damage because of greenwashing where financial products receive bogus environmental labels without sufficient sustainable criteria (Ghaemi Asl. M. et al., 2025). Standardized verification processes along with definition standards need development to achieve credibility in green financial products (Teixeira, 2025). Standardized sustainability disclosure and impact assessment frameworks should be implemented because they would help investors and policymakers evaluate investments accurately (Marín-Rodríguez et al., 2024). Strong reporting standards together with appropriate methodologies must be created to fulfill this need (IFRS Foundation 2023). The green finance sector contains numerous open and innovative spaces for future development (Fu et al., 2023). Fintech tools powered by the revolution act as strong drivers for sustainable investments by combining blockchain-based carbon trading with AI systems for ESG risk assessment while making financial services more accessible and efficient and transparent (Gopal & Pitts, 2025; Singh, 2022). Green finance reaches new audiences with consumer-focused instruments that help create sustainable behavior in individual customers (Xie et al., 2024). The proper management of challenges together with exploitation of available opportunities allows green finance to develop as a driving force behind sustainable global economic development (Peng, 2024). The quick ascent of green finance as a vital solution for worldwide sustainability problems is blocked by major obstacles that researchers must solve to maximize its power (Abro & Shehryar, 2025). Greenwashing leads to investor distrust because it involves the deceptive marketing of financial items that lack enough sustainability standards and thus harms market credibility (Barrera, 2024). Standardized verification processes along with definition standards need development to achieve credibility in green financial products (Nipper et al., 2022). Standardized sustainability disclosure and impact assessment standards are needed because they would enable better assessments and performance comparisons of sustainable investments for investors and policymakers (Amin, 2025). The creation of strong reporting standards combined with proper methodologies needs to be implemented at this time (Ahmad et al., 2025). The green finance sector contains numerous open and innovative spaces for future development. The fintech revolution functions as an empowering force through digital resources which refine financial inclusion while improving sustainable investment efficiency and transparency using blockchain carbon trading platforms and AI for ESG risk evaluation (Giudici & Wu, 2025). Green finance reaches new audiences with consumer-focused instruments that help create sustainable behavior in individual customers (Shrotriya, 2024). The proper management of challenges together with exploitation of available opportunities allows green finance to develop as a driving force behind sustainable global economic development (Abro & Shehryar, 2025). The increasing visibility of green finance encounters various impediments to its development (Chaudhary et al., 2024). The dishonest marketing technique of greenwashing jeopardizes market quality by fooling investors through false environmental claims which damages initiative trustworthiness (Passas & Garefalakis, 2025). Environmental impact assessment of financial products becomes more challenging because of the absence of standardized sustainability disclosure frameworks together with impact assessment standards which negatively affects informed decisions (Nipper, Ostermaier, & Theis, 2022). Sustainable banking practices consist of two main aspects which advance environmental sustainability: these include impact-centric financial products along with green lending policies (Saxena, 2024). From a theoretical viewpoint, we can argue that the impact of financial technology in green finance is growing significantly because of the enhancement of inclusion, efficiency, and transparency through digital systems (Li et al., 2023). The change in traditional finance with carbon trading based on blockchain technology or the assessment of ESG risks by AI systems are composite innovations of finance that allow for real time monitoring of various indicators of sustainability, elimination of deception, and self-fulfilling compliance reporting (Wang et al., 2023). Stakeholder pressure along with regulatory scrutiny is leading the adoption of sustainable business practices which use circular economy tactics like resource-efficient production and low-carbon supply chain management to reduce environmental impact (Fucà et al., 2024). Through products like green mortgages and energy-efficient housing loans, green consumer finance enables people to actively partake through green consumption (Lambert, Lyons, & Carroll, 2023). Meanwhile, personal finance applications go a step further by embedding carbon footprint monitoring and ESG investing (FinTechNews, n.d.). Public and financial entities worldwide support green finance through green banking programs combined with climate finance policy systems (Chantana et al. 2025). Central banks participate in crucial roles through integration of climate-related financial risk elements into their choice-making mechanisms (European Central Bank, 2024). Green finance serves as an innovative monetary mechanism which uses private investments to reach social and environmental targets and support economic development (Bagh & Iftikhar, 2024). The process of funding sustainable projects takes place through green bonds together with sustainability-linked investments while corporations implement regulatory policies and utilize fintech tools to fight climate change and generate sustainable development and better performance outcomes (Jasrai et al., 2024; Singh, 2022). The complete exploitation of these strategies depends on proper management of greenwashing and regulatory arbitrage and access inequalities through strong policies and transparent frameworks as well as international cooperation (Cerrato Garcia, E, 2024). Green finance will solidify its position as the sustainable economic framework for the global economy when such conditions are met (Ekué & Díaz Fajardo, 2024).

## Types of Green Finance Instruments

Green finance operates through numerous changing financial instruments that direct funds into environmentally friendly activities in order to achieve sustainable development goals (Sharma and Jain 2024). These mechanisms are vital tools in mobilizing enormous funds which address key environmental concerns and assist in achieving United Nations Sustainable Development Goals (SDGs) (Ramgopal & Mohanty, 2019). Businesses must understand different types of green finance instruments in order to comprehend how the financial industry adjusts to accommodate global economic sustainability objectives (Obadire & Moyo, 2024). The primary financial instrument in green finance sector is green bonds enabling significant funding opportunities for eligible green projects (Ojukwu et al., 2024). Debt securities function to fund new projects that select their target funding towards environmental projects across renewable energy and energy efficiency and sustainable transportation and green buildings and sustainable water management (Dambe et al., 2024). The green bond market worldwide demonstrated significant advancement because various economies from both developed and emerging areas began releasing more notes that show rising investor interest in sustainability-focused portfolio alignment (Konstantakis et al., 2023). The market includes sustainability-linked financial products that link interest rates to predefined sustainable goals instead of traditional green bonds (Addleshaw Goddard LLP, 2022). The system creates financial benefits that push organizations to boost their ESG achievements throughout their management structures which deepens sustainability integration across their strategic business plans (Stoicescu & Sima, 2024).

The green finance framework incorporates carbon pricing mechanisms as policy devices which integrate environmental expenses of greenhouse gas emissions (Global Green Growth Institute, n.d.; International Monetary Fund, 2024). These policy mechanisms establish financial penalties for pollution activities to drive investments toward environmentally-friendly solutions (Bose et al., 2019). The two main structures of carbon pricing methods involve carbon taxes that directly assign a monetary value to emissions alongside ETS which create maximum emission levels while permitting emission credit exchanges (Öztürk, S., 2024). These economic systems drive the transformation of the economy into one characterized by low carbon emissions (Parry, Black, & Zhunussova, 2022). Through sustainable banking methods combined with strong lending approaches the finance sector guides resources to sustainability initiatives (Nica, 2023). Green lending practices focus on two main elements which include financing environmentally friendly projects and adding ESG elements to risk assessment frameworks for loans and creating financial products that deliver dual benefits of wealth growth alongside societal and ecological advantages (Lapinskienė, Gudaitis, & Martišienė, 2025). Sustainable development receives support from ethical banking and microfinance programs which provide financial service to underserved communities through inclusive banking and sustainable financial resources for livelihoods (Ranabahu & Wickramasinghe, 2022).

Financial technology (Fintech) advancements transform green finance through modernization which improves sustainable investing practices across different operational areas (Arslan et al., 2024). The application of fintech solutions via blockchain technology supports better carbon trading platforms and enables AI-driven ESG assessments as well as digital platforms creating better access to green investments with enhanced sustainability reporting and verification systems (Mhlanga, D, 2025). The current level of sustainable growth receives fuel from green consumer finance that enables people to improve environmental stewardship through financial resources promoting sustainable consumption habits (Kennedy et al., 2024). The financial sector offers products such as green mortgages for eco-friendly residences along with loans for property energy conservation efforts in addition to sustainable funds and finance systems that monitor and offer environmentally sound investments (Casalini, 2025).

## Importance of Green Finance in Sustainable Development

The global drive for sustainable development has made green finance a vital aspect that gained swift importance in recent years (KV, 2024). The fundamental purpose of green finance involves providing crucial financial tools that tackle the linked problems related to climate change and natural resource limitations with social fairness issues (Sharma, H., & Jain, S., 2024). Green finance acts as the primary resource mobilization tool by attracting funds which result in dual benefits of environmental sustainability and United Nations Sustainable Development Goal achievement (Ariffin & Milala, 2023). Green finance guides economic development through capital investment into sustainable activities thus it drives economies to replace their old harmful systems with new environmentally sound systems (Fu et al., 2024). The transformation requires us to understand financial resources differently since they represent strong potential to drive beneficial change A sustainable economic model becomes essential because green finance plays a vital role in its development (Kathane et al., 2024). The necessary economic resources obtained from green finance enable us to shift toward a sustainable economy through investments in renewable energy systems and energy efficiency measures along with sustainable agricultural practices and green infrastructure construction (Shi

& Shi, 2025). The financial mechanisms of green finance through instruments such as green bonds (Khan et al. 2024) and sustainability-linked products serve to direct money flows toward sustainability targets thus creating essential economic transformation towards environmentally cautious procedures (Alamgir & Cheng, 2023). The alignment between development and sustainability interests brings dual benefits which include environmental preservation in addition to establishing new economic prospects and supporting sustainable innovation across technology and business practices Green finance works as a crucial element in reduction of climate change along with its ability to boost corporate sustainability and generate inclusive economic development (Sule et al., 2024). The minimal shift towards a low-emission economy depends heavily on financial tools and policy instruments within green finance which include carbon pricing mechanisms and green lending policies and impact-centric financial products (Heine et al., 2019). Businesses benefit from these mechanisms which drive them to minimize their environmental impact while adopting sustainable operations through the investment in clean technologies (Eyo-Udo et al., 2024). Through its environmentally beneficial operation green finance allows people to achieve sustainable development goals by including all segments of society in financial systems and ensuring ethical banking standards and promoting sustainable consumer choices (Van Niekerk, 2024). Green finance is crucial for sustainable development as it fosters architectural transformation across the financial system and stimulates innovative solutions (Chauhan et al., 2024). The system mobilizes required financing for SDG-compatible investments while creating innovative financial approaches and new technologies simultaneously (Enable.Green, 2025). Fintech solutions emerging in the market revolutionize green finance through improved sustainable investments by maintaining financial access combined with operational excellence and transparency (Patel, 2024). By means of finance innovation technologies like blockchain-based carbon market systems and AI-based ESG risk monitoring tools traditional financial systems undergo a transformation that facilitates real-time sustainability indicator tracking as well as enhanced security arrangements and enhanced accountability metrics (Saxena et al., 2024). Policy support and financial innovation together enable the release of the transformative potential of green finance that eventually leads to creating an economy which prioritizes ecological and social well-being on a sustainable basis (Fu et al., 2024).

## Greenwashing

Through sustainable banking methods combined with strong lending approaches the finance sector guides resources to sustainability initiatives (Aracil, Nájera-Sánchez, & Forcadell, 2021). Green lending policies offer two main priorities:

first, they finance environmentally sound projects then they integrate ESG factors and assessment into lending frameworks as well as develop financial products that combine economic rewards with social and environmental impact (Wang, 2023). Sustainable development receives support from ethical banking and microfinance programs which provide financial service to underserved communities through inclusive banking and sustainable financial resources for livelihoods (Gil-Lafuente & others, 2021).

Financial technology (Fintech) systems currently drive innovative changes and operational enhancements in various aspects of green finance (Areo, 2024). Blockchain technology incorporates Fintech solutions to improve carbon trading platforms along with AI-enhanced ESG risk assessment and digital platforms that accessibility green investments and advanced sustainability reporting verification capabilities (Negi et al., 2025). The current level of sustainable growth receives fuel from green consumer finance that enables people to improve environmental stewardship through financial resources promoting sustainable consumption habits (Kennedy et al., 2024). The financial sector offers products such as green mortgages for eco-friendly residences along with loans for property energy conservation efforts in addition to sustainable funds and finance systems that monitor and offer environmentally sound investments Greenwashing takes place primarily through false corporate branding that uses deceptive terminology on product labels (Jamil & Wahyuni, 2024). Financial products display eco-friendly and sustainable and green labels without standard definitions or verified environmental evidence. The ambiguous nature in these claims enables market participants to draw personal conclusions so the actual environmental consequences of investments remain unclear to investors who struggle to discover valid sustainability measures from misleading statements (Bebbington & Unerman, 2018). Organizations control what information reaches the public through selective information disclosure by presenting positive environmental aspects without showing their complete environmental effects (Agarwal et al., 2023). The manipulated information displays an inaccurate image of product sustainability making investors perceive the wrong environmental footprint(Hahn & Kühnen, 2013).

Organizations use comparative greenwashing to present themselves as green leaders by showing superior practices against competitors whose sustainability is relatively lower while their own actions fail to match true sustainable criteria (Marciniak, A.2010). By using this approach financial entities generate a misleading perception regarding their environmental leadership to deceive investors who think their products are more sustainable than they actually are (Dempere, J., Alamash, E., & Mattos, P. 2024). The situation worsens because there are no clear qualifications or verification systems in place, Poor transparency in environmental claim documentation together with absent independent verification enables greenwashing because stakeholders cannot verify the accuracy of such declarations (Mihaylova, I. M., & Blumer, A. 2025). A financial product that emphasizes one environmentally positive feature at the expense of other environmentally damaging aspects presents a deceptive impression of total sustainability (Lyon & Montgomery, 2011). The deceptive practice of greenwashing results in problems which reach past simple deceptive behavior (Gbadegesin et al., 2025). The wrong allocation of investments occurs because of greenwashing so capital ends up directing toward projects that lack genuine sustainability contribution and away from critical impactful undertakings (Flammer, 2021). The wrong allocation of resources caused by greenwashing weakens the ability of green finance to tackle important environmental concerns. For markets operating in green finance the damage to integrity leads to diminished investor trust while discouraging people from engaging further (Delmas & Burbano, 2011). Diminished trust in sustainable projects results in destructive chain reactions which therefore limit sector development together with capital distribution to true sustainability efforts, the elimination of greenwashing demands unified activities from multiple responsible parties (Ngoc Thinh, P. 2024). Establishing robust regulatory frameworks enables the development of clear definitions and standards for green financial products with effective mechanisms for enforcing regulations against environmental misinformation (Bhattacharya & Sachdev, 2024). Investors need to base their sustainability investment decisions on mandatory and standardized environmental information disclosures to evaluate investment sustainability correctly (Cifrino, D. 2023). Investors can obtain assurance about environmental claims through third-party verification schemes which offer certification yet they need transparent data access to detect and block greenwashing (Soh, B. 2024, August 3). The education of investors regarding greenwashing concepts plays an essential role together with their awareness because it equips them to detect and question greenwashing in order to discipline financial markets and enforce institutional accountability (Dempere, Alamash, & Mattos, 2024).

## Carbon Markets and Climate Finance Mechanisms: Driving the Transition to a Low-Carbon Economy

Carbon markets help mitigate climate change and transition to a low-carbon economy along with climate finance (Michaelowa, 2012).They are critical to "green finance" by funding projects that lessen the emission of GHGs and build adaptive capacities towards climate changes. A market for carbon has been created to put a dollar value on carbon emissions (Labatt & White, 2011). Emissions are reduced through internalizing the cost of carbon pollution: in systems like Emission Trading Systems (ETS) that cap total GHG emissions and permit the trading of emission allowances, or in Carbon Offset Markets that allow entities to buy carbon credits from projects that significantly reduce or remove GHG emissions (Stavins, R. N. 2023). Numerous studies carbon markets contribute to GHG emission reductions, and this is primarily ascribed to the emission reduction incentives attributed to carbon pricing; however, the effectiveness of these markets is also influenced by the give emission caps' stringency, the carbon price's rigidity, and the existence of monitoring and verification systems(Ellerman, Denny, & Montero, 2010). Climate finance includes a broader range of financial activities intended to help in mitigating and adapting to climate change, so as to catalyze the massive funding needed to shift towards a low carbon economy while building climate resilience (Mol, 2012). Important climate finance mechanisms are the Multilateral Climate Funds which include the Green Climate Fund (GCF) that offers financial support to help developing countries undertake climate-enabling activities; Bilateral Climate Finance which is direct funding of climate activities in developing countries by developed countries; and Development Finance Institutions (DFIs) like the World Bank that finance climate friendly economic activities (Michaelowa et al., 2021). These mechanisms aim to provide financial assistance to countries that are in most need, and in the case of developing countries with limited resources, this is especially critical. In the context of climate finance and carbon markets, mechanisms are critical tools for catalyzing the shift to a lower-carbon economy (Zhou & Li, 2019). While climate finance mechanisms direct funds to specific climate initiatives, carbon markets function as a cost signal for incentivizing emission reductions (Ervine, 2014). Particularly in developing economies, the mobilization of financial resources is critical, and sound implementation and governance is essential to achieve global climate objectives and a lasting future (UNFCCC, 2022).

## RULES AND REGULATIONS FOR GREEN FINANCE: ESTABLISHING A FRAMEWORK FOR INTEGRITY, IMPACT, TRANSPARENCY, AND SUSTAINABLE GROWTH.

Green finance rises to become a key solution to resolve global problems including environmental change alongside resource depletion together with social gaps which demonstrates why solid regulatory frameworks need urgent establishment (Nasir & Ahmed, 2024). This chapter demonstrates that green finance instruments such as green bonds as well as sustainability-linked instruments are gaining popularity in both developed and emerging economies and thus require modern and trustworthy regulatory frameworks for effective implementation (Del Sarto. N, 2025). Green finance sector integrity depends on rules and regulations which establish the sector's operational integrity along with maintaining genuine environmental and social impact (Jin, X., Qi, H., & Huang, X. 2024). A core responsibility of green finance regulation includes defining "green" with specific technical clarity throughout all activities. The abstract correctly names greenwashing as a major challenge which involves companies giving false environmental markers to financial products lacking actual sustainability characteristics (Ghaemi Asl & Shahzad, 2024). Standardized definitions of eligible green activities and projects along with standards for assets need to be developed under regulatory frameworks to prevent greenwashing in the market(Nipper, M., Ostermaier, A., & Theis, J. 2022). The standardized definitions serve three essential roles in investment decisions and representational clarity and sustainable development goal promotion green finance disclosure transparency depends on regulations to achieve their full purpose of ensuring proper implementation (Tang, D. Y., & Zhang, Y. (2020). Standards for sustainability reporting and impact assessment are necessary as per the abstract. All entities within both financial institutions and corporate sectors need to deliver uniform quantifiable details which clearly show the ecological and societal effects of their operational conduct and investment decisions Ioannou, I., & Serafeim, G. (2015). The transparency measures enable investors to measure sustainability performance levels in their investments and understand risks and allocate their funds properly. The system promotes both completeness and enhances oversight for tracking sustainability target achievements. Confidence of investors represents the fundamental pillar which sustains both growth and stability of the green finance market(Azad, S., & Tulasi Devi, S. L. 2025). The development of investor confidence significantly depends on the proper establishment of rules and regulations. Regulatory oversight with defined requirements and rules and enforcement protocols helps regulators stop deceptive practices and false sustainability claims and other monetary misconduct (Saeed, A., & Maryam, S. 2023). The establishment of regulatory oversight protects investors and maintains market trust while ensuring product integrity in the green financial market. Strong green finance regulations in different jurisdictions lead to increased investor confidence and enhanced market movement according to the abstract. The establishment and execution process for green finance regulations proves to be complex since they differ between nations and regions. The abstract shows that certain regions along with nations are advancing their regulatory structures yet regulatory arbitrage continues to pose difficulties for all. International regulatory standards need to be harmonized because entities would exploit such loopholes unless all nations enforce a common set of standards concerning green finance. The abstract researches the expanding position of central banks within sustainable finance initiatives. Central banks are implementing climate-related risks assessment methods for financial stability while introducing climate stress testing procedures. Mainstream financial regulation needs to incorporate sustainability considerations because this integration enables the financial system to counter systemic risks while supporting sustainability objectives. The integrity along with impact achievement of green finance requires the fundamental presence of rules and regulations (Singh, 2022). The necessary framework that these standards and policies provide enables the definition of green activities and disclosure and transparency as well as investor confidence maintenance and market stability. A robust regulatory framework combined with international collaboration stands essential to solve greenwashing problems and regulatory fragmentation in order to achieve the full potential of green finance for sustainable and resilient global economic growth.

*Figure 1. Holistic Coordination of Sustainability Tools*

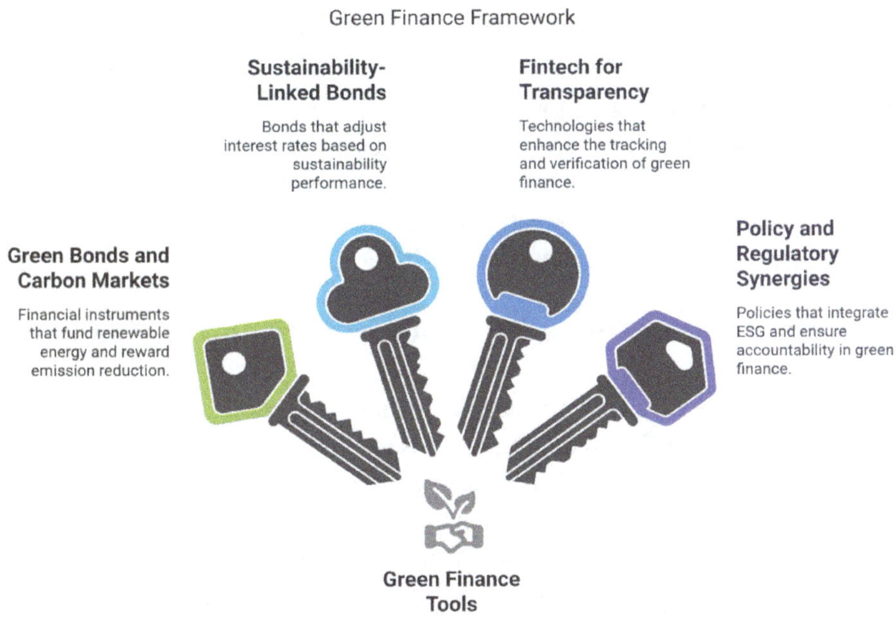


## 1. Green Bonds and Carbon Markets

Both green bonds and carbon markets are focused on getting money to climate solutions, but they use different yet connected strategies. Green bonds are used to finance projects involved in renewable energy, green transportation or efficient buildings (Stavins, R. N. 2023). From another side, carbon markets like cap-and-trade and offset systems reward companies financially for making their CO2 emissions lower.

**The connection:** Carbon reduction achievements from funded projects can be traced, giving projects the ability to be valued in carbon markets (Michaelowa, A., &

Purohit, P. 2007). In the example of a wind farm backed by green bonds, any carbon credits it generates can be used either to help companies achieve carbon neutrality or simply to remove them from the market. By doing this, a company gains bonds money and the prospect of earning through carbon offsets, making the project both more profitable and more appealing to investors.

## 2. Sustainability-Linked Bonds and Emission Metrics

SLBs differ from green bonds because they depend on results rather than how the money is used; for example, metrics such as carbon intensity, lesser emissions or greater energy efficiency (Tang, D. Y., & Zhang, Y. 2020). Very often such metrics are linked to carbon taxation or tracked in the same way as emissions trading schemes do it. As an example, a company could set it so that not meeting $CO_2$ goals results in paying a penalty rate for the rest of the loan.

**The connection:** SLBs can help carbon markets by putting corporate capital costs directly in relation to how much they reduce emissions (Reichelt, H., & Wirth, H. 2022). As a result, firms are motivated to measure their carbon outputs and realize the cost of emissions by acting responsibly in the financial market.

## 3. Fintech: Bridging Tools for Transparency and Traceability

Blockchain, AI and digital reporting platforms are the foundation that brings green financial tools together (Tapscott, D., & Tapscott, A. 2018). Thanks to blockchain and AI, it is now possible to safely track and verify carbon credits and to improve the way ESG data is measured for green bonds and SLBs. They improve how markets for carbon, loans and investment products are managed and reviewed.

**The connection:** Using fintech, green bond projects can verify the $CO_2$ savings earned by their projects eligible for carbon credits. Monitoring the use of these savings in real time benefits investors as well as regulators. It connects investing with the consequences it has on the environment.

## 4. Policy and Regulatory Synergies

Running a business in today's world means recognizing these interdependencies and legislation now reflects that. As an illustration, the EU Taxonomy and SFDR require ESG integration, green bond requirements and the same criteria for carbon market participation (Busch, T., & Lewandowski, S. 2018). New efforts by central banks include testing banks against climate risks using information from both their bond issuance and emission levels.

**The connection:** A green finance system works better when carbon markets impact behavior, green bonds support infrastructure needs, SLBs guarantee accountability and fintech guarantees openness in dealing. It strengthens the entire financial system and improves how credible sustainable finance is.

## GLOBAL GREEN INVESTMENT PERFORMANCE

Green investment refers to financial commitments aimed at supporting environmentally sustainable projects, such as renewable energy, electric vehicles (EVs), green bonds, and sustainable infrastructure (Zhang, D., Cheng, H., & Cai, W. 2022). This report presents a trend analysis of past, present, and future global green investment performance, with tables and models, supported by citations and references.

### 1. Green Investment Performance (2010-2020)

During the decade from 2010 to 2020, global green investment grew significantly due to increasing awareness of climate change and government initiatives such as the Paris Agreement 2015 (OECD, 2021).

*Table 1. Green Investment Growth (2010-2020)*

| Year | Global Green Investment ($ Billion) | Major Drivers | Leading Countries |
|---|---|---|---|
| 2010 | 200 | Renewable Energy Policies | Germany, US |
| 2012 | 350 | Feed-in Tariffs, Subsidies | China, UK |
| 2015 | 600 | Paris Agreement Commitments | EU, China |
| 2017 | 900 | Green Bonds Growth | US, France |
| 2020 | 1500 | Net-Zero Pledges, ESG Focus | China, US, EU |

Key Observations:

- Green investment grew from $200B in 2010 to $1.5T in 2020, a 650% increase (IEA, 2021).
- China and the EU emerged as top investors in renewable energy (UNEP, 2021).
- Green bonds and corporate sustainability initiatives fueled the mid-2010s surge (OECD, 2022).

*Table 2. Growth Factors Driving Green Investment (2010-20)*

| Factors | Impact Level (Low/Medium/High) | Example |
|---|---|---|
| Renewable Energy Policies | High | Germany's Renewable Energy Act |
| Green Bonds & ESG | High | EU's Sustainable Finance Plan |
| Climate Agreements | Medium | Paris Agreement 2015 |
| Technological Advances | Medium | Cost Reduction in Solar & Wind |

"The global green investment market expanded significantly between 2010 and 2020, driven by international climate policies and economic incentives." OECD (2021).

"By 2020, over 70% of green investment was directed towards renewable energy and low-carbon technologies." IEA (2021).

## 2. Green Investment Performance (2021-2024)

From 2021 to 2024, the post-pandemic recovery and energy crisis led to further acceleration in green investment (IEA, 2023).

*Table 3. Global Green Investment Trends (2021-2024)*

| Year | Global Green Investment ($ Billion) | Major Trends | Leading Countries |
|---|---|---|---|
| 2021 | 1,800 | Green Stimulus, ESG Boom | US, EU, China |
| 2022 | 2,100 | Renewable Energy Dominance | China, EU |
| 2023 | 2,400 | Climate Tech (EVs, Hydrogen) | US, Germany |
| 2024 | 2,700 (Projected) | AI in Green Finance, Carbon Markets | EU, Canada |

Key Observations:

- 50% increase from 2020 to 2024, driven by climate policies and technology (Bloomberg NEF, 2023).
- ESG investing surged, with companies shifting towards sustainable portfolios (PRI, 2023).
- China leads in renewable energy, while the US dominates climate tech innovation (IEA, 2023).

*Table 4. Key Trends Shaping Green Investment (2021-24)*

| Trends | Impact | Example |
|---|---|---|
| ESG Investment Growth | High | BlackRock's $1T ESG Portfolio |
| Hydrogen & EV Expansion | High | Tesla, Toyota's Green Vehicles |
| Green AI & Carbon Markets | Medium | EU's Carbon Pricing System |

"Global green investment reached $2.4 trillion in 2023, driven by a strong policy push towards clean energy and sustainable finance." BloombergNEF (2023).

"The rapid expansion of EVs and hydrogen energy is expected to define green investment trends through 2024." IEA (2023).

## 3. Future Green Investment Projections (2025-2035)

Over the next decade, green investment is projected to exceed $5 trillion annually by 2030 as countries aim for net-zero emissions (IEA, 2024).

*Table 5. Future Green Investment Projections (2025-2035)*

| Year | Projected Green Investment ($ Trillion) | Key Drivers | Leading Investors |
|---|---|---|---|
| 2025 | 3.2 | Green Tech Scaling | US, China, EU |
| 2027 | 4.0 | AI & Smart Grids | Canada, Japan |
| 2030 | 5.5 | Full-scale Decarbonization | EU, India |
| 2035 | 7.0 | Climate Neutral Economy | Global |

Key Observations:

- By 2030, green investment will surpass $5 trillion annually (World Bank, 2024).
- India and emerging markets will play a larger role, growing their green energy sectors (IEA, 2024).
- Green AI, carbon capture, and circular economies will be top investment areas (PwC, 2024).

*Table 6. Future Investment Growth by Sector (2025-2035)*

| Sector | Expected Growth Rate | Key Drivers |
|---|---|---|
| Renewable Energy | 12% per year | Solar, Wind Expansion |
| Electric Vehicles (EVs) | 15% per year | Lithium-ion & Hydrogen Innovation |
| Carbon Capture & Storage | 18% per year | Net-Zero Targets |

"By 2030, green investment is expected to surpass $5 trillion, driven by the energy transition and net-zero goals." World Bank (2024).

"Technologies like AI-driven green finance and smart grids will redefine the green investment landscape in the next decade." PwC (2024).

- **Year (2010-2020):** Green investment surged due to the Paris Agreement and renewable subsidies.
- **Year (2021-2024):** Investment reached $2.7T in 2024, driven by ESG growth and tech innovation.
- Year (2025-2035): Expected to exceed $5T by 2030, with key drivers including AI, EVs, and carbon capture.

## FUTURE PERSPECTIVE: GREEN INVESTMENT AFTER 2025

In the future, green investment is projected to reach over $5 trillion per year by 2030, spurred by corporate net-zero targets, government subsidies, and growing ESG requirements (IMF, 2024). Industries like carbon capture and storage (CCS), circular economy projects, and sustainable agriculture are likely to attract large investment flows (World Bank, 2024). With continued growth of green finance structures and international cooperation regarding climate policies, green investment is poised to help shape the economy of the future.

*Figure 2. Global Green Investment Performance Analysis*

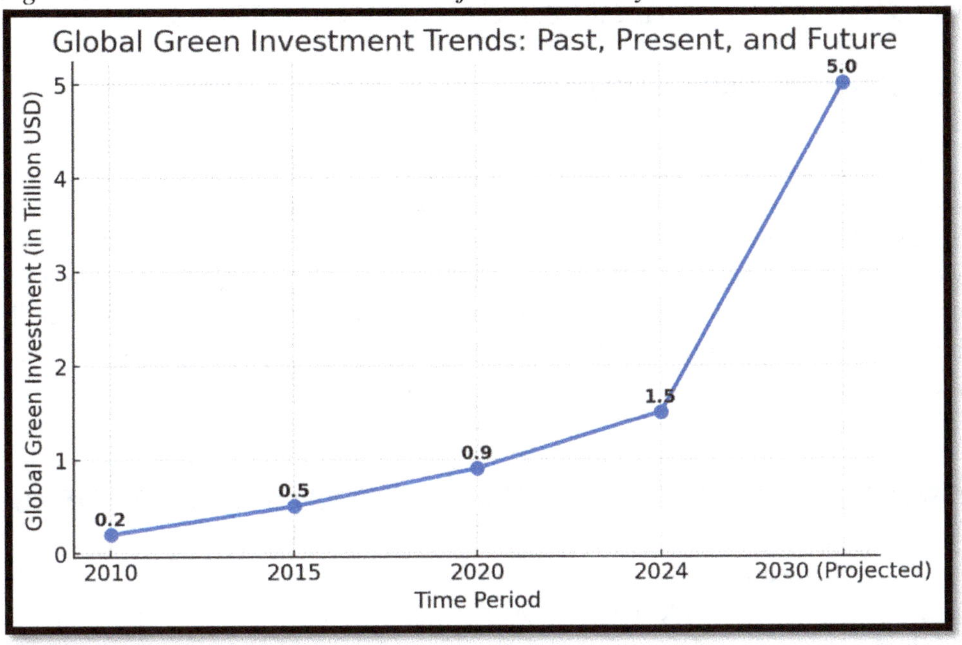


## GLOBAL GREEN INVESTMENT PERFORMANCE ANALYSIS

### 1. Year (2010-2015)

In 2010 global green investment was approximately $0.2 trillion thereby indicating a minimal financial commitment made toward sustainable development projects. By the year 2015 investments have increased to 0. 5 trillion, showing a gradual growth since increased awareness of renewable energy has led to increased initial taking up of the renewable energy market during this period.

### 2. Year (2020-2024)

By 2020 global investments in the green sector amounted to $0.9 trillion, which is due to the prevailing government policies which have granted considerable support to the sector, increasing corporate focus on sustainability goals forcing a rise in environmental, social and governance (ESG) investments. As of 2024 investors have seen an increase in investments allied by technological advancements and an international scale in climate impact agreements. More recently there has been a series of difficulties within the economy as well as a number of policies entering into uncertainties which has caused investors sentiments to fluctuate.

### 3. Future Projections (2030)

When global green investments are seeing culmination at a rate of $5 trillion annually, through this increase in green investments renewable energy transitions and aligns with the net zero commitments made by most governments in the developed world. Emerging markets will require a sum on the order of at least $2 trillion per annum to provide sufficient finance to support infrastructure and climate friendly initiatives. Innovations in AI and financial analysis will allow for enhanced investment forecasting and risk assessment and management.

## GREENWASHING, TOOL LIMITATIONS, AND SYSTEMIC RISKS

Though green finance is praised by many, we must take time to recognize its current limits and possible dangers. Greenwashing which is when certain financial products are claimed to be sustainable without meeting real environmental standards, is a big problem. Sometimes, companies claim to practice eco-friendly or green strategies without being checked by a third party which can easily confuse investors and consumers (Marquis, C., & Toffel, M. W. 2012). Such a practice causes money to be invested incorrectly and also harms the reputation of responsible financial markets. Carbon offset markets and ETS may sound helpful on paper, but they still face criticism. Often, analyses may be exaggerated, verifications may not be secure, regulations are weak and there is not one consistent standard around the world. In a few instances, firms receive carbon credits even when the projects would have been carried out anyway (Gillenwater, M., & Seres, S. 2011). Similarly, these loans and bonds could fall short of meaningful actions if the required goals are not set high or if the performance is not clearly shown.

There is also worry about systemic risk arising from the fast development of green finance without proper rules in place. Should people discover that popular environmental funds do not help enough, investors may doubt them, agencies may crack down and this could slow progress to a green economy (Campiglio, E., Dafermos, Y., & Monnin, P. (2018). So, green finance is effective when its capital build-up is matched by real benefits to the environment and society.

## CHALLENGES AND FUTURE OPPORTUNITIES IN GREEN FINANCE

The quick ascent of green finance as a vital solution for worldwide sustainability problems is blocked by major obstacles that researchers must solve to maximize its power. The market legitimacy suffers from greenwashing that occurs when financial instruments receive misleading environmental classifications lacking proper sustainability measures(Marquis, C., & Toffel, M. W. 2012). Standardized verification processes along with definition standards need development to achieve credibility in green financial products. Investors and policymakers struggle to assess and compare investment sustainability performance because there exist no standard approaches for sustainability disclosure and impact assessment. New and established reporting guidelines along with methodologies need to be established to achieve accuracy in the industry. The green finance sector contains numerous open and innovative spaces for future development. Fintech technology functions as an important accelerating force which brings digital innovations designed to increase financial access while also enhancing sustainable investment speed and openness by using blockchain carbon trading systems and AI-powered ESG risk analysis tools (Gai, K., Qiu, M., & Sun, X. 2018) Green finance reaches new audiences with consumer-focused instruments that help create sustainable behavior in individual customers. The proper management of challenges together with exploitation of available opportunities allows green finance to develop as a driving force behind sustainable global economic development.

## DIFFERENCES BETWEEN GREEN BONDS AND SUSTAINABILITY-LINKED BONDS (SLBS)

*Table 7. Two widely used financial instruments in the green finance space:*

| Feature | Green Bonds | Sustainability-Linked Bonds (SLBs) |
|---|---|---|
| **Purpose** | Fund specific environmentally sustainable projects | Encourage achievement of sustainability performance goals |
| **Use of Proceeds** | Restricted to pre-defined green projects (e.g., clean energy) | Can be used for general corporate purposes |
| **Trigger for Performance** | Project eligibility aligned with green taxonomies or frameworks | Linked to sustainability KPIs (e.g., emissions reduction targets) |

continued on following page

*Table 7. Continued*

| Feature | Green Bonds | Sustainability-Linked Bonds (SLBs) |
|---|---|---|
| **Market Regulation** | More regulated; often aligned with ICMA Green Bond Principles | Flexibly structured; varies by issuer and contract |
| **Risk of Greenwashing** | Lower due to specific use of proceeds and third-party certifications | Higher if KPIs are weak or reporting is not transparent |

## CONCLUSION

The irresponsible marketing practice known as greenwashing damages trust between investors and it weakens market legitimacy by lying about financial products' environmental friendliness. Standardized verification processes along with definition standards need development to achieve credibility in green financial products. Standards for disclosing sustainability information and assessing environmental results must be established to enable policy makers and investors to make accurate assessments concerning sustainability performance within investment options. Accurate reporting standards along with proper methodologies need immediate establishment to develop this sector (Nipper, M., Ostermaier, A., & Theis, J. (2022). The green finance sector contains numerous open and innovative spaces for future development. The fintech revolution serves as an effective agent of change that boosts sustainable investments through digital solutions which include blockchain-based carbon trading systems combined with AI technologies used for ESG risk management (Tapscott, D., & Tapscott, A. (2018). Green finance reaches new audiences with consumer-focused instruments that help create sustainable behavior in individual customers.

The proper management of challenges together with exploitation of available opportunities allows green finance to develop as a driving force behind sustainable global economic development. The quick ascent of green finance as a vital solution for worldwide sustainability problems is blocked by major obstacles that researchers must solve to maximize its power. Greenwashing poses a major problem because it damages investor trust by misleading financial consumers about environmentally friendly products without real sustainability metrics. Standardized verification processes along with definition standards need development to achieve credibility in green financial products. Significant barriers exist to accurate investment sustainability evaluation and performance comparison because of lack of standardized disclosure and impact assessment frameworks for policies and investors. Sound reporting standards together with standardized methodologies need to be established to achieve this goal. The green finance sector contains numerous open and innovative spaces for future development. The fintech revolution serves as a strong driver that uses digital tools to improve sustainable investment processes through blockchain-based carbon trading and AI algorithms which support ESG risk assessments. Green finance reaches new audiences with consumer-focused instruments that help create sustainable behavior in individual customers. The proper management of challenges together with exploitation of available opportunities allows green finance to develop as a driving force behind sustainable global economic development.

## REFERENCES


Abd Aziz, A., Ajis, M. N. E., & Mohd, A. (2025). Integrity Regulations and Corporate Governance in Government Linked Companies: Promoting Transparency and Compliance with Sustainable Development Goal 16. *Journal of Lifestyle and SDGs Review*, *5*(3), e04882–e04882. DOI: 10.47172/2965-730X.SDGsReview.v5.n03.pe04882

Abro, S., & Shehryar, Q. (2025). Advancing green finance for sustainable development: Trends, challenges, and future directions. *Dialogue Social Science Review*, *3*(5), 21–36.

Agarwal, V., Hameed, A. Z., Malhotra, S., Mathiyazhagan, K., Alathur, S., & Appolloni, A. (2023). Role of Industry 4.0 in agile manufacturing to achieve sustainable development. *Business Strategy and the Environment*, *32*(6), 3671–3688. DOI: 10.1002/bse.3321

Ahmad, V., Arora, M., Sayal, A., Kumar, R., & Kumar, P. (2025). Exploring trends in e-business and sustainable finance: An integrated analytical approach. *Frontiers in Sustainable Cities*, *7*, 1549874. DOI: 10.3389/frsc.2025.1549874

Alamgir, M., & Cheng, M.-C. (2023). Do Green Bonds Play a Role in Achieving Sustainability? *Sustainability (Basel)*, *15*(13), 10177. DOI: 10.3390/su151310177

Alves, J. M. (2023). European sustainable finance: introductory notes on the EU green deal and new green finance perspectives. (Direito Católica Teses). Universidade CatólicaEditora. DOI: 10.34632/9789725409640

Amin, M. R. (2025). Sustainability reporting and its influence on investor decision-making: Critical perspectives and empirical insights. *International Journal of Science and Research Archive*, *16*(1), 716–728. DOI: 10.30574/ijsra.2025.16.1.2085

Areo, G. (2024). Driving Sustainable Growth: The Role of Technology and Digital Transformation in Corporate Green Innovation.

Ariffin, K. M., & Milala, S. I. (2023). Advancing Sustainable Finance: A Framework for Strategic Institutional Financing. *Research in Management of Technology and Business*, *4*(2), 655–672.

Arslan, M., Faizulayev, A., Abeuova, D., & Kayani, U. N. (2024). Exploring the Risks, Challenges, and Opportunities of Using Digital Financial Technologies for Green Finance. Impact of Digitalization on Reporting, Tax Avoidance, Accounting, and Green Finance, 226-242.

Bagh, T., & Iftikhar, K. (2024). Understanding the Theoretical Context of Green Finance. In *The Palgrave Handbook of Green Finance for Sustainable Development* (pp. 49–87). Springer International Publishing. DOI: 10.1007/978-3-031-65756-6_3

Banga, C., & Afzal, M. (2025). Navigating the Green Financial Markets: Opportunities and Challenges. Exploring Pillars of Sustainability for Modern Age Improvements, 201-226.

Barrera, L. C. A. (2024). *The Law of ESG Derivatives: Risk, Uncertainty and Sustainable Finance*. Taylor & Francis. DOI: 10.4324/9781003365242

Bhattacharya, S., & Sachdev, B. K. (2024). Regulatory Challenges and Opportunities.

Binder, J., & Wade, M. (2024, Winter). Digital Sustainability for a Better Future. *Stanford Social Innovation Review*.

Bose, S., Bridges, A., & DeFrancia, K. (2019). Carbon Pricing as a Policy Instrument to Decarbonize Economies, Enel Foundation, July 2019. https://www.enelfoundation.org/content/dam/enel-found/Carbon%20Pricing%20Report%20 July%2019%202019%20FINAL1.pdf

Casalini, L. (2025). Green loans and mortgages: Harmonizing sustainability and real estate in the EU. *Uniform Law Review*, *30*(2), 250–262. DOI: 10.1093/ulr/unaf025

Cerrato Garcia, E. (2024). Navigating the landscape of EU sustainable finance regulation: challenges and imperatives to enforce sustainability financial promises in the EU through harmonized private enforcement mechanisms. (Doctoral Thesis). University of Bologna. Bologna, DOI: 10.48676/unibo/amsdottorato/11636

Chantana, B., Fu, C., Lim, W. Y. I., Cheng, K., & Khor, H. E. (2025, February 21). Green finance: Balancing sustainability and financial stability [Analytical note]. ASEAN+3 Macroeconomic Research Office. https://amro-asia.org/wp-content/uploads/2025/02/Analytical-Note_GreenFinanceBalancingSustainabilityFinancialStability.pdf

Chaudhary, M. K., Adhikari, M., & Shakya, N. (2024). Barriers to Green Financing in Developing Nation: An Investor's Perspective for Promoting Sustainable Development. *International Research Journal of MMC*, *5*(5), 195–208. DOI: 10.3126/irjmmc.v5i5.73761

Chauhan, A. S., Singh, S. K., & Gupta, S. (2024). Decoding Green Finance: Exploring Concepts, Themes, and Transformative Journey. *Delhi Business Review*, *25*(1), 55–79. DOI: 10.51768/dbr.v25i1.251202405 da Cunha, Í. G. F., Policarpo, R. V. S., de Oliveira, P. C. S., Abdala, E. C., & do Nascimento Rebelatto, D. A. (2025). A systematic review of ESG indicators and corporate performance: Proposal for a conceptual framework. *Future Business Journal, 11*(1), 106. DOI: 10.1186/s43093-025-00539-1

Dambe, D. N., Dewantara, B., Mahmudin, T., & Mere, K. (2024). Innovative Financial Instruments for Sustainable Development: A Multi-Layered Analysis of Green Bonds and Impact Investing. Dinasti International Journal of Economics, Finance & Accounting (DIJEFA), 5(4).

Del Sarto, N. (2025). The European Regulatory Framework: Policies and Regulations for Sustainable Finance. In *ESG Factors and Financial Outcomes in Banks: Quantitative Insights into the ESG-Cost of Debt Relationship* (pp. 61–94). Springer Nature Switzerland. DOI: 10.1007/978-3-031-87748-3_2

Delmas, M., & Burbano, V. (2011). The drivers of greenwashing. *California Management Review, 54*(1), 64–87. DOI: 10.1525/cmr.2011.54.1.64

Dempere, J., Alamash, E., & Mattos, P. (2024). Unveiling the truth: greenwashing in sustainable finance. Frontiers in sustainability, 5, 1362051.

Ekué, S., & Díaz Fajardo, J. (2024). *Green investment requires mobilizing global finance*. The Asset.

Ervine, K. (2014). Diminishing returns: Carbon market crisis and the future of market-dependent climate change finance. *New Political Economy, 19*(5), 723–747. DOI: 10.1080/13563467.2013.849672

Espelage, A., Ahonen, H. M., & Michaelowa, A. (2022). The role of carbon market mechanisms in climate finance. In *Handbook of International Climate Finance* (pp. 352–378). Edward Elgar Publishing.

Espelage, A., Ahonen, H. M., & Michaelowa, A. (2022). The role of carbon market mechanisms in climate finance. In *Handbook of International Climate Finance* (pp. 352–378). Edward Elgar Publishing.

Eyo-Udo, N. L., Agho, M. O., Onukwulu, E. C., Sule, A. K., & Azubuike, C. (2024). Advances in green finance solutions for combating climate change and ensuring sustainability. *Gulf Journal of Advance Business Research, 2*(6), 338–375. DOI: 10.51594/gjabr.v2i6.53

Flammer, C. (2021). Corporate greenwashing and the misallocation of capital. [link]. *Strategic Management Journal, 42*(12), 2339–2362. DOI: 10.1002/smj.3341

Fu, C., Lu, L., & Pirabi, M. (2024). Advancing green finance: A review of climate change and decarbonization. *Digital Economy and Sustainable Development*, *2*(1), 1. DOI: 10.1007/s44265-023-00026-x

Fucà, R., Cubico, S., Ardolino, P., & Rosiello, F. (2024). Evolving Sustainable Material Culture (SMC): Emerging Trends and Strategic Implications for Green Finance. *Frontiers*, *3*, 115.

Gbadegesin, O. A., Komolafe, O. S., Ayodele-Olajire, D., Omotoye, O., & Gbadegesin, A. (2025). *Unmasking Greenwashing: Strengthening Nigeria's Legal Framework for a Sustainable Green Economy*. Green and Low-Carbon Economy.

Geissdoerfer, M., Savaget, P., Bocken, N. M. P., & Hultink, E. J. (2017). The circular economy – A new sustainability paradigm? *Journal of Cleaner Production*, *143*, 757–768. DOI: 10.1016/j.jclepro.2016.12.048

Ghaemi Asl, M., & Shahzad, U. (2024). How do conventional, Islamic and green bonds idiosyncratically differ when it comes to their inherent nonlinear reliance on carbon emission future price? A novel approach to greenwashing detection. *Environment, Development and Sustainability*, *27*(9), 1–36. DOI: 10.1007/s10668-023-04351-1

Ghaemi Asl, M., Smutka, L., Nasr Isfahani, M., Raza, S. A., & Vasa, L. (2025). Can multifarious types of green bonds be accused of greenwashing with a durative analysis? Insights from a permanent causality vs. temporary causality phenomenon. *Environment, Development and Sustainability*, •••, 1–25.

Gianfrate, G., & Peri, M. (2019). Exploring the convenience of issuing green bonds: Market and corporate perspectives. *Journal of Cleaner Production*, *219*, 127–135. DOI: 10.1016/j.jclepro.2019.02.022

Giudici, P., & Wu, L. (2025). Sustainable artificial intelligence in finance: Impact of ESG factors. *Frontiers in Artificial Intelligence*, *8*, 1566197. DOI: 10.3389/frai.2025.1566197

Gopal, S., & Pitts, J. (2025). *Background and Foundations: Sustainability, Fintech, Data Science, and AI*. In *The FinTech Revolution: Bridging Geospatial Data, AI, and Sustainable Finance* (pp. 35-81). Springer. https://doi.org/DOI: 10.1007/978-3-031-74418-

Hasan, M. H., Hossain, M. Z., Hasan, L., & Dewan, M. A. (2024). FinTech and Sustainable Finance: How is FinTech Shaping the Future of Sustainable Finance? European Journal of Management. *Economics and Business*, *1*(3), 100–115.

Heine, D., Semmler, W., Mazzucato, M., Braga, J. P., Flaherty, M., Gevorkyan, A., Hayde, E., & Radpour, S. (2019). *Financing low-carbon transitions through carbon pricing and green bonds* (Policy Research Working Paper No. 8991).

IFRS. S. (2023). General requirements for disclosure of sustainability-related financial information. Доступно на: https://www. ifrs. org/content/dam/ifrs/publications/pdf-standards-issb/english/2023/issued/part-a/issb-2023-a-ifrs-slgeneral-requirements-for-disclosure-of-sustainability-related-financial-information. pdf

Jamil N. N., Wahyuni E. T. (2024). Unveiling greenwashing: Risks in sustainability and ESG reporting.

Jasrai, L., Bakshi, I., & Kaur, A. (2024). Decoding the Green Finance for India's Sustainable Growth. Alternative Finance, 104-118.

Kathane, S., Babu, N., & Ramesh, S. (2024). Conceptual Framework of Sustainability in Green Finance. 3D: IBA Journal of Management & Leadership, 15(2).

Khan, A., Arora, D., & Meena, M. K. (2024). Unlocking trends in green bonds: Navigating opportunities and challenges for sustainable development in E7 countries.

Khan, A. A., & Wahab, Y. (2025). Sustainable finance and green FinTech. [DSSR]. *Dialogue Social Science Review*, *3*(2), 874–893.

Kharche, N., & Kudal, P. (2024). Blockchain Role in Green Finance: A Pathway to Sustainable Development. In *Blockchain's Transformative Potential of Financial Technology for Sustainable Futures* (pp. 183–197). Springer Nature Switzerland. DOI: 10.1007/978-3-031-70219-8_12

Konstantakis, K. N., Koulmas, P., Michaelides, P. G., Porcher, T., & Prelorentzos, A. G. N. (2025). Green bonds & clean energy in sustainable finance: Evidence from DCC-GARCH Connectedness. *International Review of Financial Analysis*, *103*, 104168. DOI: 10.1016/j.irfa.2025.104168

Labatt, S., & White, R. R. (2011). *Carbon finance: the financial implications of climate change*. John Wiley & Sons.

Lambert, D., Lyons, P., & Carroll, J. (2023, April). *Going Green – The Growth in Green Mortgage Financing in Ireland* (Financial Stability Note 4/FS/23). Central Bank of Ireland.

Lee, J. W. (2020). Green finance and sustainable development goals: The case of China. Lee, Jung Wan (2020). Green Finance and Sustainable Development Goals: The Case of China. *The Journal of Asian Finance, Economics and Business*, *7*(7), 577–586. DOI: 10.13106/jafeb.2020.vol7.no7.577

Li, Y., Sun, G., Gao, Q., & Cheng, C. (2023). Digital financial inclusion, financial efficiency and green innovation. *Sustainability (Basel)*, *15*(3), 1879. DOI: 10.3390/su15031879

Lyon, T. P., & Montgomery, A. W. (2015). The means and end of greenwash. *Organization & Environment*, *28*(2), 223–249. DOI: 10.1177/1086026615575332

Marín-Rodríguez, N. J., Gonzalez-Ruiz, J. D., & Botero, S. (2024). Connectedness between sustainable investment indexes: The QVAR approach. *Economies*, *12*(7), 170. DOI: 10.3390/economies12070170

Mhlanga, D. (2024). The role of big data in financial technology toward financial inclusion. *Frontiers in Big Data*, *7*, 1184444. DOI: 10.3389/fdata.2024.1184444

Mhlanga, D. (2025). Leveraging Blockchain for Sustainable Finance: Insights, Challenges, and Opportunities for Africa. Financial Inclusion and Sustainable Development in Sub-Saharan Africa, 52-73.

Michaelowa, A. (2012). Carbon markets or climate finance. Low carbon and adaptation investment choices for the developing world.

Michaelowa, A., Michaelowa, K., Shishlov, I., & Brescia, D. (2021). Catalysing private and public action for climate change mitigation: The World Bank's role in international carbon markets. *Climate Policy*, *21*(1), 120–132. DOI: 10.1080/14693062.2020.1790334

Mol, A. P. (2012). Carbon flows, financial markets and climate change mitigation. *Environmental Development*, *1*(1), 10–24. DOI: 10.1016/j.envdev.2011.12.003

Nadkarni, P. (2024, June). Exploring the Role of Sustainable Green Finance in Addressing Global Economic Challenges: A Literature Review. In *International Conference on Digital Transformation in Business: Navigating the New Frontiers Beyond Boundaries (DTBNNF 2024)* (pp. 589-612). Atlantis Press.

Nasis, A. (2025). Blockchain-based compliance frameworks enhance regulatory transparency, reducing fraud in sustainable investment transactions. *National Journal of Research in Marketing. Finance & HRM*, *10*(1), 83.

Negi, L., Manpreet, M., & Singh, M. (2025). Green Finance and Digital Strategies: Catalysts for the Expansion of Circular Technologies in the Global Market. In Innovating Sustainability Through Digital Circular Economy (pp. 281-304). IGI Global Scientific Publishing.

Nica, A. (2023). The Banking System-" Limping" toward a Sustainable Future: Is Green Finance a" Thing" in Romania as of March 2023? Europolity: Continuity & Change Eur. *Governance: An International Journal of Policy, Administration and Institutions*, *17*, 209.

Nipper, M., Ostermaier, A., & Theis, J. (2022). Mandatory disclosure of standardized sustainability metrics: The case of the EU Taxonomy Regulation.

Obadire, A. M., & Moyo, V. (2024). Exploring the Dynamics of Green Banking and Finance: A Literature Review. The Palgrave Handbook of Green Finance for Sustainable Development, 723-756.

Ojukwu, P. U., Cadet, E., Osundare, O. S., Fakeyede, O. G., Ige, A. B., & Uzoka, A. (2024). Advancing green bonds through FinTech innovations: A conceptual insight into opportunities and challenges. *International Journal of Engineering Research and Development*, *20*, 565–576.

Organisation for Economic Co-operation and Development. (2021). *Green finance and investment: Mobilizing private finance for climate action in emerging economies*. OECD Publishing.

Öztürk, S. (2024). Comparative evaluation of emissions trading systems and carbon taxes: implementations in climate change mitigation through carbon pricing. Marmara Üniversitesi İktisadi ve İdari Bilimler Dergisi, (Sustainability and Green Economics Special Issue), 18-35.

Parry, I. W. H., Black, S., & Zhunussova, K. (2022). *Carbon Taxes or Emissions Trading Systems?: Instrument Choice and Design* (IMF Staff Climate Note No. 2022/006). International Monetary Fund.

Passas, I., & Garefalakis, A. (2025). The impact of fraud perception and ESG-washing on investment trust: Integrating corporate governance theory and empirical evidence. *Accounting and Auditing*, *1*(3), 9. DOI: 10.3390/accountaudit1030009

Patel, K. (2024). Digitalization and the Rise of Green Finance: Opportunities, Challenges, and the Path Forward. Impact of Digitalization on Reporting, Tax Avoidance, Accounting, and Green Finance, 179-199.

Peng, B. (2024). Navigating green horizons: An empirical exploration of business practices aligned with environmental goals in the era of sustainable economy. *MDE. Managerial and Decision Economics*, *45*(7), 4732–4752. DOI: 10.1002/mde.4284

. Puaschunder, J. (year unspecified). *Financial Social Responsibility.*

Puaschunder, J. M. (2023). The Future of Resilient Green Finance. In *The Future of Resilient Finance: Finance Politics in the Age of Sustainable Development* (pp. 185–210). Springer International Publishing. DOI: 10.1007/978-3-031-30138-4_6

Rahman, S., Hossain, I., Hassan, M., Hossain, G. S., & Perveen, R. (2022). A systematic review of green finance in the banking industry: Perspectives from a developing country. *Green Finance*, *4*(3), 347–363. DOI: 10.3934/GF.2022017

Rahman, S. U., Awan, R. U., & Azam, M. (2024). Green Finance: Tackling Sustainability Challenges in Today's Economy. In *The Palgrave Handbook of Green Finance for Sustainable Development* (pp. 779–810). Springer International Publishing. DOI: 10.1007/978-3-031-65756-6_29

Ramgopal, N. C., & Mohanty, A. K. (2019). Bridging funding gaps for climate and sustainable development: Pitfalls, progress, and potential of private finance. Dogo Rangsang Research Journal, 9(3).

Ranabahu, N., & Wickramasinghe, A. (2022). Sustainable leadership in microfinance: A pathway for sustainable initiatives in micro and small businesses? *Sustainability (Basel)*, *14*(9), 5167. DOI: 10.3390/su14095167

Sari, R. C., Sholihin, M., Cahaya, F. R., Ishola, A., Yuniarti, N., Pranesti, A., Sari, A. R., & Haryanto, . (2025). Artificial intelligence-based ESG greenwashing detection: Road to net zero carbon and its impact on corporate performance. *Business Strategy & Development*, *8*(4), e70228. DOI: 10.1002/bsd2.70228

Saxena, R. (2024). The effect of green banking practices on banks' environmental performance and green financing: An empirical study. *Journal of Electrical Systems, 20(11s).* https://doi.org/10.XXX/jes.7967

Saxena, R., Sharma, S., Saini, K. P., & Agarwal, S. (2024). From Greenwashing to Green Finance: Blockchain as a Catalyst for Transparency and Impact. Blockchain's Transformative Potential of Financial Technology for Sustainable Futures, 151-167.

Selvakumar, P., & Manjunath, T. C. (2025). *Green Finance and Investment: Explore the Role of Sustainable Finance.* In Handbook of Research on Climate Change and the Sustainable Financial Sector (pp. 138-164). IGI Global. DOI: 10.4018/979-8-3693-9750-3.ch008

Sharma, H., & Jain, S. (2024). Navigating the Green Finance Landscape: Trends, Challenges, and Future Directions in the Banking Sector. In Multidisciplinary Approaches for Sustainable Development (pp. 344-348). CRC Press.

Shi, X., & Shi, D. (2025). Impact of green finance on renewable energy technology innovation: Empirical evidence from China. *Sustainability (Basel)*, *17*(5), 2201. DOI: 10.3390/su17052201

Shrotriya, V. (2024). Consumers' behavioral willingness to use green financial products: An empirical study within a theoretical framework. *Journal of Electrical Systems*, *20*(11s).

Singh, V. K. (2022). Regulatory and legal framework for promoting green digital finance. In Taghizadeh-Hesary, F., & Hyun, S. (Eds.), *Green Digital Finance and Sustainable Development Goals: Economics, Law, and Institutions in Asia-Pacific* (pp. 3–27). Springer Singapore. DOI: 10.1007/978-981-19-2662-4_1

Sonavane, S. J. (2024). The impact of government policies on sustainable development of India Inc. Под общей редакцией Ректора КНУ Ажибаевой АА Редакционная коллегия, 328.

Steuer, S., & Tröger, T. H. (2022). The role of disclosure in green finance. *Journal of Financial Regulation*, *8*(1), 1–50. DOI: 10.1093/jfr/fjac001

Stoicescu, V., & Sima, A. G. (2024, March). Sustainable Finance as the Catalyst for ESG-Driven Organizational Design. In International Conference on Business Excellence (pp. 457-480). Cham: Springer Nature Switzerland.

Sule, A. K., Eyo-Udo, N. L., Onukwulu, E. C., Agho, M. O., & Azubuike, C. (2024). Green finance solutions for banking to combat climate change and promote sustainability. *Gulf Journal of Advance Business Research*, *2*(6), 376–410. DOI: 10.51594/gjabr.v2i6.54

Teixeira, N. (2025). The Evolution of Sustainable Investment: The Role of Decentralised Finance and Green Bonds in the Efficiency and Transparency of Green Finance. FinTech and Sustainable Innovation, 1-13.

Triggs, A. (2023). Promoting sustainable investment through financial architecture reform. *Oxford Review of Economic Policy*, *39*(2), 267–282. DOI: 10.1093/oxrep/grad009

Van Niekerk, A. J. (2024). Economic inclusion: Green finance and the SDGs. *Sustainability (Basel)*, *16*(3), 1128. DOI: 10.3390/su16031128

Volz, U. (2018). *Fostering green finance for sustainable development in Asia* (ADBI Working Paper No. 814). Asian Development Bank Institute.

Wang, J. (2023). Study on green credit policy and enterprise ESG performance. *Proceedings of the 3rd International Conference on Internet Finance and Digital Economy (ICIFDE 2023)*. Atlantis Highlights in Economics, Business and Management. DOI: 10.2991/978-94-6463-270-5_24

Wang, K., Tsai, S. B., Du, X., & Bi, D. (2019). Internet finance, green finance, and sustainability. *Sustainability (Basel), 11*(14), 3856. DOI: 10.3390/su11143856

Wang, K. H., Zhao, Y. X., Jiang, C. F., & Li, Z. Z. (2022). Does green finance inspire sustainable development? Evidence from a global perspective. *Economic Analysis and Policy, 75*, 412–426. DOI: 10.1016/j.eap.2022.06.002

Wang, Y. R., Ma, C., Ren, Y. S., & Narayan, S. (2023). Cooperative management of an emission trading system: A private governance and learned auction for a blockchain approach. *Financial Innovation, 9*(1), 122. DOI: 10.1186/s40854-023-00547-6

Wang, Y.-R., Ma, C., Ren, Y.-S., & Narayan, S. (2023). Cooperative management of an emission trading system: A private governance and learned auction for a blockchain approach. *Financial Innovation, 9*(1), 122. Advance online publication. DOI: 10.1186/s40854-023-00547-6

Xie, X., Gong, C., Su, Z., Nie, Y., & Kim, W. (2024). Consumers' behavioural willingness to use green financial products: An empirical study within a theoretical framework. *Behavioral Sciences (Basel, Switzerland), 14*(8), 634. DOI: 10.3390/bs14080634

Zhou, K., & Li, Y. (2019). Carbon finance and carbon market in China: Progress and challenges. *Journal of Cleaner Production, 214*, 536–549. DOI: 10.1016/j.jclepro.2018.12.298

## KEY TERMS AND DEFINITIONS

**Carbon Pricing:** A policy approach to internalize the external costs of carbon emissions, typically through carbon taxes or emission trading systems (ETS).

**ESG (Environmental, Social, Governance):** A set of non-financial criteria used to evaluate an organization's ethical impact and sustainability performance.

**Fintech:** Short for financial technology, referring to digital innovations such as blockchain, artificial intelligence, and mobile platforms that enhance financial services, including those aimed at promoting green finance.

**Green Bonds:** Fixed-income financial instruments used exclusively to finance new or existing environmentally friendly projects.

**Green Finance:** Financial activities that promote environmental sustainability and support climate-related investments, including renewable energy, low-carbon infrastructure, and pollution control.

**Greenwashing:** The practice of falsely marketing financial products or corporate actions as environmentally sustainable without proper evidence or verification.

**Sustainability-Linked Bonds (SLBs):** Debt instruments whose financial terms (e.g., interest rates) are tied to the issuer's ability to meet specific sustainability-related goals.

Chapter 8
# Green Finance, Green Technology Adoption, and Low-Carbon Emissions:
## Pathways to Achieving the Sustainable Development Goals

**Mohammad Rashed Hasan Polas**
https://orcid.org/0000-0002-6080-1075
*Asia Pacific University of Technology and Innovation, Malaysia*

**Saddam Hossain**
https://orcid.org/0009-0007-6897-7220
*Shanghai University of Finance and Economics, China*

**Nowshin Mahmood Tahiya**
*Shanghai University of Finance and Economics, China*

## ABSTRACT

*This chapter explores the synergistic relationship between green finance and green technology in accelerating the transition to a low-carbon, sustainable economy. Green finance through instruments such as green bonds, sustainable loans, and climate funds mobilizes capital for the development and adoption of clean technologies, including renewable energy, energy-efficient systems, and sustainable agriculture. Case studies from China and Brazil highlight successful models of policy and financial integration. However, the chapter identifies persistent barriers financial, technological, institutional, and policy-related particularly in low-income*

DOI: 10.4018/979-8-3373-8287-6.ch008

ht © 2026, IGI Global Scientific Publishing. Copying or distributing in print or electronic forms without written permission of IGI Global Scientific Publishing is prohibited. Use of this chapter to generative artificial intelligence (AI) technologies is expressly prohibited. The publisher reserves all rights to license its use for generative AI training and machine learning model development.

*countries. It offers strategic recommendations for scaling green finance, enhancing institutional capacity, and aligning national policies with global climate goals. The chapter concludes with future research directions and emphasizes the need for global collaboration to ensure equitable access to green technologies and to integrate climate action with broader sustainable development objectives.*

## 1. INTRODUCTION

Amid growing environmental challenges and global inequalities, the pursuit of sustainable development has emerged as a defining mission of our time aimed at balancing economic prosperity, social well-being, and ecological integrity (Zhang et al., 2022; Obobisa & Ahakwa, 2024). Initially articulated in the World Charter for Nature in 1982, the concept has evolved to place greater emphasis on environmental concerns within a broader development agenda. The Sustainable Development Goals (SDGs), adopted by the United Nations General Assembly in 2015, now serve as a universally recognized framework to address global challenges such as poverty, inequality, climate change, and environmental degradation (Dai et al., 2025). Central to achieving these goals is environmental sustainability, which fosters climate resilience, ecosystem preservation, and the responsible use of natural resources (Sethi et al., 2024). In this context, green finance and green technology adoption have become increasingly prominent in academic, policy, and business discourse. Green finance through investments, incentives, and responsible funding mobilizes capital toward sustainable initiatives, while green technologies offer innovative solutions to reduce emissions and support low-carbon, climate-resilient infrastructure (Sethi et al., 2024). This chapter explores the synergistic role of green finance and technology adoption in advancing the SDGs, presenting conceptual foundations, identifying key challenges, and proposing strategic pathways toward a greener, more inclusive global economy.

The relevance of environmental sustainability to the SDG framework is underscored by its cross-cutting presence across multiple goals (Bei & Wang, 2023). For example, SDG 7 (Affordable and Clean Energy) seeks to ensure access to modern and sustainable energy for all, while SDG 13 (Climate Action) calls for urgent interventions to combat climate change and its impacts. SDG 15 (Life on Land) focuses on the sustainable management of terrestrial ecosystems, reinforcing the importance of biodiversity and land preservation (Agrawal et al., 2024). Beyond these, goals like SDG 6 (Clean Water and Sanitation), SDG 11 (Sustainable Cities and Communities), and SDG 12 (Responsible Consumption and Production) also reflect the need for environmental stewardship. Climate change, largely driven by the increase in global carbon emissions, poses a severe threat to the realization of the SDGs, as it exacerbates food insecurity, health risks, and displacement, and economic instability, thereby undermining efforts to alleviate poverty (SDG 1) and improve public health (SDG 3). Consequently, environmental sustainability is not only an individual goal but a prerequisite for the overall success of the SDG agenda (Ronaldo & Suryanto, 2022).

Within this context, green finance and green technology adoption have emerged as pivotal mechanisms for operationalizing sustainable development initiatives. Green finance refers to financial investments and instruments directed toward environmentally sustainable projects, such as renewable energy infrastructure, climate adaptation programs, and energy-efficient technologies (Saleem et al., 2022). These financial tools are essential for mobilizing the vast capital required to meet climate and sustainability targets, particularly in developing and emerging economies where funding gaps are significant (Wang et al., 2022). On the other hand, green technology encompasses a range of innovations including solar and wind power, electric mobility, sustainable agriculture, and carbon capture technologies that directly contribute to lowering environmental impacts and enhancing resource efficiency. Together, these mechanisms offer scalable, market-driven solutions to environmental challenges, aligning economic activities with sustainability goals (Ali et al., 2021).

Green finance plays a foundational role by addressing the financial constraints that often impede environmental progress. Instruments such as green bonds, sustainable loans, and climate investment funds enable governments, institutions, and private actors to invest in climate-resilient infrastructure and low-carbon initiatives (Behera et al., 2024). For instance, green bonds alone rose over $269 billion globally in 2020, supporting projects in renewable energy, public transportation, and green buildings. This not only advances specific SDGs such as SDG 7 and SDG 13 but also encourages private-sector participation and innovation. Moreover, green finance can strengthen climate resilience and foster inclusive development by supporting microfinance programs and community-based investments in clean energy technologies in rural and underserved regions (Yu et al., 2022).

Simultaneously, the adoption of green technologies is crucial for decarbonizing industries and transitioning toward more sustainable modes of production and consumption (Udeagha & Ngepah, 2023). Renewable energy technologies, for example, can reduce greenhouse gas emissions by over 90% compared to fossil fuel-based power generation, significantly contributing to climate mitigation. Other technologies, such as green hydrogen, smart grids, electric vehicles, and energy-efficient building systems, further bolster progress on goals related to clean energy, sustainable cities, and responsible production. However, the uptake of green technologies often faces systemic challenges such as high upfront costs, limited infrastructure, regulatory uncertainty, and skill shortages particularly in low-income countries. Addressing these barriers requires coordinated efforts across finance, policy, and innovation ecosystems (Ma et al., 2023).

The synergy between green finance and green technology enhances the effectiveness of both. Green finance supplies the necessary capital for research, development, and deployment of innovative technologies, while the demand for such technologies stimulates investment in sustainable markets (Behera et al., 2023). Successful case studies, such as China's green finance pilot zones and Brazil's rural credit programs for sustainable agriculture, demonstrate how financial and technological interventions can reinforce each other to drive SDG outcomes. These synergies highlight the importance of integrated strategies that combine capital mobilization with technology diffusion to accelerate progress toward sustainability (Luo et al., 2021).

Crucially, reducing carbon emissions is at the core of climate action and SDG achievement. The Paris Agreement, signed in 2015, emphasizes the need to limit global warming to well below 2°C preferably 1.5°C above pre-industrial levels. Achieving this target requires a fundamental shift toward low-carbon development pathways (Olabi et al., 2023). Low-carbon strategies not only mitigate environmental damage but also enhance resilience to climate shocks, thereby protecting vulnerable populations and preserving critical ecosystems. In this regard, low-carbon emissions are both a goal and an enabler of broader development priorities. Yet, the transition to low-carbon economies must be equitable and inclusive, ensuring that emerging economies can access affordable technologies and financing mechanisms without compromising their growth potential (Li et al., 2023). The connections between green finance, green technology adoption, and low-carbon emissions form the backbone of sustainable development strategies. These elements reinforce each other in advancing environmental sustainability and accelerating the achievement of the SDGs. As the global community intensifies its commitment to the 2030 Agenda, understanding and leveraging these interconnected pathways will be essential for addressing climate risks, fostering innovation, and ensuring inclusive, sustainable growth for present and future generations (Yadav et al., 2023).

Although the importance of green finance and green technology in enhancing sustainability has been increasingly recognized, their effectiveness and their application has not been even across the board, notably in low-income and developing countries like Bangladesh, Nepal, and part of Africa south of the Sahara (Dai et al., 2025). Whereas developed economies enjoy the benefits of a mature financial system, institutional backing, and technological infrastructure, developing economies are hobbled by systemic challenges including restricted access to capital, lack of appropriate regulatory systems and poor institutional capacity (Sethi et al., 2024). Even the case in Bangladesh, where significant efforts have been made on renewable energy by means of the solar home systems, green finance efforts are fragmented and not able to address the requirements of the SMEs and the rural people, as a whole

(Fu et al., 2023). The same cases can be observed in other emerging economies where inefficiencies in institutions, policy inconsistencies, and the inability of the private sector to participate are evident factors that inhibit the incorporation of low-carbon technologies in the national development policies (Qi et al., 2023). It is the discrepancy that provokes the key research issue, namely, how green finance and technology adoption can be effectively reanimated in low-income settings to ensure significant efforts to minimize carbon emissions and meet the SDGs? To validate this issue, it is important not only to engage in theoretical revelation but also evidence based at the regional level that determines realistic pathways and government policies based on the demands in the resource-limited economies (Annu, & Tripathi, 2024).

## 1.1 Literature Gaps

Despite the increasing area of scholarly interest devoted to green finance and technology in the transnational pursuit of sustainability, a number of gaps are still unfilled (Annu, & Tripathi, 2024). First, most of the available literature is focused on developed economies or large emerging markets (e.g., China, Brazil, and India) and less on the low-income countries (Bangladesh, Nepal, or Ethiopia) where constraints on financing and technological adoption are the most relevant. Second, there is disagreement on the effectiveness of green finance tools, including green bonds and climate funds whose role and potential transformational power have been discussed as on the one hand and their accessibility and scalability in contexts of developing economies on the other (Qi et al., 2023). Third, local innovation financing and the informal green economies, where available, are poorly explored, as they sometimes are beyond the formal financial system (yet representing a close grassroots sustainability practice) (Sethi et al., 2024). Fourth, there is a dearth of regional comparative research, especially research that may explore how social political environments, governance structures and cultural norms influence adoption of green finance and technological transfer (Qi et al., 2023). Lastly, empirical policy studies on the interactions between technological adoption and finance are scattered, deficient in both case-specific and cross-nation analysis with multilateral aspects, such as institutional, social and economic factors. Judging these gaps by the possibilities of filling them, it is possible to indicate opportunities associated with the development of theory, enhanced policy design, and more inclusive routes to the achievement of the SDGs in different regional settings (Dai et al., 2025).

*Table 1. Comparative Country Data on Green Finance and Sustainability (2023)*

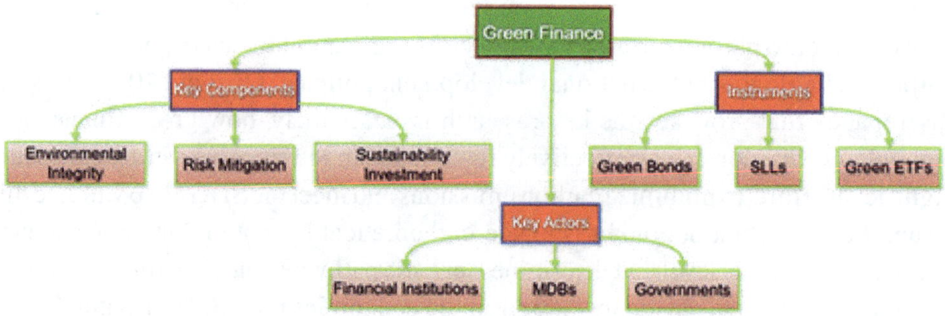


Source: International Energy Agency (IEA), World Energy Outlook 2023

## 2. CONCEPTUAL FRAMEWORK AND THEORETICAL FOUNDATIONS

### 2.1 Green Finance, Green Technology Adoption, and Low Carbon Emissions

The transition toward a sustainable and low-carbon economy is underpinned by three interrelated components: green finance, green technology adoption, and low carbon emissions (Obobisa & Ahakwa, 2024). Together, these elements constitute a triad that supports global environmental objectives, particularly the Sustainable Development Goals (SDGs). Green finance refers to the mobilization of financial resources for investments that yield environmental benefits and promote sustainable development (Hassan et al., 2023). It encompasses a broad spectrum of instruments, including green bonds, sustainable loans, carbon markets, and ESG-aligned investment funds. Unlike traditional finance, which is primarily driven by profit maximization, green finance embeds environmental and social governance principles, aiming to align financial performance with ecological stewardship. This paradigm shift signifies the financial sector's growing role in facilitating climate action and ecological transition by directing capital flows toward renewable energy, climate resilience, and other green initiatives (Lin et al., 2023).

Green technology adoption involves the diffusion and implementation of environmentally friendly technologies that mitigate ecological harm and optimize resource use (Sharif et al., 2022). These technologies span multiple domains such as energy, manufacturing, transport, and agriculture and include solar panels, electric vehicles, waste-to-energy systems, and precision farming. Adoption of such innovations is essential for decoupling economic growth from environmental degradation, a core principle of sustainability (Xia, 2023). Low carbon emissions, meanwhile, represent the outcome of a systematic shift toward cleaner production and consumption patterns. This involves reducing greenhouse gas emissions particularly carbon dioxide through structural changes in energy generation, industrial processes, and consumer behavior. A low-carbon development path not only addresses the climate crisis but also facilitates broader sustainable development by enhancing resilience, protecting ecosystems, and promoting green jobs (Agrawal et al., 2024).

These three dimensions are intricately interconnected. Green finance acts as the enabling mechanism by providing the capital necessary for the development, deployment, and scaling of green technologies. In turn, these technologies facilitate reductions in carbon emissions. This interdependence creates a virtuous cycle: financial flows empower innovation, innovation accelerates decarbonization, and decarbonization advances environmental and economic goals simultaneously. Hence, the conceptual model of sustainable transformation is anchored in the synergy between finance, technology, and emissions reduction.

## 2.2 Theoretical Foundations Guiding Green Finance and Green Technology

Understanding the roles and interactions of green finance and green technology adoption requires a multidisciplinary theoretical approach. Several theories offer valuable frameworks for interpreting these dynamics in the context of sustainable development.

### 2.2.1 Sustainable Development Theory

At the heart of environmental governance lies the theory of sustainable development, famously defined in the Brundtland Report (1987) as "development that meets the needs of the present without compromising the ability of future generations to meet their own needs." This theory emphasizes the delicate balance between economic growth, social inclusion, and environmental protection. Within this framework, green finance is essential for allocating resources in a way that supports long-term ecological and human well-being. Similarly, green technologies are viewed as instruments for enabling economic growth that does not exceed environmental thresholds, aligning with the foundational principles of sustainable development (Shi et al., 2019).

### 2.2.2 Institutional Theory

Institutional theory explains how organizational behavior is shaped by regulatory, normative, and cultural pressures within the institutional environment (Scott, 2008). In the context of sustainability, this theory elucidates why firms adopt green practices or invest in eco-friendly technologies. Regulatory mechanisms, such as carbon pricing or emission standards, act as coercive pressures that compel firms toward greener behavior. Simultaneously, normative pressures stemming from customers, investors, or civil society encourage alignment with sustainability norms. Green finance emerges as a response to these institutional forces, offering structured financial solutions that help organizations comply with or exceed environmental standards (Suddaby, 2015).

### 2.2.3 Innovation Diffusion Theory

Rogers' (2003) Innovation Diffusion Theory offers insights into how new technologies, including green technologies, are adopted across social systems. Adoption is influenced by attributes such as perceived benefits, compatibility, complexity, trialability, and observability. Green finance serves as a critical facilitator in this process, as financial support lowers the entry barriers for innovation adoption. By reducing costs and enhancing access, financial instruments accelerate the diffusion of renewable energy systems, energy-efficient infrastructure, and other green solutions within industries and communities (Ho, 2022).

### 2.2.4 Ecological Modernization Theory

Ecological Modernization Theory posits that technological advancement and environmental reform can coexist with economic development (Mol & Spaargaren, 2000). Rather than viewing economic growth and environmental protection as incompatible, this theory emphasizes the role of innovation, institutional change, and market mechanisms in driving ecological improvements. Green finance and green technology adoption embody this principle by enabling economies to grow while minimizing their ecological footprint. Investment in clean energy, green transport, and circular economy initiatives illustrates how environmental goals can be pursued through economically viable strategies (Mol & Spaargaren, 2000; Ewing, 2017).

### 2.2.5 Stakeholder Theory

Stakeholder theory broadens the focus of organizational responsibility beyond shareholders to include all parties affected by business operations, such as employees, communities, governments, and the environment (Freeman, 1984). In sustainable finance, this theory is particularly relevant, as green financial instruments are often designed not only to generate returns but also to create shared value. Green finance aligns with stakeholder interests by addressing environmental risks, promoting transparency, and delivering positive societal outcomes. Likewise, the adoption of green technologies can enhance a company's legitimacy and brand equity among environmentally conscious stakeholders (Mahajan et al., 2023).

### 2.2.6 Systems Theory

Systems theory views the economy, environment, and society as interconnected components within a holistic system. Disruptions or changes in one part inevitably affect the others. Green finance can be conceptualized as a systemic lever one that activates multiple sustainability outcomes through targeted investments. For example, funding renewable energy not only reduces emissions but also contributes to economic diversification, energy security, and job creation. This interconnectedness highlights the importance of designing integrated, cross-sectoral policies and financial mechanisms that generate systemic benefits across the SDG spectrum (Whitchurch & Constantine, 1993).

The conceptual and theoretical foundations of green finance and green technology adoption illustrate their central roles in enabling low-carbon development and achieving sustainable development goals. While green finance provides the economic engine for sustainability, green technologies serve as the technical instruments for transforming production and consumption. The theories discussed spanning development, institutions, innovation, and systems highlight the complex but mutually reinforcing relationships among financial systems, technological innovation, and ecological stability. These frameworks serve as valuable guides for policymakers, investors, and researchers in designing effective strategies for sustainable transformation (Lai & Lin, 2017).

*Figure 1. Green Finance, Technology Adoption, and SDGs (developed by authors)*

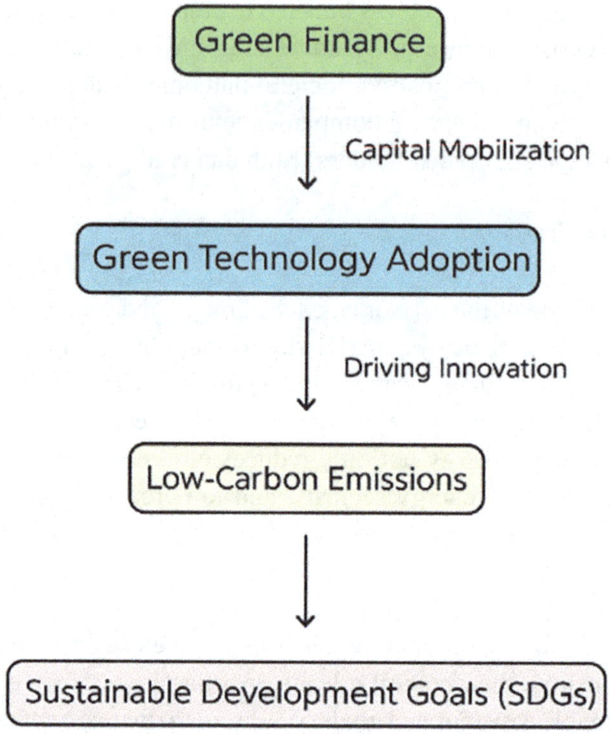


## 3. GREEN FINANCE: A CATALYST FOR SUSTAINABLE DEVELOPMENT

### 3.1 Mechanisms of Green Finance in Promoting Environmental Sustainability

Green finance plays a pivotal role in fostering environmental sustainability by directing financial flows towards environmentally beneficial projects and initiatives. It acts as a catalyst by providing the necessary capital for the transition to a low-carbon and resource-efficient economy (Ma et al., 2023). This redirection of finance is achieved through various mechanisms, including the internalization of environmental externalities into financial decision-making. Traditional finance often overlooks the environmental costs and benefits associated with economic activities, leading to under investment in green projects and over investment in polluting industries. Green finance seeks to correct this market failure by creating price signals that reflect the true value of environmental assets and the costs of environmental degradation (Dai & Chen, 2023). One key mechanism is the development of green financial instruments that specifically target environmentally sustainable activities. These instruments mobilize private capital for projects such as renewable energy, energy efficiency, and sustainable infrastructure. By increasing the availability of funding for green initiatives, green finance helps to overcome the financial barriers that often hinder their implementation. Furthermore, green finance encourages the adoption of environmentally friendly business models by making sustainable practices more financially viable. This includes supporting companies with lower energy intensity and reduced pollutant emissions, as well as those engaged in green technological innovation (Xing et al., 2024).

Financial intermediaries, such as banks and investment firms, play a crucial role in the green finance ecosystem. They facilitate the flow of capital from investors to green projects by identifying green targets and assessing the environmental credentials of potential investments (Xu et al., 2024). These intermediaries also help manage the risks associated with green investments and develop innovative financial products that attract a wider range of investors. Moreover, financial markets contribute to environmental sustainability by integrating Environmental, Social, and Governance (ESG) factors into investment decisions. This encourages companies to adopt more sustainable practices and directs capital towards environmentally responsible ventures. Regulatory frameworks and government policies also play a vital role in shaping financial markets towards environmental goals by setting standards, providing incentives, and ensuring transparency (Xing et al., 2024).

## 3.2 Green Bonds, Sustainable Investments, and Other Financial Instruments

A variety of financial instruments are utilized within green finance to promote environmental sustainability. Green bonds are a prominent example, representing debt instruments issued to finance projects with environmental benefits, such as renewable energy, energy efficiency, and sustainable transportation (Bhutta et al., 2022). The proceeds from green bonds are earmarked for environmentally friendly projects, providing investors with an opportunity to support climate change mitigation and adaptation efforts. The green bond market has seen significant growth, reflecting the increasing demand for sustainable investment options (Ye & Rasoulinezhad, 2023). Sustainable investments encompass a broader category of investments that consider ESG factors alongside traditional financial metrics. This approach recognizes that environmental and social factors can have a material impact on investment performance and seeks to align investment strategies with sustainability goals. Sustainable investments can take various forms, including green investment funds that focus on environmentally friendly companies and projects. The integration of ESG factors into investment decisions encourages companies to improve their environmental performance and contribute to a greener economy (Zhao et al., 2022).

Other green financial instruments include green loans, which are specifically designated for environmentally friendly projects like green buildings and sustainable agriculture; green venture capital funds, which provide financing for innovative green technologies; and green insurance, which can help manage environmental risks and incentivize sustainable practices. Additionally, carbon markets and carbon credits provide economic incentives for reducing greenhouse gas emissions by allowing companies to trade emission allowances. These instruments collectively contribute to mobilizing capital for a wide range of environmentally sustainable activities, driving the transition towards a low-carbon economy (Yu et al., 2022).

*Table 2. Examples of Green Financial Instruments and Their Impact*

| Instrument | Explanation | Potential Impact on Carbon Emission Reduction | Potential Impact on SDG Achievement |
|---|---|---|---|
| Green Bonds | Bonds issued to finance projects with environmental benefits. | Funds renewable energy, energy efficiency, and other climate mitigation projects, leading to reduced emissions. | Directly supports SDG 7 (Clean Energy) and SDG 13 (Climate Action), and indirectly contributes to other SDGs. |
| Green Loans | Loans specifically designated for environmentally friendly projects. | Supports investments in green buildings, sustainable agriculture, and clean transportation, reducing carbon footprints. | Contributes to SDGs related to sustainable cities (SDG 11), responsible consumption (SDG 12), and climate action (SDG 13). |
| Sustainable Investments | Investments that consider ESG factors alongside financial returns. | Directs capital towards companies and projects with strong environmental performance, encouraging lower emissions. | Supports a wide range of SDGs depending on the specific focus of the investment, including environmental and social goals. |
| Green Venture Capital Funds | Funds that invest in early-stage green technology companies. | Supports the development and deployment of innovative clean technologies, leading to long-term emission reductions. | Contributes to SDG 9 (Industry, Innovation, and Infrastructure) and SDG 13 (Climate Action). |

continued on following page

*Table 2. Continued*

| Instrument | Explanation | Potential Impact on Carbon Emission Reduction | Potential Impact on SDG Achievement |
|---|---|---|---|
| Green Insurance | Insurance products that incentivize environmentally friendly behavior and cover environmental risks. | Can encourage the adoption of cleaner technologies and practices, indirectly reducing emissions and supporting climate resilience. | Supports SDGs related to climate action (SDG 13) and sustainable consumption and production (SDG 12). |
| Carbon Markets & Credits | Market-based mechanisms that allow trading of emission allowances. | Incentivizes companies to reduce emissions by creating a financial value for carbon reductions. | Directly supports SDG 13 (Climate Action) by putting a price on carbon. |

## 3.3 Case Studies of Successful Green Finance Initiatives

Several successful green finance initiatives demonstrate the potential of financial mechanisms to drive environmental sustainability. The World Bank Green Bonds program, launched in 2008, serves as a prominent example. Through the issuance of green bonds, the World Bank raises funds from fixed-income investors to support lending for eligible projects that mitigate climate change or help people adapt to its effects. Since its inception, the program has issued over USD 20 billion equivalent in Green Bonds, supporting projects in areas such as renewable energy, energy efficiency, and sustainable transportation in developing countries. The success of the World Bank Green Bonds highlights the potential for multilateral development banks to mobilize significant capital for climate action (Nasir & Ahmed, 2024).

China's green finance policies also represent a significant initiative. The country has implemented a series of policies and institutional arrangements to attract private capital investments into green industries, including environmental protection, energy conservation, and clean energy. These policies encompass various financial services such as green credit, green bonds, and green investment funds. China's commitment to peak carbon emissions by 2035 and achieve carbon neutrality by 2060 has further driven the development of green finance in the country, including the establishment of pilot zones for green finance innovation. The scale of China's green finance efforts underscores the role of government policies in accelerating the transition to a green economy (Fu et al., 2023).

Green crowdfunding (GCF) has emerged as another successful green finance mechanism, leveraging digital platforms to raise funds for environmentally oriented and low-carbon activities from a large pool of investors. GCF offers greater accessibility and lower costs for investees, making it a valuable tool for encouraging investments in diverse sectors and addressing various environmental challenges, including those faced by Small Island Developing States (SIDs). The growing popularity of GCF demonstrates the potential of innovative financial instruments to mobilize capital for green projects and engage a wider range of stakeholders in sustainable development (Hossain et al. 2024).

## 4. GREEN TECHNOLOGY ADOPTION AND LOW CARBON EMISSIONS

The adoption of green technologies is essential in reducing carbon emissions and combating the adverse effects of climate change. Green technologies also referred to as clean or sustainable technologies play a vital role in supporting the United Nations Sustainable Development Goals (SDGs), particularly SDG 7 (Affordable and Clean Energy) and SDG 13 (Climate Action). These technologies are developed and deployed with the primary objective of minimizing environmental impact through efficient resource utilization and a shift toward renewable energy sources. Their integration into energy systems, industrial operations, agriculture, and transport has become a cornerstone in global decarbonization strategies (Javaid et al., 2022)).

### 4.1 Types of Green Technologies Contributing to Low Carbon Emissions

A wide variety of green technologies contribute significantly to carbon emissions reduction. Chief among them are renewable energy technologies, including solar, wind, hydro, geothermal, and biomass energy. These innovations harness natural resources to generate electricity with minimal greenhouse gas emissions (Habiba et al., 2022). For example, photovoltaic solar cells and solar thermal systems convert sunlight into electricity and heat, with recent advancements like perovskite cells improving their efficiency (Habiba et al., 2023). Wind energy via both onshore and offshore turbines has become one of the fastest-growing energy sources globally, benefiting from declining costs and improved technology. Hydropower, a long-established renewable source, continues to provide low-emission electricity, especially through run-of-river systems. Geothermal energy taps into subterranean heat and is particularly viable in geologically active regions. Biomass energy, when sourced sustainably, converts organic waste into power and fuel, supporting circular economy principles (Liu et al., 2024).

In addition to renewable energy, energy efficiency technologies significantly contribute to reducing carbon footprints by lowering overall energy consumption. In buildings, energy-efficient insulation, LED lighting, smart thermostats, and efficient HVAC systems reduce demand for electricity and heating (Zeng et al., 2024). In the industrial sector, process optimization, waste heat recovery, and advanced machinery have enhanced operational efficiency, cutting emissions substantially. On the consumer end, energy-efficient appliances reduce household energy use while maintaining performance standards, with programs like ENERGY STAR setting benchmarks globally (Guo & Zhang, 2023). Sustainable transportation technologies are also crucial in the fight against climate change, as the transport sector accounts for approximately 14% of global emissions. Electric vehicles (EVs), powered by renewable electricity, produce zero tailpipe emissions, while hybrid vehicles improve fuel efficiency by combining internal combustion and electric propulsion systems. Public transport, cycling, and walking infrastructure promote low-carbon urban mobility. However, the environmental benefit of EVs is maximized only when electricity grids are powered by clean energy sources (Liu et al., 2023).

Another key technological advancement is Carbon Capture and Storage (CCS), which captures $CO_2$ emissions from industrial processes and fossil fuel-based power generation and stores them underground. Though still emerging, CCS is especially vital for heavy industries like cement, steel, and chemicals, where emission reductions are otherwise difficult to achieve. It can reduce emissions from fossil-based power plants by up to 70%, although it requires significant infrastructure and may involve environmental trade-offs (Shahbaz et al., 2024). Green technologies in agriculture and land use are equally important. Practices such as precision agriculture, agroforestry, and regenerative farming reduce emissions while enhancing soil carbon sequestration and biodiversity. Methane-reducing innovations, such as improved livestock feed additives; also play a role in mitigating greenhouse gases from agricultural sources (Liu et al., 2023). Emerging technologies, including green hydrogen, tidal power, and floating solar systems, offer further potential for large-scale decarbonization as they mature and become more cost-competitive (Habiba et al., 2023).

## 4.2 Factors Influencing Green Technology Adoption in Emerging Economies

The adoption of green technologies in emerging economies is shaped by a complex interplay of barriers and enabling factors. These nations face immense pressure to grow economically while simultaneously addressing environmental challenges (Mouakket & Aboelmaged, 2023). However, structural constraints often hinder widespread adoption. Economic barriers are among the most significant, particularly the high initial investment costs associated with green technologies like solar installations or CCS systems. Access to finance remains limited in many low- and middle-income countries, especially for small and medium enterprises (SMEs) that form the backbone of their economies (Shahadat et al., 2023). In parallel, technological barriers include underdeveloped infrastructure, such as weak grid systems or poor transportation networks, and shortages of skilled labor necessary for installing, operating, and maintaining advanced green technologies (Habiba et al., 2023).

Policy and regulatory challenges further complicate adoption. Weak governance structures, inconsistent environmental regulations, and limited institutional capacity create uncertainty for investors (Makeel et al., 2025). The absence of incentives such as tax credits, feed-in tariffs, or carbon pricing also diminishes the appeal of green technology deployment. Additionally, social and cultural factors, including low public awareness and resistance to behavioral change, inhibit adoption. In some communities, skepticism about new technologies or traditional preferences for established practices slow down acceptance (Asif et al., 2023). Despite these barriers, several enablers can accelerate green technology adoption. Strong government support in the form of well-designed policies, financial incentives, and clear renewable energy targets is pivotal. For example, feed-in tariffs, low-interest green loans, and public investment in R&D can significantly enhance market readiness. International cooperation plays a crucial role through technology transfer, foreign direct investment, and capacity-building initiatives. Bilateral and multilateral partnerships, particularly under frameworks such as the UNFCCC and Paris Agreement, facilitate access to advanced technologies and funding mechanisms (Mouakket & Aboelmaged, 2022).

Market dynamics also encourage adoption. As global demand for clean technologies grows and manufacturing scales up, the costs of solar panels, batteries, and wind turbines have decreased significantly, making them more accessible to emerging markets (Kassouri & Alola, 2023). At the same time, increasing consumer awareness of environmental issues is driving demand for sustainable products and services. Local innovation and context-specific solutions such as off-grid solar systems for rural electrification demonstrate the potential of tailoring technologies to community needs. Research and development investments at the national or regional level further contribute to adaptive solutions (Bei & Wang, 2023). A relevant case is China's renewable energy strategy, which illustrates how policy frameworks can overcome economic and technological constraints. The Renewable Energy Law of 2006, combined with feed-in tariffs and mandatory grid connections, spurred exponential growth in wind and solar power. Continued support through the 14th Five-Year Plan and international collaboration has positioned China as a global leader in renewable capacity (Alam et al., 2023).

## 4.3 Role of Innovation and Policy Frameworks

Innovation and policy frameworks are twin engines of green technology adoption. Technological innovation increases the feasibility and attractiveness of low-carbon solutions by improving efficiency, reducing costs, and expanding applicability. Breakthroughs in high-efficiency solar cells, lithium-ion and solid-state batteries, and hydrogen fuel systems are transforming the renewable energy and mobility sectors (Xia et al., 2019; Alam et al., 2023). Moreover, process innovations, such as modular solar kits or circular manufacturing, and business model innovations, like pay-as-you-go energy systems, make green technologies viable for underserved populations (Uzar, 2024). Policy frameworks play a critical role in shaping the market environment and incentivizing innovation. Governments can stimulate technological progress through public R&D funding, support for startups, and public-private partnerships. Market-creating mechanisms such as renewable portfolio standards, carbon pricing, and green procurement drive demand for sustainable solutions. Regulatory standards such as minimum energy performance requirements and emission caps enforce compliance and push firms toward greener practices. International agreements like the Paris Agreement encourage nations to align domestic policies with global sustainability targets (Uzar, 2024).

A leading example is the European Union's Green Deal, which aims to achieve net-zero emissions by 2050 through a comprehensive strategy. It combines massive investment in green technologies with regulatory instruments like the Carbon Border Adjustment Mechanism and a Just Transition Fund. These tools collectively stimulate innovation while addressing economic and social disparities (Uzar, 2024). Despite the promise, challenges remain, particularly in emerging economies where financial, institutional, and infrastructural constraints persist. However, targeted strategies such as inclusive policies, international partnerships, and locally led innovations can help bridge the gap. Innovations supported by adaptive policy environments can serve as catalysts for an inclusive and resilient transition to a low-carbon future (Uzar, 2024).

## 5. GREEN FINANCE AND GREEN TECHNOLOGY SYNERGIES

The transition to a low-carbon, sustainable economy relies heavily on the synergistic relationship between green finance and green technology. Green finance defined as financial flows and instruments designed to support environmentally sustainable outcomes serves as a strategic enabler that drives the innovation, deployment, and diffusion of green technologies (Dhayal et al., 2023). These technologies, encompassing renewable energy systems, clean industrial processes, sustainable transportation, and climate-smart agricultural practices, are central to realizing the Sustainable Development Goals (SDGs), particularly SDG 7 (Affordable and Clean Energy) and SDG 13 (Climate Action). By aligning financial mechanisms with environmental objectives, green finance acts as both a catalyst and a conduit for the adoption of green innovations that contribute to significant reductions in carbon emissions and broader ecological sustainability (Nanthini et al., 2024).

## 5.1 Financial Mechanisms Enabling Green Technology Innovation and Deployment

Green finance contributes directly to the development and dissemination of green technologies by overcoming the key financial and structural challenges associated with sustainability transitions. One of its core functions is to provide capital for research, development, and deployment (RD&D) of low-carbon technologies (Feng et al., 2022). Instruments such as green bonds, sustainability-linked loans, and venture capital funds target initiatives that yield measurable environmental benefits. For instance, the global green bond market, which surpassed $269 billion in 2020, has become a major funding source for projects related to renewable energy, energy-efficient infrastructure, and sustainable urban mobility. These investments not only fund cutting-edge innovations but also help scale technologies to commercial viability (Ji & Zhang, 2024).

Small and medium-sized enterprises (SMEs), often constrained by limited financial resources, benefit significantly from green finance interventions. Favorable financing mechanisms such as concessional loans, government-backed guarantees, or blended finance help reduce capital costs and lower the risks associated with transitioning to clean technologies (Abbas & Najam, 2024). By making sustainable options more affordable, green finance democratizes access to innovation and ensures that environmentally friendly technologies reach businesses and communities that need those most. Moreover, the growing integration of Environmental, Social, and Governance (ESG) considerations into investment strategies guides capital flows toward firms demonstrating commitment to sustainability. This trend compels corporations to adopt green technologies not only for compliance but also for improved competitiveness and long-term resilience (Sampene et al., 2024).

Beyond capital provision, green finance is bolstered by policy frameworks and incentives that create an enabling ecosystem for green technology uptake. Regulatory instruments such as tax breaks, feed-in tariffs for renewable energy and carbon pricing mechanisms incentivize firms and households to invest in clean alternatives (Wang et al., 2022). National and regional initiatives such as the European Union's Green Deal or South Korea's Green New Deal mobilize public and private investments while establishing legally binding targets that drive technological innovation. Additionally, education and capacity-building programs integrated into green finance initiatives help stakeholders, from local government units to micro-enterprises; develop the technical skills and knowledge necessary for sustainable technology implementation (Wang et al., 2024). As a result, green finance not only provides monetary resources but also fosters an inclusive and informed environment for adoption and transformation. Green finance also stimulates market creation and consumer demand, both essential for the diffusion of green technologies. Investments in infrastructure such as electric vehicle charging networks, smart grids, or distributed solar power systems establish the physical foundations necessary for technology adoption (Liu et al., 2024). When financial flows support the production and availability of low-carbon goods and services, it creates positive market feedback loops, driving further innovation and lowering technology costs through economies of scale. This dynamic ensures that the impact of green finance goes beyond individual projects and contributes to structural shifts in consumption and production patterns, essential for long-term climate and sustainability goals (Lai et al., 2017).

## 5.2 Illustrative Case Studies of Finance-Technology Synergy

The synergetic relationship between green finance and green technology is best illustrated through context-specific case studies that highlight practical applications and measurable outcomes. One such example is China's Green Finance Reform and Innovation Pilot Zone (GFRIPZ), particularly in Huzhou city, Zhejiang Province. Initiated in 2017 by the People's Bank of China and provincial authorities, the pilot zone was established to test innovative green finance mechanisms that would encourage environmentally sustainable industrial transformation. In Huzhou, a combination of interest subsidies for green loans, incentives for financial product innovation, and strict anti-greenwashing regulations has catalyzed the adoption of clean technologies in industries such as textiles and battery manufacturing. Through coordinated efforts between local government and financial institutions, digital platforms have also been developed to ease access to credit for SMEs, accelerating their transition to low-emission operations (Perdana & Kulkarni, 2023).

This policy-driven financial intervention has led to tangible technological changes. In the textile industry, for example, companies have invested in water-saving dyeing technologies and energy-efficient equipment, significantly reducing their environmental footprint. In the battery sector, enterprises have adopted cleaner production methods, improving resource efficiency and lowering carbon emissions. Empirical evaluations of the GFRIPZ have shown that these financial reforms not only stimulate renewable energy innovation but also contribute to improved air quality and industrial upgrading (Kashif et al., 2024). The success of the Huzhou model offers important lessons for other emerging economies seeking to leverage finance to drive technological transformation toward sustainability. A second illustrative case is Brazil's use of climate finance to transform its land use sector a critical area given the country's high greenhouse gas emissions from agriculture and deforestation. According to the Climate Policy Initiative (2024), Brazil's climate finance for land use averaged $17.1 billion annually between 2021 and 2023, a near doubling from previous years. This investment has been predominantly domestic and private sector-driven, demonstrating strong local commitment. Key financial tools include rural credit, thematic bonds, and decarbonization credits (CBIOs). Rural credit, comprising over half of the climate finance allocation, supports sustainable farming techniques such as no-till agriculture, agroforestry, and integrated crop-livestock systems. These practices enhance soil carbon storage and biodiversity while improving productivity (Li et al., 2024).

Thematic bonds and CBIOs have also mobilized significant funding for bioenergy and reforestation projects, promoting renewable fuel sources and sustainable forest management. Low-cost credit facilities provided by the Brazilian Development Bank (BNDES) further enable access to green technologies for local producers. While these initiatives have already contributed to substantial emissions reductions over 100 million tonnes of $CO_2$ equivalent through CBIOs alone there remains vast potential for scaling. The success of Brazil's land use finance strategy underlines the importance of aligning financial tools with technological pathways that are locally relevant and environmentally impactful (Khalil et al., 2025).

## 5.3 Governance Risks and Accountability in Green Finance

Although international green finance initiatives are advancing and mapping significant success stories e.g. the eco-industrial model at Huzhou, China and biofuel proposals at Brazil, it is more important to note failures and stagnated transitions that reveal the hazards of governance, and contingent accountability (Fu et al., 2023). There are some examples demonstrating how, when improperly managed, green finance mechanisms can give rise to ineffective results. Case in point, some of the African renewable energy projects that were supported by international finance failed to work through poor institutional control and lack of investment of their own as well as inadequate management of funds leading to poor local ownership and sustainability (Li et al., 2025). Likewise, policy capture by highly influential lobbying organizations in South Asia redirected funding meant to be poured into green infrastructure to conventional fossil-based subsidies, as one example of how political economy resistance can stall a transition (Bracking & Leffel, 2021). Moreover, Green colonialism has also risen to challenge the North-South financial trends where externally funded development programs unsympathetically imposed technologies that may not congruously fit into a local setting, thus more likely deepening dependency instead of promoting self-reliance (Tan, 2022). The cases sheds light on the necessity of integrating transparency and accountability as well as context-specific design into the multilateral flows of green finances. With a lack of effective governance structures, the potential of green finance is likely to end up being compromised via corruption and elite capture with the view of structural inequities (Basak et al., 2022).

## 5.4 Toward an Integrated Framework for Sustainable Transition

The cases of Huzhou and Brazil illustrate that green finance and green technology are mutually reinforcing components of the sustainable development agenda. When aligned strategically, financial resources enable innovation, and technological progress, in turn, enhances the environmental and economic returns on investment (Bei & Wang, 2023). This integrated framework not only accelerates the pace of decarbonization but also builds resilience, improves equity, and strengthens institutional capacity. However, achieving such synergy requires deliberate coordination among financial regulators, technology developers, and policymakers. It also demands a long-term vision where investments are evaluated not only for financial yield but for ecological and societal benefits (Behera et al., 2024. As climate change intensifies and the deadline for meeting the SDGs approaches, the need for systemic solutions has never been more urgent. Green finance, when harnessed effectively, can unlock the transformative potential of green technologies and reshape the development trajectory of economies, particularly in the Global South. Through well-designed policies, targeted investments, and inclusive strategies, countries can achieve meaningful progress toward a low-carbon, sustainable future (Dai & Chen, 2023).

# 6. CHALLENGES AND BARRIERS

While the adoption of green finance and green technologies holds immense potential for advancing environmental sustainability and meeting the Sustainable Development Goals (SDGs), particularly SDG 7 (Affordable and Clean Energy) and SDG 13 (Climate Action), several formidable challenges impede their widespread implementation. These challenges are especially pronounced in emerging and low-income economies, where financial constraints, technological limitations, institutional inefficiencies, and policy gaps undermine progress. Understanding and addressing these barriers is essential to accelerate the global transition toward a low-carbon economy (Fu et al., 2023).

## 6.1 Linking Trends to Challenges

Although the chapter captures the emerging trends green finance, e.g. the growth of the green bonds, the rise of plug-in cars, and the creation of carbon markets, the description can be given an added dimension by going from description into greater depth. The inclusion of future projections on the global flows of green finance until the year 2030 or expected decline in carbon emissions under multiple adoption scenarios would give a more accurate picture of long-term effects. Meanwhile, the challenges deserve more research. In addition to the widely reported barriers of significant upfront expenses, disparate policies and insufficient capacity in low-income countries, the corruption in the arrangement of fund distribution, misuse of green bonds, and ESG related greenwashing also deserve more considerable attention. These risks are a danger to credibility and therefore limits the transformational power of green finance in realizing sustainability. Besides, the shortcomings of ESG ratings and ESG reporting standards must be intensively scrutinized to unveil drawbacks in accountability and transparency. A balanced stepped approach combining scenario-based analysis and future projections with critical reflection on systemic risks to provide a richer discussion and a more balanced and realistic appraisal of how green finance will actually create true environmental and social value.

## 6.2 Financial, Technological, and Institutional Constraints

The successful deployment of green finance mechanisms and the diffusion of green technologies are often hindered by a complex interplay of financial, technological, and institutional barriers. These challenges limit accessibility, scalability, and effectiveness, particularly in resource-constrained regions where demand for sustainable solutions is highest (Schain & Stiebale, 2021). Financial barriers are among the most significant obstacles facing the green transition. Many green technologies such as solar photovoltaic systems, wind turbines, or carbon capture and storage (CCS) require substantial upfront investment, often beyond the reach of small and medium-sized enterprises (SMEs) and governments in low-income countries (Khan et al., 2021). The long payback periods associated with such technologies further deter private investment. In addition, access to affordable capital remains limited, especially in emerging markets where financial institutions perceive green projects as high-risk ventures with uncertain returns. Despite the global growth of green bonds and sustainable loans, their availability is heavily skewed toward high-income nations. In 2020, for instance, only 3% of global green bond issuance originated from low-income economies, highlighting a substantial financing gap. Moreover, market volatility, energy price fluctuations, and currency risks add another layer of uncertainty, discouraging long-term commitments from investors (Ruiz-Palomo et al., 2022).

Technological barriers also present critical challenges to adoption. In many regions, the infrastructure needed to support renewable energy deployment such as reliable electricity grids, storage systems, and transmission lines is underdeveloped or entirely absent. In sub-Saharan Africa, for example, limited electricity access severely constrains the feasibility of deploying grid-connected green technologies (Falavigna & Ippoliti, 2022). Compounding this is the shortage of technical expertise required for installing, operating, and maintaining advanced technologies.

Many countries face significant human capital deficits, with few technical training institutions offering green energy programs. Even when advanced technologies such as next-generation batteries or CCS become available, adapting them to local conditions such as extreme weather or limited water resources adds further complexity and cost. The pace of innovation itself can also be a constraint, as the development and scaling of new technologies like green hydrogen or advanced biofuels often take years, delaying their impact on climate mitigation efforts (Amouri et al., 2021).

Institutional barriers, meanwhile, reflect the structural weaknesses within governance systems and public administration. In many emerging economies, weak regulatory frameworks, fragmented institutional responsibilities, and lack of transparency deter both domestic and international investment in green initiatives (Su et al., 2022). Corruption and mismanagement of public funds allocated for renewable energy projects have been reported in several countries, eroding trust and credibility. Regulatory inconsistencies such as abrupt changes in subsidies, tax incentives, or renewable energy targets create uncertainty for businesses and financiers (Du & Geng, 2024). Moreover, limited institutional capacity hampers the ability of public agencies to design, implement, and monitor green finance programs. For example, certifying green bonds or assessing environmental performance requires specific technical expertise that may be absent in regulatory bodies in low-income countries. These institutional inefficiencies often result in delays, duplication of efforts, and ineffective resource allocation, stalling the green transition (Du & Geng, 2024).

## 6.3 Policy Gaps and Capacity-Building Challenges in Low-Income Countries

Low-income countries face particularly acute challenges related to policy gaps and the lack of institutional and human capacity required to implement green finance and technology frameworks. These limitations constrain their ability to align with international climate targets and to benefit from global climate finance and technology transfer initiatives (Falavigna & Ippoliti, 2022). Policy gaps in these contexts are reflected in the absence of inadequacy of regulatory and fiscal mechanisms needed to foster a conducive environment for green technology and finance. Many countries lack comprehensive national policies on renewable energy, energy efficiency, or climate finance (Guo & Zhang, 2023). For instance, while nearly 90% of high-income countries had adopted renewable energy targets by 2020, only about 43% of sub-Saharan African nations had done the same. This policy vacuum results in weak investor confidence and a lack of strategic direction. Furthermore, essential financial incentives such as feed-in tariffs, carbon pricing, or tax exemptions are either underdeveloped or inconsistently applied. Even where such policies exist, their implementation is often unreliable due to budgetary constraints, administrative bottlenecks, or political instability. The misalignment of domestic policies with global frameworks like the Paris Agreement further reduces the chances of attracting international climate finance. As of 2022, only about 20% of Green Climate Fund allocations had reached least-developed countries, underscoring the limited integration between global funding mechanisms and national strategies (Hossain et al., 2024).

In parallel, capacity-building deficits present another formidable obstacle. Implementing green finance programs and deploying clean technologies requires a workforce with specialized technical, financial, and managerial expertise (Khalil et al., 2025). However, vocational and technical education systems in many low-income countries do not offer sufficient training in areas such as solar panel installation, energy auditing, or sustainable agriculture. For example, a UNEP report from 2021 noted that fewer than 10% of technical training programs in East Africa incorporated renewable energy into their curricula (Mahajan et al., 2023). Institutional knowledge gaps are also evident. Public agencies and financial regulators often lack the tools and experience necessary to assess green projects, certify green investments, or develop regulatory guidelines. This weakens the credibility of green finance initiatives and hinders access to international support. Low public and private sector awareness further compounds these issues (Mouakket & Aboelmaged, 2022). Many communities and businesses remain unaware of the potential benefits of green technologies or the availability of financing mechanisms, leading to low demand and limited adoption. For instance, a field study in rural Kenya revealed that only 30% of households were aware of solar home system financing options, despite their availability. Finally, capacity-building efforts themselves require sustained funding and infrastructural support both of which are often in short supply in low-income contexts. As a result, countries remain dependent on external development assistance, which may be irregular and insufficient for long-term transformation (Li et al., 2024).

## 6.4 Pathways Forward: Bridging Gaps through Cooperation and Innovation

Despite these challenges, several pathways can help bridge policy gaps and enhance capacity in low-income countries. International cooperation plays a central role. Technology transfer arrangements and technical assistance programs facilitated by multilateral organizations such as the United Nations Environment Programme (UNEP) and the International Renewable Energy Agency (IRENA) provide both knowledge and funding to accelerate green transitions. South-South cooperation also offers promising opportunities for peer learning and resource sharing. For example, collaborative platforms like the African Renewable Energy Initiative have enabled countries to co-develop regional strategies and share technological expertise (Perdana & Kulkarni, 2023; Obobisa & Ahakwa, 2024).

Locally tailored policy designs further enhance the effectiveness of green initiatives. Off-grid solar programs in countries such as Rwanda, which combine subsidies with private sector participation, have significantly increased access to electricity in rural communities. Similarly, investments in grassroots training and education programs can build technical capacity at the community level (Saleem et al., 2022). Notable examples include India's Barefoot College, which empowers rural women to become solar engineers through hands-on training. Such initiatives demonstrate that, with the right mix of policies, partnerships, and education, even the most constrained settings can make significant progress in adopting green finance and technology. The barriers to green technology and finance adoption are multifaceted, spanning economic, technical, and governance dimensions. While these challenges are particularly acute in low-income countries, they are not insurmountable. Strategic policy interventions, international collaboration, and investments in capacity building can create the enabling conditions necessary for a sustainable, low-carbon future (Obobisa & Ahakwa, 2024).

## 6.5 Impact Measurement in Green Finance and Technology

The frameworks to measure the impact are important considerations in the assessment of whether green finance and technologies deliver the planned sustainability effects. Financial metrics typically manage environmental and social value creation, and thus sustainability metrics are needed so that these indicators are uniformly compared (Ronaldo & Suryanto, 2022; Sethi et al., 2024). The more widely used tools are carbon intensity reduction on a dollar investment basis, energy savings, the rate of renewable energy purchases, and the increase in resource efficiency (Ronaldo & Suryanto, 2022). As an example, GHG emissions avoided, energy use per unit of output or water savings per project have been employed to measure green bonds (Annu & Tripathi, 2024). Not only do these metrics boost transparency and comparability of projects, but it also bolsters confidence in investors with the objective of attaining ESG initiatives. The impact measurement and reporting field is also guided by global frameworks like the Global Impact Investing Networks (GIIN) IRIS+ system, EU Taxonomy on sustainable activities and UN Sustainable Development Goals (SDGs) (Wang et al., 2025). It is not unclear, in the context of emerging economies such as Brazil or Bangladesh, which localized indicators (such as cleaner air, dispersal of electricity to the countryside, or increased economic empowerment of women in green SMEs) may make impact measurement more contextual and inclusive. Green finance can move beyond superficial claims of greenwashing by transforming symbolic commitments into real environmental and social impacts (Xiong & Dai, 2023).

## 6.6 Market Distortions, Political Economy Resistance, and Localized Barriers

Although financial barriers, infrastructure deficits and policy support from the crux of discussion on the green finance and sustainable transitions, there is need also to focus on the bigger picture of political economy issues that most of the time are the obstacles to significant advances (Han et al., 2025). Market failures and externalities are more comprehensive than the carbon pricing oriented, and they comprise issues of public goods, underinvestment in common resources, and disempowerment of the market with the goals of society (Hassan et al., 2024). Second, the interest of private sector actors to avoid costly green transitions is often met with counter action through lobbying, rent seeking activity or procrastination efforts in order to continue with making profits instead of focusing on the future in terms of green sustainability (Aref, 2024). The urban-rural gap exacerbates these issues as rural and informal economies can be rather limited in access to green technologies, clean energy, access to finance, and hence inequalities in transition strategies (Tsangas et al., 2022). Case studies show that a number of green processes have collapsed due to failure in overcoming these barriers on the local level and anticipated resistance by vested interests whose presence was underestimated unlike the success stories which are celebrated (Montfort et al., 2025). Thus, more substantial discussion of market distortions, political economy resistance, and implementation problems in various socio-economic settings are necessary to give a more balanced account of possibilities and limitations of green transitions.

*Figure 2. Barriers and Enablers in the Pathways from Green Finance to SDGs*

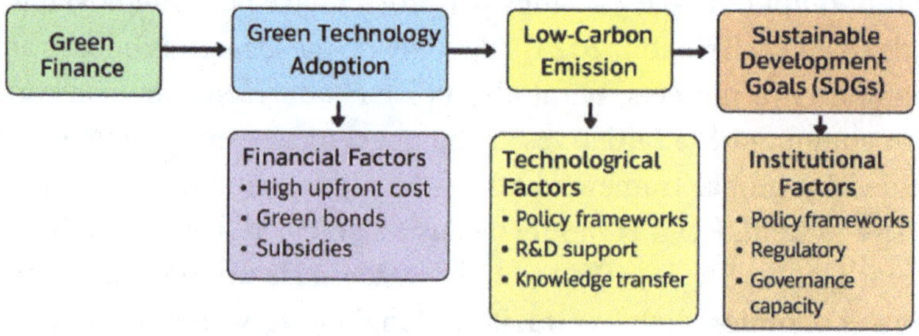


*(developed by authors)*

## 7. POLICY IMPLICATIONS AND STRATEGIC RECOMMENDATIONS

The realization of a low-carbon, sustainable global economy is deeply dependent on the successful integration of green finance and green technologies. These dual forces serve as foundational pillars in driving environmental innovation, reducing greenhouse gas emissions, and achieving Sustainable Development Goals (SDGs), especially SDG 7 (Affordable and Clean Energy) and SDG 13 (Climate Action). Nevertheless, existing financial, technological, and institutional challenges, particularly in low- and middle-income countries, necessitate strong and coherent policy frameworks to accelerate the adoption of these green solutions. Therefore, this section presents key policy implications and strategic pathways for fostering green growth, enhancing resilience, and embedding low-carbon principles into national development agendas (Shi et al., 2019; Sethi et al., 2024).

### 7.1 Strengthening Policy Support to Expand Green Finance and Technology Uptake

To enhance the flow of green investments and support the wide-scale deployment of green technologies, governments must adopt multi-pronged policy strategies that mobilize capital, provide economic incentives, and improve institutional effectiveness. One major lever is the expansion of green financial instruments, including green bonds, sustainability-linked loans, and climate-specific investment funds (Wang et al., 2022). These instruments offer targeted financial mechanisms that channel capital into renewable energy, clean transportation, and sustainable agriculture. However, as data show, low-income countries remain underrepresented in green bond issuance, accounting for merely 3% of global green bond volume in 2020 (Udeagha & Ngepah, 2023). Governments can reverse this trend by providing tax relief, credit guarantees, and co-financing schemes that reduce investment risk and encourage broader participation.

Moreover, supporting the diffusion of green technologies through favorable financing terms is essential. Microfinance and low-interest green loans enable small enterprises and rural communities to access technologies such as off-grid solar systems and clean cookstoves (Xia, 2023). Rwanda's off-grid solar program, underpinned by such financial models, successfully expanded electricity access to 67% of households by 2023 (World Bank, 2023). Complementarily, national and multilateral climate funds should prioritize low-income and vulnerable regions by simplifying application processes and increasing allocations. Beyond finance, well-calibrated economic incentives can create a level playing field for green technologies. Subsidies that reduce the upfront cost of renewable energy installations and energy-efficient devices are particularly effective in boosting consumer adoption (Xing et al., 2024). Additionally, tax exemptions or credit schemes targeting businesses that invest in clean technologies can drive private sector involvement. Carbon pricing mechanisms including carbon taxes and cap-and-trade systems have also proven successful in encouraging low-carbon transitions. The European Union's Emissions Trading System (ETS), for instance, has driven a 35% reduction in emissions in participating sectors since 2005 (Yadav et al., 2023), highlighting the importance of market-based instruments.

Robust regulatory frameworks are fundamental to fostering investor confidence and ensuring transparency. National governments should adopt standardized classifications and guidelines for green finance, adapted to local economic realities (Ye & Rasoulinezhad, 2023). The EU's Taxonomy for Sustainable Activities serves as a global benchmark, offering a classification system to prevent greenwashing and improve disclosure. Similarly, enforceable renewable energy targets and streamlined permitting processes for green infrastructure projects are essential for reducing bureaucratic delays and signaling long-term commitment to sustainability. Institutional capacity building is equally important (Zhang et al., 2022). Policymakers, regulators, and financial institutions must be equipped with the skills and knowledge to design and implement green financing programs. Investment in education and professional training, as illustrated by the UNEP's stakeholder training programs reaching over 5,000 individuals in low-income countries (Zeng et al., 2024), helps ensure sustainable program implementation. Transparency in fund management and the cultivation of public-private partnerships (PPPs), like Kenya's Lake Turkana Wind Power Project, further enhance scalability and attract global investors (Schain & Stiebale, 2021).

Lastly, international cooperation must remain a central pillar. Technology transfer agreements, such as those under the African Renewable Energy Initiative, play a pivotal role in making advanced solutions like solar PV and hydrogen fuel cells accessible in the Global South. Global financial commitments including the Paris Agreement's $100 billion annual climate finance goal must be met with equity and urgency, as only 20% of Green Climate Fund allocations currently reach the least-developed countries (Green Climate Fund, 2022). South-South cooperation and regional green finance networks, such as those established within ASEAN, also offer valuable platforms for knowledge exchange and joint investment (Ronaldo & Suryanto, 2022).

## 7.2 Strategic Frameworks for Integrating Low-Carbon Principles into SDG Achievement

Integrating low-carbon strategies within the broader framework of the SDGs requires the development of strategic frameworks that align national and international priorities, foster multi-stakeholder collaboration, and ensure equitable and inclusive outcomes. A core component of this integration lies in aligning national development policies with global commitments, particularly through the enhancement of Nationally Determined Contributions (NDCs). By embedding specific renewable energy targets and emission reduction goals within NDCs, countries can contribute directly to climate action while supporting other development objectives (Yadav et al., 2023). India's revised NDC, which commits to generating 50% of its energy from renewable sources by 2030, offers a strong example of how national action can align with international climate ambitions (Tan et al., 2017). National SDG strategies should explicitly integrate low-carbon pathways, ensuring coherence across energy, environmental, and economic policies. Morocco's Solar Plan, for instance, aligns renewable energy development with employment generation and poverty alleviation, illustrating how integrated planning can achieve multiple SDGs simultaneously (IRENA, 2020). At the policy level, coherence is critical to avoid conflicting objectives. The European Union's Green Deal, which unites climate, energy, and finance agendas under a common roadmap toward carbon neutrality by 2050, exemplifies the benefits of coordinated policy-making (Kobayakawa, 2021).

Public-private partnerships are vital for achieving scale and fostering innovation. These partnerships can mobilize resources, share risks, and catalyze technology deployment. Governments can enhance private-sector participation by offering blended finance, risk-sharing facilities, or investment guarantees. Brazil's successful use of thematic bonds to rise over $2.5 billion annually for forestry and bioenergy projects demonstrates the effectiveness of such mechanisms (Liang et al., 2024). Collaborative research hubs that bring together governments, universities, and businesses such as Singapore's Clean Energy Research Programme also accelerate the development of cutting-edge green technologies. Equally important is engaging communities in project design and implementation, as seen in Kenya's off-grid solar initiatives that integrate community cooperatives. Capacity building and education remain indispensable for empowering stakeholders at all levels. Expanding vocational training in green skills such as solar engineering, sustainable farming, and climate finance will create a workforce capable of leading low-carbon transitions. India's Barefoot College, which has trained over 15,000 rural women across 90 countries as solar engineers, highlights the transformative potential of inclusive, grassroots education models (Di Vaio et al., 2024). Public awareness campaigns, like Rwanda's national solar campaign that increased household adoption by 40% between 2018 and 2022, also demonstrate the importance of outreach and education in fostering behavioral change (Shang & Lv, 2023).

Data and digital technologies offer powerful tools for tracking progress and ensuring accountability. Digital finance platforms, such as the SME green financing portal in Huzhou, China, streamline access to funds while providing real-time data on project performance (Abubakar et al., 2023). Emission monitoring systems, like those embedded in the EU's ETS, enable policymakers to adjust strategies based on empirical evidence. National SDG dashboards, such as Bhutan's integrated reporting system, offer a model for linking climate performance with socioeconomic development indicators (Zhu & Li, 2024). Finally, ensuring equity and a just transition must be central to all strategic frameworks. The shift to a low-carbon economy should not exacerbate existing social inequalities. Mechanisms like the EU's Just Transition Fund are essential to support workers and communities affected by the decline of carbon-intensive industries. Similarly, gender-inclusive policies that empower women in green technology sectors can lead to more equitable and impactful outcomes. Ensuring that climate finance reaches the most vulnerable regions, and designing policies with marginalized communities in mind, will be critical in fostering sustainable development that is both inclusive and resilient (Evro et al., 2024).

## 8. RESEARCH GAPS AND FUTURE DIRECTIONS

Although literature on the topic of sustainable finance and green investment is increasing, one can still point out several gaps that have not been covered yet, which restrict the degree of its theory and practical implementation. First, there is no comparative analysis between good and flawed cases and this limits the capability of policymakers to draw balanced lessons across contexts. The majority of the existing works single out the success stories without highlighting stalled or unsuccessful initiatives and thus lessening invaluable insight regarding core factors explaining the lacklustre performance. Second, considerable portions of related literature have been based largely on descriptive accounts, making little use of the more rigorous methodological approaches like econometric modelling, structural equation modelling or comparative case analysis that can be used to identify causality and the decision relationship process. Third, these processes lack unanimous theoretical and conceptual frameworks that relate green finance mechanisms to governance, accountability and local socio-economic realities. Moreover, policy capture and transparency risks, as well as misplaced funds have not received sufficient scrutiny especially in multilateral green finance mechanisms that are vital in ensuring equitable and efficient application of resources.

Future studies considering more empirically tangible measures are needed to close these gaps; they should include longitudinal trend effects, comparing nations, and multi-level governance. Productive visual decision-making frameworks, such as flowcharts that profile important participants, responsibility matrices, and their financial allocations, can complement policymakers in more thoroughly appreciating complex green finance systems. Likewise, empirical tables on country-level progress in the areas of green investment, regulatory innovation, and governance accountability can give a systematic layout for both theoreticians and activists. Introducing critical synthesis into methodological rigor, the future research could provide more than description and could offer actionable models toward effective, transparent, and inclusive green finance approaches.

## 9. CONCLUSION

The twin pillars of green finance and green technology adoption are indispensable in the global quest for sustainable development and climate resilience. Their interconnection fosters a transformative pathway that supports low-carbon innovation, enhances energy efficiency, and advances the Sustainable Development Goals (SDGs), particularly SDG 7 (Affordable and Clean Energy) and SDG 13 (Climate Action). By channeling financial flows into environmentally sound investments and facilitating the widespread use of renewable and clean technologies, this synergistic approach not only mitigates greenhouse gas emissions but also contributes to inclusive and sustainable economic growth (Asif et al., 2023).

This chapter has emphasized that green finance acts as a catalyst in mobilizing the necessary capital to drive technological transformation. Financial tools such as green bonds, sustainable loans, and climate investment funds have proven effective in enabling the deployment of technologies like solar photovoltaics, wind turbines, energy-efficient systems, and sustainable agriculture. Equally, green technologies themselves play a pivotal role in emission reduction, offering scalable alternatives to fossil-fuel-based systems and creating co-benefits such as improved air quality, job creation, and energy access. The synergy between financial innovation and technological progress is evident in case examples from across the globe, from China's green finance zones to Brazil's climate-smart land use strategies (Behera et al., 2023).

However, the potential of these mechanisms is constrained by multiple barriers, particularly in low-income and emerging economies. High upfront investment costs, limited access to affordable capital, underdeveloped infrastructure, skills shortages, and weak institutional capacity continue to hamper adoption. Moreover, fragmented policy environments and the lack of coherent regulatory frameworks further deter investors and slow down the transition. These findings underscore the critical need for comprehensive, context-sensitive policy reforms and robust capacity-building initiatives. Global frameworks such as the EU Green Deal and China's Renewable Energy Law illustrate how integrated policy action can serve as a replicable model for other regions (Di Vaio et al., 2024).

Looking ahead, future research must focus on deepening our understanding of the long-term impacts and scalability of green finance and technologies, particularly in resource-constrained contexts. There is a pressing need to explore how these mechanisms can be tailored to ensure equity, resilience, and inclusion especially for marginalized populations and vulnerable geographies. Evaluating the effectiveness of policy instruments in low-income settings, and understanding their interplay with broader development goals such as poverty alleviation, urban sustainability, and gender empowerment, will be vital for maximizing their transformative potential (Feng et al., 2022).

Finally, the journey toward a green and sustainable future cannot be undertaken in isolation. Global cooperation encompassing technology transfer, climate finance commitments, and South-South partnerships is essential for bridging the implementation gap. As the world faces intensifying environmental, economic, and social challenges, the integration of green finance and technology offers not just a solution, but a roadmap toward a just, inclusive, and climate-resilient global economy. The time to act collectively and decisively is now.

## REFERENCES


Abbas, J., & Najam, H. (2024). Role of environmental decentralization, green human capital, and digital finance in firm green technological innovation for a sustainable society. *Environment, Development and Sustainability*, *27*(8), 1–15. DOI: 10.1007/s10668-024-04783-3

Abubakar, I. R., & Alshammari, M. S. (2023). Urban planning schemes for developing low-carbon cities in the Gulf Cooperation Council region. *Habitat International*, *138*, 102881. DOI: 10.1016/j.habitatint.2023.102881

Agrawal, R., Agrawal, S., Samadhiya, A., Kumar, A., Luthra, S., & Jain, V. (2024). Adoption of green finance and green innovation for achieving circularity: An exploratory review and future directions. *Geoscience Frontiers*, *15*(4), 101669. DOI: 10.1016/j.gsf.2023.101669

Alam, S. S., Masukujjaman, M., Ahmed, S., Kokash, H. A., & Khattak, A. (2024). Towards a circular economy: Cleaner production technology adoption among small and medium enterprises in an emerging economy. *Circular Economy and Sustainability*, *4*(2), 1357–1386. DOI: 10.1007/s43615-023-00341-7

Ali, E. B., Anufriev, V. P., & Amfo, B. (2021). Green economy implementation in Ghana as a road map for a sustainable development drive: A review. *Scientific African*, *12*, e00756. DOI: 10.1016/j.sciaf.2021.e00756

Amouri, A., Festa, G., Shams, S. R., Sakka, G., & Rossi, M. (2021). Technological propensity, financial constraints, and entrepreneurial limits in young entrepreneurs' social business enterprises: The tunisian experience. *Technological Forecasting and Social Change*, *173*, 121126. DOI: 10.1016/j.techfore.2021.121126

Annu & Tripathi, R. (2024). Framework of green finance to attain sustainable development goals: an empirical evidence from the TCCM approach. *Benchmarking: An International Journal, 31*(9), 3130-3153.

Aref, M. (2024). Sharing economy from the sustainable development goals perspective: A path to global prosperity. *Journal of Internet and Digital Economics*, *4*(2), 116–138. DOI: 10.1108/JIDE-02-2024-0007

Asif, M. H., Zhongfu, T., Dilanchiev, A., Irfan, M., Eyvazov, E., & Ahmad, B. (2023). Determining the influencing factors of consumers' attitude toward renewable energy adoption in developing countries: A roadmap toward environmental sustainability and green energy technologies. *Environmental Science and Pollution Research International*, *30*(16), 47861–47872. DOI: 10.1007/s11356-023-25662-w

Basak, R., Karlsson-Vinkhuyzen, S., & Termeer, K. J. (2022). Information for climate finance accountability regimes: Proposed framework and case study of the Green Climate Fund. *Public Administration and Development, 42*(5), 261–280. DOI: 10.1002/pad.2000

Behera, B., Behera, P., & Sethi, N. (2024). Decoupling the role of renewable energy, green finance and political stability in achieving the sustainable development goal 13: Empirical insight from emerging economies. *Sustainable Development (Bradford), 32*(1), 119–137. DOI: 10.1002/sd.2657

Behera, P., Haldar, A., & Sethi, N. (2023). Achieving carbon neutrality target in the emerging economies: Role of renewable energy and green technology. *Gondwana Research, 121*, 16–32. DOI: 10.1016/j.gr.2023.03.028

Bei, J., & Wang, C. (2023). Renewable energy resources and sustainable development goals: Evidence based on green finance, clean energy and environmentally friendly investment. *Resources Policy, 80*, 103194. DOI: 10.1016/j.resourpol.2022.103194

Bhutta, U. S., Tariq, A., Farrukh, M., Raza, A., & Iqbal, M. K. (2022). Green bonds for sustainable development: Review of literature on development and impact of green bonds. *Technological Forecasting and Social Change, 175*, 121378. DOI: 10.1016/j.techfore.2021.121378

Bracking, S., & Leffel, B. (2021). Climate finance governance: Fit for purpose? *Wiley Interdisciplinary Reviews: Climate Change, 12*(4), e709. DOI: 10.1002/wcc.709

Brundtland, G. H. (1987). Brundtland report. Our common future. *Comissão Mundial, 4*(1), 17–25.

Dai, B., Zhang, J., & Hussain, N. (2025). Policy pathways through FinTech and green finance for low-carbon energy transition in BRICS nations. *Energy Strategy Reviews, 57*, 101603. DOI: 10.1016/j.esr.2024.101603

Dai, B., Zhang, J., & Hussain, N. (2025). Policy pathways through FinTech and green finance for low-carbon energy transition in BRICS nations. *Energy Strategy Reviews, 57*, 101603. DOI: 10.1016/j.esr.2024.101603

Dai, Y., & Chen, X. (2023). Evaluating green financing mechanisms for natural resource management: Implications for achieving sustainable development goals. *Resources Policy, 86*, 104160. DOI: 10.1016/j.resourpol.2023.104160

Dhayal, K. S., Giri, A. K., Kumar, A., Samadhiya, A., Agrawal, S., & Agrawal, R. (2023). Can green finance facilitate Industry 5.0 transition to achieve sustainability? A systematic review with future research directions. *Environmental Science and Pollution Research International*, *30*(46), 102158–102180. DOI: 10.1007/s11356-023-29539-w

Di Vaio, A., Zaffar, A., & Chhabra, M. (2024). Intellectual capital through decarbonization for achieving Sustainable Development Goal 8: A systematic literature review and future research directions. *Journal of Intellectual Capital*, *25*(7), 54–86. DOI: 10.1108/JIC-05-2024-0131

Du, L., & Geng, B. (2024). Financial technology and financing constraints. *Finance Research Letters*, *60*, 104841. DOI: 10.1016/j.frl.2023.104841

Evro, S., Oni, B. A., & Tomomewo, O. S. (2024). Global strategies for a low-carbon future: Lessons from the US, China, and EU's pursuit of carbon neutrality. *Journal of Cleaner Production*, *461*, 142635. DOI: 10.1016/j.jclepro.2024.142635

Ewing, J. A. (2017). Hollow ecology: Ecological modernization theory and the death of nature. *Journal of World-systems Research*, *23*(1), 126–155. DOI: 10.5195/jwsr.2017.611

Falavigna, G., & Ippoliti, R. (2022). Financial constraints, investments, and environmental strategies: An empirical analysis of judicial barriers. *Business Strategy and the Environment*, *31*(5), 2002–2018. DOI: 10.1002/bse.2995

Feng, S., Zhang, R., & Li, G. (2022). Environmental decentralization, digital finance and green technology innovation. *Structural Change and Economic Dynamics*, *61*, 70–83. DOI: 10.1016/j.strueco.2022.02.008

Freeman, R. B. (1984). Longitudinal analyses of the effects of trade unions. *Journal of Labor Economics*, *2*(1), 1–26. DOI: 10.1086/298021

Fu, C., Lu, L., & Pirabi, M. (2023). Advancing green finance: A review of sustainable development. *Digital Economy and Sustainable Development*, *1*(1), 20. DOI: 10.1007/s44265-023-00020-3

Fu, C., Lu, L., & Pirabi, M. (2023). Advancing green finance: A review of sustainable development. *Digital Economy and Sustainable Development*, *1*(1), 20. DOI: 10.1007/s44265-023-00020-3

Guo, Z., & Zhang, X. (2023). Carbon reduction effect of agricultural green production technology: A new evidence from China. *The Science of the Total Environment*, *874*, 162483. DOI: 10.1016/j.scitotenv.2023.162483

Habiba, U., Xinbang, C., & Ali, S. (2023). Investigating the impact of financial development on carbon emissions: Does the use of renewable energy and green technology really contribute to achieving low-carbon economies? *Gondwana Research, 121*, 472–485. DOI: 10.1016/j.gr.2023.05.013

Habiba, U. M. M. E., Xinbang, C., & Anwar, A. (2022). Do green technology innovations, financial development, and renewable energy use help to curb carbon emissions? *Renewable Energy, 193*, 1082–1093. DOI: 10.1016/j.renene.2022.05.084

Han, J., Zhang, W., Liu, X., Huang, H., & Isik, C. (2025). The role of green finance in energy transition: Regional variations and the moderating impact of women political participation. *Energy Policy, 207*, 114817. DOI: 10.1016/j.enpol.2025.114817

Hassan, S. A., Haq, I., Khattak, E. A., Nassani, A. A., Zaman, K., & Haffar, M. (2024). Transitioning from gridlock to sustainability: Advancing transport strategies for eco-friendly solutions in high-income countries. *Environmental Science and Pollution Research International, 31*(47), 58152–58175. DOI: 10.1007/s11356-024-34997-x

Hassan, T., Khan, Y., Safi, A., Chaolin, H., Wahab, S., Daud, A., & Tufail, M. (2023). Green financing strategy for low-carbon economy: The role of high-technology imports and institutional strengths in China. *Journal of Cleaner Production, 415*, 137859. DOI: 10.1016/j.jclepro.2023.137859

Ho, J. C. (2022). Disruptive innovation from the perspective of innovation diffusion theory. *Technology Analysis and Strategic Management, 34*(4), 363–376. DOI: 10.1080/09537325.2021.1901873

Hossain, M. R., Rao, A., Sharma, G. D., Dev, D., & Kharbanda, A. (2024). Empowering energy transition: Green innovation, digital finance, and the path to sustainable prosperity through green finance initiatives. *Energy Economics, 136*, 107736. DOI: 10.1016/j.eneco.2024.107736

Javaid, M., Haleem, A., Singh, R. P., Suman, R., & Gonzalez, E. S. (2022). Understanding the adoption of Industry 4.0 technologies in improving environmental sustainability. *Sustainable operations and computers, 3*, 203-217.

Ji, M., & Zhang, X. (2024). Assessing the impacts and mechanisms of green bond financing on the enhancement of green management and technological innovation in environmental conservation enterprises. *Journal of the Knowledge Economy, 15*(3), 12709–12750. DOI: 10.1007/s13132-023-01594-1

Kashif, M., Pinglu, C., Ullah, S., & Zaman, M. (2024). Evaluating the influence of financial technology (FinTech) on sustainable finance: A comprehensive global analysis. *Financial Markets and Portfolio Management, 38*(1), 123–155. DOI: 10.1007/s11408-023-00439-w

Kassouri, Y., & Alola, A. A. (2023). Examining the interaction of technology adoption-diffusion and sectoral emission intensity in developing and emerging countries. *Journal of Cleaner Production, 405*, 136920. DOI: 10.1016/j.jclepro.2023.136920

Khalil, M. A., Sinliamthong, P., & Khalil, R. (2025). From paper to pixels for a world of purpose: A systematic review of sustainable finance, blockchain, and digital assets. *Sustainable Financing—A Contemporary Guide for Green Finance, Crowdfunding and Digital Currencies: Sustainable Financing*, 61-78.

Khan, S. U., Shah, A., & Rizwan, M. F. (2021). Do financing constraints matter for technological and non-technological innovation? A (re) examination of developing markets. *Emerging Markets Finance & Trade, 57*(9), 2739–2766. DOI: 10.1080/1540496X.2019.1695593

Kobayakawa, T. (2021). Country diagnostics for low carbon development: Can developing countries pursue simultaneous implementation of the Sustainable Development Goals and the Paris Agreement? *Business Strategy & Development, 4*(3), 294–312. DOI: 10.1002/bsd2.159

Lai, C. H., & Lin, S. H. (2017). Systems theory. *The international encyclopedia of organizational communication, 41*, 1-18.

Li, B., Rahman, M. M., & Haneklaus, N. (2024). Assessing China's energy transition pathway: Insights from the synergistic effects of key drivers. *Energy Strategy Reviews, 55*, 101528. DOI: 10.1016/j.esr.2024.101528

Li, G., Wu, H., Jiang, J., & Zong, Q. (2023). Digital finance and the low-carbon energy transition (LCET) from the perspective of capital-biased technical progress. *Energy Economics, 120*, 106623. DOI: 10.1016/j.eneco.2023.106623

Li, T., Lau, W. T., & Dato Haji Yahya, M. H. (2025). Blockchain Applications in Green Finance for Transparency and Accountability in Sustainable Investments. *Sustainability (Basel), 17*(6), 2520. DOI: 10.3390/su17062520

Liang, X., Liu, M., & Huang, Y. (2024). Studying financial development with low-carbon architecture development and green technological innovation: Sustaining SDG-9. *Environmental Science and Pollution Research International, 31*(2), 2009–2025. DOI: 10.1007/s11356-023-31155-7

Lin, Z., Liao, X., & Jia, H. (2023). Could green finance facilitate low-carbon transformation of power generation? Some evidence from China. *International Journal of Climate Change Strategies and Management, 15*(2), 141–158. DOI: 10.1108/IJCCSM-03-2022-0039

Liu, M., Baisheng, S., Alharthi, M., Hassan, M. S., & Hanif, I. (2023). The role of natural resources, clean energy and technology in mitigating carbon emissions in top populated countries. *Resources Policy, 83*, 103705. DOI: 10.1016/j.resourpol.2023.103705

Liu, Y., Lei, P., & He, D. (2024). Endogenous green technology progress, green transition and carbon emissions. *International Review of Economics & Finance, 91*, 69–82. DOI: 10.1016/j.iref.2023.12.007

Liu, Z., Zheng, H., Gu, J., Xu, S., & Ye, Y. (2024). Exploring the nexus between green finance and energy efficiency: Unravelling the impact through green technology innovation and energy structure. *Heliyon, 10*(9), e30141. DOI: 10.1016/j.heliyon.2024.e30141

Ma, M., Zhu, X., Liu, M., & Huang, X. (2023). Combining the role of green finance and environmental sustainability on green economic growth: Evidence from G-20 economies. *Renewable Energy, 207*, 128–136. DOI: 10.1016/j.renene.2023.02.046

Mahajan, R., Lim, W. M., Sareen, M., Kumar, S., & Panwar, R. (2023). Stakeholder theory. *Journal of Business Research, 166*, 114104. DOI: 10.1016/j.jbusres.2023.114104

Makeel, R., Syed, Z. A., & Zhao, S. (2025). Unlocking green technology adoption: Exploring influential factors and the moderating influence of environmentally responsible behaviour. *Behaviour & Information Technology*, 1–19. DOI: 10.1080/0144929X.2025.2515450

Mol, A. P., & Spaargaren, G. (2000). Ecological modernisation theory in debate: A review. *Environmental Politics, 9*(1), 17–49. DOI: 10.1080/09644010008414511

Montfort, S., Fesenfeld, L., Ingold, K., Lamb, W. F., & Andrijevic, M. (2025). Political enablers of ambitious climate policies: A framework and thematic review. *npj. Npj Climate Action, 4*(1), 14. DOI: 10.1038/s44168-024-00206-1

Mouakket, S., & Aboelmaged, M. (2022). Drivers and outcomes of green information technology adoption in service organizations: An evidence from emerging economy context. *Journal of Science and Technology Policy Management, 13*(4), 898–924. DOI: 10.1108/JSTPM-09-2020-0137

Mouakket, S., & Aboelmaged, M. (2023). Factors influencing green information technology adoption: A multi-level perspective in emerging economies context. *Information Development, 39*(4), 699–719. DOI: 10.1177/02666669211048489

Nanthini, M., Vinumon, V. S., Thomas, A. A., & Sheshu, A. (2024). Green Finance 2.0: Harnessing Fintech for Sustainable Investments in Industry 5.0. In *Anticipating Future Business Trends: Navigating Artificial Intelligence Innovations* (Vol. 1, pp. 195–204). Springer Nature Switzerland. DOI: 10.1007/978-3-031-63569-4_17

Nasir, N., & Ahmed, W. (2024). Green Finance Initiatives and Their Potential to Drive Sustainable Development. In *Climate Change and Finance: Navigating the Challenges and Opportunities in Capital Markets* (pp. 3–29). Springer Nature Switzerland. DOI: 10.1007/978-3-031-56419-2_1

Obobisa, E. S., & Ahakwa, I. (2024). Stimulating the adoption of green technology innovation, clean energy resources, green finance, and environmental taxes: The way to achieve net zero CO2 emissions in Europe? *Technological Forecasting and Social Change, 205*, 123489. DOI: 10.1016/j.techfore.2024.123489

Olabi, A. G., Abdelkareem, M. A., Mahmoud, M. S., Elsaid, K., Obaideen, K., Rezk, H., Wilberforce, T., Eisa, T., Chae, K.-J., & Sayed, E. T. (2023). Green hydrogen: Pathways, roadmap, and role in achieving sustainable development goals. *Process Safety and Environmental Protection, 177*, 664–687. DOI: 10.1016/j.psep.2023.06.069

Perdana, A., & Kulkarni, M. S. (2023). Exploring the synergy between financial technologies and financial inclusion: What we know and where we should be heading? *Pacific Asia Journal of the Association for Information Systems, 15*(1), 4.

Qi, H., Huang, X., & Sheeraz, M. (2023). Green financing for renewable energy development: Driving the attainment of zero-emission targets. *Renewable Energy, 213*, 30–37. DOI: 10.1016/j.renene.2023.05.111

Rogers, E. M. (2003). Diffusion networks. *Networks in the knowledge economy, 10.*

Ronaldo, R., & Suryanto, T. (2022). Green finance and sustainability development goals in Indonesian Fund Village. *Resources Policy, 78*, 102839. DOI: 10.1016/j.resourpol.2022.102839



Ronaldo, R., & Suryanto, T. (2022). Green finance and sustainability development goals in Indonesian Fund Village. *Resources Policy, 78*, 102839. DOI: 10.1016/j.resourpol.2022.102839

Ruiz-Palomo, D., Fernández-Gámez, M. Á., & León-Gómez, A. (2022). Analyzing the effect of financial constraints on technological and management innovation in SMEs: A gender perspective. *SAGE Open*, *12*(1). DOI: 10.1177/21582440221079925

Saleem, H., Khan, M. B., & Mahdavian, S. M. (2022). The role of green growth, green financing, and eco-friendly technology in achieving environmental quality: Evidence from selected Asian economies. *Environmental Science and Pollution Research International*, *29*(38), 57720–57739. DOI: 10.1007/s11356-022-19799-3

Sampene, A. K., Li, C., & Nsiah, T. K. (2024). Catalyzing renewable energy deployment in the Mercosur economies: A synthesis of human capital, technological innovation and green finance. *Energy Strategy Reviews*, *53*, 101388. DOI: 10.1016/j.esr.2024.101388

Schain, J. P., & Stiebale, J. (2021). Innovation, institutional ownership and financial constraints. *Empirical Economics*, *61*(3), 1689–1697. DOI: 10.1007/s00181-020-01909-0

Scott, W. R. (2008). Approaching adulthood: The maturing of institutional theory. *Theory and Society*, *37*(5), 427–442. DOI: 10.1007/s11186-008-9067-z

Sethi, L., Behera, B., & Sethi, N. (2024). Do green finance, green technology innovation, and institutional quality help achieve environmental sustainability? Evidence from the developing economies. *Sustainable Development (Bradford)*, *32*(3), 2709–2723. DOI: 10.1002/sd.2811

Sethi, L., Behera, B., & Sethi, N. (2024). Do green finance, green technology innovation, and institutional quality help achieve environmental sustainability? Evidence from the developing economies. *Sustainable Development (Bradford)*, *32*(3), 2709–2723. DOI: 10.1002/sd.2811

Shahadat, M. H., Nekmahmud, M., Ebrahimi, P., & Fekete-Farkas, M. (2023). Digital technology adoption in SMEs: What technological, environmental and organizational factors influence in emerging countries? *Global Business Review*. DOI: 10.1177/09721509221137199

Shahbaz, M., Patel, N., Du, A. M., & Ahmad, S. (2024). From black to green: Quantifying the impact of economic growth, resource management, and green technologies on CO2 emissions. *Journal of Environmental Management*, *360*, 121091. DOI: 10.1016/j.jenvman.2024.121091

Shang, W. L., & Lv, Z. (2023). Low carbon technology for carbon neutrality in sustainable cities: A survey. *Sustainable Cities and Society*, *92*, 104489. DOI: 10.1016/j.scs.2023.104489

Sharif, A., Saqib, N., Dong, K., & Khan, S. A. R. (2022). Nexus between green technology innovation, green financing, and CO2 emissions in the G7 countries: The moderating role of social globalisation. *Sustainable Development (Bradford), 30*(6), 1934–1946. DOI: 10.1002/sd.2360

Shi, L., Han, L., Yang, F., & Gao, L. (2019). The evolution of sustainable development theory: Types, goals, and research prospects. *Sustainability (Basel), 11*(24), 7158. DOI: 10.3390/su11247158

Su, Y., Liu, B., Yang, X., & Wang, E. (2022). Research on technological innovation investment, financing constraints, and corporate financial risk: Evidence from China. *Mathematical Problems in Engineering, 2022*(1), 5052274. DOI: 10.1155/2022/5052274

Suddaby, R. (2015). Can institutional theory be critical? *Journal of Management Inquiry, 24*(1), 93–95. DOI: 10.1177/1056492614545304

Tan, C. (2022). Audit as accountability: Technical authority and expertise in the governance of private financing for development. *Social & Legal Studies, 31*(1), 3–26. DOI: 10.1177/0964663921992100

Tan, S., Yang, J., Yan, J., Lee, C., Hashim, H., & Chen, B. (2017). A holistic low carbon city indicator framework for sustainable development. *Applied Energy, 185*, 1919–1930. DOI: 10.1016/j.apenergy.2016.03.041

Udeagha, M. C., & Ngepah, N. (2023). The drivers of environmental sustainability in BRICS economies: Do green finance and fintech matter? *World Development Sustainability, 3*, 100096. DOI: 10.1016/j.wds.2023.100096

Uzar, U. (2024). The critical role of green innovation technologies and democracy in the transition to sustainability: A study on leading emerging market economies. *Technology in Society, 78*, 102622. DOI: 10.1016/j.techsoc.2024.102622

Wang, C., Rahman, M. M., Siddik, A. B., Wen, Z. G., & Sobhani, F. A. (2024). Exploring the synergy of logistics, finance, and technology on innovation. *Scientific Reports, 14*(1), 21918. DOI: 10.1038/s41598-024-72409-9

Wang, K. H., Zhao, Y. X., Jiang, C. F., & Li, Z. Z. (2022). Does green finance inspire sustainable development? Evidence from a global perspective. *Economic Analysis and Policy, 75*, 412–426. DOI: 10.1016/j.eap.2022.06.002

Wang, X., Sun, X., Zhang, H., & Xue, C. (2022). Does green financial reform pilot policy promote green technology innovation? Empirical evidence from China. *Environmental Science and Pollution Research International, 29*(51), 77283–77299. DOI: 10.1007/s11356-022-21291-x

Whitchurch, G. G., & Constantine, L. L. (1993). Systems theory. In *Sourcebook of family theories and methods: A contextual approach* (pp. 325–355). Springer US. DOI: 10.1007/978-0-387-85764-0_14

Xia, D., Zhang, M., Yu, Q., & Tu, Y. (2019). Developing a framework to identify barriers of Green technology adoption for enterprises. *Resources, Conservation and Recycling*, *143*, 99–110. DOI: 10.1016/j.resconrec.2018.12.022

Xia, Q. (2023). Does green technology advancement and renewable electricity standard impact on carbon emissions in China: Role of green finance. *Environmental Science and Pollution Research International*, *30*(3), 6492–6505. DOI: 10.1007/s11356-022-22517-8

Xing, L., Chang, B. H., & Aldawsari, S. H. (2024). Green Finance Mechanisms for Sustainable Development: Evidence from Panel Data. *Sustainability (Basel)*, *16*(22), 9762. DOI: 10.3390/su16229762

Xu, T., Yang, G., & Chen, T. (2024). The role of green finance and digital inclusive finance in promoting economic sustainable development: A perspective from new quality productivity. *Journal of Environmental Management*, *370*, 122892. DOI: 10.1016/j.jenvman.2024.122892

Yadav, S., Samadhiya, A., Kumar, A., Majumdar, A., Garza-Reyes, J. A., & Luthra, S. (2023). Achieving the sustainable development goals through net zero emissions: Innovation-driven strategies for transitioning from incremental to radical lean, green and digital technologies. *Resources, Conservation and Recycling*, *197*, 107094. DOI: 10.1016/j.resconrec.2023.107094

Ye, X., & Rasoulinezhad, E. (2023). Assessment of impacts of green bonds on renewable energy utilization efficiency. *Renewable Energy*, *202*, 626–633. DOI: 10.1016/j.renene.2022.11.124

Yu, M., Zhou, Q., Cheok, M. Y., Kubiczek, J., & Iqbal, N. (2022). Does green finance improve energy efficiency? New evidence from developing and developed economies. *Economic Change and Restructuring*, *55*(1), 1–25. DOI: 10.1007/s10644-021-09355-3

Zeng, S., Li, T., Wu, S., Gao, W., & Li, G. (2024). Does green technology progress have a significant impact on carbon dioxide emissions? *Energy Economics*, *133*, 107524. DOI: 10.1016/j.eneco.2024.107524

Zhang, L., Saydaliev, H. B., & Ma, X. (2022). Does green finance investment and technological innovation improve renewable energy efficiency and sustainable development goals. *Renewable Energy*, *193*, 991–1000. DOI: 10.1016/j.renene.2022.04.161

Zhao, L., Chau, K. Y., Tran, T. K., Sadiq, M., Xuyen, N. T. M., & Phan, T. T. H. (2022). Enhancing green economic recovery through green bonds financing and energy efficiency investments. *Economic Analysis and Policy*, *76*, 488–501. DOI: 10.1016/j.eap.2022.08.019

Zhu, X., & Li, D. (2024). How to promote the construction of low-carbon cities in China? An urban complex ecosystem perspective. *Sustainable Development (Bradford)*, *32*(5), 4354–4373. DOI: 10.1002/sd.2897

# Chapter 9
# The Triple Bottom Line of Green Finance:
## Profitability, Planet, and People in the Context of SDGs

**Shivangi Kashyap**
https://orcid.org/0009-0002-1685-330X
*University of Hyderabad, India*

**R. Prasantha Kumar**
https://orcid.org/0000-0001-5299-7701
*University of Hyderabad, India*

## ABSTRACT

*This chapter discusses how the Triple Bottom Line (TBL) model—People, Planet, Profit—has been implemented in the emerging dynamics of green financing. It discusses how financial instruments, which are in line with environmental and social goals, can create a long-term economic payoff, and simultaneously respond to climate change, social equity, and inclusive development. Based on case studies and practices around the world, the chapter will make a case of how green finance can define sustainable economies, minimize inequalities, and promote climate resilience. It also speaks of the issues like greenwashing and the gaps in measures implying the necessity to standardize, innovate, and constructive policy models.*

## 1. INTRODUCTION

For the past 30 years, the blending of finance and sustainability has dominated discussions of global development. Green finance was a niche issue, outside of

DOI: 10.4018/979-8-3373-8287-6.ch009

ht © 2026, IGI Global Scientific Publishing. Copying or distributing in print or electronic forms without written permission of IGI Global Scientific Publishing is prohibited. Use of this chapter to generative artificial intelligence (AI) technologies is expressly prohibited. The publisher reserves all rights to license its use for generative AI training and machine learning model development.

traditional economic considerations. However, climate change, significant environmental degradation, and inequality have shown limitations of existing paradigms of economic growth. Green finance has now transformed from an environmental issue to one of systemic importance. The evolution of finance as a system, rather than just an ecological issue, represents a major shift in how economies consider development, stability, and sustainability in the future.

## 1.1 Evolution of Green Finance: 1990s to Present

In the early 1990s, development finance was principally based upon profit maximization, with environmental and social impacts characterized as external costs of achieving economic growth and often neglected because they were "externalities." The lag of traditional finance perspectives shifted markedly at the Rio Earth Summit in 1992, with other consequential international agreements taking place in 1997 (Kyoto Protocol) and 2016 (Paris Agreement) that challenged the efficacy of traditional financial practices (Sachs et al., 2019; Skea et al., 2021) and initiated a process of calling for environmental accountability in finance organizations through integrated environmental responsibility considerations for introducing environmental accountabilities into finance instruments (Citaristi, 2022).

During the early 2000s, corporate social responsibility maintained a focus on philanthropy but developed into measurable industry standards. Throughout this period, a variety of new green finance instruments were created as overlays and offshoots—green bond investment funds, sustainable lending practices, and ESG investment funds—with a focus on enabling financial sustainability while addressing climate-risk (Flammer, 2021; Hadaś-Dyduch et al., 2022). Then in 2008, the financial crisis spurred further discussion on how financial "value" should be redefined from the pursuit of short-term profits for shareholders to creating sustainable value that would include all stakeholders over a longer-term horizon (Clark et al., 2015; Eccles et al., 2014).

Since 2015, the introduction of the United Nations Sustainable Development Goals (SDGs) and the Paris Agreement have provided an international context for directing capital flows towards sustainability (Sachs et al., 2019). The level of climate-aligned finance reached USD 600 billion per year by 2020, according to the Climate Policy Initiative (Galindo-Gutiérrez, 2024). Financial institutions have been increasingly forced to disclose climate-related risks through frameworks such as the Task Force on Climate-related Financial Disclosures (Kotsantonis et al., 2016; Pucker, 2021).

## 1.2 Limitations of Profit-Only Finance Models

At their core, conventional finance systems are inevitably built on neoclassical economic assumptions that set economic growth through capital accumulation as the supreme goal, neglecting any ecological boundaries (Tietenberg & Lewis, 2023; Khan et al., 2016). Such a short-term, risk-discounting model, all the while ignoring environmental degradation, also needs to be blamed for making social inequalities even worse (Nguyen & Khominich, 2023; Weber, 2017). For instance, wealth has increased on a global scale, yet income and opportunity disparities have the latter being mostly in the Global South (Malik & Sharma, 2025; Renneboog et al., 2008).

Profit-only models also don't consider any planetary boundaries—with the carbon budgets, availability of water, or biodiversity thresholds taken as examples—when making investment decisions, resulting in further unsustainable industrial expansion, resource depletion, and climate vulnerabilities in disguise of economic development, sometimes even financing these factors (Boiral & Heras-Saizarbitoria, 2020; Awazu & Samama-Romain, 2020).

On top of everything else, COVID-19 vividly illustrated how fragile and unresilient an economy turned excessively extractive and linear growth-based could be. It gave way to a conscientious demand for resilient systems that promote ecosystem protection, community empowerment, and inclusive growth (Jeucken, 2010; Ghosh & Dutta, 2023).

## 1.3 Definition and Scope of Green Finance

Green finance refers to any investment wherein the public and private sectors may be allocated to projects with positive environmental outputs. The term covers a whole gamut of services, including green bonds, climate funds, sustainability-linked loans, carbon markets, and ESG investments (HLEG, 2018; Flammer, 2021). It may be used for anything from climate mitigation and adaptation to biodiversity, pollution, and a low-carbon economy (Inderst et al., 2012; Zadek & Flynn, 2013). Whereas traditional finance sets the limits based on environmental integrity and the long-term value of society, green finance does not imply "doing less harm" but rather propagating systems that are regenerative and restorative (Elkington & Rowlands, 1999; Bocken et al., 2014).

"Green finance has not emerged separately, but has been bolstered by regulatory and institutional frameworks. The European Union's Taxonomy for Sustainable Activities, the OECD guidelines on sustainable finance, and frameworks in national policies, such as India's SEBI green bond regulations, provide important standardization and credibility. These initiatives help establish market norms, minimize the risk of greenwashing, and enhance capital flows dedicated to truly sustainable activities.

## 1.4 The Triple Bottom Line (TBL) as a Response to Sustainable Development Complexity

In 1994, Elkington's Triple Bottom Line (TBL) was conceived as a paradigm shift to address the broad nature of 21st-century problems. Apart from profit, the environmental, social, and economic performances of an organization should be equally considered, i.e., "People," "Planet," and "Profit" (Elkington & Rowlands, 1999). Thus, these frameworks must be based on stakeholder theory, which recognizes that people and businesses are mutually dependent upon each other, as are ecosystems and communities (Khan et al., 2016; Malik & Sharma, 2025). In addition to its theoretical moorings, the TBL framework has a wider theoretical background. Stakeholder theory explains how firms engage with their community and environmental systems, asserting the interdependence of firms, communities, and ecosystems (Freeman & Phillips, 2002), whereas institutional theory explains how forces of policy and governance (and the structures they produce) influence organizations (Scott, 2005). While the environment ("Planet") and economics ("Profit") dimensions typically receive more attention (Bocken et al., 2014; Elkington, 1999), the social ("People") pillar, as it pertains to labour rights, equity, and community resilience, is often marginal at best. Exploring the social dimension is an important premise to help ensure (and hopefully create) just and inclusive sustainability transitions. Green finance, in particular, poses a triple bottom line problem by welding together economic performance with environmental responsibility and social equity (Bocken et al., 2014; Cornell & Damodaran, 2020). This triad offers a holistic picture in weighing the cost and value of a financial measure (Kotsantonis et al., 2016; Kathane et al., 2024).

## 1.5 Relevance to the 2030 Agenda and SDGs

The 2030 Agenda for Sustainable Development and its 17 goals envision a world in which prosperity is shared, environmental degradation is reversed, and social injustices are remedied (Sachs et al., 2019). Green finance acts as a vehicle to promote achievement in SDG-13 (Climate Action) while also promoting SDG-7 (Affordable and Clean Energy) and SDG-8 (Decent Work and Economic Growth) (Yadav et al.,2024; Ghosh & Dutta,2023). The TBL framework goes deeply into the integrated approach inherent in the SDGs. For example:

- Under "Planet," it supports SDG 13 (Climate Action), SDG 6 (Clean Water and Sanitation), and SDG 15 (Life on Land) (Tietenberg & Lewis, 2023; Skea et al., 2021).

- Under "People," it supports SDG 5 (Gender Equality), SDG 10 (Reduced Inequalities) and SDG 1 (No Poverty) (Malik et al., 2022; Malik & Sharma, 2025).
- Under "Profit," it supports SDG 8 (Decent Work and Economic Growth) and SDG 9 (Industry, Innovation, and Infrastructure) (Clark et al., 2015; Wang et al., 2023).

Thus, by linking TBL with green finance, financial systems can work toward meeting the mutually reinforcing global development goals that strive to simultaneously improve economic growth, environmental resilience, and human well-being (Jeucken, 2010; Zadek & Flynn, 2013).

Consequently, this chapter seeks to explore how green finance intersects with the Triple Bottom Line framework which identifies overlaps in profitability, ecosystem performance, and social fairness. By engaging with the context of regulatory frameworks, governance models, and debates about labour transition, the chapter makes a meaningful contribution to viewing sustainable finance purely from a system-wide perspective; it builds from contributions that unite finance with the Sustainable Development Goals. The next section reviews the academic and policy literature with a view to articulating gaps and openings that shape the conceptual and analytical contributions of this piece.

## 2. CONCEPTUAL FRAMEWORK: GREEN FINANCE AND TBL INTEGRATION

In their pursuit of an environmentally sustainable economic transformation, green finance and the Triple Bottom Line (TBL) combine to offer a comprehensive framework that guides investment decisions, institutional policies, and stakeholder actions (Eccles et al., 2014; Dell'Erba & Doronzo, 2023). This section thus sets the theoretical underpinning for green finance, traces the genesis and structure of the TBL framework, and further illustrates how the integration of the two abreast with the SDGs, particularly with SDGs 7, 8, and 13 (Sachs et al., 2019; HLEG, 2018).

### 2.1 Green Finance: A Theoretical Foundation

Green finance (See Figure 1) is associated with the financing of investments, which, in effect, render environmental benefits within the broader context of sustainable development. Further, it encompasses a variety of financial instruments and mechanisms, such as green bonds, climate-focused venture capital, sustainability-linked loans, and ESG-compliant funds (Flammer, 2021; Martini, 2020). Essentially, green finance is a conscious shift in capital allocation strategies towards environmental health on a long-run basis, thereby joining economic returns (Kotsantonis et al., 2016; Ghosh & Dutta, 2023).

Key Components of Green Finance:

- **Environmental Integrity**: Investments must produce documentable, clear, and measurable benefits to environmental objectives such as climate change and emissions reduction, renewable energy deployment or construction, biodiversity protection and management, or waste management (Tietenberg & Lewis, 2023; Sra & Deo, 2024).
- **Risk Mitigation**: Green finance considers environmental risk scenarios in its pricing models and credit assessment. This requires more than just financial scenario testing; climate disclosures and climate-risk-based financial disclosures must also be assessed. There is the additional factor of nature-based risks as well (Awazu & Samama-Romain, 2020; De Silva Lokuwaduge & De Silva, 2022).
- **Sustainability Investment**: It can extend beyond being a "do no harm" model (Cornell & Damodaran, 2020) and possibly result in an outcome that can produce both social and environmental positive impacts (Boiral & Heras-Saizarbitoria, 2020).

*Figure 1. Green Finance Framework*

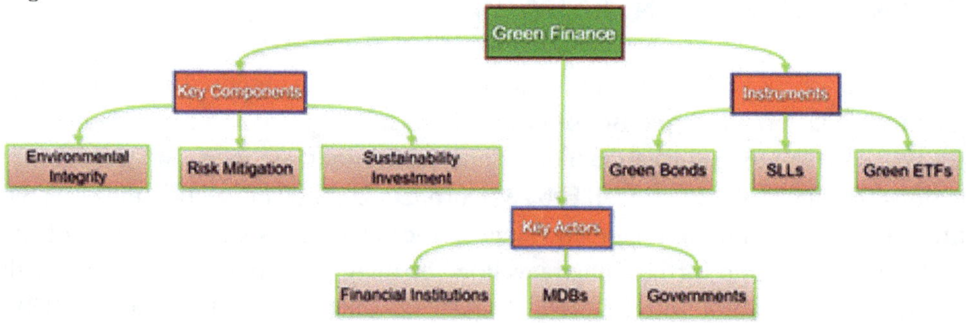


*Source: Author's Work*

Key Actors:

- **Financial Institutions**: In addition to policy-driven incentives, financial institutions (including banks, insurers, and asset managers) are increasingly implementing some level of green standards in their underwriting through lending and asset management (Weber, 2017; Shroff-Mehta et al., 2024).

- **Multilateral Development Banks (MDBs)**: To the extent that Multilateral Development Banks such as the World Bank, Asian Development Bank, or African Development Bank have a role in green infrastructure capital, their ability to issue guarantees by MDBs to de-risk their green investments to emerging markets dented some form of critical and catalytic player in the provision of green infrastructure capital (Galindo-Gutiérrez, 2024; Inderst et al., 2012).
- **Regulators and Governments:** Regulation and governments create famous ecosystem enablers (e.g., taxonomies, green standards, green bonds, and carbon price frameworks that create operational incentives) (HLEG, 2018; Martini, 2020).

### Instruments in Green Finance

In 2023, the global green bond market surpassed USD 2 trillion in total cumulative issuance (Flammer, 2021; Hadaś-Dyduch et al., 2022). Green Bonds represent debt securities raised to fund environmental activity. Sustainability-Linked Loans (SLLs) are loans that will incentivize the borrowers to do so by meeting their respective performance objectives based on ESG requirements (Cornell & Damodaran, 2020; Ghosh & Dutta, 2023). There can be no reasonable restrictions to the quantity and kinds of green financing products that attempt to benefit from a quickly growing market and rising interest in sustainable financing commodities (Renneboog et al., 2008; Clark et al., 2015) since Green Mutual Funds and ETFs are made to invest in companies that influence the environment positively or have sustainable business strategies. An indicator of systemic change in financing is the orientation towards sustainability financing due to integrating the concepts of risks, returns, and the real-world outcomes (Kotsantonis et al., 2016; Dell'Erba & Doronzo, 2023).

## 2.2 The Triple Bottom Line (TBL) Theory

The concept of triple bottom line, coined by John Elkington in the year 1994, has been disruptive in thinking about corporate performance (Elkington & Rowlands, 1999). According to this framework, people, planet, and profit are the aspects that businesses should consider, not only attempts to gain profits but also with the floors of social rights and environmental safety (Khan et al., 2016; Bocken et al., 2014).

## The Three Pillars of TBL

1. **People (Social Dimension):** The social dimension is focused on human well-being, labor rights, community involvement, and diversity/equity/inclusivity. This dimension also requires organizations and financial institutions to consider their effects on employees' well-being, clients' outcomes, and overall well-being in society (Malik et al., 2022; Malik & Sharma, 2025).
2. **Planet (Environmental Dimension):** The environmental pillar focuses on environmental stewardship via the sustainable use of resources and minimal ecological impact, maintenance of biodiversity, and adoption of new ecosystems (Tietenberg & Lewis, 2023; Skea et al., 2021).
3. **Profit (Economic Dimension):** Whereas the need to remain profitable should be an absolute priority, this dimension implies that the money-making strategy should focus on long-term economic sustainability as regards prudent risks, innovative practices, and development of enduring value to workers, stakeholders, and consumers (Eccles et al., 2014; Wang et al., 2023).

## TBL in Practice

The TBL model has eventually led to sustainability reporting guidelines, corporate social responsibility models, and ESG factors in investment decision-making (Boiral & Heras-Saizarbitoria, 2020; De Silva Lokuwaduge & De Silva, 2022). It is well-complemented by:

- **Circular Economy Models:** Reducing resource usage while maximizing recycling and reuse across production and consumption pathways (Pucker, 2021; Kathane et al., 2024).
- **Stakeholder Capitalism:** Realizing that value creation is not just for shareholders but also customers, employees, communities, governments, environmental systems, and more (Kotsantonis et al., 2016; Shroff-Mehta et al., 2024).

TBL seriously disrupts how we choose to measure success and introduces accountability systems that reward inclusive and regenerative economic development strategies (Jeucken, 2010; Zadek & Flynn, 2013).

## 2.3 Alignment of TBL and SDGs through Green Finance

The incorporation of the Triple Bottom Line (TBL) framework in conjunction with green finance, shown in Table 1, allows financial instruments to correspond with direct contributions to certain Sustainable Development Goals (SDGs):

- **SDG 7 (Affordable and Clean Energy):** The green finance sector can enhance investment in renewable energy projects, rural electrification, and clean cooking devices by developing innovative sourcing instruments such as solar bonds, energy efficiency loans, and blended finance (Yadav et al., 2024; Inderst et al., 2012).
- **SDG 8 (Decent Work and Economic Growth):** Green finance is currently having, and will continue to have, a significant impact in terms of stimulating sustainable industries and generating green jobs mainly through focused investments into the energy transition and climate-resilient agriculture, creating jobs, links, economic resilience, and innovation (Clark et al., 2015; Malik & Sharma, 2025).
- **SDG 13 (Climate Action):** Green finance can drive growth in sustainable industries and create decent jobs, and contribute to sustainable economic growth, by directing investment toward energy transition activities and climate-smart agriculture practices, which lead to job creation, economic resilience, and new technology (Clark et al., 2015; Malik & Sharma, 2025).

*Table 1. Mapping TBL to SDGs:*

| TBL Dimension | Relevant SDGs | Green Finance Interventions |
|---|---|---|
| People | SDG 1, 5, 8, 10 | Microfinance, inclusive lending, green jobs, and rural credit |
| Planet | SDG 6, 7, 13, 15 | Green bonds, climate funds, carbon markets, and reforestation |
| Profit | SDG 8, 9, 12 | ESG investing, impact funds, innovation finance |

Source – Author's work

### Climate-Resilient and Inclusive Economies

Green finance has a principal role in the effort at developing climate-adaptive and socially inclusive economies, using the TBL framework as a vehicle the TBL framework (Sachs et al., 2019; Khan et al., 2016).

Notable examples include:

- Investing in off-grid solar installations, which reduce emissions and increase access to electricity for remote communities, which then helps to improve education and health (Yadav et al., 2024; Inderst et al., 2012).
- Funding sustainable agriculture relates to smallholder finance, but also helps smallholders expose themselves to eco-friendly practices, which helps ensure food security and improves rural livelihoods (Nguyen & Khominich, 2023; Ghosh & Dutta, 2023).
- Green municipal bonds can help sustainability infrastructure (flood resiliency, water treatment plants, transit low emissions) in cities and result in better ecological resiliency and quality of life (Flammer, 2021; Hadaś-Dyduch et al., 2022).

These are examples that illustrate the potential of green finance to create shared value using TBL frameworks, as it is no longer being measured just by profit margin but also by measurable ecosystem services, community well-being, and intergenerational equity (Elkington & Rowlands, 1999; Bocken et al., 2014).

Although green finance allows putting capital in a strategic position to achieve sustainable results, the Triple Bottom Line model highlights one important point among them: environmental sustainability alone is not enough. Sustainable development would require a balance between three interdependent aspects, namely, environmental protection, economic viability, and social responsibility (Jeucken, 2010; Malik and Sharma, 2025). The two complementary strategies create a strong structure when reimagining financial systems as systems producing collective economic wealth and acting as custodians of environmental sustainability (Eccles et al., 2014; Dell'Erba and Doronzo, 2023).Green finance and TBL frameworks theoretically come together to provide a fantastic scaffold for sustainable development (Kotsantonis et al., 2016; Kathane et al., 2024).

In this chapter, case studies will be examined and evaluated using this integrated conceptual framework to understand the extent to which green finance is contributing to achieving the 2030 Agenda for Sustainable Development.

## 3. LITERATURE REVIEW

The obligations of law and policy make the pending transition to sustainable financial systems an enforcer behind a burgeoning research literature on green finance, operation of the Triple Bottom Line, and in conformity with the Sustainable Development Goals (Sachs et al., 2019; De Silva Lokuwaduge & De Silva, 2022). This section attempts to maintain an introspective perspective on how the academic, policy, and institutional environment has fostered the evolution of these themes.

## 3.1 Evolution of Green Finance in Scholarly Discourse

The early literature on green finance was mainly concerned with environmental externalities and the associated market failures arising from issues such as pollution, resource depletion, and ecosystem degradation (Tietenberg & Lewis, 2023). These issues found their expression mainly in the "polluter pays" principle and the full internalization of environmental costs into market mechanisms. Initially, green finance was therefore looked upon by scholars and policy thinkers as some sort of occasional corrective mechanism to align private interests with public environmental goals (Jeucken, 2010).

With the growth of the discourse, green finance came to be linked with the broader sustainability paradigms. The advent of corporate social responsibility and sustainable development frameworks brought about a gradual dislocationist thought between environmental protection and social equity, and the long-term stabilization of the economy (Khan et al., 2016; Malik & Sharma, 2025). Subsequently, financial scholars started developing market mechanisms that reward environmentally responsible behavior and mechanisms that allow green investments to compete in rate of return (Kotsantonis et al., 2016; Clark et al., 2015).

Following the worldwide financial crisis, a definite literature shift did occur towards issues of risk and resilience. Green Finance then transmuted to mean as much the restoration of the environment as risk reduction in an unstable global economy (Flammer, 2021; Awazu & Samama-Romain, 2020). This heralded the prominence of instruments such as green bonds, sustainability-linked loans, and ESG-oriented asset classes (Hadaś-Dyduch et al., 2022; Weber, 2017). This opened a greater scope for scholarly research with topics that include matters of fiduciary duty, regulatory incentives, disclosure practices concerning climate issues, and the role of institutional investors (Dell'Erba & Doronzo, 2023; Boiral & Heras-Saizarbitoria, 2020).

Modern research studies continue to unravel how green finance can be systemically integrated into mainstream economic systems. It includes tampering with taxonomies, green rating schemes, and factoring environmental performance into central banking policy (HLEG, 2018; Martini, 2020). Discussions have consequently widened to include digital finance issues on how fintech, blockchain, and AI will support transparency, traceability, and access in green finance (Ghosh & Dutta, 2023; Shroff-Mehta et al., 2024).

## 3.2 The Triple Bottom Line (TBL) in Financial Literature

The Triple Bottom Line framework generated a very important evolutionary window in the conceptualization of organizational success. The concept was first proposed as a sort of heresy to the conventional capitalism-based sole measure of firm performance (Elkington & Rowlands, 1999). Therefore, it was embraced in academe and business alike as a more ethical and comprehensive performance measure (Bocken et al., 2014).

Such early literature primarily deals with theoretical arguments concerning the legitimacy and measurement of social and environmental ends. Scholars considered whether social value could be quantified; whether the environment is relevant to, or in conflict with, financial ends; and to what extent TBL can be or ought to be integrated within the traditional business paradigm (Cornell & Damodaran, 2020; Khan et al., 2016). The trade-offs between the three pillars, i.e., people, planet, and profit, seemed to be a recurring theme (Malik & Sharma, 2025).

Consequently, with the coming of defined empirical research, several studies highlighted that there exists a positive relationship between managers employing a triple bottom line approach and firm performance. It was shown that sustainability practices provided companies with a reputation benefit along with operational efficiencies, resilience from the fine-tuning of loyal consumers, and long-term investors' interest (Eccles et al., 2014; Wang et al., 2023). The financial literature gradually ceased to conceive of TBL as an expense and began to consider it as a strategic resource (Clark et al., 2015).

Yet, the criticisms were still doled out against the model. Some scholars argued that TBL was never clear in its measurements and thus could be adopted only superficially or even for greenwashing (De Silva Lokuwaduge & De Silva, 2022; Pucker, 2021). Others would find the application of TBL inconsistent across industries and countries, and within the world of finance, issues would remain about whether principles of sustainability could be scaled up in capital markets and whether ESG could be integrated realistically (Renneboog et al., 2008; Dell'Erba & Doronzo, 2023).

Despite such critiques, the TBL framework has made an impact on how sustainability reporting frameworks, non-financial disclosures, and integrated reporting standards are structured today (Boiral & Heras-Saizarbitoria, 2020; Sra & Deo, 2024). With responsible investment practices now well entrenched, the Triple Bottom Line has established itself as a baseline assessment basis for green finance initiatives attempting to achieve environmental, economic, and social goals (Kathane et al., 2024; Jeucken, 2010).

The practical application of the TBL framework in green finance is deeply conditioned by institutional and regulatory arrangements that define the boundaries of sustainable practice. Thus, green finance closely depends on how such practices evolve and how governance structures and regulatory frameworks shape them.

### 3.2.1 Theoretical Foundations for Green Finance and TBL

While a large portion of the literature has been focused on the operationalization of TBL and green finance, there is potential to deepen our conceptualization by placing green finance in relation to larger theories. The theory of ecological modernization posits environmental purposes can fit into the economy through innovation, regulation, and institutional change; in this theory, green finance can function as corrective, and enable change (ecological) within modern institutions as a feature of capitalism. On the other hand, the socio-technical transitions theory (Geels, 2002) draws attention to the systemic, multi-level nature of change and emphasizes that financial instruments are only one element of an impending transition involving technology, policy (or governance more broadly), markets, and social practices.

On the one hand, and in connection with the presuppositions of the stakeholder theory, it is noted that there is a relationship between companies, communities, financial systems, as well as ecosystems, and that the decisions taken financially must benefit different actors (Freeman & Phillips, 2002). Institutional theory supplements this observation by showing the impact of financial behavior decision-making making to "rules, norms and governance structures" (Scott, 2005). These theories integrate the critique of green finance and move beyond the accounts of its description. Most importantly, these theories shed light on the imbalance between ecological modernization's hopeful perspective on solutions that cost nothing and can bring multiple benefits, and the political economy theories that speak of greenwashing, capture, and unequal capital (Jackson, 2017). In relation to the TBL theory, the use of these theoretical arguments improves its critique and defines the theory in relation to other academic debates.

## 3.3 Institutional and Regulatory Approaches

The growth of green finance cannot take place in a contextual vacuum but must be viewed against home country institutional and regulatory measures that influence green finance. Regulations provide the definitional clarity and market legitimacy needed to help make sustainable finance mainstream. At a supranational level, regulations and standards such as the EU Green Taxonomy have been promising in facilitating the standardisation of classifications of sustainable economic activities and alleviating concerns of greenwashing by providing a legally binding classification for capital seekers to use in the event execution of investments (European Commission 2020, p.3). The OECD, to provide the public with another comprehensive starting point, developed some Guidelines for Sustainable Finance (OECD 2019) and stressed that the establishment of common reporting frameworks and disclosure regimes could improve trust between participants in the same sustainable financial markets.

At the national level, emerging economies have also developed frameworks to give investors some confidence that financial activities are directed towards long-term sustainability goals. For example, the Securities and Exchange Board of India (SEBI) guided the concept of issuing green bonds, and provided much-needed procedural specifics that could drive and steer the growth of a sustainable debt market in India, (SEBI 2017). Institutional measures de-risk reputational and financial risks and indicate to potential capital seekers their respective country's long-term commitment to some aspects of sustainability.

From a theoretical standpoint, institutional theory provides the opportunity to explain the meanings inherent to these developments. As Scott (2005) suggests, institutions provide organizational behavior guidance by offering regulatory, normative, and cognitive frameworks through which actors act. Regulatory processes concerning green finance are, amongst others, institutional "rules of the game," and through these regulatory frameworks actors are required, or heavily influenced, to make environmentally and/or socially responsible investment choices and corporate decisions. Institutional and regulatory mechanisms are not a footnote, but rather an undeniable part of how green finance systems emerging in particular territorial and industrial domains progress, and help us frame how they interact with existing systems of finance.

In addition to international taxonomies and regulatory frameworks, the geographic/territorial dimension of governance has come to be the focus of researchers as publicity is slowly being developed to inform citizens of this strand of governance. Examples of regional and municipal governance mechanisms include the EU Green Deal's cohesion policy, the C40 Cities Finance Facility, and municipal funds for climate adaptation. These structures of governance exemplify how financial regulation and policy engage with territorial actions that lead to different, and often disparate, outcomes depending on local resources, coalitions, and policy conditions. The practice of territorial governance reinforces the potential for green finance to result in practices of circular economies located in community-level transitions that utilize broad local inclusion, instead of being treated primarily as a national or corporate concern.

## 3.4 Linking Green Finance to the SDGs

The onset of the Sustainable Development Goals in 2015 was nothing short of a sundering of the landscape for sustainability-oriented financial research (Sachs et al., 2019). Thereafter, scholars began framing finance not only as a vector for economic growth but also as an instrument to achieve global development objectives (Yadav et al., 2024).

The SDGs brought forth a common language toward aligning capital allocation with inclusive and environmentally sound outcomes. The literature points to the necessity of green finance being an enabler across SDGs, and green finance instruments have been the subject of research as a potential contributor to renewable energy scale-up (SDG 7), employment and economic inclusion (SDG 8), and climate resilience (SDG 13) (Inderst et al., 2012; HLEG, 2018).

In addition, researchers are examining the degree to which the design, regulation, and implementation of green finance instruments affect access and outcomes (Flammer, 2021; Ghosh & Dutta, 2023).

The scholarly literature has focused particularly on multilateral institutions and their ability to fund SDG-related projects. Authors have examined the feasibility of climate funds and concessional financing models as well as the relevance and effectiveness of public-private partnerships (Galindo-Gutiérrez, 2024; Zadek & Flynn, 2013). A parallel corpus of literature examines national financing instruments, including green taxonomies, green budgets, and sovereign green bonds (Martini, 2020; Awazu & Samama-Romain, 2020).

The other main areas of research deal with the integration of SDGs into the private finance sector. This also includes analyses at the level of institutional investors, banks, and corporations of the embedding of SDG criteria into their decision-making processes (Clark et al., 2015; Malik et al., 2022). Researchers hence are looking into ways of measuring impact, investigating the use of sustainability indices, and alignment mechanisms that map financial flows to SDG targets (Dell'Erba & Doronzo, 2023; Wang et al., 2023).

The literature emphasizes the complexity of financing projects that fit the SDGs, in part, because sustainable development is complex and multi-dimensional (Nguyen & Khominich, 2023). Still, the literature does recognize that green finance—potentially including the TBL framework—has great promise to act as an accelerant for attaining these global development objectives (Kotsantonis et al., 2016; Khan et al., 2016).

## 3.5 Thematic Insights

As green finance and TBL principles mature, several cross-cutting themes (Fig. 2) have emerged in the literature.

### Greenwashing

One topic of concern in both the academic and practitioner literature is greenwashing. The literature documents how companies and financial institutions can overstate the sustainability credentials of their projects or investment products, and the overall lack of standardized definitions and measurable metrics means that the risk of greenwashing remains high (Pucker, 2021; De Silva Lokuwaduge & De Silva, 2022). Experts are investigating methods of greenwashing detection and mitigation even more, particularly through third-party assurance, independent rating agencies, and rule-making (Boiral & Heras-Saizarbitoria, 2020; Dell'Erba & Doronzo, 2023).

## Access and Equity

Various studies and literature are addressing the distributional implications of green finance in terms of access and equity. Although there is a lot of capital moving into sustainable activities, access to this capital is still unevenly distributed (often depending on whether the firm is a micro, small, and medium-size enterprise (MSME), or located in rural areas, etc.), and many groups (including women and racialized communities) have earned little capital (Malik et al., 2022; Malik & Sharma, 2025). There is a body of research, and local research, looking at the structural and institutional constraints that the research is referring to, and clarifying that focused policy and innovations (e.g., microfinance, community investment, gender responsive financial products) can allow for more accessible financial opportunities for individuals (Shroff-Mehta et al., 2024; Ghosh & Dutta, 2023).

## Metrics and Measurability

Measurement is an enduring issue with green finance. The lack of harmonized indicators that collect and measure environmental, social, and economic outcomes is recognised in the literature as a challenge (Kotsantonis et al., 2016; Khan et al., 2016). Many ESG metrics exist but differ, and vary significantly in type, methodology, and scope. Lack of similarity and comparability results in lower confidence among investors and accountability. Furthermore, the literature has evidenced, and has demanded, greater standardization, disclosure, and utilization of quantitative as well as qualitative indicators (Sra & Deo, 2024; Boiral & Heras-Saizarbitoria, 2020).

*Figure 2. Themes of Green Finance*

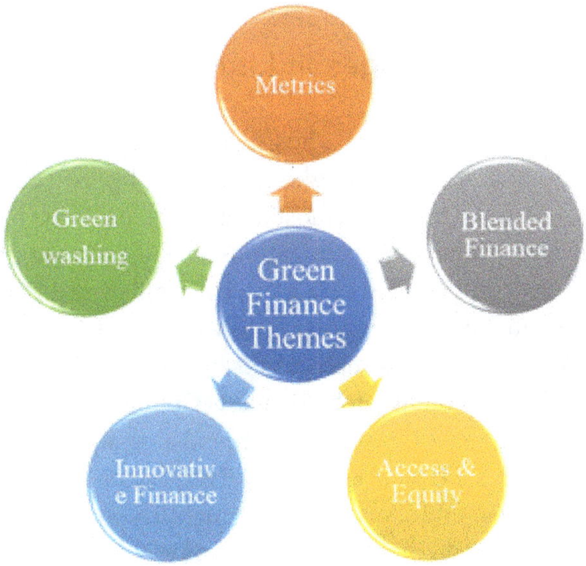


*Source- Author's Work*

## Innovative Finance

New studies explore the use of financial innovation in increasing the reach and effectiveness of green finance. These subjects include carbon trading systems powered by blockchain, risk assessment systems powered by artificial intelligence, and microfinance focused on the environment, but using mobile banking (Shroff-Mehta et al., 2024; Ghosh and Dutta, 2023). It is acknowledged that these technological breakthroughs have become the key to the reduction of transaction costs, increase of data visibility, and expansion of financial services to attention-deficit groups (Dell'Erba & Doronzo, 2023; Martini, 2020).

## Blended Finance

Researchers examine the strategic application of philanthropic and public capital to leverage private investment in sustainable development. Blended finance structures are examined to de-risk green projects and enhance their bankability (Zadek & Flynn, 2013; HLEG, 2018). The literature assesses the performance of such instruments in delivering environmental and social impact without sacrificing financial returns (Clark et al., 2015; Flammer, 2021).

## 3.6 Green Finance: Challenges in Literature

On one hand, the literature reflects a positive outlook about the future of green finance; on the other hand, it also highlights a number of persistent challenges that also limit its full realization. One of the most notable issues is that of greenwashing, when companies or even financial organizations lose their representation of their engagements to the environment and care areas by simply making superficial marketing statements and not taking any actual action to change the nature of what they do. As a result, market integrity is compromised and information asymmetries arise that diminish the willingness of investors to invest (Delmas & Burban, 2011). When standards and disclosure requirements are not pre-existing and universally accepted, institutions inevitably fall back on fragmented, divergent practices in meaningfully reducing carbon emissions, and the consequent inability to comparably assess the performance of initiatives reducing GHG emissions across geographical locations and sectors exacerbates the challenge.

Another theme speaks directly to measurement and data gaps. Measurement implies a variety of approaches for determining environmental performance. Although there exist many forms for assessing environmental performance as it applies to finance, the distinction is not limited to the ability to measure the overarching gamut of economic, social, and environmental consequences, or aspects of each. Importantly, because there is no standardized form, the existence of a contradictory tension also exists between shared compliance in name only to avoid sceptics and return only profitable outcomes or environmentally advantageous outcomes that also count as beneficial changes made by commitment to sustainability.

Whatever the structural limitations of the different areas of literature on green finance, it remains an open inquiry on several fronts, with less work attending to equity and inclusiveness. Most literature focuses on environmental as well as financial aspects of green finance, and little assessment of social responsibilities such as labour rights and practices, community resilience, and distributive or procedural justice. Thus, green finance will ultimately have beneficial/sustainable outcomes to the extent of redressing capitalistic projects, returning profit and environmental limb, and addressing (notably, that social considerations are included).

These issues are undoubtedly well-recognized, but the academic discourse has not addressed them systematically. This means there are several research questions that need more scrutiny, both to resolve fundamental issues and to improve the aspects of green finance that functionally matter.

## 3.7 Gaps in Existing Research

The review of the literature explored progress in the understanding of green finance, but there are still gaps that limit theoretical clarity and practical relevance. First, while green finance has been extensively discussed with environmental and economic performance in mind, the social dimension of the Triple Bottom Line is underrepresented. Themes of labour transition, distributive justice, and equity are often absent or limited in review when it is considered how finance could facilitate truly sustainable development across triple dimensions.

Second, as regulatory approaches such as the European Union's Green taxonomy, OECD guidelines, and India's SEBI green bond processes are starting to structure the field, the academic literature has moved modestly with respect to addressing the institutional and regulatory contexts in which it is developing. If the author has to integrate literature on institutional pressures, regulatory and governance models, it would be better positioned to assess how market regulation and governance are influencing organizational behaviour in particular territorial contexts.

Third, the literature on green finance continues to face measurement and methodological issues. Few standardized frameworks exist to assess social, environmental, and economic outcomes, and this leads to fragmented approaches and a challenge to evaluate impact and, subsequently, intensified risk of greenwashing as well as undermining the credibility and quality of sustainable/green financial instruments.

In the same vein, the empirical documentation shows a striking regional bias. There is a greater focus on developed countries while the Global South is almost ignored, as the Global South's regions' sustainable finance is barely represented in the debate. Emerging and developing markets are underrepresented in empirical research, limiting understanding of how structural and financial constraints and local governance models impact the uptake of green finance in those countries.

When combined, the identified gaps necessitate research attention that can be anchored in stakeholder and institutional theories, conducted in a range of environments, and attentive to socio-cultural and equity issues. Overcoming these limitations will be essential in advancing the green finance scholarship as well as its practical impact in facilitating a just and sustainable transition.

# 4. METHODOLOGY

This paper takes a qualitative study, an exploratory-descriptive research design, to look at the association between green finance and the Triple Bottom Line (TBL) framework. It employs a theoretical perspective of sustainable finance, which appreciates its changing definitions, international contextual differences, and complex effects. The analysis is not intended to measure results but to develop a detailed picture of how the environmental, economic, and social pillars may be integrated into the financial systems.

The secondary sources were fully used as data and they included peer-reviewed academic articles, policy reports of the organizations such as UN, World Bank and OECD, industry reports, the NGO reporting as well as real life case studies. These include sources in different fields (e.g. energy, agriculture, housing), in financial instruments (e.g. green bonds, ESG investing, microfinance) and regions of the world (Asia, Africa, Latin America).

Although chosen case studies were not created to be replicated, they were specifically selected to exemplify best practices and organizational issues. We applied thematic analysis to sort out results under the three pillars of the TBL, that is, Profit, Planet, People, and again divided into sub-themes, including job creation, emission reduction, gender equity, and financial inclusion. Triangulation between the literature sources contributed to the increase in the validity of findings, whereas comparative and systems thinking methods were used to examine the cross-sectoral dynamics and/or long-term effects.

Even though the research does not involve primary data and it is restricted to the conceptualization which is supported by examples, it is quite appropriate due to the scope of the conceptual and example-based research to frame an all-sided vision of the nature in which green finance can be the Hallmark of the TBL framework with its economic, ecological and social stock.

## 5. PROFITABILITY: ECONOMIC VIABILITY OF GREEN FINANCE

The belief that green finance, being compassionate towards nature, is conducted at the expense of real financial returns is instead being challenged. The markets and ever-growing empirical evidence suggest that. Now considered by investors, corporates, and governments as investments meant to endure and generate returns for the long run, they are no longer viewed as a trade-off but as an opportunity (Clark et al., 2015; Khan et al., 2016). This section discusses green finance from an economic point of view, particularly profitability, green bond performance, macroeconomic considerations, and corporate approach to environmental, social, and governance (ESG) issues.

### 5.1 Myth vs. Reality: Return on Sustainable Investment

Sustainable investing was believed to bring about sub-par returns; even today, certain site manuals float authoritatively in that perception. Data from the global financial markets has slowly proven the contrary (Renneboog et al., 2008; Cornell & Damodaran, 2020). Green financial products are fast gaining ground, competing with or even surpassing the best of their conventional counterparts. Sustainable investments generally perform well in the long run as they are less exposed to the problems triggered by regulatory, reputational, or environmental risks (Kotsantonis et al., 2016; Wang et al., 2023).

In reality, the risk-adjusted return profiles of green investments have been observed to show more resilience, particularly during periods of economic turbulence. For instance, companies that take proactive steps in managing climate risks and observe ESG conformity tend to be less susceptible to shocks arising out of supply-chain disruptions, regulatory fines, consumer sentiment changes, etc. (Eccles et al., 2014; Weber, 2017). They also tend to attract investors who are in it for long-term value creation rather than short-term speculative gains (Clark et al., 2015).

Also, investors are now taking climate risk increasingly seriously within their decision-making frameworks. This change in orientation fosters financial innovation, creates newer possibilities for capital deployment in the sustainable sectors, and, in turn, exerts a positive feedback on green investments' performance and attractiveness (Shroff-Mehta et al., 2024; Ghosh & Dutta, 2023).

## 5.2 Green Bonds and Profitability

Green bonds are the vehicle par excellence of green finance, channeling billions every year into climate and sustainability programs (Flammer, 2021; Hadaś-Dyduch et al., 2022). In contrast to conventional bonds, these bonds are targeted at financing projects that generate some sort of environmental benefit, e.g., renewable energy, green buildings, and sustainable transport.

The growth of the green bond market has been exponential. Institutional investors are attracted not just by the ethical proposition but by consideration of their stability and performance (Clark et al., 2015; Boiral & Heras-Saizarbitoria, 2020). According to several studies and market analyses, green bonds tend to have less volatility, tighter spreads, and lower default rates vis-à-vis classical corporate bonds (Dell'Erba & Doronzo, 2023; Kotsantonis et al., 2016).

Case studies from different regions illustrate how green bonds can bolster financial and reputational performance. As an example, when a key state actor, especially a large, publicly-traded institution, emits green bonds to finance renewable infrastructure, the direct capital allocation to climate-oriented projects increases investor confidence, spurs market activity, and narrows pricing spreads. The result of this demand-related market mechanism is that US issuers can obtain the capital at a lower price, which enhances the market economic competitiveness of sustainable debt instruments (Yadav et al., 2024; Ghosh and Dutta, 2023).

More than that, this ecosystem of green bonds is supported by governments and regulatory authorities at the level of special tax breaks, profound issuance schemes, and market streamlining (HLEG, 2018; Martini, 2020).This reduces issuance costs and increases transparency, which in turn further builds investor trust and market performance (Inderst et al., 2012).

## 5.3 Impact on Job Creation and GDP Growth

Furthermore, while considering how to make green finance economically viable, one has to weigh the fact that, in the larger scheme of things, it contributes to the economy at a macro level. Job creation is one of the major avenues of impact. Investment in green technologies is highly labor-intensive, given that renewable energy, sustainable farming, and energy efficiency sectors provide tokenistic employment potential across skill levels (Nguyen & Khominich, 2023; Ghosh & Dutta, 2023).

Upon an analysis of relevant studies, the renewable power sector is found to generate more jobs per dollar invested than does the fossil fuel sector (Sachs et al., 2019; Yadav et al., 2024). Investment in solar power plants, wind farms, and energy retrofitting cuts emissions and, on the other hand, creates employment prospects in engineering, construction, maintenance, and technology development. These jobs are selling two local economic boundaries and thereby support local development, reducing pressure on economic migration (Malik & Sharma, 2025; Shroff-Mehta et al., 2024).

In addition, the multiplier impact of green finance sustains GDP growth. Capital formation in sustainable infrastructure has benefits radiating throughout the economy that spill over into supply chains, increase productivity, and foster innovation (Eccles et al., 2014; Khan et al., 2016). For example, green urban development projects set in motion job creation that improves the quality of life, diminishes health care costs, and enhances environmental resilience—all of which contribute to economic stability.

The other great economic advantage is lower long-term costs. By taking up sustainable technologies now, economies can avoid the higher costs a climate disaster would bring in the future—health costs resulting from pollution, plus those from scarce resources (Awazu & Samama-Romain, 2020; Tietenberg & Lewis, 2023). In this way, green finance contributes to fiscal sustainability by preempting crisis expenditures (Clark et al., 2015).

## 5.4 ESG Integration in Corporate Strategy

Over the recent years, ESG integration has been positioned as the modern form of corporate finance. Companies have transformed through this consideration: When weighing risks, measuring performance, and communicating with stakeholders, financial profitability is no longer seen in isolation but as part of a comprehensive framework defined under ethical governance, environmental compliance, and social responsibility (Kotsantonis et al., 2016; Malik & Sharma, 2025).

Research has shown that those that put ESG into practice tend to deliver better returns to shareholders and operate with a lower cost of capital than their peers (Clark et al., 2015; Khan et al., 2016). Increasingly, ESG compliance is being viewed as an indicator of good management and corporate governance. It says to investors that a company understands long-term threats and will manage such a threatening signal through a complex and changing landscape (Eccles et al., 2014; Wang et al., 2023).

Another outcome of ESG integration is financial resilience. Firms with strong environmental policies are less likely to be hit by, say, regulatory penalties, supply chain interruptions, or consumer boycotts (Weber, 2017; Ghosh & Dutta, 2023). On the same vein, better-governed companies with solid relationships and employee-engagement programs face less employee turnover, suffer fewer productivity lags, and encounter fewer reputational issues (Shroff-Mehta et al., 2024; Malik et al., 2022).

On the flip side, investors have also begun demanding more ESG accountability. Shareholder resolutions, proxy voting, and investor coalitions are demanding transparency relative to climate targets, diversity metrics, and ethical conduct (Dell'Erba & Doronzo, 2023; De Silva Lokuwaduge & De Silva, 2022). Therefore, a large number of companies began to publish integrated reports that report on both financial and non-financial performance in terms of sustainability, and most firms now based their disclosures on a framework, typically either Global Reporting Initiative or Sustainability Accounting Standards Board (Sra & Deo, 2024; Boiral and Heras-Saizarbitoria, 2020).

The connection between ESG and profitability will also be enhanced by the development of the client's profile of investors selling the stocks. Pension funds and sovereign wealth funds become institutional investors whose portfolio more and more aligns with ESG. Since their mandates are often long-term in orientation and focus more on intergenerational equity, they would perceive firms that adhere to ESG principles as more deserving of an inflow of capital and market valuation (Renneboog et al., 2008; Cornell & Damodaran, 2020).

Now, there is no question about profitability in green finance; it is a reality cemented with market data and strategic behavior. Sustainable investments yield competitive returns, incur lower risks, and promote long-term stability. Green bonds are proving profitable, companies with better ESG ratings substantially outshine their peers, and green sectors are big job creators, with the largest contribution to GDP (Flammer, 2021; Yadav et al., 2024).

As financial markets evolve further, the very emphasis placed on profitability must be shifted away from short-term gains alone and towards sustained value creation in all spheres: economic, social, and environmental (Elkington & Rowlands,

1999). If green finance is based on the triple bottom line, then it presents a robust and inclusive economic pathway that shall cater to humanity and the environment.

## 6. PLANET: ENVIRONMENTAL SUSTAINABILITY AND CLIMATE ACTION

The Triple Bottom Line framework on the environmental dimension is based on the concept of ecological balance, where the health and environmental stability of long-term planetary well-being are core factors of sustained development of an economy and social prosperity (Tietenberg and Lewis, 2023).Green finance is an effective tool to reduce climate change and restore biodiversity, and make the transition to sustainable use of resources possible (Sachs et al., 2019; Khan et al., 2016). This section examines the role that financial mechanisms are playing in serving environmental goals, including climate solutions, carbon markets, transition finance, and environmental impact measurement.

### 6.1 Financing Climate Solutions

To tackle the climate crisis, the mobilization of huge capital is needed to solve mitigation and adaptation. Green finance is central to shifting flows of resources towards climate-resilient infrastructure, renewable energy, sustainable agriculture, and nature-based solutions (Yadav et al., 2024; Inderst et al., 2012).

Not only are investments in low-carbon infrastructure essential to decarbonization, but they also offer long-term cost savings and environmental degradation reduction (Flammer, 2021; Awazu & Samama-Romain, 2020). Green finance mechanisms such as concessional loans, blended finance tools, municipal green bonds, etc., make the investment process possible (HLEG, 2018; Zadek and Flynn, 2013). Green energy is still one of the main beneficiaries of green financing. The utility-scale solar and wind power projects have become cheaper to finance with the decline in costs of technologies and government incentives for such projects (Martini, 2020; Ghosh & Dutta, 2023). Both independent power producers and national governments are embracing green bonds and climate funds to install clean energy systems that push back fossil-fuel dependence (Flammer, 2021; Skea et al., 2021).

Green finance also enhances nature-based solutions, such as afforestation, restoration of wetlands, sustainable land management, and others. These measures sequester carbon, water balances, and facilitate biodiversity, and provide a high payoff ecologically and economically (Tietenberg & Lewis, 2023; Sra & Deo, 2024).

Asia and African case studies show evidence of the effectiveness of climate funds in spurring national climate plans. This money goes to the community adaptation plans, preparedness system towards disasters, and climate-resistant infrastructure in the most vulnerable areas of the climate risks (Yadav et al., 2024; Sachs et al., 2019). Such financing allows a long-term sustainability of cities and rural areas by increasing resilience and decreasing vulnerability (Weber, 2017).

## 6.2 Carbon Markets and Financial Innovation

Carbon markets form an active nexus between finances and environmental regulation. These markets put a price on the carbon emitted, and there is an economic incentive to cut the carbon footprint of the emitter (Cornell & Damodaran, 2020; Malik & Sharma, 2025).

A good example is that cap-and-trade systems impose a cap on total emissions, and companies can trade emissions based on the extent to which they emit. The firms that minimize emissions act within the agreed cap can auction excess allowances and make a profit, and those that surpass the cap should either buy credits or pay fines. This market-based solution brings in innovation of low-carbon technology and promotes behavioral change (Sachs et al., 2019; HLEG, 2018).

The voluntary carbon trade has also been an accelerating growth, with corporations and individuals buying carbon credits to compensate for their emissions. Financial innovation, such as platforms enabled by blockchain technology to make credit creation and usage traceable and transparent are example of financial innovation in this field (Shroff-Mehta et al., 2024; Ghosh and Dutta, 2023). These platforms eliminate fraud, make verification easy, and create confidence between buyers and regulators (Dell'Erba & Doronzo, 2023).

The third new technology is a climate risk price. Those financial institutions are devising ways to measure the financial risk attributed to climate-related aspects, such as stranded asset, losses caused by extreme climatic weather, and regulatory liability and take them into account in credit rating, premiuming and valuing the portfolios (Awazu & Samama-Romain, 2020; Khan et al., 2016). Such manipulation of assets based on environmental performance will offer incentives to individual firms to be sustainable.

Fintech solutions are more easily helping maintain carbon neutrality. Through AI-based analytics and digital wallets, as well as mobile applications, consumers and investors can monitor and keep track of their carbon footprint and reduce it (Shroff-Mehta et al., 2024; Ghosh and Dutta, 2023). These are the tools of environmental finance that are democratic, those that promote both personal accountability and institutional action.

## 6.3 Transition Finance and Energy Shift

The movement towards a low-emission future and a carbon-intensive economy is a complicated process that has financial, technical, and even social aspects to it. Transition finance. The term transition finance can be defined as the financial flows that help industries and countries transition to sustainability gradually and credibly (Martini, 2020; Awazu & Samama-Romain, 2020).

Transition finance is especially applicable to the steel, cement, aviation, and oil and gas industries, among others, that have high emissions. Carbon neutrality is a huge technological and economic challenge to these industries. As opposed to divestment in general, the role of green finance is gradually changing to provide conditional subsidies to companies making long-term commitments to transition plans that are "scientifically credible" (Cornell & Damodaran, 2020; HLEG, 2018).

Financial institutions are coming up with just transition frameworks that will see no vulnerable communities left behind with the shift to the low-carbon economy. It involves retraining of the workers in the fossil-based area, related community projects, and protection against energy poverty during the transition period (Sachs et al., 2019; Shroff-Mehta et al., 2024).

More recent types of financial instruments are transition bonds, meant to support projects that can eliminate emissions in the firm, although not necessarily pure green (Yadav et al., 2024; Ghosh & Dutta, 2023). The instruments are especially relevant in new markets whose full transition to renewable energy is not yet possible, yet a significant decrease in emissions can be achieved.

Blended finance structures are also a major part of transition finance, as they create a lower risk element and encourage the attachment of private capital to the projects (Zadek & Flynn, 2013; Inderst et al., 2012). The first risk is absorbed or a guarantee given by the state-owned organizations, which motivates the individual investors to contribute to the effect and enhancement of infrastructure systems, fuel replacement technologies, and clean production technologies.

A nascent strand of literature empathetically discusses the financing of circular economy transitions that address resource-efficient, waste-reducing, and closed-loop systems of production and consumption beyond carbon mitigation. (Geissdoerfer et al., 2017). Green finance instruments like recycling bonds, eco-design innovation fund schemes, and investment in industrial symbiosis activities are being identified to drive circular business models. Circular economy finance seeks to help finance regenerative systems, not extractive systems, linking the Planet and Profit elements of the TBL, creating local employment, and potentially reducing reliance bias to material inputs. This fundamental shift in the view of the environmental pillar situates the circular economy transition regardless of the increase in climate mitigation, instead of more systemic resource management resilience that diversifies and builds long-term resilience for businesses of territorial economies.

## 6.4 Monitoring and Measuring Environmental Outcomes

The environmental outcome must be quantified to measure the finances of green financing and to make it accountable. Nevertheless, it is a complicated task to assess environmental impact because of a lack of enough data, differences in measuring methods, and regulatory disunity (Boiral & Heras-Saizarbitoria, 2020; Dell'Erba & Doronzo, 2023).

The commonly used measures are:

- **Avoided emissions:** Determines the quantity of emissions that have been forestalled via particular initiatives or interventions that reduce greenhouse gas emissions.
- **Carbon intensity:** How much carbon was released as compared to the output or revenue?
- **Biodiversity effect:** Indices like species richness, ecosystem connectivity, and an index on the restoration of habitats.
- **Water use efficiency:** Determination of water used per point of an output or service.

The range of satellite information, on-ground evaluation, external supplier audits, and computerized tracking can be required to monitor the environmental effects (Sra & Deo, 2024; Ghosh & Dutta, 2023). New technologies—remote sensing, drones, and machine learning—are also assisting in increasing the named frequency and quality of data collection (Shroff-Mehta et al., 2024; Tietenberg & Lewis, 2023).

Although this is advancing, data transparency and standardisation are key obstacles. The unanimity over standards of environmental impact also has its holes because the lack of such standards means that anyone can exaggerate or make false claims at the expense of the environment (De Silva Lokuwaduge & De Silva, 2022; Pucker, 2021). In response to this, several initiatives have been started globally to develop taxonomies, reporting frameworks, and verification protocols capable of achieving credibility in environmental finance (Martini, 2020; HLEG, 2018).

Green rating agencies and ESG data providers are also changing, and the newer types are issuing more sophisticated ratings that factor in indirect impacts in addition to direct impacts (Dell'Erba & Doronzo, 2023; Kotsantonis et al., 2016). These ratings are being increasingly used in investment analysis, credit decisions, and risk modeling by financial institutions (Weber, 2017; Wang et al., 2023).

Green finance mechanisms are causing meaningful activation when it comes to this environmental pillar of the Triple Bottom Line. Green finance is turning out to be a critical tool leading to environmental change since it can finance renewable energy and climate adaptation, among other things, to support carbon markets and transition pathways (Flammer, 2021; Sachs et al., 2019). Nevertheless, data systems need to be strengthened, impact measurement practices standardized, and equal access to climate finance encouraged in efforts to maximize the potential of this new resource.

With the heightening of the climate emergency, the significance of finance in the redemption of the degradation of the environment cannot be underrated. Once green financial transparency and integrity are provided, there is a good basis (environmental restoration, ecological management, and sustainable future) towards the planetary boundaries (Elkington and Rowlands 1999; Tietenberg and Lewis 2023).

## 7. PEOPLE: SOCIAL IMPACT AND INCLUSIVITY

Although quite a lot of green finance discussion has been paralleled into what happens environmentally and on economic sustainability grounds, the social dimension, which is represented by the People, is equally important (Elkington & Rowlands, 1999; Malik & Sharma, 2025). Financial systems have no right to say that they are sustainable when they do everything to include marginalized groups, promote inequality, or do not promote human well-being. This section will consider how green finance has an impact on employment, financial inclusion, and social equity, and how to make a difference in the real world.

### 7.1 Social Sustainability in Green Finance

Social sustainability emphasizes the capacity of financial systems to promote inclusivity, equality, and human well-being in the green transition. Financial institutions are increasingly expected to engage with not only environmental performance but also with social and ethical responsibilities (Khan et al., 2016; Kotsantonis et al., 2016).

Green finance mechanisms are causing meaningful activation when it comes to this environmental pillar of the Triple Bottom Line. Green finance is turning out to be a critical tool leading to environmental change since it can finance renewable energy and climate adaptation, among other things, to support carbon markets and transition pathways (Ghosh & Dutta, 2023; Sachs et al., 2019). Nevertheless, data systems need to be strengthened, impact measurement practices standardized, and equal access to climate finance encouraged in efforts to maximize the potential of this new resource (Dell'Erba & Doronzo, 2023; Sra & Deo, 2024).

With the heightening of the climate emergency, the significance of finance in the redemption of the degradation of the environment cannot be underrated. When transparency and integrity are ensured in green finance, this provides a strong ground for environmental restoration, ecological management, and a future that is considerate about the planetary limits (Pucker, 2021; De Silva Lokuwaduge & De Silva, 2022).

One important aspect of consideration in the social pillar is how labour transitions happen with the green shift. Coal, steel, and non-renewable energy-led industries, as they diminish, pose huge dislocation challenges for workers and communities. Scholars examining the "just transition" framework express the critical nature of assessing how to either mitigate or proactively plan into workers' lives, active re-training programming, income supports, and social dialogue to address and prevent new exclusionary inroads. Green finance could assist in this transition through funding training programs, community development funds, and skills retraining programs, all of which would help to integrate economic objectives with social objectives within the TBL.

Secondly, the gendered implications of green finance merit explicit attention. Studies illustrate how women entrepreneurs, informal workers, and rural households experience exclusion from the norms of the financial world by both formal and informal financial systems. If financial instruments were to include examples of gender-responsive issues, for example, providing microcredit financing for women-led green enterprises or guarantees or subsidies for women farmers adopting climate-adaptive technologies, green finance provides opportunities not just for environmental resilience, but also contributes to social equity, too(UN Women, 2021).

Finally, the idea of social resilience expands on the "People" pillar by looking at community organization and your willingness to adapt as a group or community when adapting to climate and market shocks. Providing inclusive financial products, governance by participatory processes, and encouraging local ownership of green infrastructure projects all serve to entwine finance with community capacity building in terms of resilience building.

## 7.2 Financial Inclusion through Green Products

One important impediment towards social equity is the lack of coverage of mainstream financial systems by the rural communities, the small-scale enterprises, and the informal workers (Malik et al., 2022; Ghosh & Dutta, 2023). The gap in meeting the needs of underserved communities can be closed by using green finance, which is designed inclusively to formulate products that can suit the needs of underserved communities.

Green microfinance is a good example of innovation that lends small amounts to individuals or cooperatives to use on green activities—buying solar panels, clean cookstoves, water-saving irrigation systems, or even biodegradable packaging materials (Shroff-Mehta et al., 2024; Yadav et al., 2024). Such loans do not only enable individuals to practice sustainability, but also enhance livelihoods and decrease living conditions of being at risk to environmental circumstances.

Another example would be community solar models, which include smaller-scale solar systems in a community that are owned or used by the entire community. These models allow self-sustaining and empower the community by lowering energy prices and improving access to quality electricity (Inderst et al., 2012; Zadek & Flynn, 2013).

The horizon of green financial services has been further extended due to the use of mobile banking and digital wallets. With the help of local cooperatives, fintech platforms are making it quite possible today that rural households have access to climate insurance, pay-as-you-go solar kits, or crowd-sourced loans to purchase sustainable agricultural inputs, all on the easy-to-use mobile interfaces (Ghosh & Dutta, 2023; Shroff-Mehta et al., 2024).

Democratization of green finance is therefore dependent on the process to design affordable, available, and culturally relevant products, and at the same time, developing financial literacy and technical capacity of local people (Malik & Sharma, 2025; Boiral & Heras-Saizarbitoria, 2020).

## 7.3 Equity and Environmental Justice

The central concept of the pillar of the people is equity. The key consideration of green finance should be who does the investment activities and who takes the risks (Malik & Sharma, 2025; Khan et al., 2016). Environmental justice insists that no group, least of all historically disadvantaged groups, should be disproportionately exposed to environmental damage or lose out in the move to sustainability (Cornell & Damodaran, 2020).

Frontline groups—people who live close to pollution-intensive areas or in vulnerable areas to climate change—are the most affected by these two factors. They live under the yoke of environmental destruction and economic marginalization in most areas and usually have no political capital or institutional frameworks to be involved in land use, development project decision-making, or environmental remediation (Sachs et al., 2019; Weber, 2017).

Green finance presents a chance to re-balance these imbalances through directing investments in inclusive infrastructure, decentralized energy supply, and ownership of community-based projects (Yadav et al., 2024; Zadek & Flynn, 2013). It also promotes partnerships between the public and the private sector, involving social safeguards, community consultations, and mechanisms for sharing benefits (HLEG, 2018; Inderst et al., 2012).

This, in practice, may involve investing in climate-resilient and affordable housing in coastal slums, sustainable mass transit that takes shantytown dwellers to workplaces in cities, or initiatives such as Indigenous-run eco-tourism (Shroff-Mehta et al., 2024; Sra & Deo, 2024). Such interventions are not only good as they improve the environmental outcome, but they also improve social cohesion and intergenerational justice (Elkington & Rowlands, 1999).

Equity is an international issue, too. Access to green finance has become severely North–South lopsided. The developing nations, which generate a minimal contribution to past emissions, are usually the most vulnerable to the effects of climate and the weakest to fund adaptation practices (Sachs et al., 2019; Malik & Sharma, 2025). Climate change can only be reasonably addressed in a truly fair green finance system where world imbalances are reduced through higher concessional flows, lower cost of borrowing of low-income countries, and honoring local knowledge in project planning (Galindo-Gutiérrez, 2024; Yadav et al., 2024).

## 7.4 Case Examples

Case studies present an idea of how green finance can be effectively used in the interests of serving the social agenda because it is embedded in inclusive patterns.

***The IDCOL Solar Home System Program of Bangladesh:*** This is an off-grid solar program that has become one of the most successful in the world and enjoys green finance provided by international development partners. The program has installed solar home systems for millions of people in the rural areas of Bangladesh, benefiting more than 20 million people (Sachs et al., 2019; Inderst et al., 2012). It has brought thousands of jobs from installation and maintenance, enhanced the quality of education by making evening studies possible due to the availability of electricity, and also eliminated the wasteful use of kerosene—enhancing health and safety. Notably, gender targets were set in the program and local entrepreneurs were involved a majority of whom are women.

***South African Just Energy Transition***: Green finance is also finding application in South Africa, where the country is dropping coal to fund retraining of workers, growth of new livelihoods, and expansion of clean energy in ex-coal towns. The government, together with international climate funds, has come up with structures to make sure that the displaced workers are not left in the back seat. The TBL is demonstrated through an all-inclusive approach encompassing both environmental, economic, and social desires (HLEG, 2018; Zadek & Flynn, 2013).

***Clean Cookstove Finance Initiatives in India***: In the Indian states where indoor air pollution is a major health concern, clean cookstoves have been introduced with the help of microfinance institutions that have tied with green technology producers to finance clean cookstoves among poor households (Ghosh & Dutta, 2023; Weber, 2017). Not only does it lessen the cases of respiratory diseases—especially among women and children—but also saves time and income, giving an added flow of productivity and school attendance. These projects set out the picture of how local green finance can result in huge social benefits (Boiral & Heras-Saizarbitoria, 2020; Malik & Sharma, 2025).

***Latin American Community Forestry Projects:*** Elsewhere, including Guatemala and Mexico, green finance has been channeled into Indigenous-led forestry cooperatives that are used to sustainably harvest the native forest resources and their sustainable management as a source of revenue. The models safeguard biodiversity, strengthen cultural heritage, and offer sustainable employment. Financial institutions have a facilitating role in availing credit lines, insurance products, as well as capacity-building grants towards these community enterprises.

The social pillar of the Triple Bottom Line requires that, in addition to its contribution to profit and restoration of the environment, finance should also contribute to human development (Elkington & Rowlands, 1999; Khan et al., 2016). Green finance has proved to create years of employment, minimize inequalities, and foster inclusive growth when carefully crafted to be people-oriented (Clark et al., 2015; Malik et al., 2022).

Inclusivity should not become an additional feature, though. It must be imbibed in the architecture of financial systems, which must be accessible equally, participatory governance, and the community at large. The future of green finance is in its ability to empower the frailest in the world, to mend economic disparities, and to make sure that sustainability is not a privilege, but everybody born with a right.

## 8. CHALLENGES AND LIMITATIONS

Although the green finance movement shows a strong potential and congruence with the Triple Bottom Line (TBL), multiple barriers are still holding it back. Such issues pertain to the nexus of regulating, measuring, accessibility, and frameworks of institutions. Otherwise, they can jeopardize the credibility, scale, and inclusiveness of green finance.

## 8.1 Greenwashing and Mislabeling

Another potential threat of greenwashing to green finance is that it removes an opportunity to misrepresent financial products to be environmentally friendly. This consists of such things as labeling unproven or controversial bonds as green, overstating ESG performance, or marketing projects with a marginally better climate impact as climate positive. This issue is exacerbated by the lack of uniformity in definition and variability in the way the ESG rating is compiled, which allows the disclosures to be selective. Regulation systems are poor and inconsistent in providing deterrence to such practices. Enhanced disclosure requirements, third-party validation, and enforcement are needed to fight greenwashing, or the hue and cry of green finance can be defeated, and the movement will not succeed in making the environment cleaner.

## 8.2 Impact Measurement Deficiency

The inability to quantify the effect of green finance on the environment, society, and economy is another major setback in this kind of finance. In contrast to the financial returns, the results of sustainability are multidimensional, complex, and often delayed. Although different reporting tools, such as ESG scores and climate disclosures, exist, the improvement in the quality of data is unequal and cannot be compared because there are no standardized tools. Most of the existing measurements do not pay attention to qualitative indicators like community well-being and ecosystem health, which are essential to the Triple Bottom Line (TBL) concept. This unreliable data is a loss to the confidence of the investors and the appropriateness of the climate funds. This should be handled with integrated reporting systems, a weaker data structure, independent oversight, and instantaneous analytics to increase credibility and impact measurement.

## 8.3 Accessibility and Affordability of Green Finance

While the sphere of green finance is expanding globally, it remains unevenly distributed, especially among small businesses, low-income populations, and developing countries. Numerous obstructions to green finance remain, including high transaction costs, cumbersome eligibility criteria, and work-perceived high risk. The MSMEs, in most cases, do not have credit backgrounds, securities, or technical skills to obtain a green loan or subsidies. The certification, reporting, and compliance costs are prohibitive even in circumstances where they are not compulsory. This creates a false impression that only midsize corporations and financially sound governments are capable of engaging in green capital markets. Green finance programmes, as a rule, pay no attention to the informal sectors that constitute quite an important part of most developing economies. Formal financial systems and these sectors tend to be pretty obscure, leaving lenders with dangerous exposure when such sectors could contribute to grassroots sustainability. There is also a difference between the Global North and the Global South. Though the number of ESG investments and green bonds is becoming exponentially higher in developed countries, in developing countries, people are usually dependent on donor funds and concession financing. Another disadvantage that has affected them is a low credit rating, currency risk, and low institutional capacity to coordinate and report on sustainability activities, which increases the difficulty of getting access to affordable green finance. Such hurdles can be overcome by investing in financial infrastructure to foster financial literacy, simplify application procedures, lower transaction costs, and subsidize impact-oriented lending. Additionally, access can be improved through innovative mechanisms like de-risking tools, blended finance, and results-based financing, which support underserved sectors and regions.

## 8.4 Institutional and Policy Gaps

Good implementation of green finance is being slowed by poor institutional coordination and a lack of uniformity across policies. In many more than enough countries, policy, finance, and economic plans are not tied together in this climate course of action leading to wastefulness.Even though central banks start to react to climate risks, green mandates are usually voluntary, and the financial community continues to be focused on making a profit in the short-term perspective. The lack of specific guidelines and intersectoral cooperation suffocates innovation in green finance, leading to fragmented work and some inhibition of the overall effect. The systems of donors are not usually geographically local and sustainable. The solution to these issues is that governments are forced to adopt national green finance policies, establish cross-sectoral working groups, and enshrine sustainability into the frameworks of publicly provided finance. To achieve a sustainable and fair world economy, green finance must cease being a pipe dream and adopt a more workable, transparent, and responsible regime that can be achieved only through political will, institutional transformation, and popular uprising.

When put together, greenwashing, weaknesses in measurements, accessibility, and disconnected policies are not separate obstacles, but instead issues that are interdependent and complementary. As an example, the lack of oversight and enforcement of regulation on greenwashing only further exacerbates the lack of accountability that relates to a lack of standardised metrics, which also leads to a trust deficit from investors looking for interconnected sustainability impacts that validate their funding. Additionally, discriminatory access to finance is reinforced with policy loopholes that advantage larger existing firms and developed economies. These complex linkages emphasise the need for as systemic and coherent reforms as possible, which, collectively, build a governance architecture for green finance markets, which improves transparency, provides equal access, and integrates ecological and social impacts for the long term. Otherwise, green finance as a systemic principle and practice will always continue to poorly translate into incremental and largely symbolic behavioural changes.

## 9. POLICY AND PRACTICAL IMPLICATIONS

A multi-stakeholder, multi-level strategy is what is needed to achieve a long-term, sustainable financing future that is centered on the TBL. The green finance ecosystem needs to be reinforced by policymakers, regulators, investors, businesses, academic institutions, and civil society.

### 9.1 Role of Policymakers and Regulators

Fiscal administrators and financial managers are also crucial to the creation of a conducive environment for green finance. They can increase transparency and minimize greenwashing by demanding ESG disclosures in the form of standardized reporting and thereby facilitate allocation of the capital to genuinely sustainable projects. The central banks can also further incorporate climate risks in monetary policies and stress testing, and also encourage low-carbon lending via amended capital requirements. Green taxonomies are important because they can clearly define sustainable activities and curb confusion in the market and cooperation in international investments. Also, the fiscal instruments, such as carbon pricing, green subsidies, and tax incentives, can shift the public and private finance in the direction of sustainability. As the leader of change, the involvement of public institutions in the top-down change encouraging (TBL) principles in budgeting, purchasing, and investing can be the driver to transform a system.

### 9.2 Enhancing the Green Finance Ecosystem

Expansion of a robust green finance environment must go beyond regulation; it should be innovative, collaborative, and inclusive. In this, de-risking sustainable investment by use of financial products such as guarantees, first-loss, and political risk insurance is crucial to the case in emerging markets. By absorbing the risk at an early stage, development finance institutions can generate some private investment. A strong solution that achieves impact and financial sustainability, especially in such spheres as renewable energy and climate adaptation, is blended finance using a combination of government (public), private, and philanthropic capital.

Fintech is changing the availability of green finance as it facilitates such models as crowdfunding, peer-to-peer lending, and impact investment platforms, establishing a connection between capital and green projects at the grassroots level. Mobile banking, satellite monitoring, and blockchain are the technologies that make an impact easier to track, cost less, and tend to be more transparent. In this regard, to enhance this ecosystem, governments and institutions should invest in education, training, and awareness, as this will ultimately provide all the stakeholders involved, including the investor and the community, with the knowledge and tools to participate and be involved in sustainable finance.

## 9.3 Corporate and Investor Engagement

Corporations and investors are responsible for aligning finance with the Triple Bottom Line. To do this, on the firm side, being sustainability-driven at the core of the strategy entails the whole picture, generally all with the understanding of gaining trust and reducing risks towards just forming sustainable profit for the company, such as sustainable procurement processes, energy efficiency, paying fair wages, community engagement, and so on. The TBL metrics also make their way into performance management, executive remuneration, and investor relations for enhanced accountability and funneling purpose-driven capital into the company.

On the investor side, the shift of capital toward ESG-compliant portfolios is the impetus behind impact investing. Institutional investors can set standards for sustainability and invest in green instruments while practicing shareholder activism to influence corporate conduct. Strengthening the stewardship code and demanding clear, third-party-verified impact disclosures will also help to end cases of greenwashing. International collaborative platforms—green finance hubs, sustainability indices, and industry alliances—support the sharing of knowledge, co-standardization, and the creation of a credible green investment pipeline as an accelerant for systemic change across financial markets.

## 9.4 Academic and Institutional Collaboration

Academic institutions as well as think tanks are critical to the growth of green finance by providing research, innovation, and talent development. Universities can integrate sustainability across all the disciplines and set up specialized programs in green finance, ESG analytics, and climate leadership to train the workforce of the future. Think tanks, on the other hand, assist in the development of policy experiments, taxonomies at the localized level, and in modeling financial approaches tailored to specific developmental needs.

Other than these roles, they foster cross-sector collaboration in an independent environment to carry out participative research infused with grassroots views and inclusive solutions. This will enable them to create standard measurements for TBL and serve as independent assessors against the act of greenwashing due to their expertise.

Finally, to have a green and inclusive economy, all the sectors need to operate in sync. Patronizing laws and fiscal instruments, financial services will need to reach more people and become creative; corporations will need to make sustainability a central theme; and investors will need to calibrate capital and lasting influence. Senating institutions provide the necessary foundation towards this transformation through building systems thinking, policy, and practice. Green finance can be regarded as one of the pillars of sustainable world progress when all stakeholders support the idea of the Triple Bottom Line.

## 9.5 Governance Models and Multi-stakeholder Coalitions

The effectiveness of green finance depends not just on instruments and regulatory change, but on the governance models of collective action. Research into sustainability transitions has shown that multidisciplinary coalitions involving government, private investors, civil society, and labour are instrumental in shaping the nature and legitimacy of green financial systems (Swilling et al., 2016). For example, the South African Just Energy Transition Partnership illustrates how international finance, domestic government policy, and the position of local labour unions may intersect to create socially inclusive decarbonization pathways. Similar to the European Green Deal, the Just Energy Transition Partnership highlights how regional and city-level collaboration and coalition building can help to structure finance within broader territorial development efforts.

Coalition-based governance has many advantages, not the least of which can avoid and mitigate conflicts of interest, distribute risk, and ensure that, as the finance model is implemented, additional voices are included who are often at the margins of decision-making. What is especially important is that coalition-based governance responds to the political nature of green finance and can incorporate distributive justice imperatives into investment decision-making. The goal is to refocus on the socio-political nature of sustainability transitions, which can ensure that coalition-based governance can strengthen the potential of green finance to fulfil the full promise of the Triple Bottom Line.

## 10. CONCLUSION

For the Triple Bottom Line (TBL) framework, green finance has mesmerized attention as "socially just" or morally inclined; however, its very core is in securing long-term profitability, ecological resilience, and social equity. This chapter exemplified how green finance instruments such as green bonds and other ESG-compliant investment tools have been providing steady returns while even supporting climate mitigation, resource efficiency, and inclusive development. When the case studies in Bangladesh, South Africa, India, and Latin America evidence TBL, then the financial system will promote innovation and raise the levels of the poor and, thereby, tackle systemic barriers arising out of inequality and energy poverty. Until then, to realize their full potential, green finance in the courts will have to demand continuous redress and stronger regulation regarding issues of greenwashing, data voids, and access inequity.

## 11. FUTURE SCOPE

Green finance can metamorphose in the coming days when a few things are to be set in place: setting clear yet verifiable standards for measurement vis-à-vis environmental and social outcomes; using modern technology to stay transparent and explicative; and inclusive financial products, which organizations can use to reach underserved communities. Equally, policy and regulatory interventions ought to be aligned cross-sectorally such that the sustainability agenda is endorsed for the long run. Research ought also to expand, especially in the Global South, to comprehend local needs while developing suitably contextualized financial models. The future of green finance lies in making the core architecture of finance sustainable, where profit, people, and planet cannot be competing priorities but interconnected, resilient development.

## REFERENCES


Awazu, P. B. M. D. L., & Samama-Romain, P. D. S. F. (2020). The green swan-central banking and financial stability in the age of climate change.

Bocken, N. M., Short, S. W., Rana, P., & Evans, S. (2014). A literature and practice review to develop sustainable business model archetypes. *Journal of Cleaner Production*, *65*, 42–56. DOI: 10.1016/j.jclepro.2013.11.039

Boiral, O., & Heras-Saizarbitoria, I. (2020). Sustainability reporting assurance: Creating stakeholder accountability through hyperreality? *Journal of Cleaner Production*, *243*, 118596. DOI: 10.1016/j.jclepro.2019.118596

Citaristi, I. (2022). United Nations Environment Programme—UNEP. In *The Europa directory of international organizations 2022* (pp. 193–199). Routledge. DOI: 10.4324/9781003292548-46

Clark, G. L., Feiner, A., & Viehs, M. (2015). From the stockholder to the stakeholder: How sustainability can drive financial outperformance. *Available at SSRN* 2508281.

Cornell, B., & Damodaran, A. (2020). *Valuing ESG: Doing good or sounding good?* NYU Stern School of Business.

De Silva Lokuwaduge, C. S., & De Silva, K. M. (2022). ESG risk disclosure and the risk of green washing. *Australasian Accounting. Business and Finance Journal*, *16*(1), 146–159.

Dell'Erba, M., & Doronzo, M. (2023). Sustainability gatekeepers: ESG ratings and data providers. *U. Pa. J. Bus. L.*, *25*, 355.

Eccles, R. G., Ioannou, I., & Serafeim, G. (2014). The impact of corporate sustainability on organizational processes and performance. *Management Science*, *60*(11), 2835–2857. DOI: 10.1287/mnsc.2014.1984

Elkington, J., & Rowlands, I. H. (1999). Cannibals with forks: The triple bottom line of 21st century business. *Alternatives Journal*, *25*(4), 42.

Flammer, C. (2021). Corporate green bonds. *Journal of Financial Economics*, *142*(2), 499–516. DOI: 10.1016/j.jfineco.2021.01.010

Freeman, R. E., & Phillips, R. A. (2002). Stakeholder theory: A libertarian defense. *Business Ethics Quarterly*, *12*(3), 331–349. DOI: 10.2307/3858020

Galindo-Gutiérrez, J. (2024). The World Bank and 'Maximizing Finance for Development': Talk the talk but not walk the walk. *Journal of International Relations and Development, 27*(4), 391–413. DOI: 10.1057/s41268-024-00333-6

Geels, F. W. (2002). Technological transitions as evolutionary reconfiguration processes: A multi-level perspective and a case-study. *Research Policy, 31*(8-9), 1257–1274. DOI: 10.1016/S0048-7333(02)00062-8

Geissdoerfer, M., Savaget, P., Bocken, N. M., & Hultink, E. J. (2017). The Circular Economy–A new sustainability paradigm? *Journal of Cleaner Production, 143*, 757–768. DOI: 10.1016/j.jclepro.2016.12.048

Ghosh, A., & Dutta, S. (2023). Green Finance–Integral Adaptation to Climate Change. *Perspectives in Sustainable Management Practices*, 42-51.

Hadaś-Dyduch, M., Puszer, B., Czech, M., & Cichy, J. (2022). Green bonds as an instrument for financing ecological investments in the V4 countries. *Sustainability (Basel), 14*(19), 12188. DOI: 10.3390/su141912188

HLEG. (2018). Financing a sustainable European economy. *Final Report.*

Inderst, G., Kaminker, C., & Stewart, F. (2012). Defining and measuring green investments.

Jeucken, M. (2010). *Sustainable finance and banking: The financial sector and the future of the planet*. Routledge. DOI: 10.4324/9781849776264

Kathane, S., Babu, N., & Ramesh, S. (2024). Conceptual Framework of Sustainability in Green Finance. *3D: IBA Journal of Management & Leadership, 15*(2).

Khan, M., Serafeim, G., & Yoon, A. (2016). Corporate sustainability: First evidence on materiality. *The Accounting Review, 91*(6), 1697–1724. DOI: 10.2308/accr-51383

Kotsantonis, S., Pinney, C., & Serafeim, G. (2016). ESG integration in investment management: Myths and realities. *The Bank of America Journal of Applied Corporate Finance, 28*(2), 10–16. DOI: 10.1111/jacf.12169

Malik, A. H., Jais, M. B., Md Isa, A. H., & Rehman, A. U. (2022). Role of social sustainability for financial inclusion and stability among Asian countries. *International Journal of Social Economics, 49*(9), 1324–1348. DOI: 10.1108/IJSE-08-2021-0458

Malik, K., & Sharma, S. (2025). Role of ESG and private equity on environmental degradation: A nexus of opportunity and responsibility for developing and developed countries. *Journal of Economic Studies (Glasgow, Scotland), 52*(3), 532–548. DOI: 10.1108/JES-11-2023-0672

Martini, M. (2020). Developing sustainable finance definitions and taxonomies.

Nguyen, D. H. H., & Khominich, I. P. (2023). The measurement of green economic quality in the BRICS countries: Should they prioritize financing for environmental protection, economic growth, or social goals? *Russian Journal of Economics*, *9*(2), 183–200. DOI: 10.32609/j.ruje.9.101612

Pucker, K. P. (2021). Overselling sustainability reporting. *Harvard Business Review*, *99*(3), 134–143.

Renneboog, L., Ter Horst, J., & Zhang, C. (2008). Socially responsible investments: Institutional aspects, performance, and investor behavior. *Journal of Banking & Finance*, *32*(9), 1723–1742. DOI: 10.1016/j.jbankfin.2007.12.039

Sachs, J. D., Schmidt-Traub, G., Mazzucato, M., Messner, D., Nakicenovic, N., & Rockström, J. (2019). Six transformations to achieve the sustainable development goals. *Nature Sustainability*, *2*(9), 805–814. DOI: 10.1038/s41893-019-0352-9

Scott, W. R. (2005). Institutional theory: Contributing to a theoretical research program. *Great minds in management: The process of theory development, 37*(2), 460-484.

Shroff-Mehta, P., Thakur, S., Viswanathan, V., & Lemal-Brown, P. (2024). ESG Maturity Mapping: Sustainability in Legacy, New Age, and Start-Up Organizations. In *The Routledge Handbook of Global and Digital Governance Crossroads* (pp. 441-460). Routledge India.

Skea, J., Shukla, P., Al Khourdajie, A., & McCollum, D. (2021). Intergovernmental Panel on Climate Change: Transparency and integrated assessment modeling. *Wiley Interdisciplinary Reviews: Climate Change*, *12*(5), e727. DOI: 10.1002/wcc.727

Sra, J., & Deo, B. (2024). GRI Standards for Environmental Sustainability–A Brief Review. In *IISE Annual Conference. Proceedings* (pp. 1-6). Institute of Industrial and Systems Engineers (IISE). DOI: 10.21872/2024IISE_6407

Swilling, M., Musango, J., & Wakeford, J. (2016). Developmental states and sustainability transitions: Prospects of a just transition in South Africa. *Journal of Environmental Policy and Planning*, *18*(5), 650–672. DOI: 10.1080/1523908X.2015.1107716

Tietenberg, T., & Lewis, L. (2023). *Environmental and natural resource economics*. Routledge. DOI: 10.4324/9781003213734

Wang, K., Li, T., San, Z., & Gao, H. (2023). How does corporate ESG performance affect stock liquidity? Evidence from China. *Pacific-Basin Finance Journal, 80*, 102087. DOI: 10.1016/j.pacfin.2023.102087

Weber, O. (2017). Corporate sustainability and financial performance of Chinese banks. *Sustainability Accounting. Management and Policy Journal*, *8*(3), 358–385.

Women, U. N. (2021). Women's representation in local government: A global analysis. *Hämtad*, *27*, 2022–01.

Yadav, A., Gyamfi, B. A., Asongu, S. A., & Behera, D. K. (2024). The role of green finance and governance effectiveness in the impact of renewable energy investment on CO2 emissions in BRICS economies. *Journal of Environmental Management*, *358*, 120906. DOI: 10.1016/j.jenvman.2024.120906 PMID: 38636419

Zadek, S., & Flynn, C. (2013). South-originating green finance. *Exploring Its Potential.*

# Compilation of References


Abbas, J., & Najam, H. (2024). Role of environmental decentralization, green human capital, and digital finance in firm green technological innovation for a sustainable society. *Environment, Development and Sustainability*, *27*(8), 1–15. DOI: 10.1007/s10668-024-04783-3

Abbott, K. W. (2012). Engaging the public and the private in global sustainability governance. *International Affairs*, *88*(3), 543–564. DOI: 10.1111/j.1468-2346.2012.01088.x

Abd Aziz, A., Ajis, M. N. E., & Mohd, A. (2025). Integrity Regulations and Corporate Governance in Government Linked Companies: Promoting Transparency and Compliance with Sustainable Development Goal 16. *Journal of Lifestyle and SDGs Review*, *5*(3), e04882–e04882. DOI: 10.47172/2965-730X.SDGsReview.v5.n03.pe04882

Abdel-Aziem, A. H., & Soliman, T. H. M. (2023). The Regulatory Landscape of Green Finance: An Improved Approach for Market Development. *Financial Technology and Innovation*, *2*(1), 26–34. DOI: 10.54216/FinTech-I.020103

Abrell, J., & Kosch, M. (2022). The impact of carbon prices on renewable energy support. *Journal of the Association of Environmental and Resource Economists*, *9*(3), 531–563. DOI: 10.1086/717417

Abro, S., & Shehryar, Q. (2025). Advancing green finance for sustainable development: Trends, challenges, and future directions. *Dialogue Social Science Review*, *3*(5), 21–36.

Abubakar, I. R., & Alshammari, M. S. (2023). Urban planning schemes for developing low-carbon cities in the Gulf Cooperation Council region. *Habitat International*, *138*, 102881. DOI: 10.1016/j.habitatint.2023.102881

Adisa, O., Ilugbusi, B. S., & Obi, O. C. (2024). Green bonds in climate finance: A review of USA and African initiatives. *International Journal of Science and Development.*

African Development Bank. (2024). Climate Change and Green Growth at the African Development Bank, Annual Report 2022 https://www.afdb.org/fr/documents/climate-change-and-green-growth-2022-annual-report

Agarwal, M. (2020). Green economy research paper. *The International journal of analytical and experimental modal analysis, Volume XII, Issue* IV.

Agarwal, V., Hameed, A. Z., Malhotra, S., Mathiyazhagan, K., Alathur, S., & Appolloni, A. (2023). Role of Industry 4.0 in agile manufacturing to achieve sustainable development. *Business Strategy and the Environment*, *32*(6), 3671–3688. DOI: 10.1002/bse.3321

Agence France Trésor. (2025). *Green OATs overview*. https://www.aft.gouv.fr/en/green-oat

Agrawal, R., Agrawal, S., Samadhiya, A., Kumar, A., Luthra, S., & Jain, V. (2024). Adoption of green finance and green innovation for achieving circularity: An exploratory review and future directions. *Geoscience Frontiers*, *15*(4), 101669. DOI: 10.1016/j.gsf.2023.101669

Ahamed, A. J. (2025). Chapter-1 Financial Literacy. Social Science Research Network. DOI: 10.2139/ssrn.5084835

Ahmad, V., Arora, M., Sayal, A., Kumar, R., & Kumar, P. (2025). Exploring trends in e-business and sustainable finance: An integrated analytical approach. *Frontiers in Sustainable Cities*, *7*, 1549874. DOI: 10.3389/frsc.2025.1549874

Akita, N., & Ohe, Y. (2021). Sustainable forest management evaluation using carbon credits: From production to environmental forests. *Forests*, *12*(8), 1016. DOI: 10.3390/f12081016

Akrofi, M. M. (2025). Green hotspots? Unveiling global hotspots and shifting trends in carbon credit projects. *Sustainable Development (Bradford)*, *33*(2), 1782–1796. DOI: 10.1002/sd.3209

Alamgir, M., & Cheng, M.-C. (2023). Do Green Bonds Play a Role in Achieving Sustainability? *Sustainability (Basel)*, *15*(13), 10177. DOI: 10.3390/su151310177

Alam, S. S., Masukujjaman, M., Ahmed, S., Kokash, H. A., & Khattak, A. (2024). Towards a circular economy: Cleaner production technology adoption among small and medium enterprises in an emerging economy. *Circular Economy and Sustainability*, *4*(2), 1357–1386. DOI: 10.1007/s43615-023-00341-7

Alharbi, S. S., Al Mamun, M., Boubaker, S., & Rizvi, S. K. A. (2023). Green finance and renewable energy: A worldwide evidence. *Energy Economics*, *118*, 106499. DOI: 10.1016/j.eneco.2022.106499

Alhejaili, M. O. (2024). Integrating Climate Change Risks and Sustainability Goals into Saudi Arabia's Financial Regulation: Pathways to Green Finance. *Sustainability (Basel)*, *16*(10), 4159. Advance online publication. DOI: 10.3390/su16104159

Ali, E., Anshari, M., Hamdan, M., Ahmad, N., &Surieshtino, Y. (2023). Green Finance for Sustainable Development: A Bibliographic Analysis. 46–49. DOI: 10.1109/SIBF60067.2023.10379915

Ali, E. B., Anufriev, V. P., & Amfo, B. (2021). Green economy implementation in Ghana as a road map for a sustainable development drive: A review. *Scientific African*, *12*, e00756. DOI: 10.1016/j.sciaf.2021.e00756

Almazrouei, H., & Nobanee, H. (2021). *Green Finance and Sustainable Growth.*

Alnassar, W. (2022). THE EFFECT OF GREEN LOAN AND ECOLOGICAL SUSTAINABILITY ON POLLUTION DEPLETION: PRACTICAL EVALUATION IN DEVELOPING AND OECD ECONOMIES. *Academy of Strategic Management Journal*, *20*, 2021.

Al-Swidi, A. K., Al-Hakimi, M. A., & Al-Hattami, H. M. (2024). Fostering environmental preservation: Exploring the synergy of green human resource management and corporate environmental ethics. *The Bottom Line (New York, N.Y.)*, *37*(1), 1–26. DOI: 10.1108/BL-06-2023-0191

Alves, J. M. (2023). European sustainable finance: introductory notes on the EU green deal and new green finance perspectives. (Direito Católica Teses). Universidade CatólicaEditora. DOI: 10.34632/9789725409640

Alves, L. L. M., Angelo, H., Almeida, A. N., Silva, G. F., Matricardi, E. A. T., Nunes, A., & Souza Júnior, C. V. N. (2024). Strategic analysis of the forest carbon market in Brazil. *Sustainability (Basel)*, *16*(16), 6898. DOI: 10.3390/su16166898

Amendolagine, V., Lema, R., & Rabellotti, R. (2021). Green foreign direct investments and the deepening of capabilities for sustainable innovation in multinationals: Insights from renewable energy. *Journal of Cleaner Production*, *310*, 127381. DOI: 10.1016/j.jclepro.2021.127381

Amin, M. R. (2025). Sustainability reporting and its influence on investor decision-making: Critical perspectives and empirical insights. *International Journal of Science and Research Archive, 16*(1), 716–728. DOI: 10.30574/ijsra.2025.16.1.2085

Amouri, A., Festa, G., Shams, S. R., Sakka, G., & Rossi, M. (2021). Technological propensity, financial constraints, and entrepreneurial limits in young entrepreneurs' social business enterprises: The tunisian experience. *Technological Forecasting and Social Change, 173*, 121126. DOI: 10.1016/j.techfore.2021.121126

Amram, M., & Kulatilaka, N. (2009). The Invisible Green Hand: How Individual Decisions and Markets Can Reduce Greenhouse Gas Emissions. *California Management Review, 51*(2), 194–218. DOI: 10.2307/41166486

Andrada, I. (2015). Incentives for financing sustainable development. Annals - Economy Series, 1(2), 312–317. https://www.utgjiu.ro/revista/ec/pdf/2015-02/45_Moldovan.pdf

Annu & Tripathi, R. (2024). Framework of green finance to attain sustainable development goals: an empirical evidence from the TCCM approach. *Benchmarking: An International Journal, 31*(9), 3130-3153.

Antonelli, A., Rueda, X., Calcagno, R., & Kalunda, P. N. (2024). How biodiversity credits could help to conserve and restore nature. *Nature, 634*(8036), 1045–1049. DOI: 10.1038/d41586-024-03475-2 PMID: 39468324

Anyiam-Osigwe, T., & Ibrahim, S. E. (2024). Across the boards: Corporate governance and access to climate finance. *Academy of Management Proceedings.* Retrieved from https://journals.aom.org

Aref, M. (2024). Sharing economy from the sustainable development goals perspective: A path to global prosperity. *Journal of Internet and Digital Economics, 4*(2), 116–138. DOI: 10.1108/JIDE-02-2024-0007

Areo, G. (2024). Driving Sustainable Growth: The Role of Technology and Digital Transformation in Corporate Green Innovation.

Ariffin, K. M., & Milala, S. I. (2023). Advancing Sustainable Finance: A Framework for Strategic Institutional Financing. *Research in Management of Technology and Business, 4*(2), 655–672.

Arslan, M., Faizulayev, A., Abeuova, D., & Kayani, U. N. (2024). Exploring the Risks, Challenges, and Opportunities of Using Digital Financial Technologies for Green Finance. Impact of Digitalization on Reporting, Tax Avoidance, Accounting, and Green Finance, 226-242.

Asif, M. H., Zhongfu, T., Dilanchiev, A., Irfan, M., Eyvazov, E., & Ahmad, B. (2023). Determining the influencing factors of consumers' attitude toward renewable energy adoption in developing countries: A roadmap toward environmental sustainability and green energy technologies. *Environmental Science and Pollution Research International, 30*(16), 47861–47872. DOI: 10.1007/s11356-023-25662-w

Asimiyu, Z. (2024). Fintech solutions to overcome financing constraints in corporate green innovation. *ResearchGate*. Retrieved from https://www.researchgate.net

Auzepy, A., Bannier, C. E., & Gärtner, F. (2024). Looking beyond ESG preferences: The role of sustainable finance literacy in sustainable investing. Social Science Research Network. DOI: 10.2139/ssrn.4773211

Awazu, P. B. M. D. L., & Samama-Romain, P. D. S. F. (2020). The green swan-central banking and financial stability in the age of climate change.

Azad, S., & Devi, S. L. T. (2024). Sustainable development and investor confidence: The safe-haven appeal of green-bond issuing firms. *Sustainable Development*. Advance online publication. DOI: 10.1002/sd.3172

Bagh, T., & Iftikhar, K. (2024). Understanding the Theoretical Context of Green Finance. In *The Palgrave Handbook of Green Finance for Sustainable Development* (pp. 49–87). Springer International Publishing. DOI: 10.1007/978-3-031-65756-6_3

Bai, X. (2024). Post-2030 global goals need explicit targets for cities and businesses. *Science, 385*(6714), eadq4993. Advance online publication. DOI: 10.1126/science.adq4993

Balative, M. I., Hariyanto, E., Sholikhah, A., & Prayoga, R. G. (2025). A closer look at Indonesia's experience in developing green sukuk. In Taghizadeh-Hesary, F., Thaker, H. M. T., Bhatti, M. I., & Thaker, M. A. M. T. (Eds.), *Islamic finance and sustainability: A research companion* (pp. 441–464). Routledge. DOI: 10.4324/9781003518617-23

Balmford, A., Keshav, S., Venmans, F., Coomes, D., Groom, B., & Madhavapeddy, A.. (2023). Realising the social value of impermanent carbon credits. *Cambridge Open Engage*. DOI: 10.33774/coe-2023-5v93l-v3

Balsalobre-Lorente, D., Shahbaz, M., Roubaud, D., & Farhani, S. (2020). How economic growth, renewable electricity and natural resources contribute to CO2 emissions? *Energy Policy, 113*, 356–367. DOI: 10.1016/j.enpol.2017.10.050

Bamgbose, O. (2024, June 24). Bridging faith and sustainability: Unlocking Islamic sustainable finance. *Global Ethical Finance Initiative (GEFI) Insights Series,* https://www.globalethicalfinance.org/2024/06/26/bridging-faith-and-sustainability-unlocking-islamic-sustainable-finance/

Banga, C., & Afzal, M. (2025). Navigating the Green Financial Markets: Opportunities and Challenges. Exploring Pillars of Sustainability for Modern Age Improvements, 201-226.

Barral, S., Ghosh, R., & Corbera, E. (2025). The politics of influence in biodiversity offsetting. *Nature Sustainability, 8*(4), 350–357. DOI: 10.1038/s41893-025-01514-y

Barrera, L. C. A. (2024). *The Law of ESG Derivatives: Risk, Uncertainty and Sustainable Finance*. Taylor & Francis. DOI: 10.4324/9781003365242

Basak, R., Karlsson-Vinkhuyzen, S., & Termeer, K. J. (2022). Information for climate finance accountability regimes: Proposed framework and case study of the Green Climate Fund. *Public Administration and Development, 42*(5), 261–280. DOI: 10.1002/pad.2000

Bassey, K. E., Aigbovbiosa, J., & Agupugo, C. (2024). Risk management strategies in renewable energy investment. *International Journal of Novel Research in Engineering and Science, 11*(1), 138–148. DOI: 10.5281/zenodo.13311076

BBVA. (2019). *BBVA issues the first blockchain-supported structured green bond for MAPFRE.* https://www.bbva.com/en/sustainability/bbva-issues-the-first-blockchain-supported-structured-green-bond-for-mapfre/

Behera, B., Behera, P., & Sethi, N. (2024). Decoupling the role of renewable energy, green finance and political stability in achieving the sustainable development goal 13: Empirical insight from emerging economies. *Sustainable Development (Bradford), 32*(1), 119–137. DOI: 10.1002/sd.2657

Behera, P., Haldar, A., & Sethi, N. (2023). Achieving carbon neutrality target in the emerging economies: Role of renewable energy and green technology. *Gondwana Research, 121*, 16–32. DOI: 10.1016/j.gr.2023.03.028

Bei, J., & Wang, C. (2023). Renewable energy resources and sustainable development goals: Evidence based on green finance, clean energy and environmentally friendly investment. *Resources Policy, 80*, 103194. DOI: 10.1016/j.resourpol.2022.103194

Beisembina, A., Gizzatova, A., Kunyazov, Y., Ernazarov, T., Mashrapov, N., & Dontsov, S. (2023). Investing in human capital for green and sustainable development. *Journal of Environmental Management and Tourism, 14*(5), 2300. DOI: 10.14505/jemt.v14.5(69).11

Beisenbina, M., Fabregat-Aibar, L., Barberà-Mariné, M. G., & Sorrosal-Forradellas, M. T. (2022). The burgeoning field of sustainable investment: Past, present and future. *Sustainable Development (Bradford), 31*(2), 649–667. DOI: 10.1002/sd.2422

Bengo, I., Boni, L., & Sancino, A. (2022). EU financial regulations and social impact measurement practices: A comprehensive framework on finance for sustainable development. *Corporate Social Responsibility and Environmental Management, 29*(4), 809–819. DOI: 10.1002/csr.2235

Bennett, M., & Coyle, H. (2025, March 4). State of the sukuk market and prospects for growth. *World Bank,* https://blogs.worldbank.org/en/allaboutfinance/state-of-the-sukuk-market-and-prospects-for-growth

Berensmann, K., & Lindenberg, N. (2016). Green Finance: across the universe. In WorldScientific eBooks (pp. 305–332). DOI: 10.1142/9789811206887_0011

Bhandary, R. R., Gallagher, K. S., & Zhang, F. (2021). Climate finance policy in practice: A review of the evidence. *Climate Policy, 21*(4), 529–545. DOI: 10.1080/14693062.2020.1871313

Bhattacharya, S., & Sachdev, B. K. (2024). Regulatory Challenges and Opportunities.

Bhattacharyya, R. (2021). Green finance for energy transition, climate action and sustainable development: Overview of concepts, applications, implementation and challenges. *Green Finance, 4*(1), 1–35. DOI: 10.3934/GF.2022001

Bhattacherjee, P., Mishra, S., Bouri, E., & Wee, J. B. (2024). ESG, clean energy, and petroleum futures markets: Asymmetric return connectedness and hedging effectiveness. *International Review of Economics & Finance, 94*, 103375. DOI: 10.1016/j.iref.2024.103375

Bhutta, U. S., Tariq, A., Farrukh, M., Raza, A., & Iqbal, M. K. (2022). Green bonds for sustainable development: Review of literature on development and impact of green bonds. *Technological Forecasting and Social Change, 175*, 121378. DOI: 10.1016/j.techfore.2021.121378

Binder, J., & Wade, M. (2024, Winter). Digital Sustainability for a Better Future. *Stanford Social Innovation Review.*

Biswas, B., & Gupta, R. P. (2023). Global ESG Regulatory Framework and Sustainability: Issues and Prospects (pp. 20–32). DOI: 10.31674/book.2023srdsi003

Blended Finance Taskforce. (2017). *Better finance, better world.* Consultation paper of the Blended Finance Task Force in partnership with the Business & Sustainable Development Commission and SYSTEMIQ. http://s3.amazonaws.com/aws-bsdc/BFT_BetterFinance_final_01192018.pdf

Bloomberg New Energy Finance. (2025). Global Investment in the Energy Transition Exceeded $2 Trillion for the First Time in 2024, BloombergNEF Report Retrieved from: https://about.bnef.com/blog/global-investment-in-the-energy-transition-exceeded-2-trillion-for-the-first-time-in-2024-according-to-bloombergnef-report/

Bocken, N. M., Short, S. W., Rana, P., & Evans, S. (2014). A literature and practice review to develop sustainable business model archetypes. *Journal of Cleaner Production*, *65*, 42–56. DOI: 10.1016/j.jclepro.2013.11.039

Boiral, O., & Heras-Saizarbitoria, I. (2020). Sustainability reporting assurance: Creating stakeholder accountability through hyperreality? *Journal of Cleaner Production*, *243*, 118596. DOI: 10.1016/j.jclepro.2019.118596

Bolton, P., Després, M., da Silva, L. A. P., Samama, F., & Svartzman, R. (2020). *The green swan.* https://www.bis.org/publ/othp31.htm

Bortz, P. G. (2024). Green and sustainable taxonomies: Dimensions, challenges, and difficulties. *UNSAM*. Retrieved from https://www.unsam.edu.ar

Bose, S., Bridges, A., & DeFrancia, K. (2019). Carbon Pricing as a Policy Instrument to Decarbonize Economies, Enel Foundation, July 2019. https://www.enelfoundation.org/content/dam/enel-found/Carbon%20Pricing%20Report%20 July%2019%202019%20FINAL1.pdf

Bowley, T., & Hill, J. G. (2024). The Global ESG Stewardship Ecosystem. *European Business Organization Law Review*, *25*(2), 229–268. Advance online publication. DOI: 10.1007/s40804-024-00316-7

Bracking, S., & Leffel, B. (2021). Climate finance governance: Fit for purpose? *Wiley Interdisciplinary Reviews: Climate Change*, *12*(4), e709. DOI: 10.1002/wcc.709

Brears, R. (2022). *Financing nature-based solutions: Exploring public, private, and blended finance models and case studies.* Springer International Publishing AG. DOI: 10.1007/978-3-030-93325-8

Brown, P. (2018). Environmental Sustainability Factors Impact on Financial Performance in Materials Industry. *Journal of International Business and Economics*, *18*(4), 49–53. DOI: 10.18374/JIBE-18-4.5

Brożek, J., Kożuch, A., Wieruszewski, M., Jaszczak, R., & Adamowicz, K. (2024). Taxonomy Regulation as a New Instrument for the Sustainable Management of the Forest Environment in Europe. *Sustainability (Basel), 16*(20), 8799. DOI: 10.3390/su16208799

Brühl, V. (2022). Green Financial Products in the EU — A Critical Review of the Status Quo. *Inter Economics, 57*(4), 252–259. DOI: 10.1007/s10272-022-1057-2

Brundtland, G. H. (1987). Brundtland report. Our common future. *Comissão Mundial, 4*(1), 17–25.

Brunnhuber, S. (2023). *Financing our anthropocene: How wall street, main street and central banks can manage, fund and hedge our global commons*. Springer. DOI: 10.1007/978-3-031-23285-5

Buana, G. K., & Musari, K. (2020, December 28). A new sphere of sukuk: Linking pandemic to Paris agreement. *The World Financial Review,* November-December Edition, Islam Finance, pp. 59-61. https://worldfinancialreview.com/a-new-sphere-of-sukuk-linking-the-pandemic-to-the-paris-agreement/

Bule, T., & Less, C. T. (2016). Promoting sustainable development through responsible business conduct. *Diseases of the Colon and Rectum,* •••, 119–136. DOI: 10.1787/dcr-2016-12-en

Burgess, N. D., Ali, N., Bedford, J., Bhola, N., Brooks, S., Cierna, A., Correa, R., Harris, M., Hargey, A., Hughes, J., McDermott-Long, O., Miles, L., Ravilious, C., Rodrigues, A. R., van Soesbergen, A., Sihvonen, H., Seager, A., Swindell, L., Vukelic, M., & Butchart, S. H. M. (2024). Global metrics for terrestrial biodiversity. *Annual Review of Environment and Resources, 49*(1), 673–709. DOI: 10.1146/annurev-environ-121522-045106

Busch, T., Bauer, R., & Orlitzky, M. (2015). Sustainable development and financial markets. *Business & Society, 55*(3), 303–329. DOI: 10.1177/0007650315570701

Cabiyo, B., & Field, C. B. (2025). Embracing imperfection: Carbon offset markets must learn to mitigate the risk of over-crediting. *PNAS Nexus, 4*(5), pgaf091. Advance online publication. DOI: 10.1093/pnasnexus/pgaf091 PMID: 40352644

Caetano, R. V., Marques, A. C., & Afonso, T. L. (2022). How Can Foreign Direct Investment Trigger Green Growth? The Mediating and Moderating Role of the Energy Transition. *Economies, 10*(8), 8. Advance online publication. DOI: 10.3390/economies10080199

Cai, X., & Song, X.-F. (2022). Towards sustainable environment: Unleashing the mechanism between green finance and corporate social responsibility. 0958305X2211332. DOI: 10.1177/0958305X221133258

Caldecott, B. (Ed.). (2018). *Ullahtranded assets and the environment: Risk, resilience and opportunity*. Routledge. DOI: 10.4324/9781315651606

Calel, R., & Dechezleprêtre, A. (2016). Environmental policy and directed technological change: Evidence from the European carbon market. *The Review of Economics and Statistics*, *98*(1), 173–191. DOI: 10.1162/REST_a_00470

Camilleri, L. (2024). The EU's green agenda: An analysis of green finance efforts to date and expectations for the new EU Green Bond Standard. *UM Theses*. Retrieved from https://www.um.edu.mt

Camilleri, M. A. (2020). The market for socially responsible investing: A review of the developments. *Social Responsibility Journal*, *17*(3), 412–428. DOI: 10.1108/SRJ-06-2019-0194

Carney, M. (2015). Breaking the tragedy of the horizon—Climate change and financial stability. *Bank of England Speech*. Retrieved from https://www.bankofengland.co.uk

Casalini, L. (2025). Green loans and mortgages: Harmonizing sustainability and real estate in the EU. *Uniform Law Review*, *30*(2), 250–262. DOI: 10.1093/ulr/unaf025

Cerrato Garcia, E. (2024). Navigating the landscape of EU sustainable finance regulation: challenges and imperatives to enforce sustainability financial promises in the EU through harmonized private enforcement mechanisms. (Doctoral Thesis). University of Bologna. Bologna, DOI: 10.48676/unibo/amsdottorato/11636

Cetindamar, D., Shdifat, B., & Erfani, S. (2020). Assessing big data analytics capability and sustainability in supply chains. Proceedings of the . . . *Annual Hawaii International Conference on System Sciences/Proceedings of the Annual Hawaii International Conference on System Sciences*. DOI: 10.24251/HICSS.2020.026

Chala, V., & Demidov, B. (2024). Theoretical Aspects of Green Financing for Providing Sustainable Development. *Economic Scope*, *193*(193), 37–45. DOI: 10.30838/EP.193.37-45

Chandrashekara, T. (2022). Green finance and sustainable investment: Trends, challenges, and opportunities. *International Journal of Research and Analytical Reviews*, *9*(4), 282. https://www.ijrar.org

Chan, K. H., Chong, L. L., Ng, T. H., & Ong, W. L. (2022). A model of green investment decision making for societal well-being. *Heliyon*, *8*(8), e10024. DOI: 10.1016/j.heliyon.2022.e10024

Chantana, B., Fu, C., Lim, W. Y. I., Cheng, K., & Khor, H. E. (2025, February 21). Green finance: Balancing sustainability and financial stability [Analytical note]. ASEAN+3 Macroeconomic Research Office. https://amro-asia.org/wp-content/uploads/2025/02/Analytical-Note_GreenFinanceBalancingSustainabilityFinancialStability.pdf

Chaudhary, M. K., Adhikari, M., & Shakya, N. (2024). Barriers to Green Financing in Developing Nation: An Investor's Perspective for Promoting Sustainable Development. *International Research Journal of MMC*, *5*(5), 195–208. DOI: 10.3126/irjmmc.v5i5.73761

Chauhan, R. (2024). Sustainable finance and green investing: Navigating the future of ethical capital markets. *ITM University*. Retrieved from https://mis.itmuniversity.ac.in

Chauhan, A. S., Singh, S. K., & Gupta, S. (2024). Decoding Green Finance: Exploring Concepts, Themes, and Transformative Journey. *Delhi Business Review*, *25*(1), 55–79. DOI: 10.51768/dbr.v25i1.251202405

Chausson, A., Welden, E. A., Melanidis, M. S., Gray, E., Hirons, M., & Seddon, N. (2023). Going beyond market-based mechanisms to finance nature-based solutions and foster sustainable futures. *PLOS Climate*, *2*(4), e0000169. DOI: 10.1371/journal.pclm.0000169

Cheteni, P., Matsongoni, H., & Umejesi, I. (2025). South Africa's green bond market: Financing sustainable development. *Cogent Economics & Finance*. Retrieved from https://www.tandfonline.com

Cho, K. Q. (2023, December 1). Malaysia's progress in green sukuk. *Phillip Invest,* Finance, Investments, https://www.phillipinvest.com.my/malaysias-progress-in-green-sukuk/

Choi, D., Gao, Z., & Jiang, W. (2020). Attention to global warming. *Review of Financial Studies*, *33*(3), 1112–1145. DOI: 10.1093/rfs/hhz086

Chua, F., & Ho, J. (2023). Assessing the potential of green finance in supporting environmental sustainability. *International Journal of Geography Geology and Environment*, *5*(1), 266–269. DOI: 10.22271/27067483.2023.v5.i1c.271

Citaristi, I. (2022). United Nations Environment Programme—UNEP. In *The Europa directory of international organizations 2022* (pp. 193–199). Routledge. DOI: 10.4324/9781003292548-46

Clark, G. L., Feiner, A., & Viehs, M. (2015). From the stockholder to the stakeholder: How sustainability can Drive financial Outperformance. SSRN Electronic Journal. DOI: 10.2139/ssrn.2508281

Clark, G. L., Feiner, A., & Viehs, M. (2015). From the stockholder to the stakeholder: How sustainability can drive financial outperformance. *Available at SSRN* 2508281.

Clark, R., Reed, J., & Sunderland, T. (2018). Bridging funding gaps for climate and sustainable development: Pitfalls, progress and potential of private finance. *Land Use Policy*, *71*, 335–346. DOI: 10.1016/j.landusepol.2017.12.013

Clifton, J., & Schwerdtner Mánez, K. (2025). A framework based on payments for ecosystem services to support the delivery of high integrity carbon and biodiversity credits. *Ecosystem Services*, *73*, 101724. DOI: 10.1016/j.ecoser.2025.101724

Climate Bonds Initiative. (2017). Green bond highlights 2017. https://www.climatebonds.net/resources/reports/green-bond-highlights-2017

Climate Bonds Initiative. (2023). Green bond market summary. Retrieved from https://www.climatebonds.net

Cornell, B., & Damodaran, A. (2020). *Valuing ESG: Doing good or sounding good?* NYU Stern School of Business.

Cort, T. L. (2023). The Pragmatist's Guide to ESG. *Environment*, *65*(4), 10–17. DOI: 10.1080/00139157.2023.2205346

Cui, H. D., Rokicki, B., & M'Barek, R. (2025). *European green bonds, carbon tax, and crowding-out: The economic, social, and environmental impacts of the EU's green investments under different scenarios. Renewable and Sustainable Energy Reviews.* Retrieved from ScienceDirect.

D'Orazio, P., Schäfer, D., & Stephan, A. (2024). *Macro-financial policy at the crossroad: addressing climate change, biodiversity loss, and environmental degradation - introduction to the special issue*. Eurasian Economic Review., DOI: 10.1007/s40822-024-00265-z

da Cunha, Í. G. F., Policarpo, R. V. S., de Oliveira, P. C. S., Abdala, E. C., & do Nascimento Rebelatto, D. A. (2025). A systematic review of ESG indicators and corporate performance: Proposal for a conceptual framework. *Future Business Journal*, *11*(1), 106. DOI: 10.1186/s43093-025-00539-1

Dahlgren, H., & Santesson, P. (2024). Lost in translation: Bridging the gap between climate change and municipal bonds. *Diva Portal*. Retrieved from https://www.diva-portal.org

Dai, B., Zhang, J., & Hussain, N. (2025). Policy pathways through FinTech and green finance for low-carbon energy transition in BRICS nations. *Energy Strategy Reviews*, *57*, 101603. DOI: 10.1016/j.esr.2024.101603

Dai, Y., & Chen, X. (2023). Evaluating green financing mechanisms for natural resource management: Implications for achieving sustainable development goals. *Resources Policy*, *86*, 104160. DOI: 10.1016/j.resourpol.2023.104160

Damak, M., Jagtiani, S., Lescova, T., & Ozyavuz, A. (2025, January 13). Sukuk market: Strong performance set to continue in 2025. *S&P Global,* https://www.spglobal.com/ratings/en/research/articles/250113-sukuk-market-strong-performance-set-to-continue-in-2025-13377916

Dambe, D. N., Dewantara, B., Mahmudin, T., & Mere, K. (2024). Innovative Financial Instruments for Sustainable Development: A Multi-Layered Analysis of Green Bonds and Impact Investing. Dinasti International Journal of Economics, Finance & Accounting (DIJEFA), 5(4).

de Mariz, F. (2022). The Promise of Sustainable Finance: Lessons from Brazil. *Georgetown Journal of International Affairs*, *23*(2), 185–190. DOI: 10.1353/gia.2022.0030

De Silva Lokuwaduge, C. S., & De Silva, K. M. (2022). ESG risk disclosure and the risk of green washing. *Australasian Accounting. Business and Finance Journal*, *16*(1), 146–159.

Dechezleprêtre, A., & Sato, M. (2017). The impacts of environmental regulations on competitiveness. *Review of Environmental Economics and Policy*, *11*(2), 183–206. DOI: 10.1093/reep/rex013

Del Sarto, N. (2025). The European Regulatory Framework: Policies and Regulations for Sustainable Finance. In *ESG Factors and Financial Outcomes in Banks: Quantitative Insights into the ESG-Cost of Debt Relationship* (pp. 61–94). Springer Nature Switzerland. DOI: 10.1007/978-3-031-87748-3_2

Delacote, P., L'Horty, T., Kontoleon, A., West, T. A. P., Creti, A., Filewod, B., LeVelly, G., Guizar-Coutiño, A., Groom, B., & Elias, M. (2024). Strong transparency required for carbon credit mechanisms. *Nature Sustainability*, *7*(6), 706–713. DOI: 10.1038/s41893-024-01310-0

Dell'Erba, M., & Doronzo, M. (2023). Sustainability gatekeepers: ESG ratings and data providers. *U. Pa. J. Bus. L.*, *25*, 355.

Delmas, M., & Burbano, V. (2011). The drivers of greenwashing. *California Management Review*, *54*(1), 64–87. DOI: 10.1525/cmr.2011.54.1.64

Dempere, J., Alamash, E., & Mattos, P. (2024). Unveiling the truth: greenwashing in sustainable finance. Frontiers in sustainability, 5, 1362051.

Derrick, M. (2024). Top 10: Energy Industry Associations. *Energy Digital.* https://energydigital.com/top10/top-10-energy-industry-associations

DFI. (2023). *DFI working group on blended concessional finance for private sector projects.* Joint Report, March. https://idbinvest.org/en/publications/dfi-working-group-blended-concessional-finance-private-sector-projects-2023

Dhayal, K. S., Giri, A. K., Kumar, A., Samadhiya, A., Agrawal, S., & Agrawal, R. (2023). Can green finance facilitate Industry 5.0 transition to achieve sustainability? A systematic review with future research directions. *Environmental Science and Pollution Research International, 30*(46), 102158–102180. DOI: 10.1007/s11356-023-29539-w

Di Vaio, A., Zaffar, A., & Chhabra, M. (2024). Intellectual capital through decarbonization for achieving Sustainable Development Goal 8: A systematic literature review and future research directions. *Journal of Intellectual Capital, 25*(7), 54–86. DOI: 10.1108/JIC-05-2024-0131

Dial, A. (2025, March 31). Blended finance & impact investing in the global south. *Yale School of Management,* https://som.yale.edu/story/2025/blended-finance-impact-investing-global-south

Digitemie, W. N., & Ekemezie, I. O. (2024). Assessing the role of carbon pricing in global climate change mitigation strategies. *Magna Scientia Advanced Research and Reviews, 10*(2), 22-31. DOI: 10.30574/msarr.2024.10.2.0040

Dimmelmeier, A. (2023). Expanding the politics of measurement in sustainable finance: Reconceptualizing environmental, social and governance information as infrastructure. Environment And Planning C: Politics and Space. DOI: 10.1177/23996544231209149

Dordi, T., Gehricke, S. A., Naef, A., & Weber, O. (2022). Ten financial actors can accelerate a transition away from fossil fuels. *Environmental Innovation and Societal Transitions, 44*, 60–78. DOI: 10.1016/j.eist.2022.05.006

Du, L., & Geng, B. (2024). Financial technology and financing constraints. *Finance Research Letters, 60*, 104841. DOI: 10.1016/j.frl.2023.104841

Dupuy, P. (2024). Finance literacy and sustainable finance literacy. Bankers, Markets, Investors/RB Bankers, Markets. *Investors, 178*(3). 0031.doi.org/10.54695/bmi.178.0031

Eccles, R. G., Ioannou, I., & Serafeim, G. (2014). The impact of corporate sustainability on organizational processes and performance. *Management Science*, *60*(11), 2835–2857. DOI: 10.1287/mnsc.2014.1984

Ehlers, T., & Packer, F. (2017). Green bond finance and certification. *BIS Quarterly Review*. Retrieved from https://www.bis.org

Ekué, S., & Díaz Fajardo, J. (2024). *Green investment requires mobilizing global finance*. The Asset.

El Madnaoui, A., Cheedella, S. S., Okolo, K., Wang, K., Jatin, P., Agrawal, A., & Priya, S. (2021). *The Case for a Green Economy*. DOI: 10.5281/ZENODO.4740628

Elkington, J., & Rowlands, I. H. (1999). Cannibals with forks: The triple bottom line of 21st century business. *Alternatives Journal*, *25*(4), 42.

ElMassah, S., & Hassanein, E. A. (2023). Economic development and environmental sustainability in the GCC countries: New insights based on the economic complexity. *Sustainability (Basel)*, *15*(10), 7987. DOI: 10.3390/su15107987

Emirates News Agency – WAM. (2023, February 6). *UAE foreign trade achieved AED2.233 trillion in 2022 with growth rate of 17%: Mohammed bin Rashid.* https://www.wam.ae/en/details/1395303125677

Ergun, H. (2023). Yellow sukuk unveiled: Harnessing agricultural commodity trade for islamic finance and paradigm shift in commodity exchanges. *Al Qasimia University (AQU). Journal of Islamic Economics*, *3*(1), 81–114. DOI: 10.52747/aqujie.3.1.229

Ervine, K. (2014). Diminishing returns: Carbon market crisis and the future of market-dependent climate change finance. *New Political Economy*, *19*(5), 723–747. DOI: 10.1080/13563467.2013.849672

Eskerkhanova, L. T., Zaripova, R. S., & Mitrofanov, S. V. (2024). Sustainable development and investment in the green economy: The role of the private and public sectors. *Ekonomikaiupravlenieproblemyresheniya*, *3/4*(144), 85–91. DOI: 10.36871/ek.up.p.r.2024.03.04.011

Espelage, A., Ahonen, H. M., & Michaelowa, A. (2022). The role of carbon market mechanisms in climate finance. In *Handbook of International Climate Finance* (pp. 352–378). Edward Elgar Publishing.

Evro, S., Oni, B. A., & Tomomewo, O. S. (2024). Global strategies for a low-carbon future: Lessons from the US, China, and EU's pursuit of carbon neutrality. *Journal of Cleaner Production*, *461*, 142635. DOI: 10.1016/j.jclepro.2024.142635

Ewing, J. A. (2017). Hollow ecology: Ecological modernization theory and the death of nature. *Journal of World-systems Research, 23*(1), 126–155. DOI: 10.5195/jwsr.2017.611

Eyo-Udo, N. L., Agho, M. O., Onukwulu, E. C., Sule, A. K., & Azubuike, C. U. (2024). Advances in green finance solutions for combating climate change and ensuring sustainability. 2(6), 338–375. DOI: 10.51594/gjabr.v2i6.53

Falavigna, G., & Ippoliti, R. (2022). Financial constraints, investments, and environmental strategies: An empirical analysis of judicial barriers. *Business Strategy and the Environment, 31*(5), 2002–2018. DOI: 10.1002/bse.2995

Falcone, P. M., & Sica, E. (2019). Assessing the Opportunities and Challenges of green finance in Italy: An analysis of the biomass production sector. *Sustainability (Basel), 11*(2), 517. DOI: 10.3390/su11020517

Feng, K., Yang, Z., Zhuo, Y., Jiao, L., Wang, B., & Liu, Z. (2024). Impact of Carbon Tax on Renewable Energy Development and Environmental–Economic Synergies. *Energies, 17*(21), 5347. DOI: 10.3390/en17215347

Feng, S., Zhang, R., & Li, G. (2022). Environmental decentralization, digital finance and green technology innovation. *Structural Change and Economic Dynamics, 61*, 70–83. DOI: 10.1016/j.strueco.2022.02.008

Fiegenbaum, H. (2024). Complementing carbon credits from forest-related activities with biodiversity insurance and resilience value. *arXiv*. DOI: 10.31219/osf.io/buvzy

Filewod, B., & McCarney, G. (2023). Avoiding carbon leakage from nature-based offsets by design. *One Earth, 6*(7), 790–802. DOI: 10.1016/j.oneear.2023.05.024

Filippini, M., Leippold, M., &Wekhof, T. (2024). Sustainable Finance Literacy and the Determinants of Sustainable Investing. DOI: 10.1016/j.jbankfin.2024.107167

Finvizier. (2024). *Sustainable sukuk: Global trends and market overview.* https://www.finvizier.com/wp-content/uploads/2024/07/sustainable-sukuk-global-trends-and-market-overview-upd.pdf

Fitch Rating. (2025, January 21). *ESG sukuk to cross usd50 billion in 2025: Key ESG funding role in emerging markets.* https://www.fitchratings.com/research/non-bank-financial-institutions/esg-sukuk-to-cross-usd50-billion-in-2025-key-esg-funding-role-in-emerging-markets-21-01-2025

Flammer, C. (2021). Corporate green bonds. *Journal of Financial Economics, 142*(2), 499–516. DOI: 10.1016/j.jfineco.2021.01.010

Flammer, C. (2021). Corporate greenwashing and the misallocation of capital. [link]. *Strategic Management Journal*, *42*(12), 2339–2362. DOI: 10.1002/smj.3341

Folke, C., Carpenter, S. R., Walker, B., Scheffer, M., Chapin, T., & Rockström, J. (2010). Resilience thinking: Integrating resilience, adaptability and transformability. *Ecology and Society*, *15*(4), art20. Advance online publication. DOI: 10.5751/ES-03610-150420

Freeman, R. B. (1984). Longitudinal analyses of the effects of trade unions. *Journal of Labor Economics*, *2*(1), 1–26. DOI: 10.1086/298021

Freeman, R. E., & Phillips, R. A. (2002). Stakeholder theory: A libertarian defense. *Business Ethics Quarterly*, *12*(3), 331–349. DOI: 10.2307/3858020

Friede, G. (2019). Why don't we see more action? A meta synthesis of the investor impediments to integrate environmental, social, and governance factors. *Business Strategy and the Environment*, *28*(6), 1260–1282. DOI: 10.1002/bse.2346

Fu, C., Lu, L., & Pirabi, M. (2023). Advancing green finance: A review of sustainable development. *Digital Economy and Sustainable Development*, *1*(1), 20. DOI: 10.1007/s44265-023-00020-3

Fu, C., Lu, L., & Pirabi, M. (2024). Advancing green finance: A review of climate change and decarbonization. *Digital Economy and Sustainable Development*, *2*(1), 1. DOI: 10.1007/s44265-023-00026-x

Fucà, R., Cubico, S., Ardolino, P., & Rosiello, F. (2024). Evolving Sustainable Material Culture (SMC): Emerging Trends and Strategic Implications for Green Finance. *Frontiers*, *3*, 115.

Fuerst, F. (2015). The Financial Rewards of Sustainability: A Global Performance Study of real estate investment trusts. SSRN Electronic Journal. DOI: 10.2139/ssrn.2619434

Fu, X., Qian, Q. K., Liu, G. R., Zhuang, T., Visscher, H., & Huang, R. (2023). Overcoming inertia for sustainable urban development: Understanding the role of stimuli in shaping residents' participation behaviors in neighborhood regeneration projects in China. *Environmental Impact Assessment Review*, *103*, 107252. Advance online publication. DOI: 10.1016/j.eiar.2023.107252

Galindo-Gutiérrez, J. (2024). The World Bank and 'Maximizing Finance for Development': Talk the talk but not walk the walk. *Journal of International Relations and Development*, *27*(4), 391–413. DOI: 10.1057/s41268-024-00333-6

Gao, Z., Luo, Y., Tian, G., & Yang, H. (2023). Green preference, green investment. SSRN Electronic Journal. DOI: 10.2139/ssrn.4655538

Garsous, G., & Kozluk, T. (2017). Foreign direct investment and the pollution haven hypothesis: Evidence from listed firms (OECD Economics Department Working Papers No. 1379). OECD Publishing. https://doi.org/DOI: 10.1787/5jlv2g5b3w9n-en

Gbadegesin, O. A., Komolafe, O. S., Ayodele-Olajire, D., Omotoye, O., & Gbadegesin, A. (2025). *Unmasking Greenwashing: Strengthening Nigeria's Legal Framework for a Sustainable Green Economy*. Green and Low-Carbon Economy.

Geddes, A., Schmidt, T. S., & Steffen, B. (2018). The multiple roles of state investment banks in low-carbon energy finance: An analysis of Australia, the UK and Germany. *Energy Policy*, *115*, 158–170. DOI: 10.1016/j.enpol.2018.01.009

Geels, F. W. (2002). Technological transitions as evolutionary reconfiguration processes: A multi-level perspective and a case-study. *Research Policy*, *31*(8-9), 1257–1274. DOI: 10.1016/S0048-7333(02)00062-8

GEFI. (2024). Green and sustainability sukuk report 2024: Crossing borders. *Global Ethical Finance Initiative (GEFI),* https://www.globalethicalfinance.org/2024/11/28/green-and-sustainability-sukuk-report-2024-crossing-borders

Geissdoerfer, M., Savaget, P., Bocken, N. M. P., & Hultink, E. J. (2017). The circular economy – A new sustainability paradigm? *Journal of Cleaner Production*, *143*, 757–768. DOI: 10.1016/j.jclepro.2016.12.048

Ge, P., Liu, Y., Tang, C., & Zhu, R. (2024). Green bonds and corporate Environmental social and governance performance: Innovative approaches to identifying greenwashing in green bond markets. *Corporate Social Responsibility and Environmental Management*. Advance online publication. DOI: 10.1002/csr.3005

GGGI. (2023). Role of green bonds and sukuk in unlocking climate finance in Arab countries: International experiences in issuing green bonds and policy implications. *Global Green Growth Institute (GGGI),* https://climate2023.arabfund.org/wp-content/uploads/2023/08/163INT1.pdf

Ghaemi Asl, M., & Shahzad, U. (2024). How do conventional, Islamic and green bonds idiosyncratically differ when it comes to their inherent nonlinear reliance on carbon emission future price? A novel approach to greenwashing detection. *Environment, Development and Sustainability*, *27*(9), 1–36. DOI: 10.1007/s10668-023-04351-1

Ghaemi Asl, M., Smutka, L., Nasr Isfahani, M., Raza, S. A., & Vasa, L. (2025). Can multifarious types of green bonds be accused of greenwashing with a durative analysis? Insights from a permanent causality vs. temporary causality phenomenon. *Environment, Development and Sustainability*, •••, 1–25.

Ghosh, A., & Dutta, S. (2023). Green Finance–Integral Adaptation to Climate Change. *Perspectives in Sustainable Management Practices*, 42-51.

Gianfrate, G., & Peri, M. (2019). Exploring the convenience of issuing green bonds: Market and corporate perspectives. *Journal of Cleaner Production*, *219*, 127–135. DOI: 10.1016/j.jclepro.2019.02.022

Gigliotti, M., Schmidt-Traub, G., & Bastianoni, S. (2019). The sustainable development goals. In Elsevier eBooks (pp. 426–431). DOI: 10.1016/B978-0-12-409548-9.10986-8

Giudici, P., & Wu, L. (2025). Sustainable artificial intelligence in finance: Impact of ESG factors. *Frontiers in Artificial Intelligence*, *8*, 1566197. DOI: 10.3389/frai.2025.1566197

Global Commission on Adaptation. (2019). *Adapt now: A global call for leadership on climate resilience*. Retrieved from https://gca.org

Global Green Growth Institute. (2023). Principles of Green Finance. Retrieved from https://gggi.org/

Golub, S., Kauffmann, C., & Yeres, P. (2011). Defining And Measuring Green FDI: An Exploratory Review Of Existing Work And Evidence. *OECD Working Papers On International Investment*. DOI: 10.1787/18151957

Gomes, A., Islam, N. M., & Karim, M. R. (2024). Data-Driven Environmental Risk Management and Sustainability Analytics. *Non-Human Journal.*, *1*(01), 100–113. DOI: 10.70008/jmldeds.v1i01.46

Gonzalez-Arcos, C., Meath, C., Leszczyc, P. P., Haruvy, E., & An, J. (2023). Fostering sustainable investments through micro-investing platforms. *Scientific Reports*, *13*(1), 21194. Advance online publication. DOI: 10.1038/s41598-023-48452-3

Gopal, S., & Pitts, J. (2025). *Background and Foundations: Sustainability, Fintech, Data Science, and AI*. In *The FinTech Revolution: Bridging Geospatial Data, AI, and Sustainable Finance* (pp. 35-81). Springer. https://doi.org/DOI: 10.1007/978-3-031-74418-

Gul, R., & Hussain, S. (2024). Unlocking sustainable futures: Exploring the non-linear linkages between green finance and environmental sustainability in developing countries. *Journal of Environmental Management, 370*, 122971. 122971.doi.org/10.1016/j.jenvman.2024.122971. DOI: 10.1016/j.jenvman.2024.122971

Guo, Z., & Zhang, X. (2023). Carbon reduction effect of agricultural green production technology: A new evidence from China. *The Science of the Total Environment, 874*, 162483. DOI: 10.1016/j.scitotenv.2023.162483

Gupta, S., Kaur, G., Kumari, I., & Kalra, D. S. (2023). *Exploration of Opportunities and Challenges in Green Finance*. IGI Global., DOI: 10.4018/979-8-3693-1388-6.ch018

Gutsche, G., Wetzel, H., & Ziegler, A. (2023). Determinants of individual sustainable investment behavior - A framed field experiment. *Journal of Economic Behavior & Organization, 209*, 491–508. DOI: 10.1016/j.jebo.2023.03.016

Habiba, U. M. M. E., Xinbang, C., & Anwar, A. (2022). Do green technology innovations, financial development, and renewable energy use help to curb carbon emissions? *Renewable Energy, 193*, 1082–1093. DOI: 10.1016/j.renene.2022.05.084

Habiba, U., Xinbang, C., & Ali, S. (2023). Investigating the impact of financial development on carbon emissions: Does the use of renewable energy and green technology really contribute to achieving low-carbon economies? *Gondwana Research, 121*, 472–485. DOI: 10.1016/j.gr.2023.05.013

Hachigian, H., & McGill, S. M. (2012). Reframing the governance challenge for sustainable investment. *Journal of Sustainable Finance & Investment, 2*(3-4), 166–178. DOI: 10.1080/20430795.2012.742632

Hadad-Zervos, F. (2017, July 31). Malaysia launches the world's first green Islamic bond. *World Bank,* Blog, https://blogs.worldbank.org/en/eastasiapacific/malaysia-launches-the-worlds-first-green-islamic-bond?

Hadaś-Dyduch, M., Puszer, B., Czech, M., & Cichy, J. (2022). Green bonds as an instrument for financing ecological investments in the V4 countries. *Sustainability (Basel), 14*(19), 12188. DOI: 10.3390/su141912188

Hafenstein, A., & Bassen, A. (2016). Influences for using sustainability information in the investment decision-making of non-professional investors. *Journal of Sustainable Finance & Investment, 6*(3), 186–210. DOI: 10.1080/20430795.2016.1203598

Haggag Kotb Kholaif, M. M. N., & Tang, X. (2024). The role of green finance to achieve sustainability through green supply chain management and innovative technologies. *Sustainable Development*. Advance online publication. DOI: 10.1002/sd.3176

Hai, W. (2024). Development and Future Trends of Green Finance from an ESG Perspective. *Frontiers in Business, Economics and Management, 16*(1), 351–354. DOI: 10.54097/0hkacp17

Hamid, N. A., Muda, R., Alam, M. M., Omar, N., & Nadzri, F. A. A. (2019). Contribution of Islamic social capital on green economic growth in Malaysia. *International Journal of Business and Management Science*, *9*(2), 239–256.

Han, J., Zhang, W., Liu, X., Huang, H., & Isik, C. (2025). The role of green finance in energy transition: Regional variations and the moderating impact of women political participation. *Energy Policy*, *207*, 114817. DOI: 10.1016/j.enpol.2025.114817

Hasan, M. H., Hossain, M. Z., Hasan, L., & Dewan, M. A. (2024). FinTech and Sustainable Finance: How is FinTech Shaping the Future of Sustainable Finance? European Journal of Management, Economics and Business. 1(3), 100–115.doi.org/10.59324/ejmeb.2024.1(3).09

Hasan, M. H., Hossain, M. Z., Hasan, L., & Dewan, M. A. (2024). FinTech and Sustainable Finance: How is FinTech Shaping the Future of Sustainable Finance? European Journal of Management. *Economics and Business*, *1*(3), 100–115.

Hassan, S. A., Haq, I., Khattak, E. A., Nassani, A. A., Zaman, K., & Haffar, M. (2024). Transitioning from gridlock to sustainability: Advancing transport strategies for eco-friendly solutions in high-income countries. *Environmental Science and Pollution Research International*, *31*(47), 58152–58175. DOI: 10.1007/s11356-024-34997-x

Hassan, T., Khan, Y., Safi, A., Chaolin, H., Wahab, S., Daud, A., & Tufail, M. (2023). Green financing strategy for low-carbon economy: The role of high-technology imports and institutional strengths in China. *Journal of Cleaner Production*, *415*, 137859. DOI: 10.1016/j.jclepro.2023.137859

Heine, D., Semmler, W., Mazzucato, M., Braga, J. P., Flaherty, M., Gevorkyan, A., Hayde, E., & Radpour, S. (2019). *Financing low-carbon transitions through carbon pricing and green bonds* (Policy Research Working Paper No. 8991).

Helali, L. (2024, May 2). Green sukuk as an alternative to green bonds – opportunities and challenges. *Islamic Business and Financial Law,* https://blogs.helsinki.fi/islamic-business-financial-law/2024/05/02/green-sukuk-as-an-alternative-to-green-bonds-opportunities-and-challenges/

Heras-Saizarbitoria, I., Sáez, L., Allur, E., & Morandeira, J. (2018). The emergence of renewable energy cooperatives in Spain: A review. *Renewable & Sustainable Energy Reviews*, *94*, 1036–1043. DOI: 10.1016/j.rser.2018.06.049

Hidayat, S. E., Musari, K., Masrohatin, S., & Smolo, E. (2024). The future of Islamic finance. In Smolo, E., & Raheem, M. M. (Eds.), *The future of Islamic finance: From shari'ah law to fintech* (pp. 221–242). Emerald Publishing Limited. DOI: 10.1108/978-1-83549-906-120241014

HLEG. (2018). Financing a sustainable European economy. *Final Report.*

Ho, J. (2025, January 22). Global ESG sukuk market to surpass US$50 bil in 2025. *Singapore News Yahoo,* https://sg.news.yahoo.com/global-esg-sukuk-market-surpass-140000332.html

Ho, J. C. (2022). Disruptive innovation from the perspective of innovation diffusion theory. *Technology Analysis and Strategic Management, 34*(4), 363–376. DOI: 10.1080/09537325.2021.1901873

Hossain, M. R., Rao, A., Sharma, G. D., Dev, D., & Kharbanda, A. (2024). Empowering energy transition: Green innovation, digital finance, and the path to sustainable prosperity through green finance initiatives. *Energy Economics, 136*, 107736. DOI: 10.1016/j.eneco.2024.107736

Huang, Y., & Xu, J. (2024). Public development banks and green bond market development. *SSRN.* Retrieved from https://papers.ssrn.com DOI: 10.2139/ssrn.4972418

Hughes, A., Urban, M. A., & Wójcik, D. (2021). Alternative ESG Ratings: How Technological Innovation is reshaping Sustainable investment. *Sustainability (Basel), 13*(6), 3551. DOI: 10.3390/su13063551

Hunt, K. J. (2022). Sustainable Finance. *Review of Finance, 26*(6), 1309–1313. DOI: 10.1093/rof/rfac069

ICMA, IsDB, & LSEG. (2024). *Guidance on green, social and sustainability sukuk.* International Capital Market Association (ICMA), the Islamic Development Bank (IsDB), and the London Stock Exchange Group (LSEG).

IFRS. S. (2023). General requirements for disclosure of sustainability-related financial information. Доступно на: https://www. ifrs. org/content/dam/ifrs/publications/pdf-standards-issb/english/2023/issued/part-a/issb-2023-a-ifrs-slgeneral-requirements-for-disclosure-of-sustainability-related-financial-information. pdf

IISD. (2015). Islamic climate change declaration calls for zero emissions strategy. *International Institute for Sustainable Development (IISD),* https://sdg.iisd.org/news/islamic-climate-change-declaration-calls-for-zero-emissions-strategy/

Inderst, G., Kaminker, C., & Stewart, F. (2012). Defining and measuring green investments.

Indonesia, U. N. D. P. (2020, November 11). Pioneering the green sukuk in Indonesia. *United Nations Development Programme (UNDP),* https://www.undp.org/content/undp/en/home/stories/pioneering-the-green-sukok-in-indonesia.html

In, S. Y., & Schumacher, K. (2021). Carbonwashing: A new type of carbon data-related ESG greenwashing. DOI: 10.2139/ssrn.3901278

International Capital Market Association. (2023). Green Bond Principles. Retrieved from https://www.icmagroup.org/sustainable-finance/the-principles-guidelines-and-handbooks/green-bond-principles-gbp/

International Energy Agency. (2024), *Renewables 2024*, IEA, Paris, Retrieved from: https://www.iea.org/reports/renewables-2024

International Monetary Fund. (n.d.). *Climate Finance Indicators.* Retrieved from: https://climatedata.imf.org/pages/climate-finance

International Renewable Energy Agency. (2023). Renewable Energy. Retrieved from https://www.irena.org/

Intonti, M., De Leonardis, M., & Starace, G. (2025). *Enhancing circular practices in olive oil production: The role of green finance. Sustainability*. MDPI.

IPCC. (2021). *The physical science basis*. Sixth assessment report of the Intergovernmental Panel on Climate Change. Retrieved from https://www.ipcc.ch

Iqbal, Z. (January 23, 2024). Islamic Development Bank | Expert Insights | The Knowledge Portal. https://ukifc.com/2024/01/23/islamic-development-bank-expert-insights-the-knowledge-portal/

IsDB. (2020). Annual Impact Report on IsDB Debut Green Sukuk. Islamic Development Bank (IsDB), https://www.isdb.org/publications/annual-impact-report-on-isdb-debut-green-sukuk-dec-2020

Jain, K., Gangopadhyay, M., & Mukhopadhyay, K. (2022). Prospects and challenges of green bonds in renewable energy sector: Case of selected Asian economies. *Journal of Sustainable Finance & Investment, 14*(3), 708–731. DOI: 10.1080/20430795.2022.2034596

Jamil N. N., Wahyuni E. T. (2024). Unveiling greenwashing: Risks in sustainability and ESG reporting.

Janicka, M. (2016). Financial markets and the challenges of sustainable growth. *Comparative Economic Research Central and Eastern Europe, 19*(2), 27–41. DOI: 10.1515/cer-2016-0011

Jasrai, L., Bakshi, I., & Kaur, A. (2024). Decoding the Green Finance for India's Sustainable Growth. Alternative Finance, 104-118.

Jaumotte, F., Kim, J., Pienknagura, S., & Schwerhoff, G. (2024). *Policies to foster green FDI: Best practices for emerging market and developing economies (IMF Staff Climate Notes 2024/004)*. International Monetary Fund., DOI: 10.5089/9798400289927.066

Javaid, M., Haleem, A., Singh, R. P., Suman, R., & Gonzalez, E. S. (2022). Understanding the adoption of Industry 4.0 technologies in improving environmental sustainability. *Sustainable operations and computers, 3*, 203-217.

Jednak, D., & Jednak, S. (2019). Socially responsible financial markets. In *Palgrave studies in impact finance* (pp. 103–125). DOI: 10.1007/978-3-030-16522-2_5

Jeucken, M. (2010). *Sustainable finance and banking: The financial sector and the future of the planet*. Routledge. DOI: 10.4324/9781849776264

Ji, M., & Zhang, X. (2024). Assessing the impacts and mechanisms of green bond financing on the enhancement of green management and technological innovation in environmental conservation enterprises. *Journal of the Knowledge Economy, 15*(3), 12709–12750. DOI: 10.1007/s13132-023-01594-1

Johnson, L., Sachs, L., & Lobel, N. (2019). Aligning International Investment Agreements with the Sustainable Development Goals. SSRN Electronic Journal. DOI: 10.2139/ssrn.3452070

Johnstone, N., Serravalle, C., Scapecchi, P., & Labonne, J. (2007). *Public environmental policy and corporate behaviour: Project background, overview of the data and summary results* (OECD Working Paper). Organisation for Economic Co-operation and Development.

Jones, E.-A., Paige, L., Smith, A., Worth, A., Betts, L., & Stafford, R. (2024). Potential for carbon credits from conservation management: Price and potential for multi-habitat nature-based carbon sequestration in Dorset, UK. *Sustainability (Basel), 16*(3), 1268. DOI: 10.3390/su16031268

Joshipura, M., Mathur, S., & Kedia, N. (2024). Sustainable investing and financing for sustainable development: A hybrid review. *Sustainable Development (Bradford), 32*(5), 4469–4485. Advance online publication. DOI: 10.1002/sd.2912

Judijanto, L., Yoga, T., & Wijayanti, I. O. (2024). Bibliometric analysis of green finance and sustainable investment strategies. *West Science Social and Humanities Studies, 2*(12), 1965–1980. DOI: 10.58812/wsshs.v2i12.1487

Jun, N. H. H. (2013). Investing Well by Investing for good? Exploring the motivations of socially responsible investors. *Asian International Studies Review, 14*(1), 29–56. DOI: 10.1163/2667078X-01401002

Karumanchi, L. (2024). The role of green financing in accelerating sustainable economic development in emerging economies. *International Journal of Trade and Business Management*. Retrieved from https://ijtbm.com

Kashif, M., Pinglu, C., Ullah, S., & Zaman, M. (2024). Evaluating the influence of financial technology (FinTech) on sustainable finance: A comprehensive global analysis. *Financial Markets and Portfolio Management, 38*(1), 123–155. DOI: 10.1007/s11408-023-00439-w

Kassouri, Y., & Alola, A. A. (2023). Examining the interaction of technology adoption-diffusion and sectoral emission intensity in developing and emerging countries. *Journal of Cleaner Production, 405*, 136920. DOI: 10.1016/j.jclepro.2023.136920

Kathane, S., Babu, N., & Ramesh, S. (2024). Conceptual Framework of Sustainability in Green Finance. 3D: IBA Journal of Management & Leadership, 15(2).

Kerr, T. M., & Avendano, F. (2020). Green loans and multinational corporations. *Natural Resources and Environment, 35*(2), 46–49. https://www.jstor.org/stable/e27010659

Khalil, M. A., Sinliamthong, P., & Khalil, R. (2025). From paper to pixels for a world of purpose: A systematic review of sustainable finance, blockchain, and digital assets. *Sustainable Financing—A Contemporary Guide for Green Finance, Crowdfunding and Digital Currencies: Sustainable Financing*, 61-78.

Khan, A., Arora, D., & Meena, M. K. (2024). Unlocking trends in green bonds: Navigating opportunities and challenges for sustainable development in E7 countries.

Khan, A. A., & Wahab, Y. (2025). Sustainable finance and green FinTech. [DSSR]. *Dialogue Social Science Review, 3*(2), 874–893.

Khan, M., Serafeim, G., & Yoon, A. (2016). Corporate sustainability: First evidence on materiality. *The Accounting Review, 91*(6), 1697–1724. DOI: 10.2308/accr-51383

Khan, S. U., Shah, A., & Rizwan, M. F. (2021). Do financing constraints matter for technological and non-technological innovation? A (re) examination of developing markets. *Emerging Markets Finance & Trade*, *57*(9), 2739–2766. DOI: 10.1080/1540496X.2019.1695593

Kharche, N., & Kudal, P. (2024). Blockchain Role in Green Finance: A Pathway to Sustainable Development. In *Blockchain's Transformative Potential of Financial Technology for Sustainable Futures* (pp. 183–197). Springer Nature Switzerland. DOI: 10.1007/978-3-031-70219-8_12

Khoa, D. D., & Anh, D. N. (2024). Integrating green finance for sustainable agricultural practices and economic diversification in rural Vietnam. *Organizational Committee Proceedings*. Retrieved from https://duan.edu.ua

Kirby, D., MacMahon, C. H., & Thompson, S. E. (2024). *The co-evolution of sustainable finance stakeholders under the EU taxonomy for sustainable activities: an exploratory study of Irish disclosure experiences*. Sustainability Accounting, Management and Policy Journal., DOI: 10.1108/SAMPJ-11-2023-0842

Klaus, V. H., Schaub, S., Séchaud, R., Fabian, Y., Jeanneret, P., Lüscher, A., & Huguenin-Elie, O. (2024). Upscaling of ecosystem service and biodiversity indicators from field to farm to inform agri-environmental decision- and policy-making. *Ecological Indicators*, *163*, 112104. DOI: 10.1016/j.ecolind.2024.112104

Kobayakawa, T. (2021). Country diagnostics for low carbon development: Can developing countries pursue simultaneous implementation of the Sustainable Development Goals and the Paris Agreement? *Business Strategy & Development*, *4*(3), 294–312. DOI: 10.1002/bsd2.159

Kohli, S., & Al Taitoon, J. (2025, February 17). Why ESG sukuk has the wind in its sails. *London Stock Exchange Group (LSEG) Insights,* https://www.lseg.com/en/insights/why-sustainable-sukuk-has-wind-in-its-sails

Konstantakis, K. N., Koulmas, P., Michaelides, P. G., Porcher, T., & Prelorentzos, A. G. N. (2025). Green bonds & clean energy in sustainable finance: Evidence from DCC-GARCH Connectedness. *International Review of Financial Analysis*, *103*, 104168. DOI: 10.1016/j.irfa.2025.104168

Kotsantonis, S., Pinney, C., & Serafeim, G. (2016). ESG integration in investment management: Myths and realities. *The Bank of America Journal of Applied Corporate Finance*, *28*(2), 10–16. DOI: 10.1111/jacf.12169

Koumpli, V. (2024). EU ETS and voluntary carbon markets: Key features and current challenges. *Journal of World Energy Law and Business, 17*(1), 87–93. DOI: 10.1093/jwelb/jwad034

Kozlovska, A., & Kirilieva, A. (2020). Formation of an Effective Policy of "Green" Investment as A Priority Direction Of Sustainable Development of National Economy. *Pryazovskyi Economic Herald*, (2(19)). Advance online publication. DOI: 10.32840/2522-4263/2020-2-30

Kreibich, N., & Ossenbrink, J. (2021). The role of blockchain in the sustainable development goals: A case study of green bond issuance. *Journal of Cleaner Production, 303*, 127015. DOI: 10.1016/j.jclepro.2021.127015

Krueger, P., Sautner, Z., & Starks, L. T. (2020). The importance of climate risks for institutional investors. *Review of Financial Studies, 33*(3), 1067–1111. DOI: 10.1093/rfs/hhz137

Kruse, T., Mohnen, M., & Sato, M. (2023). Do Financial Markets Respond to Green Opportunities? *Journal of the Association of Environmental and Resource Economists*. Advance online publication. DOI: 10.1086/727370

Kumar, R. S. P., & Sheela, P. (2023). Can Islamic banks be sustainable with a simultaneously strong conventional banking counterpart? A comparative study of the financial performance of Islamic and conventional banks in Bahrain. *International Journal of Business Excellence, 30*(2), 133–159. DOI: 10.1504/IJBEX.2023.132063

Kurniawan, E., Nastiti, H. M., & Ali, R. A. (2024). Zakat environment: A bibliometric analysis. *Indonesian Conference of Zakat - Proceedings,* 398-405. DOI:DOI: 10.37706/iconz.2023.587

Labatt, S., & White, R. R. (2011). *Carbon finance: the financial implications of climate change*. John Wiley & Sons.

Lai, C. H., & Lin, S. H. (2017). Systems theory. *The international encyclopedia of organizational communication, 41*, 1-18.

Lakasse, S., Amril, A., Syamsuri, H., & Jusman, I. A. (2024). The Role of Green Finance in Sustainable Business Strategies: Opportunities and Challenges for Business Organizations. *JurnalPenelitianInovatif, 4*(2), 665–672. DOI: 10.54082/jupin.379

Lambert, D., Lyons, P., & Carroll, J. (2023, April). *Going Green – The Growth in Green Mortgage Financing in Ireland* (Financial Stability Note 4/FS/23). Central Bank of Ireland.

Langford, M. (2016). Lost in transformation? The politics of the sustainable development goals. *Ethics & International Affairs, 30*(2), 167–176. DOI: 10.1017/S0892679416000058

Larsen, M. L. (2019, November 22). *A growing toolbox of sustainable finance instruments – Green Finance & Development Center*. https://greenfdc.org/a-growing-toolbox-of-sustainable-finance-instruments/

Larsen, M. L. (2022). Driving Global Convergence in Green Financial Policies: China as Policy Pioneer and the EU as Standard Setter. *Global Policy, 13*(3), 358–370. DOI: 10.1111/1758-5899.13105

Law, K. (2025). Biodiversity credits are more problematic than carbon credits. *Nature, 637*(8045), 272. DOI: 10.1038/d41586-025-00017-2 PMID: 39774804

Lee, E., Kim, J. Y., & Lee, Y. (2025). A comparative analysis of green sukuk and green bonds. *International Journal of Islamic and Middle Eastern Finance and Management*. .DOI: 10.1108/IMEFM-12-2024-0609

Lee, C. C., Wang, F., & Chang, Y. F. (2023). Does green finance promote renewable energy? Evidence from China. *Resources Policy, 82*, 103439. Advance online publication. DOI: 10.1016/j.resourpol.2023.103439

Lee, J. W. (2020). Green finance and sustainable development goals: The case of China. Lee, Jung Wan (2020). Green Finance and Sustainable Development Goals: The Case of China. *The Journal of Asian Finance, Economics and Business, 7*(7), 577–586. DOI: 10.13106/jafeb.2020.vol7.no7.577

Liang, X., Liu, M., & Huang, Y. (2024). Studying financial development with low-carbon architecture development and green technological innovation: Sustaining SDG-9. *Environmental Science and Pollution Research International, 31*(2), 2009–2025. DOI: 10.1007/s11356-023-31155-7

Li, B. (2023). The role of financial markets in the energy transition: An analysis of investment trends and opportunities in renewable energy and clean technology. *Environmental Science and Pollution Research International, 30*(43), 97948–97964. DOI: 10.1007/s11356-023-29014-6 PMID: 37599346

Li, B., Rahman, M. M., & Haneklaus, N. (2024). Assessing China's energy transition pathway: Insights from the synergistic effects of key drivers. *Energy Strategy Reviews, 55*, 101528. DOI: 10.1016/j.esr.2024.101528

Li, C., Zhang, Y., Hou, G., & Ma, M. (2023). Analysis of Driving Factors and Action Path of Green Investment Behavior of Individual Investors. Highlights in Business. *Economics and Management, 9*, 33–43. DOI: 10.54097/hbem.v9i.7767

Li, G., Wu, H., Jiang, J., & Zong, Q. (2023). Digital finance and the low-carbon energy transition (LCET) from the perspective of capital-biased technical progress. *Energy Economics*, *120*, 106623. DOI: 10.1016/j.eneco.2023.106623

Lindenberg, N. (2014). Definition of Green Finance. Environmental Anthropology eJournal.

Lininger, K. B., & Lave, R. (2024). River restoration can increase carbon storage but is not yet a suitable basis for carbon credits. *Bioscience*, *74*(10), 717–724. DOI: 10.1093/biosci/biae083 PMID: 39444511

Lin, Z., Liao, X., & Jia, H. (2023). Could green finance facilitate low-carbon transformation of power generation? Some evidence from China. *International Journal of Climate Change Strategies and Management*, *15*(2), 141–158. DOI: 10.1108/IJCCSM-03-2022-0039

Li, T., Lau, W. T., & Dato Haji Yahya, M. H. (2025). Blockchain Applications in Green Finance for Transparency and Accountability in Sustainable Investments. *Sustainability (Basel)*, *17*(6), 2520. DOI: 10.3390/su17062520

Liu, M., Baisheng, S., Alharthi, M., Hassan, M. S., & Hanif, I. (2023). The role of natural resources, clean energy and technology in mitigating carbon emissions in top populated countries. *Resources Policy*, *83*, 103705. DOI: 10.1016/j.resourpol.2023.103705

Liu, Y., Lei, P., & He, D. (2024). Endogenous green technology progress, green transition and carbon emissions. *International Review of Economics & Finance*, *91*, 69–82. DOI: 10.1016/j.iref.2023.12.007

Liu, Z., Zheng, H., Gu, J., Xu, S., & Ye, Y. (2024). Exploring the nexus between green finance and energy efficiency: Unravelling the impact through green technology innovation and energy structure. *Heliyon*, *10*(9), e30141. DOI: 10.1016/j.heliyon.2024.e30141

Li, X., & Liu, X. (2005). Foreign direct investment and economic growth: An increasingly endogenous relationship. *World Development*, *33*(3), 393–407. https://doi.org/ https://doi.org/10.1016/j.worlddev.2004.11.001. DOI: 10.1016/j.worlddev.2004.11.001

Li, Y., Sun, G., Gao, Q., & Cheng, C. (2023). Digital financial inclusion, financial efficiency and green innovation. *Sustainability (Basel)*, *15*(3), 1879. DOI: 10.3390/su15031879

Lone, F. A., Aggarwal, S., & Jain, S. (2024). Retail investors' perception towards green bonds in advancing sustainability: Evidence from India. *Asia-Pacific Financial Markets*. Retrieved from https://link.springer.com

LSEG Data & Analytics, LSE, UKIFC, & GEFI. (2024). *Green and sustainability sukuk update 2023: Financing a sustainable future.* Refinitiv, London Stock Exchange Group (LSEG) Data & Analytics, London Stock Exchange (LSE), Islamic Finance Council United Kingdom (UKIFC), and the Global Ethical Finance Initiative (GEFI).

Luurila, K. (2022). Green finance research around the world: A review of literature. *International Journal of Green Economics, 16*(1), 56. DOI: 10.1504/IJGE.2022.125554

Lv, Y. (2023). Transitioning to sustainable energy: Opportunities, challenges, and the potential of blockchain technology. *Frontiers in Energy Research, 11*, 1258044. DOI: 10.3389/fenrg.2023.1258044

Lyon, T. P., & Montgomery, A. W. (2015). The means and end of greenwash. *Organization & Environment*, *28*(2), 223–249. DOI: 10.1177/1086026615575332

Mahajan, R., Lim, W. M., Sareen, M., Kumar, S., & Panwar, R. (2023). Stakeholder theory. *Journal of Business Research, 166*, 114104. DOI: 10.1016/j.jbusres.2023.114104

Mahmood, S., Sun, H., Iqbal, A., Alhussan, A. A., & El-kenawy, E.-S. M. (2024). Green finance, sustainable infrastructure, and green technology innovation: Pathways to achieving sustainable development goals in the Belt and Road Initiative. *Environmental Research Communications*, *6*(10), 105036. Advance online publication. DOI: 10.1088/2515-7620/ad898f

Mahn, K. D. (2016). The impact of sustainable investment strategies. *Journal of Investing*, *25*(2), 96–102. DOI: 10.3905/joi.2016.25.2.096

Makeel, R., Syed, Z. A., & Zhao, S. (2025). Unlocking green technology adoption: Exploring influential factors and the moderating influence of environmentally responsible behaviour. *Behaviour & Information Technology*, 1–19. DOI: 10.1080/0144929X.2025.2515450

Malaysia, B. I. X. (2023, January 3). *The state of Islamic sustainable finance in Malaysia and Indonesia, according to the legal community.* https://www.bixmalaysia.com/learning-center/articles-tutorials/the-state-of-islamic-sustainable-finance-in-malaysia-and-indonesia,-according-to-the-legal-community

Malik, A. H., Jais, M. B., Md Isa, A. H., & Rehman, A. U. (2022). Role of social sustainability for financial inclusion and stability among Asian countries. *International Journal of Social Economics*, *49*(9), 1324–1348. DOI: 10.1108/IJSE-08-2021-0458

Malik, K., & Sharma, S. (2025). Role of ESG and private equity on environmental degradation: A nexus of opportunity and responsibility for developing and developed countries. *Journal of Economic Studies (Glasgow, Scotland)*, *52*(3), 532–548. DOI: 10.1108/JES-11-2023-0672

Maltais, A., & Nykvist, B. (2020). Understanding the role of green bonds in advancing sustainability. *Environmental Innovation and Societal Transitions*, *27*, 1–8. DOI: 10.1016/j.eist.2017.10.003

Ma, M., Zhu, X., Liu, M., & Huang, X. (2023). Combining the role of green finance and environmental sustainability on green economic growth: Evidence from G-20 economies. *Renewable Energy*, *207*, 128–136. DOI: 10.1016/j.renene.2023.02.046

Manaswi, K., Singh, A., & Gupta, V. (2023). Building a Better Future with Sustainable Investments: Insights from Recent Research. *Indian Journal of Human Development*, *17*(2), 320–343. DOI: 10.1177/09737030231194836

Manfrino, M. (2024). Beyond carbon: Navigating the path to biodiversity credits for climate action and ecosystem conservation. DOI: 10.2139/ssrn.4687255

Mani, V., Delgado, C., Hazen, B., & Patel, P. (2017). Mitigating Supply Chain Risk via Sustainability Using Big Data Analytics: Evidence from the Manufacturing Supply Chain. *Sustainability (Basel)*, *9*(4), 608. DOI: 10.3390/su9040608

Marín-Rodríguez, N. J., González-Ruíz, J. D., & Botero-Botero, S. (2025). Towards New Strategies for Investing: Insights on Sustainable Exchange-Traded Funds (ETFs). *WORLD (Oakland, Calif.)*, *6*(1), 8. DOI: 10.3390/world6010008

Marín-Rodríguez, N. J., Gonzalez-Ruiz, J. D., & Botero, S. (2024). Connectedness between sustainable investment indexes: The QVAR approach. *Economies*, *12*(7), 170. DOI: 10.3390/economies12070170

Marín-Rodríguez, N. J., González-Ruiz, J. D., & Valencia-Arias, A. (2023). Incorporating Green Bonds into Portfolio Investments: Recent Trends and Further Research. *Sustainability (Basel)*, *15*(20), 14897. Advance online publication. DOI: 10.3390/su152014897

Market Research Future. (2025). *Global Green Finance Market Overview* Retrieved from: https://www.marketresearchfuture.com/reports/green-finance-market-24469]

Markina, T. A. (2022). Defining a sustainable development target space for 2030 and 2050. *One Earth*, *5*(2), 142–156. DOI: 10.1016/j.oneear.2022.01.003

Martin, V. (2023). Green Finance: Regulation and Instruments. *Journal of Central Banking Theory and Practice*. DOI: 10.2478/jcbtp-2023-0019

Martini, M. (2020). Developing sustainable finance definitions and taxonomies.

Meng, X. L., & Shaikh, G. M. (2023). Evaluating Environmental, Social, and Governance Criteria and Green Finance Investment Strategies Using Fuzzy AHP and Fuzzy WASPAS. *Sustainability (Basel)*, *15*(8), 6786. DOI: 10.3390/su15086786

Mhlanga, D. (2025). Leveraging Blockchain for Sustainable Finance: Insights, Challenges, and Opportunities for Africa. Financial Inclusion and Sustainable Development in Sub-Saharan Africa, 52-73.

Mhlanga, D. (2024). The role of big data in financial technology toward financial inclusion. *Frontiers in Big Data*, *7*, 1184444. DOI: 10.3389/fdata.2024.1184444

Michaelowa, A. (2012). Carbon markets or climate finance. Low carbon and adaptation investment choices for the developing world.

Michaelowa, A., Michaelowa, K., Shishlov, I., & Brescia, D. (2021). Catalysing private and public action for climate change mitigation: The World Bank's role in international carbon markets. *Climate Policy*, *21*(1), 120–132. DOI: 10.1080/14693062.2020.1790334

Middle East Briefing. (2025, January 23). ESG Sukuk to Cross US$50 Billion in 2025, Key Funding Tool in Emerging Markets. https://www.middleeastbriefing.com/news/esg-sukuk-to-cross-usd50-billion-in-2025-key-global-funding-tool/

Mishra, M. S. N. (2021). *Future of Green Financing: Challenges and Opportunities. 1*(1).

Mitchell Aide, T. (2024). The Biodiversity Credit Market needs rigorous baseline, monitoring, and validation practices. *npj. Npj Biodiversity*, *3*(1), 30. DOI: 10.1038/s44185-024-00062-6

Mittal, H. (2023). Exploring How Financial Literacy Affects University Students' Sustainable Investment Decisions. Educational Administration: Theory and Practice.

Miyan, M., Cheong, C. W. H., Sharif, A., & Afshan, S. (2024). Three Decades of Green Finance: The State of the Art and Way Forward. *International Journal of Energy Economics and Policy*, *14*(6), 88–105. DOI: 10.32479/ijeep.16718

Mnif, E., Jarboui, A., & Mouakhar, K. (2024). Strategic insights into carbon markets, digital finance and geopolitical risks for advancing green sustainability investments. *Management of Environmental Quality*, *35*(7), 1622–1649. Advance online publication. DOI: 10.1108/MEQ-10-2023-0369

MOCCAE. (2020, December 16). Ministry of Climate Change and Environment Launches UAE Environmental Policy. https://www.moccae.gov.ae/en/media-center/news/16/12/2020/ministry-of-climate-change-and-environment-launches-uae-environmental-policy.aspx#page=1

MOCCAE. (2021). *UAE sustainable finance framework 2021-2031*. United Arab Emirates (UAE) Ministry of Climate Change and Environment (MOCCAE), https://www.moccae.gov.ae/assets/24b84d14/UAE_Sustainable_framework_21.pdf.aspx

MOCCAE. (2022). *UAE green bond and sukuk program development situation analysis report.* United Arab Emirates (UAE) Ministry of Climate Change and Environment (MOCCAE), https://www.moccae.gov.ae/assets/download/a36ce910/UAE%20Green%20Bond%20and%20Sukuk%20Program%20Development.pdf.aspx

MoF & UNDP Indonesia. (2018). *Indonesia's green bond & green sukuk initiative.* Ministry of Finance Republic of Indonesia (MoF of Indonesia), Jakarta.

MoF of Indonesia. (2019). *Green sukuk, allocation and impact report – February 2019.* Ministry of Finance Republic of Indonesia (MoF of Indonesia), Jakarta.

MoF of Indonesia. (2020). *Green sukuk, allocation and impact report – March 2020.* Ministry of Finance (MoF), Republic of Indonesia, Jakarta.

MoF of Indonesia. (2024). Green sukuk, allocation and impact report 2024. Ministry of Finance Republic of Indonesia (MoF of Indonesia), Jakarta.

MoF of Saudi Arabia. (2024). *Kingdom of Saudi Arabia Green Financing Framework March 2024.* Ministry of Finance Kingdom of Saudi Arabia (MoF of Saudi Arabia).

Mol, A. P. (2012). Carbon flows, financial markets and climate change mitigation. *Environmental Development*, *1*(1), 10–24. DOI: 10.1016/j.envdev.2011.12.003

Mol, A. P., & Spaargaren, G. (2000). Ecological modernisation theory in debate: A review. *Environmental Politics*, *9*(1), 17–49. DOI: 10.1080/09644010008414511

Montfort, S., Fesenfeld, L., Ingold, K., Lamb, W. F., & Andrijevic, M. (2025). Political enablers of ambitious climate policies: A framework and thematic review. *npj. Npj Climate Action*, *4*(1), 14. DOI: 10.1038/s44168-024-00206-1

Moriarty, P., & Honnery, D. (2016). Can renewable energy power the future? *Energy Policy*, *93*, 3–7. DOI: 10.1016/j.enpol.2016.02.051

Mouakket, S., & Aboelmaged, M. (2022). Drivers and outcomes of green information technology adoption in service organizations: An evidence from emerging economy context. *Journal of Science and Technology Policy Management*, *13*(4), 898–924. DOI: 10.1108/JSTPM-09-2020-0137

Mouakket, S., & Aboelmaged, M. (2023). Factors influencing green information technology adoption: A multi-level perspective in emerging economies context. *Information Development, 39*(4), 699–719. DOI: 10.1177/02666669211048489

Muganyi, T., Yan, L., & Sun, H. (2021). Green finance, fintech and environmental protection: Evidence from China. *International Journal of Environmental Research and Public Health, 18*(9), 4771. DOI: 10.3390/ijerph18094771 PMID: 33947122

Muniasamy, I. G. (2024). Digital platform dynamics: Governance, market design and AI integration. *Purdue University*. Retrieved from https://hammer.purdue.edu

Musari, K. (2020a, January 7). Measuring the opportunities of white sukuk for SDGs. *Bisnis Indonesia,* Opini, 2.

Musari, K. (2020b, April 14). Pandemic and catastrophe sukuk. *Bisnis Indonesia,* Opini, 2.

Musari, K., & Khan, T. (2023). *Sustainable development and circular economy in the GCC countries.* A paper was presented at the Workshop "Circular Economy and Sustainable Development Model: It's Role in the GCC States' National Visions" held by Gulf Research Centre Cambridge (GRCC), University of Cambridge, Cambridge – United Kingdom, July, 11th -13th

Musari, K. (2021). Green sukuk, Islamic green financing: A lesson learned from Indonesia. In Olarewaju, O. M., & Ganiyu, I. O. (Eds.), *Climate change and the sustainable financial sector* (pp. 1–16). IGI Global. DOI: 10.4018/978-1-7998-7967-1.ch001

Musari, K. (2025). Towards the perpetual sustainable sukuk through Islamic blended finance: Lesson from green sukuk and blue sukuk in Indonesia. In de Pablos, P. O., Lytras, M., & Malik, S. (Eds.), *Securing sustainable futures through blue and green economies* (pp. 381–402). IGI Global. DOI: 10.4018/979-8-3693-7893-9.ch015

Musari, K., & Hidayat, S. E. (2023). The role of green sukuk in maqasid al-shariah and SDGs: Evidence from Indonesia. In Jumat, Z. H., Khateeb, S. H., & Ali, S. N. (Eds.), *Islamic finance, fintech, and the road to sustainability: Reframing the approach in the post-pandemic era* (pp. 181–203). Palgrave CIBFR Studies in Islamic Finance. Palgrave Macmillan. DOI: 10.1007/978-3-031-13302-2_9

Mutambatsere, E., & Schellekens, P. (2020). *The why and how of blended finance.* A Discussion Paper of International Finance Corporation (IFC) World Bank Group, November

Nadkarni, P. (2024, June). Exploring the Role of Sustainable Green Finance in Addressing Global Economic Challenges: A Literature Review. In *International Conference on Digital Transformation in Business: Navigating the New Frontiers Beyond Boundaries (DTBNNF 2024)* (pp. 589-612). Atlantis Press.

Nanthini, M., Vinumon, V. S., Thomas, A. A., & Sheshu, A. (2024). Green Finance 2.0: Harnessing Fintech for Sustainable Investments in Industry 5.0. In *Anticipating Future Business Trends: Navigating Artificial Intelligence Innovations* (Vol. 1, pp. 195–204). Springer Nature Switzerland. DOI: 10.1007/978-3-031-63569-4_17

Nasir, N., & Ahmed, W. (2024). *Green finance initiatives and their potential to drive sustainable development*. Springer. DOI: 10.1007/978-3-031-56419-2_1

Nasis, A. (2025). Blockchain-based compliance frameworks enhance regulatory transparency, reducing fraud in sustainable investment transactions. *National Journal of Research in Marketing. Finance & HRM*, *10*(1), 83.

Negi, L., Manpreet, M., & Singh, M. (2025). Green Finance and Digital Strategies: Catalysts for the Expansion of Circular Technologies in the Global Market. In Innovating Sustainability Through Digital Circular Economy (pp. 281-304). IGI Global Scientific Publishing.

Nevatia, V. (2024). Sovereign green bonds: Reducing climate capital costs in emerging markets. *SSRN*. Retrieved from https://papers.ssrn.com DOI: 10.2139/ssrn.4983252

Ng, T. H., & Tao, J. Y. (2016). Bond financing for renewable energy in Asia. *Energy Policy*, *95*, 509–517. https://doi.org/10. DOI: 10.1016/j.enpol.2016.03.015

Nguyen, D. H. H., & Khominich, I. P. (2023). The measurement of green economic quality in the BRICS countries: Should they prioritize financing for environmental protection, economic growth, or social goals? *Russian Journal of Economics*, *9*(2), 183–200. DOI: 10.32609/j.ruje.9.101612

Nguyen, D. T., Oanh, T. T. K., Bui, T. D., & Dao, L. K. O. (2024). The impact of green finance on green growth: The role of green energy and green production. *Heliyon*, *10*(16), e36639. DOI: 10.1016/j.heliyon.2024.e36639 PMID: 39262964

Nica, A. (2023). The Banking System-" Limping" toward a Sustainable Future: Is Green Finance a" Thing" in Romania as of March 2023? Europolity: Continuity & Change Eur. *Governance: An International Journal of Policy, Administration and Institutions*, *17*, 209.

Nile, I. V. E., Udo, E. S., Jack, A. E., & Abner, I. P. (2024), Green Finance and Sustainable Development Nexus in Sub-Saharan Africa. FWU Journal of Social Sciences, 78–90. DOI: 10.51709/19951272/Summer2024/8

Nippa, M., Patnaik, S., & Taussig, M. (2021). MNE responses to carbon pricing regulations: Theory and evidence. *Journal of International Business Studies*, *52*(5), 904–929. DOI: 10.1057/s41267-021-00403-8

Nipper, M., Ostermaier, A., & Theis, J. (2022). Mandatory disclosure of standardized sustainability metrics: The case of the EU Taxonomy Regulation.

Nordea (2023). What are green loans? Retrieved from: https://www.nordea.com/en/news/what-are-green-loans

O'Sullivan, N. (2024). *Sustainable investment.* Edward Elgar Publishing., DOI: 10.4337/9781800880344.ch39

Obadire, A. M., & Moyo, V. (2024). Exploring the Dynamics of Green Banking and Finance: A Literature Review. The Palgrave Handbook of Green Finance for Sustainable Development, 723-756.

Obobisa, E. S., & Ahakwa, I. (2024). Stimulating the adoption of green technology innovation, clean energy resources, green finance, and environmental taxes: The way to achieve net zero CO2 emissions in Europe? *Technological Forecasting and Social Change*, *205*, 123489. DOI: 10.1016/j.techfore.2024.123489

OECD (2018), *Making Blended Finance Work for the Sustainable Development Goals.* Organisation for Economic Co-operation and Development (OECD) Publishing. DOI: 10.1787/9789264288768-en

OECD. (2021). *Mobilising Bond Markets for a Low-Carbon Transition.* https://www.oecd.org/en/publications/mobilising-bond-markets-for-a-low-carbon-transition_9789264272323-en.html

OECD. (2021). The OECD DAC blended finance guidance. Organisation for Economic Co-operation and Development (OECD) Development Co-operation Directorate, Paris

OECD. (2022). *Global outlook on financing for sustainable development 2023: No sustainability without equity.* Organisation for Economic Co-operation and Development (OECD) Publishing. DOI: 10.1787/fcbe6ce9-en

Ofori, I. K., Figari, F., & Ojong, N. (2023). Towards sustainability: The relationship between foreign direct investment, economic freedom and inclusive green growth. *Journal of Cleaner Production*, *406*, 137020. DOI: 10.1016/j.jclepro.2023.137020

Ojukwu, P. U., Cadet, E., Osundare, O. S., Fakeyede, O. G., Ige, A. B., & Uzoka, A. (2024). Advancing green bonds through FinTech innovations: A conceptual insight into opportunities and challenges. *International Journal of Engineering Research and Development, 20*, 565–576.

Okeke, N. I., Bakare, O. A., &Achumie, G. O. (2024). Integrating policy incentives and risk management for effective green finance in emerging markets. International Journal of Frontiers in Science and Technology Research, 7(1), 076–088. DOI: 10.53294/ijfstr.2024.7.1.0050

Olabi, A. G., Abdelkareem, M. A., Mahmoud, M. S., Elsaid, K., Obaideen, K., Rezk, H., Wilberforce, T., Eisa, T., Chae, K.-J., & Sayed, E. T. (2023). Green hydrogen: Pathways, roadmap, and role in achieving sustainable development goals. *Process Safety and Environmental Protection, 177*, 664–687. DOI: 10.1016/j.psep.2023.06.069

Ongsakul, V., & Sen, S. K. (2018). Creating shared value through big-data analytics: a aleResearch, 12(04). DOI: 10.24052/JBRMR/V12IS04/ART-10

Organisation for Economic Co-operation and Development. (2021). *Green finance and investment: Mobilizing private finance for climate action in emerging economies*. OECD Publishing.

Ottinger, R. L., & Bowie, J. (2014). Innovative Financing for Renewable Energy. *Academy of Environmental Law Colloquium*. DOI: 10.2139/ssrn.2497175

Owadally, I., Mwizere, J., Kalidas, N., Murugesu, K., & Kashif, M. (2021). Long-Term sustainable investment for retirement. *Sustainability (Basel), 13*(9), 5000. DOI: 10.3390/su13095000

Öztürk, S. (2024). Comparative evaluation of emissions trading systems and carbon taxes: implementations in climate change mitigation through carbon pricing. Marmara Üniversitesi İktisadi ve İdari Bilimler Dergisi, (Sustainability and Green Economics Special Issue), 18-35.

Palea, V. (2021). Accounting for sustainable finance: Does fair value measurement fit for long-term equity investments? *Meditari Accountancy Research, 30*(1), 22–38. DOI: 10.1108/MEDAR-07-2020-0965

Panfilov, M. A., Nikishova, N. V., & Logutenkov, A. V. (2024). Impact of green bond issuance on the company's efficiency. In *Creation of green finance frameworks*. Springer. DOI: 10.1007/978-3-031-70962-3_21

Parry, I. W. H., Black, S., & Zhunussova, K. (2022). *Carbon Taxes or Emissions Trading Systems?: Instrument Choice and Design* (IMF Staff Climate Note No. 2022/006). International Monetary Fund.

Passas, I., & Garefalakis, A. (2025). The impact of fraud perception and ESG-washing on investment trust: Integrating corporate governance theory and empirical evidence. *Accounting and Auditing, 1*(3), 9. DOI: 10.3390/accountaudit1030009

Patel, K. (2024). Digitalization and the Rise of Green Finance: Opportunities, Challenges, and the Path Forward. Impact of Digitalization on Reporting, Tax Avoidance, Accounting, and Green Finance, 179-199.

Pelling, M., O'Brien, K., & Matyas, D. (2015). Adaptation and transformation. *Climatic Change, 133*(1), 113–127. DOI: 10.1007/s10584-014-1303-0

Peng, B. (2024). Navigating green horizons: An empirical exploration of business practices aligned with environmental goals in the era of sustainable economy. *MDE. Managerial and Decision Economics, 45*(7), 4732–4752. DOI: 10.1002/mde.4284

Perdana, A., & Kulkarni, M. S. (2023). Exploring the synergy between financial technologies and financial inclusion: What we know and where we should be heading? *Pacific Asia Journal of the Association for Information Systems, 15*(1), 4.

Pizzani, L. (2015). Expanding ESG Coverage. *CFA Institute Magazine, 26*(6), 30–31. DOI: 10.2469/cfm.v26.n6.12

PME. (2023, November 7). *Green bonds and sukuk in the UAE: Legal framework and considerations.* Prudential Middle East (PME) Global LLC, https://www.linkedin.com/pulse/green-bonds-sukuk-uae-legal-framework-znmff/

Polzin, F., Sanders, M., & Tauebe, F. (2017). A diverse and resilient financial system for investments in the energy transition. *Current Opinion in Environmental Sustainability, 28*, 24–32. DOI: 10.1016/j.cosust.2017.07.004

Pramitasari, D. A. (2024). ESG Investing: Evaluating the financial performance of sustainable portfolios. [EJME]. *Equator Journal of Management and Entrepreneurship, 12*(4), 332–340. DOI: 10.26418/ejme.v12i4.82793

Probst, B. S., Toetzke, M., Kontoleon, A., Anadón, L. D., Minx, J. C., & Haya, B. K.. (2024). Systematic assessment of the achieved emission reductions of carbon crediting projects. *Nature Communications, 15*(9562), 1–14. DOI: 10.1038/s41467-024-53645-z PMID: 39543137

Puaschunder, J. M. (2023). The Future of Resilient Green Finance. In *The Future of Resilient Finance: Finance Politics in the Age of Sustainable Development* (pp. 185–210). Springer International Publishing. DOI: 10.1007/978-3-031-30138-4_6

Pucker, K. P. (2021). Overselling sustainability reporting. *Harvard Business Review, 99*(3), 134–143.

Qadri, H. M. U. D., Ali, H., Abideen, Z. U., & Jafar, A. (2024). Mapping the evolution of green finance research and development in emerging green economies. *Resources Policy, 91*, 104943. DOI: 10.1016/j.resourpol.2024.104943

Qi, H., Huang, X., & Sheeraz, M. (2023). Green financing for renewable energy development: Driving the attainment of zero-emission targets. *Renewable Energy, 213*, 30–37. DOI: 10.1016/j.renene.2023.05.111

Rahman, S., Hossain, I., Hassan, M., Hossain, G. S., & Perveen, R. (2022). A systematic review of green finance in the banking industry: Perspectives from a developing country. *Green Finance, 4*(3), 347–363. DOI: 10.3934/GF.2022017

Raji. (2024). Sustainable Finance in Action: Exploring Green Loans in Promoting Environmental Responsibility. Kristu Jayanti Journal of Management Sciences (KJMS), 14–25. DOI: 10.59176/kjms.v2i1.2348

Ramakrishna, D. (2023). *Emerging Trends of Green Finance in India: Challenges and Opportunities*. International Journal for Multidisciplinary Research., DOI: 10.36948/ijfmr.2023.v05i05.7224

Raman, R., Ray, S., Das, D., & Nedungadi, P. (2025). Innovations and barriers in sustainable and green finance for advancing sustainable development goals. *Frontiers in Environmental Science, 12*, 1513204. Advance online publication. DOI: 10.3389/fenvs.2024.1513204

Ramgopal, N. C., & Mohanty, A. K. (2019). Bridging funding gaps for climate and sustainable development: Pitfalls, progress, and potential of private finance. Dogo Rangsang Research Journal, 9(3).

Ranabahu, N., & Wickramasinghe, A. (2022). Sustainable leadership in microfinance: A pathway for sustainable initiatives in micro and small businesses? *Sustainability (Basel), 14*(9), 5167. DOI: 10.3390/su14095167

Rasoulinezhad, E., & Taghizadeh-Hesary, F. (2022). Role of green finance in improving energy efficiency and renewable energy development. *Energy Efficiency, 15*(2), 14. DOI: 10.1007/s12053-022-10021-4 PMID: 35529528

Ratnakaram, S., Manikeswari, D., Babu, M., & Paluri, S. (2025). *Islamic Banking, Environmental Social Governance (ESG) Ingredients for Enhanced Sustainability in the Banking Sector*. Digital Transformation and Sustainability of Business. DOI: 10.1201/9781003606185-49

Raut, R. D., Narkhede, B., & Gardas, B. B. (2017). To identify the critical success factors of sustainable supply chain management practices in the context of oil and gas industries: ISM approach. *Renewable & Sustainable Energy Reviews*, *68*, 33–47. DOI: 10.1016/j.rser.2016.09.067

Refinitiv, LSE, UKIFC, & GEFI. (2022). *Green and sustainability sukuk report 2022*. Refinitiv, London Stock Exchange (LSE), Islamic Finance Council United Kingdom (UKIFC), and the Global Ethical Finance Initiative (GEFI).

Renneboog, L., Ter Horst, J., & Zhang, C. (2008). Socially responsible investments: Institutional aspects, performance, and investor behavior. *Journal of Banking & Finance*, *32*(9), 1723–1742. DOI: 10.1016/j.jbankfin.2007.12.039

Riaz, T., Selamat, A. I., Nor, N. M., & Hassan, A. F. S. (2024). Do investors get benefits from corporate green sukuk issuance. *Journal of Islamic Monetary Economics and Finance*, *10*(3), 445–470. DOI: 10.21098/jimf.v10i3.1944

Richardson, B. J. (2014). The Evolving Marketscape of Climate Finance. *Climate Law*, *4*(1-2), 94–106. DOI: 10.1163/18786561-00402008

Ringe, W. (2023). Investor Empowerment for sustainability. *Review of Economics*, *74*(1), 21–52. DOI: 10.1515/roe-2023-0016

Risalvato, G., Venezia, C., & Maggio, F. (2018). Social Responsible Investments and performance. *International Journal of Financial Research*, *10*(1), 10. DOI: 10.5430/ijfr.v10n1p10

Rockström, J., Steffen, W., Noone, K., Persson, Å., Chapin, F. S., Lambin, E., & Schellnhuber, H. J. (2009). A safe operating space for humanity. *Nature*, *461*(7263), 472–475. DOI: 10.1038/461472a PMID: 19779433

Rogers, E. M. (2003). Diffusion networks. *Networks in the knowledge economy, 10.*

Rohith, N. R., & Patil, N. H. (2025). Awareness of investors toward green finance initiatives. [PEN]. *Periodicals of Engineering and Natural Sciences*, *13*(2), 337–348. DOI: 10.21533/pen.v13.i2.283

Ronaldo, R., & Suryanto, T. (2022). Green finance and sustainability development goals in Indonesian Fund Village. *Resources Policy*, *78*, 102839. DOI: 10.1016/j.resourpol.2022.102839

Rossberg, A. G., O'Sullivan, J. D., Malysheva, S., & Shnerb, N. M. (2024). A metric for tradable biodiversity credits quantifying impacts on global extinction risk. *Journal of Industrial Ecology*, *28*(4), 1009–1021. DOI: 10.1111/jiec.13518

Roy, P. K. (2023). Enriching the green economy through sustainable investments: An ESG-based credit rating model for green financing. *Journal of Cleaner Production*, *420*, 138315. DOI: 10.1016/j.jclepro.2023.138315

Ruiz-Palomo, D., Fernández-Gámez, M. Á., & León-Gómez, A. (2022). Analyzing the effect of financial constraints on technological and management innovation in SMEs: A gender perspective. *SAGE Open*, *12*(1). DOI: 10.1177/21582440221079925

Sachs, J. D., Schmidt-Traub, G., Mazzucato, M., Messner, D., Nakicenovic, N., & Rockström, J. (2019). Six transformations to achieve the sustainable development goals. *Nature Sustainability*, *2*(9), 805–814. DOI: 10.1038/s41893-019-0352-9

Saleem, H., Khan, M. B., & Mahdavian, S. M. (2022). The role of green growth, green financing, and eco-friendly technology in achieving environmental quality: Evidence from selected Asian economies. *Environmental Science and Pollution Research International*, *29*(38), 57720–57739. DOI: 10.1007/s11356-022-19799-3

Saliou, P., Muller, V., & Rocha, F. (2025). Green Finance: The role of the EU, US and China, and how Securitization can unlock the market potential. *Ernest & Young*. Luxembourg. Retrieved from: https://www.ey.com/en_lu/insights/securitization/green-finance-the-role-of-the-eu-us-china

Sampene, A. K., Li, C., & Nsiah, T. K. (2024). Catalyzing renewable energy deployment in the Mercosur economies: A synthesis of human capital, technological innovation and green finance. *Energy Strategy Reviews*, *53*, 101388. DOI: 10.1016/j.esr.2024.101388

Saraji, S., & Borowczak, M. (2024). A Blockchain-based carbon credit ecosystem. *arXiv*.

Sari, R. C., Sholihin, M., Cahaya, F. R., Ishola, A., Yuniarti, N., Pranesti, A., Sari, A. R., & Haryanto, . (2025). Artificial intelligence-based ESG greenwashing detection: Road to net zero carbon and its impact on corporate performance. *Business Strategy & Development*, *8*(4), e70228. DOI: 10.1002/bsd2.70228

Sasongko, A., & Sakti, A. (2020). *Sovereign green sukuk: Environmental risk model development*. Working Paper of Bank Indonesia Number WP/2/2020, https://publication-bi.org/repec/idn/wpaper/WP022020.pdf

Saxena, R. (2024). The effect of green banking practices on banks' environmental performance and green financing: An empirical study. *Journal of Electrical Systems, 20(11s)*. https://doi.org/10.XXX/jes.7967

Saxena, R., Sharma, S., Saini, K. P., & Agarwal, S. (2024). From Greenwashing to Green Finance: Blockchain as a Catalyst for Transparency and Impact. Blockchain's Transformative Potential of Financial Technology for Sustainable Futures, 151-167.

SC. (2019). *Sustainable and responsible investment sukuk framework: An overview.* Securities Commission (SC) Malaysia. S&P Global. (2025, March 25). *Sustainability insights: Sustainable bond outlook 2025: Middle east issuance to remain high.* https://www.spglobal.com/ratings/en/research/articles/250304-sustainability-insights-sustainable-bond-outlook-2025-middle-east-issuance-to-remain-high-13424912

Schain, J. P., & Stiebale, J. (2021). Innovation, institutional ownership and financial constraints. *Empirical Economics*, *61*(3), 1689–1697. DOI: 10.1007/s00181-020-01909-0

Schoenmaker, D., & Schramade, W. (2019). Investing for long-term value creation. *Journal of Sustainable Finance & Investment*, *9*(4), 356–377. DOI: 10.1080/20430795.2019.1625012

Schwerdtner Mánez, K., & Clifton, J. (2025). *Biodiversity credits: A new currency to support nature conservation?* Fauna & Flora International. DOI: 10.1017/S0030605324001467

Scott, W. R. (2005). Institutional theory: Contributing to a theoretical research program. *Great minds in management: The process of theory development, 37*(2), 460-484.

Scott, W. R. (2008). Approaching adulthood: The maturing of institutional theory. *Theory and Society*, *37*(5), 427–442. DOI: 10.1007/s11186-008-9067-z

Seidl, A., Cumming, T., Arlaud, M., Crossett, C., & van den Heuvel, O. (2024). Investing in the wealth of nature through biodiversity and ecosystem service finance solutions. *Ecosystem Services*, *66*, 101601. DOI: 10.1016/j.ecoser.2024.101601

Selvakumar, P., & Manjunath, T. C. (2025). *Green Finance and Investment: Explore the Role of Sustainable Finance*. In Handbook of Research on Climate Change and the Sustainable Financial Sector (pp. 138-164). IGI Global. DOI: 10.4018/979-8-3693-9750-3.ch008

Senaya, N. G. M.Glenda M Senaya. (2024). Financial literacy and its role in promoting sustainable investment. *World Journal of Advanced Research and Reviews*, *24*(1), 212–232. DOI: 10.30574/wjarr.2024.24.1.2986

Sethi, L., Behera, B., & Sethi, N. (2024). Do green finance, green technology innovation, and institutional quality help achieve environmental sustainability? Evidence from the developing economies. *Sustainable Development (Bradford), 32*(3), 2709–2723. DOI: 10.1002/sd.2811

Shahadat, M. H., Nekmahmud, M., Ebrahimi, P., & Fekete-Farkas, M. (2023). Digital technology adoption in SMEs: What technological, environmental and organizational factors influence in emerging countries? *Global Business Review*. DOI: 10.1177/09721509221137199

Shahbaz, M., Patel, N., Du, A. M., & Ahmad, S. (2024). From black to green: Quantifying the impact of economic growth, resource management, and green technologies on CO2 emissions. *Journal of Environmental Management, 360*, 121091. DOI: 10.1016/j.jenvman.2024.121091

Shah, D. (2024). Sustainable Finance and ESG Investing. *International Journal for Research in Applied Science and Engineering Technology, 12*(2), 412–416. Advance online publication. DOI: 10.22214/ijraset.2024.58346

Shajar, S. N., Kashif, M., George, J., & Nasir, S. (2024). *The Future of Green Finance*. IGI Global., DOI: 10.4018/979-8-3693-1878-2.ch013

Shalhoob, H. (2023). Green sukuk in Saudi Arabia: Challenges and potentials of sustainability in the light of Saudi Vision 2030 . *Journal of Governance & Regulation, 12*(4), 351–360. DOI: 10.22495/jgrv12i4siart15

Shang, W. L., & Lv, Z. (2023). Low carbon technology for carbon neutrality in sustainable cities: A survey. *Sustainable Cities and Society, 92*, 104489. DOI: 10.1016/j.scs.2023.104489

Sharif, A., Saqib, N., Dong, K., & Khan, S. A. R. (2022). Nexus between green technology innovation, green financing, and CO2 emissions in the G7 countries: The moderating role of social globalisation. *Sustainable Development (Bradford), 30*(6), 1934–1946. DOI: 10.1002/sd.2360

Sharma, H., & Jain, S. (2024). Navigating the Green Finance Landscape: Trends, Challenges, and Future Directions in the Banking Sector. 344–348.doi.org/10.1201/9781003543633-55

Sharma, H., & Jain, S. (2024). Navigating the Green Finance Landscape: Trends, Challenges, and Future Directions in the Banking Sector. In Multidisciplinary Approaches for Sustainable Development (pp. 344-348). CRC Press.

Shefy, D., Rossi, S., & Rinkevich, B. (2025). Not just carbon: Biodiversity credits for restoration of the marine animal forests. *Ecosystems and People (Abingdon, England)*, *21*(1), 2488350. DOI: 10.1080/26395916.2025.2488350

Shi, L., Han, L., Yang, F., & Gao, L. (2019). The evolution of sustainable development theory: Types, goals, and research prospects. *Sustainability (Basel)*, *11*(24), 7158. DOI: 10.3390/su11247158

Shi, X., & Shi, D. (2025). Impact of Green Finance on Renewable Energy Technology Innovation: Empirical Evidence from China. *Sustainability (Basel)*, *17*(5), 2201. DOI: 10.3390/su17052201

Shi, Z., & Shao, T. (2024). *The Development Status*. Challenges and Problems of Green Finance in Different Countries., DOI: 10.54097/j8jyvd42

Shroff-Mehta, P., Thakur, S., Viswanathan, V., & Lemal-Brown, P. (2024). ESG Maturity Mapping: Sustainability in Legacy, New Age, and Start-Up Organizations. In *The Routledge Handbook of Global and Digital Governance Crossroads* (pp. 441-460). Routledge India.

Shrotriya, V. (2024). Consumers' behavioral willingness to use green financial products: An empirical study within a theoretical framework. *Journal of Electrical Systems*, *20*(11s).

Sikken, B. J. (2011). Accelerating the transition towards sustainable investing - strategic options for investors, corporations, and other key stakeholders. SSRN Electronic Journal. DOI: 10.2139/ssrn.1891834

Singhania, M., Bhan, I., & Chadha, G. K. (2023). Sustainable investments: A scientometric review and research agenda. *Managerial Finance*, *50*(1), 266–294. DOI: 10.1108/MF-04-2023-0238

Singh, V. K. (2022). Regulatory and legal framework for promoting green digital finance. In Taghizadeh-Hesary, F., & Hyun, S. (Eds.), *Green Digital Finance and Sustainable Development Goals: Economics, Law, and Institutions in Asia-Pacific* (pp. 3–27). Springer Singapore. DOI: 10.1007/978-981-19-2662-4_1

Sinha, A., Mishra, S., Sharif, A., & Yarovaya, L. (2021). Does green financing help to improve environmental & social responsibility? Designing SDG framework through advanced quantile modelling. *Journal of Environmental Management*, *292*, 112751. DOI: 10.1016/j.jenvman.2021.112751

Skea, J., Shukla, P., Al Khourdajie, A., & McCollum, D. (2021). Intergovernmental Panel on Climate Change: Transparency and integrated assessment modeling. *Wiley Interdisciplinary Reviews: Climate Change*, *12*(5), e727. DOI: 10.1002/wcc.727

Solecki, W., Leichenko, R., & O'Brien, K. (2017). Climate change adaptation strategies and disaster risk reduction in cities: Connections, contentions, and synergies. *Current Opinion in Environmental Sustainability*, *19*, 1–7. DOI: 10.1016/j.cosust.2015.08.001

Sonavane, S. J. (2024). The impact of government policies on sustainable development of India Inc. Под общей редакцией Ректора КНУ Ажибаевой АА Редакционная коллегия, 328.

Soundarrajan, P., & Vivek, N. (2016). Green finance for sustainable green economic growth in India. [ZemědělskáEkonomika]. *Zemedelská Ekonomika*, *62*(1), 35–44. DOI: 10.17221/174/2014-AGRICECON

Spalding, M. D., Ruffo, S., Lacambra, C., Meliane, I., Zeitlin, H., & Hale, L. Z. (2014). The role of ecosystems in coastal protection: Adapting to climate change and coastal hazards. *Ocean and Coastal Management*, *90*, 50–57. DOI: 10.1016/j.ocecoaman.2013.09.007

Sra, J., & Deo, B. (2024). GRI Standards for Environmental Sustainability–A Brief Review. In *IISE Annual Conference. Proceedings* (pp. 1-6). Institute of Industrial and Systems Engineers (IISE). DOI: 10.21872/2024IISE_6407

Sruthi, S. (2024). The role of financial institutions in promoting green finance for sustainable development. *Redshine Archive*. Retrieved from https://chapters.redshine.in

Stafford Smith, M., Cook, C., Sokona, Y., Elmqvist, T., Fukushi, K., Broadgate, W., & Jarzebski, M. P. (2018). Advancing sustainability science for the SDGs. *Sustainability Science*, *13*(6), 1483–1487. DOI: 10.1007/s11625-018-0645-3

Steuer, S., & Tröger, T. H. (2022). The role of disclosure in green finance. *Journal of Financial Regulation*, *8*(1), 1–50. DOI: 10.1093/jfr/fjac001

Stoicescu, V., & Sima, A. G. (2024, March). Sustainable Finance as the Catalyst for ESG-Driven Organizational Design. In International Conference on Business Excellence (pp. 457-480). Cham: Springer Nature Switzerland.

Strauß, N. (2021). Communicating Sustainable Responsible Investments as Financial Advisors: Engaging Private Investors with Strategic Communication. *Sustainability (Basel)*, *13*(6), 3161. DOI: 10.3390/su13063161

Suddaby, R. (2015). Can institutional theory be critical? *Journal of Management Inquiry*, *24*(1), 93–95. DOI: 10.1177/1056492614545304

Sule, A. K., Eyo-Udo, N. L., Onukwulu, E. C., Agho, M. O., & Azubuike, C. (2024). Green finance solutions for banking to combat climate change and promote sustainability. *Gulf Journal of Advance Business Research*, *2*(6), 376–410. DOI: 10.51594/gjabr.v2i6.54

Suminto. (2024). Preface. In Musari, K. (Ed.), *Series 3 of IAEI east java writes: Searching for the opportunity of Islamic sustainable financing* (pp. iii-vii). Jakad Media Publishing.

Su, Y., Liu, B., Yang, X., & Wang, E. (2022). Research on technological innovation investment, financing constraints, and corporate financial risk: Evidence from China. *Mathematical Problems in Engineering*, *2022*(1), 5052274. DOI: 10.1155/2022/5052274

Swallow, T. (2022). Top 10: largest renewable energy organisations in the world. *Sustainability Magazine*. https://sustainabilitymag.com/renewable-energy/10-largest-renewable-energy-organisations-in-the-world

Swilling, M., Musango, J., & Wakeford, J. (2016). Developmental states and sustainability transitions: Prospects of a just transition in South Africa. *Journal of Environmental Policy and Planning*, *18*(5), 650–672. DOI: 10.1080/1523908X.2015.1107716

Taghizadeh-Hesary, F., & Yoshino, N. (2020). Sustainable solutions for green financing and investment in renewable energy projects. *Energies*, *13*(4), 788. DOI: 10.3390/en13040788

Tan, C. (2022). Audit as accountability: Technical authority and expertise in the governance of private financing for development. *Social & Legal Studies*, *31*(1), 3–26. DOI: 10.1177/0964663921992100

Tang, P., Ma, H., Sun, Y., & Xu, X. (2024). *Exploring the role of Fintech, green finance and natural resources towards environmental sustainability: A study on ASEAN economies. Resources Policy*. Retrieved from Elsevier.

Tan, S., Yang, J., Yan, J., Lee, C., Hashim, H., & Chen, B. (2017). A holistic low carbon city indicator framework for sustainable development. *Applied Energy*, *185*, 1919–1930. DOI: 10.1016/j.apenergy.2016.03.041

Tao, Z., & Chao, J. (2024). Investing in green, sustaining the planet: The role of fintech in promoting corporate green investment in the Chinese energy industry. *Journal of Environmental Management*, *370*, 122990. DOI: 10.1016/j.jenvman.2024.122990

Tedersoo, L., Sepping, J., Morgunov, A. S., Kiik, M., Esop, K., Rosenvald, R., Hardwick, K., Breman, E., Purdon, R., Groom, B., Venmans, F., Kiers, E. T., & Antonelli, A. (2024). Towards a co-crediting system for carbon and biodiversity. *Plants, People, Planet*, *6*(1), 18–28. DOI: 10.1002/ppp3.10405

Teixeira, N. (2025). The Evolution of Sustainable Investment: The Role of Decentralised Finance and Green Bonds in the Efficiency and Transparency of Green Finance. FinTech and Sustainable Innovation, 1-13.

The UAE's Government portal. (2024). The UAE's Green Agenda – 2030. https://u.ae/en/about-the-uae/strategies-initiatives-and-awards/strategies-plans-and-visions/environment-and-energy/the-uaes-green-agenda-2030

Tietenberg, T., & Lewis, L. (2023). *Environmental and natural resource economics*. Routledge. DOI: 10.4324/9781003213734

Trencher, G., Nick, S., Carlson, J., & Johnson, M. (2024). Demand for low-quality offsets by major companies undermines climate integrity of the voluntary carbon market. *Nature Communications*, *15*(1), 6863. DOI: 10.1038/s41467-024-51151-w PMID: 39127784

Triggs, A. (2023). Promoting sustainable investment through financial architecture reform. *Oxford Review of Economic Policy*, *39*(2), 267–282. DOI: 10.1093/oxrep/grad009

Trukhachev, V., & Dzhikiya, M. (2023). Development of environmental economy and management in the age of AI based on green finance. *Frontiers in Environmental Science*, *10*, 1087034. Advance online publication. DOI: 10.3389/fenvs.2022.1087034

Tufail, M., Song, L., & Khan, Z. (2024). Green finance and green growth nexus: Evaluating the role of globalization and human capital. *Journal of Applied Econometrics*, *27*(1), 2309437. DOI: 10.1080/15140326.2024.2309437

Tung, P.-H., Chiu, Y.-H., & Huang, C.-H. (2025). Exploring the research development trajectory and trends of green finance. *Asia Pacific Management Review, 30*(3), 100329. https://doi.org/ https://doi.org/10.1016/j.apmrv.2024.10.001

Twidell, J. (2021). *Institutional and Economic Factors. Renewable energy resources* (4th ed.). Routledge. DOI: 10.4324/9780429452161

Udeagha, M. C., & Ngepah, N. (2023). The drivers of environmental sustainability in BRICS economies: Do green finance and fintech matter? *World Development Sustainability*, *3*, 100096. DOI: 10.1016/j.wds.2023.100096

Ullah, A., Liu, X., Zeeshan, M., & Shah, W. U. (2024). Evaluating growth and crisis risk dynamics of sustainable climate Exchange-Traded Funds. *Sustainability (Basel), 16*(22), 10049. DOI: 10.3390/su162210049

UN Principles for Responsible Investment. (2023). The Six Principles for Responsible Investment. Retrieved from https://www.unpri.org/

UNCTAD. (2014). World investment report 2014 - Investing in the SDGs: An action plan. *United Nations Conference on Trade and Development (UNCTAD)*, New York & Geneva.

UNCTAD. (2023). *World Investment Report 2023: Investing in sustainable energy for all.* United Nations Conference on Trade and Development. https://unctad.org/publication/world-investment-report-2023

UNDP in Asia and the Pacific. (2020, November 9). Footing the bill: Innovative financing for climate action in Indonesia and the pioneering of green sukuk. *United Nations Development Programme Indonesia (UNDP) in Asia and the Pacific.* https://undpasiapac.medium.com/footing-the-bill-innovative-financing-for-climate-action-in-indonesia-and-the-pioneering-of-green-bbee3262047

United Nations Environment Programme (UNEP). (2021). *Adaptation gap report 2021: The gathering storm.* UNEP. Retrieved from https://www.unep.org

United Nations Environment Programme Finance Initiative. (2023). Principles for Responsible Banking. Retrieved from https://www.unepfi.org/banking/bankingprinciples/

Urwin, R. (2010). Sustainable Investing Practice: Simplified complexity. SSRN Electronic Journal. DOI: 10.2139/ssrn.1656988

Uzar, U. (2024). The critical role of green innovation technologies and democracy in the transition to sustainability: A study on leading emerging market economies. *Technology in Society, 78*, 102622. DOI: 10.1016/j.techsoc.2024.102622

Valadkhani, A., & O'Mahony, B. (2024). Sustainable investing in extreme market conditions: Doing well while doing good. *Journal of Economics*. Studies.doi.org/10.1108/jes-11-2023-0626

Van Niekerk, A. J. (2024). Economic inclusion: Green finance and the SDGs. *Sustainability (Basel), 16*(3), 1128. DOI: 10.3390/su16031128

Volz, U. (2018). *Fostering green finance for sustainable development in Asia* (ADBI Working Paper No. 814). Asian Development Bank Institute.

Vorisek, D. L., & Yu, S. (2020). *Understanding the cost of achieving the sustainable development goals.* World Bank Policy Research Working Paper No. 9164. https://ssrn.com/abstract=3545657

Vorontsova, A., Agafonova, E. O., & Bilan, S. A. (2023). *Directions of regulatory coordination of responsible (esg) investment in the world: fragmentation or unification?* Economics & Law., DOI: 10.15407/econlaw.2023.03.091

Wadhwani, D., & Malpani, P. (2023). United Nations Sustainable Goals: Global to local Need of the hour. SSRN Electronic Journal. DOI: 10.2139/ssrn.4426147

Waidelich, P., & Steffen, B. (2024). Renewable energy financing by state investment banks: Evidence from OECD countries. *Energy Economics, 133*, 107455. https://doi.org/ https://doi.org/10.1016/j.eneco.2024.107455. DOI: 10.1016/j.eneco.2024.107455

Wang, J. (2023). Study on green credit policy and enterprise ESG performance. *Proceedings of the 3rd International Conference on Internet Finance and Digital Economy (ICIFDE 2023).* Atlantis Highlights in Economics, Business and Management. DOI: 10.2991/978-94-6463-270-5_24

Wang, C., Rahman, M. M., Siddik, A. B., Wen, Z. G., & Sobhani, F. A. (2024). Exploring the synergy of logistics, finance, and technology on innovation. *Scientific Reports, 14*(1), 21918. DOI: 10.1038/s41598-024-72409-9

Wang, K. H., Zhao, Y. X., Jiang, C. F., & Li, Z. Z. (2022). Does green finance inspire sustainable development? Evidence from a global perspective. *Economic Analysis and Policy*, *75*, 412–426. DOI: 10.1016/j.eap.2022.06.002

Wang, K., Li, T., San, Z., & Gao, H. (2023). How does corporate ESG performance affect stock liquidity? Evidence from China. *Pacific-Basin Finance Journal*, *80*, 102087. DOI: 10.1016/j.pacfin.2023.102087

Wang, K., Tsai, S. B., Du, X., & Bi, D. (2019). Internet finance, green finance, and sustainability. *Sustainability (Basel)*, *11*(14), 3856. DOI: 10.3390/su11143856

Wang, X., Sun, X., Zhang, H., & Xue, C. (2022). Does green financial reform pilot policy promote green technology innovation? Empirical evidence from China. *Environmental Science and Pollution Research International*, *29*(51), 77283–77299. DOI: 10.1007/s11356-022-21291-x

Wang, Y. R., Ma, C., Ren, Y. S., & Narayan, S. (2023). Cooperative management of an emission trading system: A private governance and learned auction for a blockchain approach. *Financial Innovation*, *9*(1), 122. DOI: 10.1186/s40854-023-00547-6

Wang, Z., Peng, M. Y. P., Anser, M. K., & Chen, Z. (2023). Research on the impact of green finance and renewable energy on energy efficiency: The case study E– 7 economies. *Renewable Energy, 205*, 166–173. DOI: 10.1016/j.renene.2022.12.077

Webb, J., Fujii, H., Rowlings, D., Grace, P., Mundree, S., Managi, S., & Wilson, C. (2025). Prospects for integration of carbon and biodiversity credits: An Australian case study review. *Sustainability Science*. Advance online publication. DOI: 10.1007/s11625-024-01603-5

Weber, O. (2017). Corporate sustainability and financial performance of Chinese banks. *Sustainability Accounting. Management and Policy Journal, 8*(3), 358–385.

WEF & McKinsey. (2024). Biodiversity credits: Demystifying metrics for nature markets. https://www3.weforum.org/docs/WEF_Biodiversity_Credits_2024.pdf

West, T. A. P., Wunder, S., Sills, E. O., Börner, J., Rifai, S. W., Neidermeier, A. N., Frey, G. P., & Kontoleon, A. (2023). Action needed to make carbon offsets from tropical forest conservation work for climate change mitigation. *Science, 877*(6660), 873–877. DOI: 10.1126/science.ade3535 PMID: 37616370

Whitchurch, G. G., & Constantine, L. L. (1993). Systems theory. In *Sourcebook of family theories and methods: A contextual approach* (pp. 325–355). Springer US. DOI: 10.1007/978-0-387-85764-0_14

Women, U. N. (2021). Women's representation in local government: A global analysis. *Hämtad, 27*, 2022–01.

World Bank Documents and Reports the basic green finance reference guide -, accessed April 16, 2025. Retrieved from: https://documents1.worldbank.org/curated/en/099126011232333546/pdf/IDU132f9c75017b0314d0e1bedb16cb861caace2.pdf

World Bank Group. (2021). *What You Need to Know About Green Loans.* Retrieved from: https://www.worldbank.org/en/news/feature/2021/10/04/what-you-need-to-know-about-green-loans

World Bank Treasury. (2024). *Green Bonds* Retrieved from https://treasury.worldbank.org/en/about/unit/treasury/ibrd/ibrd-green-bonds

World Bank. (2023). Green Finance. Retrieved from https://documents1.worldbank.org/curated/zh/148291573020848322/pdf/Executive-Summary.pdf

World Economic Forum. (2020). *What is green finance and why is it important?* (Green Horizon Summit: The Pivotal Role of Finance). Cologny, Switzerland. https://www.weforum.org/stories/2020/11/what-is-green-finance/

World Economic Forum. (2024). *3 financing trends to watch that can propel a clean energy revolution in the Global South.* Retrieved from: https://www.weforum.org/stories/2024/12/3-financing-trends-to-watch-that-can-propel-a-clean-energy-revolution-in-the-global-south/

Wunder, S., Fraccaroli, C., Bull, J. W., Dutta, T., Eyres, A., & Evans, M. C.. (2025). Biodiversity credits: An overview of the current State, future opportunities, and potential pitfalls. *Business Strategy and the Environment.*

Xia, D., Zhang, M., Yu, Q., & Tu, Y. (2019). Developing a framework to identify barriers of Green technology adoption for enterprises. *Resources, Conservation and Recycling, 143*, 99–110. DOI: 10.1016/j.resconrec.2018.12.022

Xiao, R., Deng, J., Zhou, Y., & Chen, M. (2023). Analyzing contemporary trends in sustainable finance and ESG investment. *Law And Economy, 2*(11), 44–52. DOI: 10.56397/LE.2023.11.06

Xia, Q. (2023). Does green technology advancement and renewable electricity standard impact on carbon emissions in China: Role of green finance. *Environmental Science and Pollution Research International, 30*(3), 6492–6505. DOI: 10.1007/s11356-022-22517-8

Xie, Q., Hao, J., Li, K., & Zheng, X. (2022). Carbon price prediction considering climate change: A text-based framework. *Economic Analysis and Policy, 74*, 382–401. DOI: 10.1016/j.eap.2022.02.010

Xie, X., Gong, C., Su, Z., Nie, Y., & Kim, W. (2024). Consumers' behavioural willingness to use green financial products: An empirical study within a theoretical framework. *Behavioral Sciences (Basel, Switzerland), 14*(8), 634. DOI: 10.3390/bs14080634

Xing, L., Chang, B. H., & Aldawsari, S. H. (2024). Green Finance Mechanisms for Sustainable Development: Evidence from Panel Data. *Sustainability (Basel), 16*(22), 9762. DOI: 10.3390/su16229762

Xu, D., Corbet, S., Lang, C., & Hu, Y. (2024). Understanding dynamic return connectedness and portfolio strategies among international sustainable exchange-traded funds. *Economic Modelling, 141*, 106864. DOI: 10.1016/j.econmod.2024.106864

Xu, L., & Xu, C. (2022). Does green finance and energy policy paradox demonstrate green economic recovery: Role of social capital and public health. *Frontiers in Public Health, 10*, 843314. DOI: 10.3389/fpubh.2022.951527 PMID: 36438284

Xu, T., Yang, G., & Chen, T. (2024). The role of green finance and digital inclusive finance in promoting economic sustainable development: A perspective from new quality productivity. *Journal of Environmental Management*, *370*, 122892. DOI: 10.1016/j.jenvman.2024.122892

Yadav, A. P. (2024). Changing Dynamics of Sustainable Investing: Emerging Trends. Journal of Informatics Education and Research. DOI: 10.52783/jier.v3i2.467

Yadav, A., Gyamfi, B. A., Asongu, S. A., & Behera, D. K. (2024). The role of green finance and governance effectiveness in the impact of renewable energy investment on CO2 emissions in BRICS economies. *Journal of Environmental Management*, *358*, 120906. DOI: 10.1016/j.jenvman.2024.120906 PMID: 38636419

Yadav, S., Samadhiya, A., Kumar, A., Majumdar, A., Garza-Reyes, J. A., & Luthra, S. (2023). Achieving the sustainable development goals through net zero emissions: Innovation-driven strategies for transitioning from incremental to radical lean, green and digital technologies. *Resources, Conservation and Recycling*, *197*, 107094. DOI: 10.1016/j.resconrec.2023.107094

Yan, N., Liu, G., Ulgiati, S., & Yang, Z. (2024). Biodiversity conservation strategies from No Net Loss to Net Gain. A multidimensional accounting method. *Earths' Future, 12*(10), e2024EF004652. DOI: 10.1029/2024EF004652

Ye, X., & Rasoulinezhad, E. (2023). Assessment of impacts of green bonds on renewable energy utilization efficiency. *Renewable Energy*, *202*, 626–633. DOI: 10.1016/j.renene.2022.11.124

Yong, J. Y., Yusliza, M., Ramayah, T., Chiappetta Jabbour, C. J., Sehnem, S., & Mani, V. (2019). Pathways towards sustainability in manufacturing organizations: Empirical evidence on the role of green human resource management. *Business Strategy and the Environment*. Advance online publication. DOI: 10.1002/bse.2359

Yu, Y. (2016). *Climate finance in and beyond the Paris agreement: Implementing climate finance commitments in Asia and the Pacific*. A Discussion Paper of Macroeconomic Policy and Financing for Development Division at First High-Level Follow-up Dialogue on Financing for Development in Asia and the Pacific, March 30th-31th, Incheon.

Yuan, X., Shang, L., & Xu, J. (2024). Green Financial Policy, Resource Allocation and Corporate Environmental Responsibility. *Sustainability (Basel)*, *16*(15), 6273. DOI: 10.3390/su16156273

Yu, M., Zhou, Q., Cheok, M. Y., Kubiczek, J., & Iqbal, N. (2022). Does green finance improve energy efficiency? New evidence from developing and developed economies. *Economic Change and Restructuring*, *55*(1), 1–25. DOI: 10.1007/s10644-021-09355-3

Yumnam, G., Gyanendra, Y., & Ibohal Singh, C. (2024). A Systematic Bibliometric Review of the Global Research Dynamics of United Nations Sustainable Development Goals 2030. *Sustainable Futures : An Applied Journal of Technology, Environment and Society*, *7*, 100192. Advance online publication. DOI: 10.1016/j.sftr.2024.100192

Yun, X., & Hu, Y. (2024). An Overview of the Evolution in the Research Landscape of Green Finance. *WORLD (Oakland, Calif.)*, *5*(4), 1335–1366. DOI: 10.3390/world5040068

Yu, R., & Li, J. (2024). Does fintech influence sustainable development under natural resource constraints: Insights from 270 Chinese cities. *Resources Policy*, *91*, 104924. Advance online publication. DOI: 10.1016/j.resourpol.2024.104924

Zadek, S., & Flynn, C. (2013). South-originating green finance. *Exploring Its Potential.*

Zairis, G., Liargovas, P., & Apostolopoulos, N. (2024). Sustainable Finance and ESG Importance: A Systematic Literature Review and Research Agenda. *Sustainability (Basel)*, *16*(7), 2878. Advance online publication. DOI: 10.3390/su16072878

Zakari, A., & Khan, I. (2021). *The introduction of green finance: a curse or a benefit to environmental sustainability?* Energy Research Letters., DOI: 10.46557/001c.29977

ZAWYA. (2024, September 25). Saudi Arabia leads GCC in sustainable sukuk issuances. https://www.zawya.com/en/economy/islamic-economy/saudi-arabia-leads-gcc-in-sustainable-sukuk-issuances-smnx5ezs

ZAWYA. (2025, January 21). ESG sukuk to cross $50bln in 2025: Key ESG Funding Role in Emerging Markets. https://www.zawya.com/en/press-release/research-and-studies/esg-sukuk-to-cross-50bln-in-2025-fo768f6h

Zeng, S., Li, T., Wu, S., Gao, W., & Li, G. (2024). Does green technology progress have a significant impact on carbon dioxide emissions? *Energy Economics*, *133*, 107524. DOI: 10.1016/j.eneco.2024.107524

Zerbib, O. D. (2019). The effect of pro-environmental preferences on bond prices: Evidence from green bonds. *Journal of Banking & Finance*, *98*, 39–60. DOI: 10.1016/j.jbankfin.2018.10.012

Zhang, L., Saydaliev, H. B., & Ma, X. (2022). Does green finance investment and technological innovation improve renewable energy efficiency and sustainable development goals. *Renewable Energy*, *193*, 991–1000. DOI: 10.1016/j.renene.2022.04.161

Zhang, Y. (2022). How Economic Performance of OECD economies influences through Green Finance and Renewable Energy Investment Resources? *Resources Policy*, *79*, 102925. DOI: 10.1016/j.resourpol.2022.102925

Zhang, Y., & Umar, M. (2023). Examining the interconnectedness of green finance: An analysis of dynamic spillover effects among green bonds, renewable energy, and carbon markets. *Environmental Science and Pollution Research International*, *30*(31), 1–17. DOI: 10.1007/s11356-023-27870-w

Zhao, L., Chau, K. Y., Tran, T. K., Sadiq, M., Xuyen, N. T. M., & Phan, T. T. H. (2022). Enhancing green economic recovery through green bonds financing and energy efficiency investments. *Economic Analysis and Policy*, *76*, 488–501. DOI: 10.1016/j.eap.2022.08.019

Zhao, Y. (2024). Empowering Sustainable finance: The convergence of AI, blockchain, and big data analytics. *Advances in Economics Management and Political Sciences*, *85*(1), 267–273. DOI: 10.54254/2754-1169/85/20240925

Zhong, W. (2023). An analysis of focusing on ESG investment. *Highlights in Business Economics and Management*, *17*, 8–13. DOI: 10.54097/hbem.v17i.11016

Zhou, K., & Li, Y. (2019). Carbon finance and carbon market in China: Progress and challenges. *Journal of Cleaner Production*, *214*, 536–549. DOI: 10.1016/j.jclepro.2018.12.298

Zhu, H., Feng, T., & Li, X. (2024). Green finance, green development and decarbonization of the energy consumption structure. PLOS ONE, 19. e.0300579DOI: <ALIGNMENT.qj></ALIGNMENT>10.1371/journal.pon

Zhu, X., & Li, D. (2024). How to promote the construction of low-carbon cities in China? An urban complex ecosystem perspective. *Sustainable Development (Bradford)*, *32*(5), 4354–4373. DOI: 10.1002/sd.2897

Zioło, M., Bąk, I., & Spoz, A. (2024). Literature review of greenwashing research: State of the art. *Corporate Social Responsibility and Environmental Management*, *31*(6), 5343–5356. DOI: 10.1002/csr.2842

Zioło, M., Bąk, I., & Spoz, A. (2024). The Role of Financial Markets in Energy Transitions. *Energies*, *17*(24), 6315. DOI: 10.3390/en17246315 zu Ermgassen, S. O. S. E., Hawkins, I., Lundhede, T., Liu, Q., Thorsen, B. J., & Bull, J. W. (2025). The current state, opportunities and challenges for upscaling private investment in biodiversity in Europe. *Nature Ecology & Evolution*, *9*(3), 515–524. DOI: 10.1038/s41559-024-02632-0 PMID: 39910373

# About the Contributors

**Karima Sayari** is an Associate Professor in Managerial and Financial Sciences Department at Al Zahra College for Women. She holds a bachelor's degree in international trade, a master's degree in economics and international finance, and a PhD in Finance and Economic Sciences in 2012. Dr. Sayari has over 10 years of teaching experience and has published extensively in reputable international journals indexed in Scopus and Web of Science and served as Reviewer and Editor in various international journals. Her research focuses on economics, finance, banking, and digital finance. She is an active peer reviewer in various academic journals.

**Revenio C. Jalagat, Jr.** is presently employed in Al Zahra College for Women in the Sultanate of Oman since 2013 and as Associate Professor in 2023. He had a total accumulated experience of 18 years in both the industry serving as Accountant, Chief Accountant, Finance Manager, and in the Academe as Lecturer, Assistant Professor and Dean in the Philippines. Dr. Jalagat was also a lecturer at Gulf College in Oman for almost two and a half years. He is a Certified Public Accountant (CPA) in the Philippines and graduated Doctor of Management at Capitol University, Philippines. He has published research in internationally reputed journals, including Scopus and Web of Science indexed journals, and served as Reviewer and Editorial Member in various international journals.

**Rafat Al Batayneh** is currently employed as the Head of the Department and Associate Professor in the Managerial and Financial Sciences at Al Zahra College for Women, Sultanate of Oman. He finished his PhD in Finance in 2014 and worked in professorial capacities in different Universities for more than 10 years in Jordan and overseas. In the field of research, he has published and presented papers in international fora including Scopus and Web of Science indexes as well as serving as editor and reviewers in various international peer-reviewed journals. As an experienced academician, he has also supervised theses and dissertations as proof of his expertise in the field of finance.

* * *

**Qasim Albaqali** is a senior Lecturer in Accounting and Finance and the Program Manager (Banking and Finance). His areas of interest include sustainability reporting, assurance and corporate governance.

**Huda AlNajjar** is the Accounting Program Manager and a Lecturer at Bahrain Polytechnic's Business School. Huda holds a Master's degree in Law and Accounting from the London School of Economics and Political Sciences and a Bachelor degree in Accounting, Business Finance and Management from the University of York. With over 15 years of professional experience, she specializes in strategy consulting, business development, and financial analysis, with a focus on projects involving public and private companies, as well as SMEs. Her research interests include auditors independence, taxation, strategic management, corporate finance and financial regulation.

**Tiago Jordão Cardoso** is a Specialized Technical Officer at the General Secretariat of the Environment in Portugal, where he focuses on the integration of artificial intelligence and chatbots within public administration. Currently completing a master's in public administration, his research centers on technological acceptance, particularly in the public sector's use of AI to enhance sustainability and resilience. With strong involvement in climate change initiatives, Tiago explores the intersection of AI-driven innovation and sustainable practices, co-authoring articles on these topics and preparing additional proposals on AI's role in environmental resilience.

**Pedro Pinheiro Gomes** is a Technical Adviser at the Secretary General for the Environment in Portugal, where he currently focuses on project management and communication within the Environment Programme of the EEA Grants. He holds a master's degree in Environmental Engineering, specializing in environmental systems and policy. His professional journey also includes extensive experience in statistics and data analysis within the European Comparison Programme (ECP) for Purchasing Power Parities. In addition to his core roles, Pedro has authored multiple publications, including chapters in scientific books on environmental management, policy, and the integration of Artificial Intelligence in sustainability. He has contributed to high-impact projects, such as the development of mobile applications for coastal and tourism analysis aligned with the Inspire Directive, as well as tools for natural disaster alerts and forecasting.

**Hani Hamaidan** is a qualified CPA(USA) and currently working as a Tutor in Bahrain Polytechnic. He has vast experience in teaching and his areas of research include Accounting, Banking, IFRS, Green Finance, and Sustainability.

**Saddam Hossain** is a postgraduate student at the Shanghai University of Finance and Economics.

**Vishal Jain** is presently working as a Professor at the Department of Computer Science & Engineering, School of Engineering & Technology, Vivekananda Institute of Professional Studies - Technical Campus, New Delhi. Before that, he worked as Professor at Sharda University, Greater Noida and Associate Professor at Bharati Vidyapeeth's Institute of Computer Applications and Management (BVICAM), New Delhi. He has associated as a member of the Faculty Board, Board of Planning and Management, Executive Council, Academic Council, Curriculum Development and Review Committee and Academic Audit of various higher education Institutions. He is associated with Kuala Lumpur University of Science and Technology (KLUST), Malaysia, Lincoln University College, Malaysia and Research Institute of IoT Cybersecurity, Department of Electronic Engineering, National Kaohsiung University of Science and Technology, Taiwan for research oriented activities.

**Ganesha K. S.** is an Assistant Professor in the Department of Management Studies, at Dayananda Sagar College of Engineering, Bangalore, India. He has 15 years of experience in Corporate, Teaching and Research. He is a Member of the International Safety Quality Environment Management Association (ISQEM), UK. His primary research interests are tourist behavior, social media, sentiment analysis, human resource management, and labor studies. He has presented at multiple conferences and published articles in Scopus and other International Indexed journals. He has conducted FDP, workshops, and training in the areas of Digital Marketing, Statistical Analysis using SPSS, Project Management, Research Methodology, Entrepreneurship, etc.

**Shivangi Kashyap**, a skillful academician, holds a Bachelor's degree in Commerce with Honours in Accounts and an MBA in Financial Management. She is currently pursuing a PhD at the University of Hyderabad. Earlier, she worked as an Assistant Professor at Brainware University, Barasat, Kolkata, where she passionately imparted her expertise in finance and management to aspiring minds. With a commitment to academic excellence, she also embraces online education, leveraging technology to ensure effective and engaging learning experiences.

**Devi Manikeswari**, currently serving as an Assistant Professor, is an accomplished higher education academic who possesses extensive teaching experience across 3 countries. She is also a certified Psychometric Test User and has published in renowned journals in the field of higher education, psychometric testing, HR and OB. She has served as a resource person in several Faculty Develop Programs and delivered guest lectures in several renowned universities.

**Khairunnisa Musari** is an Assistant Professor at Faculty of Islamic Economics and Business (FEBI) & Postgraduate Program, Kiai Haji Achmad Siddiq State Islamic University (UIN KHAS), Jember, Indonesia. She is a Secretary of the Indonesian Association of Islamic Economists (IAEI) for the Provincial Board of East Java and a member of the International Association for Islamic Economics (IAIE). Her research interests in sukuk, waqf, esham, fiscal & monetary policies, circular economy, halal logistics, sustainable finance, climate change, and Islamic microfinance & nanofinance. She has several book chapters with international reputable publishers such as IGI Global, Emerald Publishing Limited, World Scientific Publishing, Routledge, Springer, and Palgrave Macmillan. She has experience as a Senior Specialist for Islamic Finance of United Nations Development Programme (UNDP) Indonesia and was listed as one of the Top 300 Most Influential Women in Islamic Business & Finance 2019, 2020, 2021, WOMANi Significancica 2022, and WOMANi Academica 2023, 2024, by Cambridge-IFA.

**Satya Pavan Kumar Ratnakaram** is an accomplished academician currently employed as an Assistant Professor in the Faculty of Business and Logistics, Bahrain Polytechnic since September 2022. Prior to this, he has worked as a Program Manager and IQA member in the Commercial Studies Division, Bahrain Training Institute, Kingdom of Bahrain for more than 16 years. With over two decades of teaching/training/industry experience across three countries, presented/published more than 25 articles in national and international conferences/journals in the field of banking, insurance, accounting, CSR, and ESG.

**Jyoti Tyagi** is an Assistant Professor in the Department of management at IAMR Group of Institution, Ghaziabad. Her research interests include Financial technology, Digital Payments, and operation Management, AI. She has contributed to academic publications and actively engages in interdisciplinary research that bridges theory and practice in Finance.

# Index

## G



## I



## L

## T

www.ingramcontent.com/pod-product-compliance
Lightning Source LLC
LaVergne TN
LVHW060006031026
849161LV00025B/1531